Element Line

Element Line Volume 2
Created by Mamiya Takizaki

Translation - Claire de Dobay Rifelj
English Adaptation - Christine Boylan
Copy Editor - Shannon Wattes
Retouch and Lettering - Star Print Brokers
Production Artist - Jennifer M. Sanchez
Graphic Designer - John Lo

Editor - Nikhil Burman
Digital Imaging Manager - Chris Buford
Pre-Production Supervisor - Vicente Rivera, Jr.
Production Specialist - Lucas Rivera
Managing Editor - Vy Nguyen
Art Director - Al-Insan Lashley
Editor-in-Chief - Rob Tokar
Publisher - Mike Kiley
President and C.O.O. - John Parker
C.E.O. and Chief Creative Officer - Stu Levy

A **TOKYOPOP** Manga

TOKYOPOP and are trademarks or registered trademarks of TOKYOPOP Inc.

TOKYOPOP Inc.
5900 Wilshire Blvd. Suite 2000
Los Angeles, CA 90036

E-mail: info@TOKYOPOP.com
Come visit us online at www.TOKYOPOP.com

Element Line vol. 2
© 2004 Mamiya Takizaki / Ki-oon
All rights reserved.
First published in France in 2004 by Ki-oon Ltd.
English translation rights arranged through Ki-oon Ltd.
English text copyright © 2008 TOKYOPOP Inc.

ISBN: 978-1-4278-0528-7

First TOKYOPOP printing: August 2008
10 9 8 7 6 5 4 3 2 1
Printed in the USA

vol.2
By Mamiya Takizaki

HAMBURG // LONDON // LOS ANGELES // TOKYO

The Characters

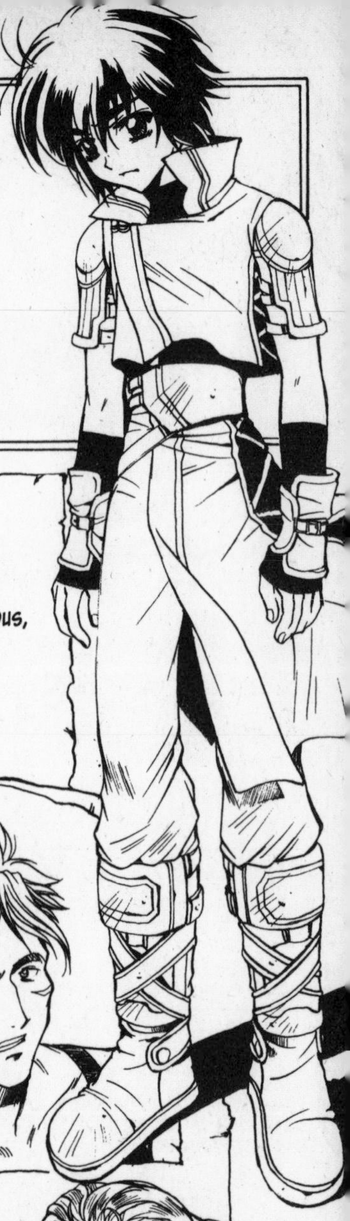

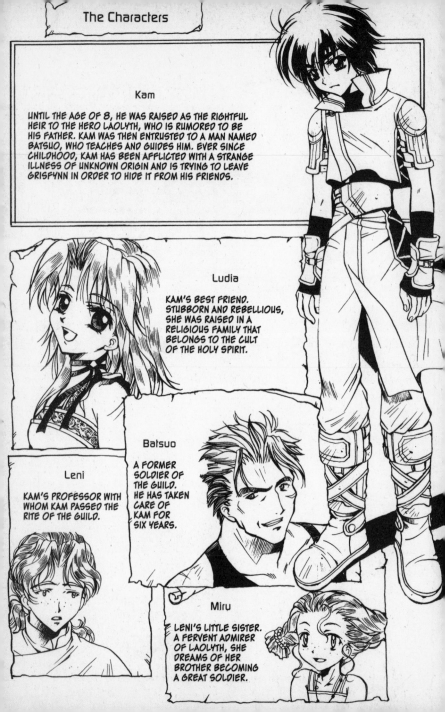

Kam

UNTIL THE AGE OF 8, HE WAS RAISED AS THE RIGHTFUL HEIR TO THE HERO LAOLYTH, WHO IS RUMORED TO BE HIS FATHER. KAM WAS THEN ENTRUSTED TO A MAN NAMED BATSUO, WHO TEACHES AND GUIDES HIM. EVER SINCE CHILDHOOD, KAM HAS BEEN AFFLICTED WITH A STRANGE ILLNESS OF UNKNOWN ORIGIN AND IS TRYING TO LEAVE GRISFYNN IN ORDER TO HIDE IT FROM HIS FRIENDS.

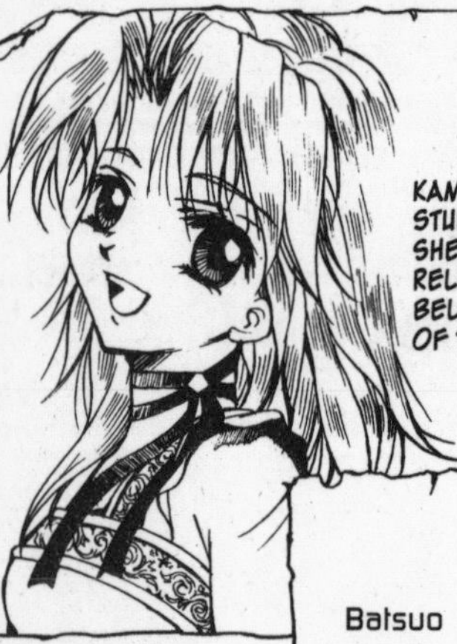

Ludia

KAM'S BEST FRIEND. STUBBORN AND REBELLIOUS, SHE WAS RAISED IN A RELIGIOUS FAMILY THAT BELONGS TO THE CULT OF THE HOLY SPIRIT.

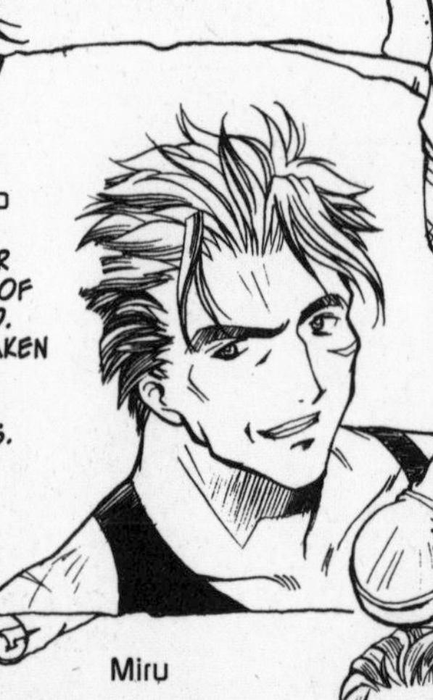

Batsuo

A FORMER SOLDIER OF THE GUILD. HE HAS TAKEN CARE OF KAM FOR SIX YEARS.

Leni

KAM'S PROFESSOR WITH WHOM KAM PASSED THE RITE OF THE GUILD.

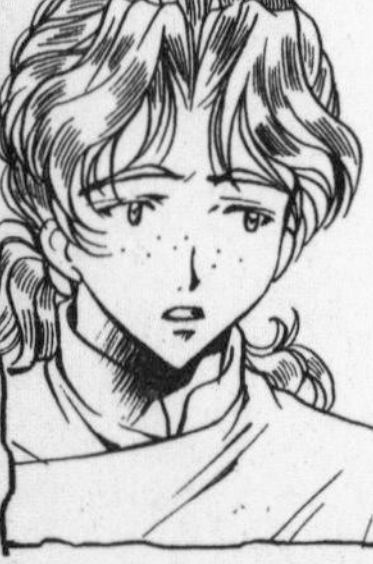

Miru

LENI'S LITTLE SISTER. A FERVENT ADMIRER OF LAOLYTH, SHE DREAMS OF HER BROTHER BECOMING A GREAT SOLDIER.

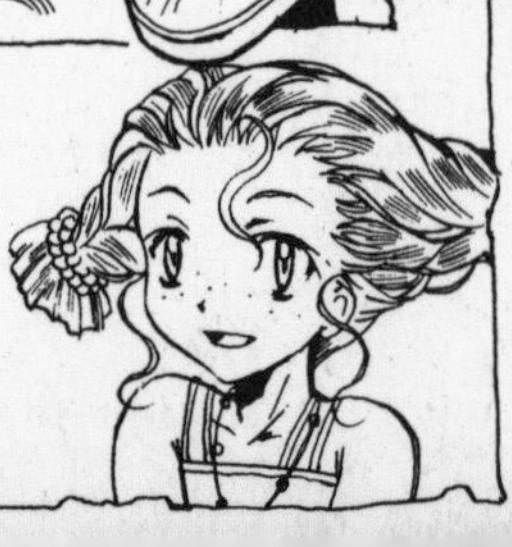

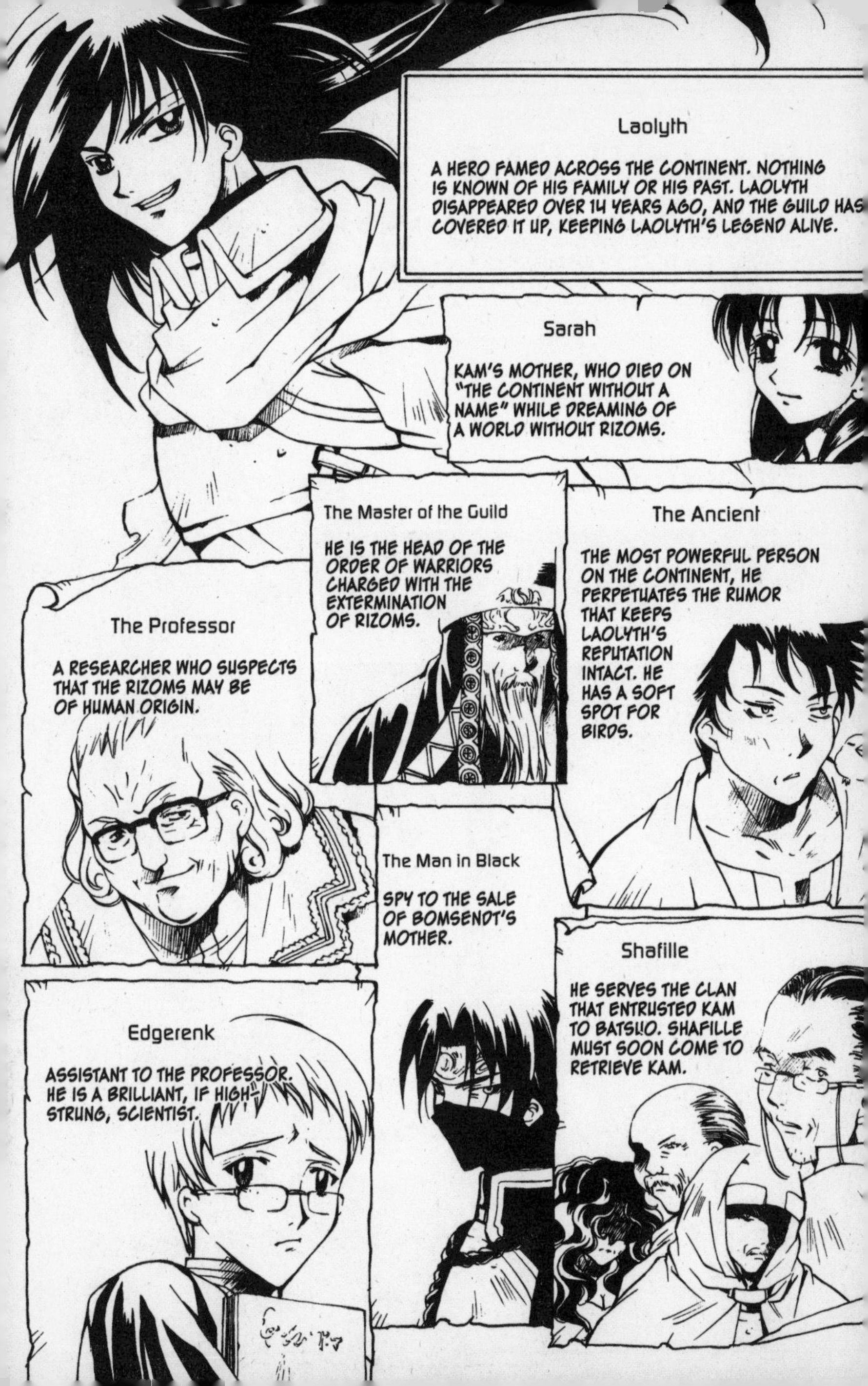

Laolyth
A HERO FAMED ACROSS THE CONTINENT. NOTHING IS KNOWN OF HIS FAMILY OR HIS PAST. LAOLYTH DISAPPEARED OVER 14 YEARS AGO, AND THE GUILD HAS COVERED IT UP, KEEPING LAOLYTH'S LEGEND ALIVE.
Sarah
KAM'S MOTHER, WHO DIED ON "THE CONTINENT WITHOUT A NAME" WHILE DREAMING OF A WORLD WITHOUT RIZOMS.
The Ancient
THE MOST POWERFUL PERSON ON THE CONTINENT, HE PERPETUATES THE RUMOR THAT KEEPS LAOLYTH'S REPUTATION INTACT. HE HAS A SOFT SPOT FOR BIRDS.
The Master of the Guild
HE IS THE HEAD OF THE ORDER OF WARRIORS CHARGED WITH THE EXTERMINATION OF RIZOMS.
The Professor
A RESEARCHER WHO SUSPECTS THAT THE RIZOMS MAY BE OF HUMAN ORIGIN.
The Man in Black
SPY TO THE SALE OF BOMSENDT'S MOTHER.
Shafille
HE SERVES THE CLAN THAT ENTRUSTED KAM TO BATSUO. SHAFILLE MUST SOON COME TO RETRIEVE KAM.
Edgerenk
ASSISTANT TO THE PROFESSOR. HE IS A BRILLIANT, IF HIGH-STRUNG, SCIENTIST.

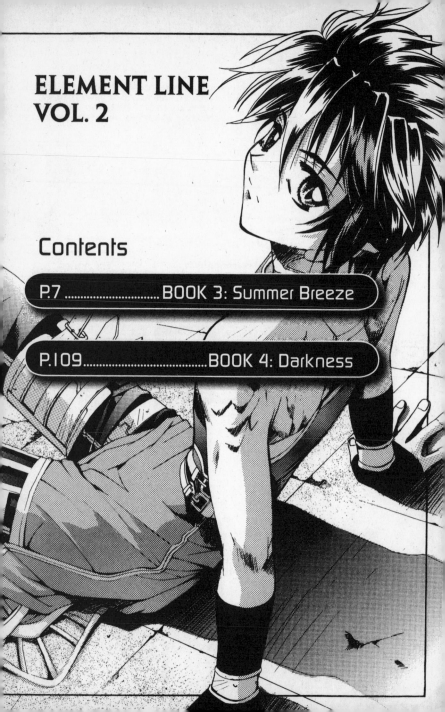

ELEMENT LINE
VOL. 2

Contents

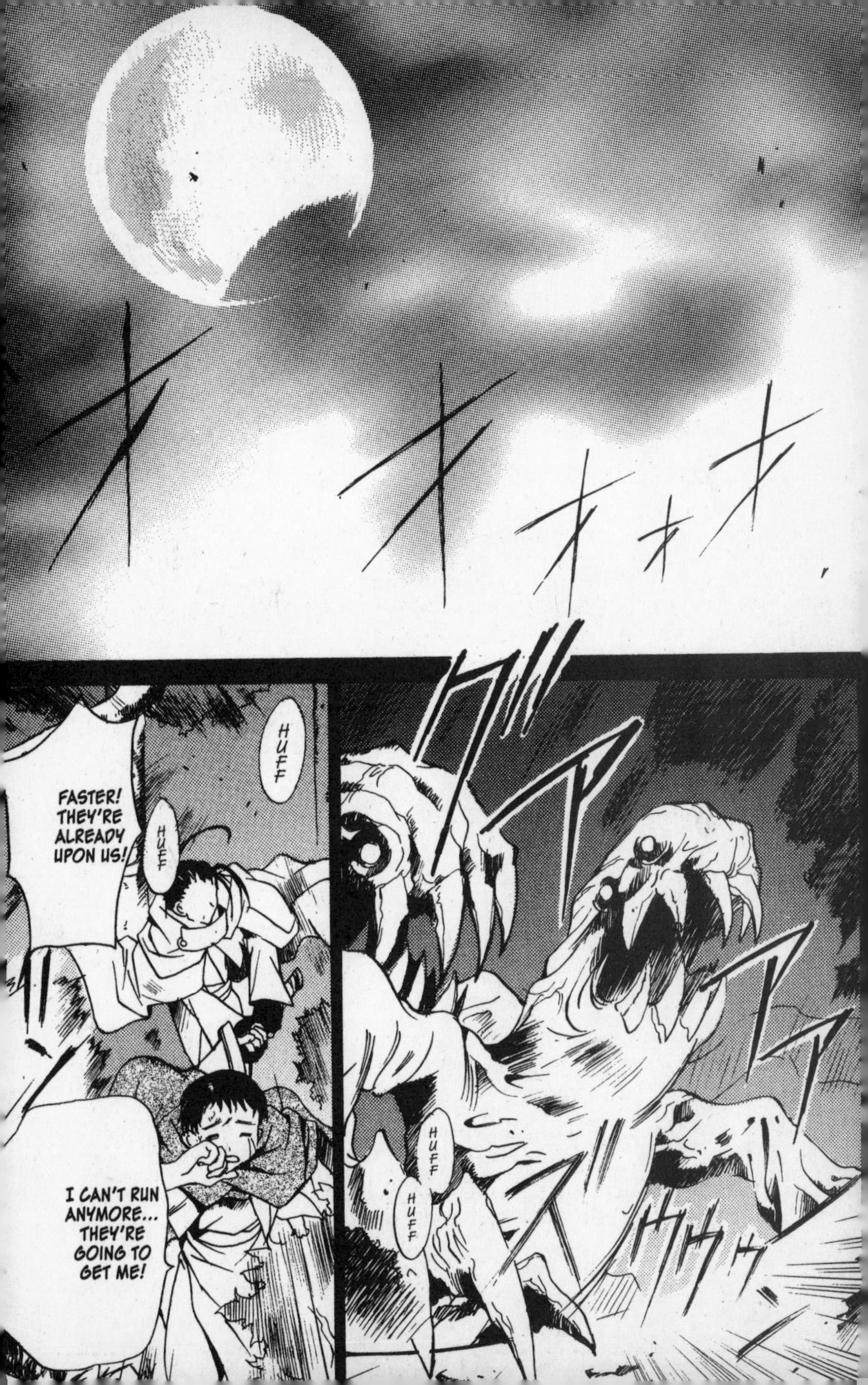
HUFF
HUFF
HUFF
FASTER! THEY'RE ALREADY UPON US!
HUFF
I CAN'T RUN ANYMORE... THEY'RE GOING TO GET ME!

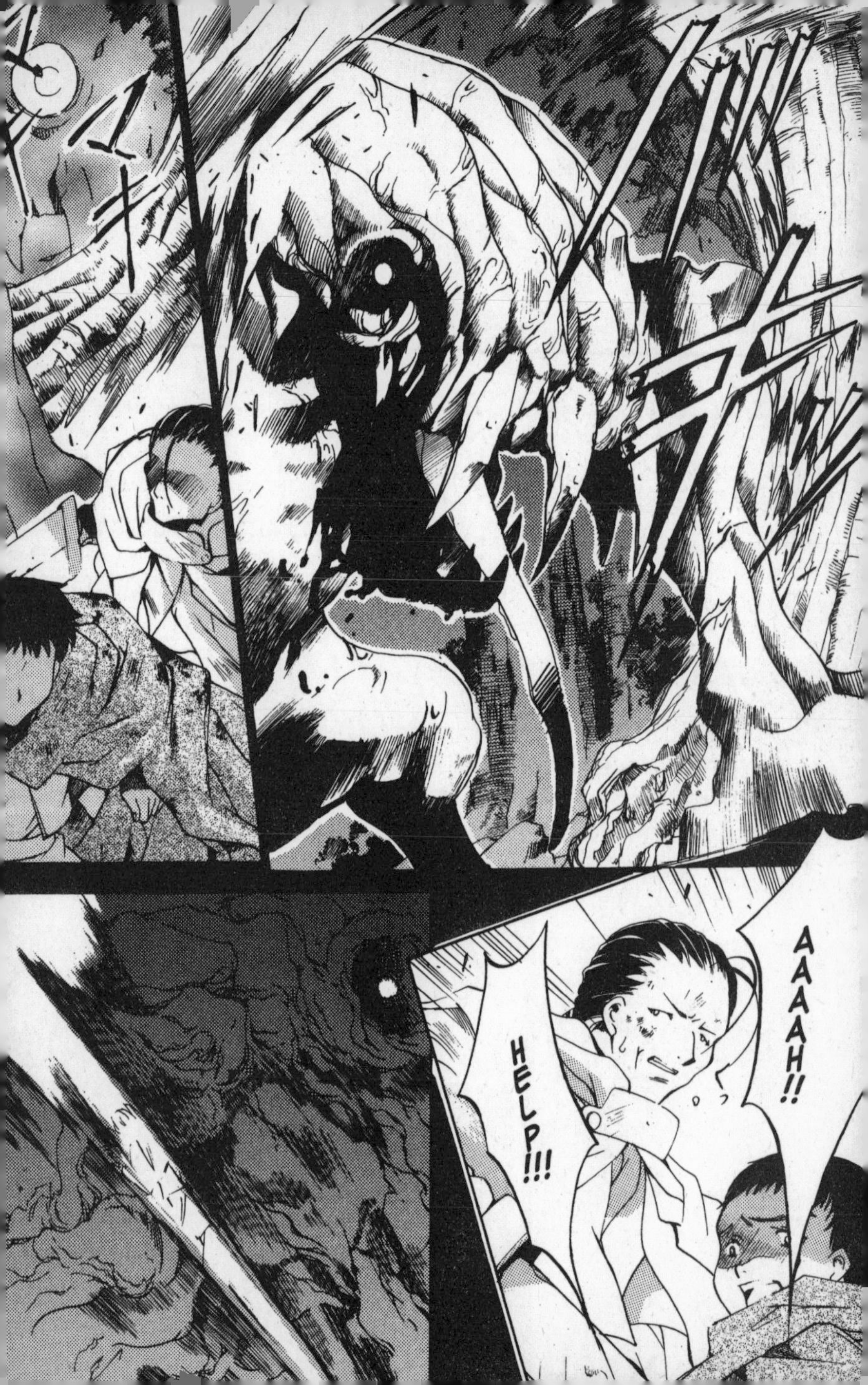
AAAAH!!
HELP!!!

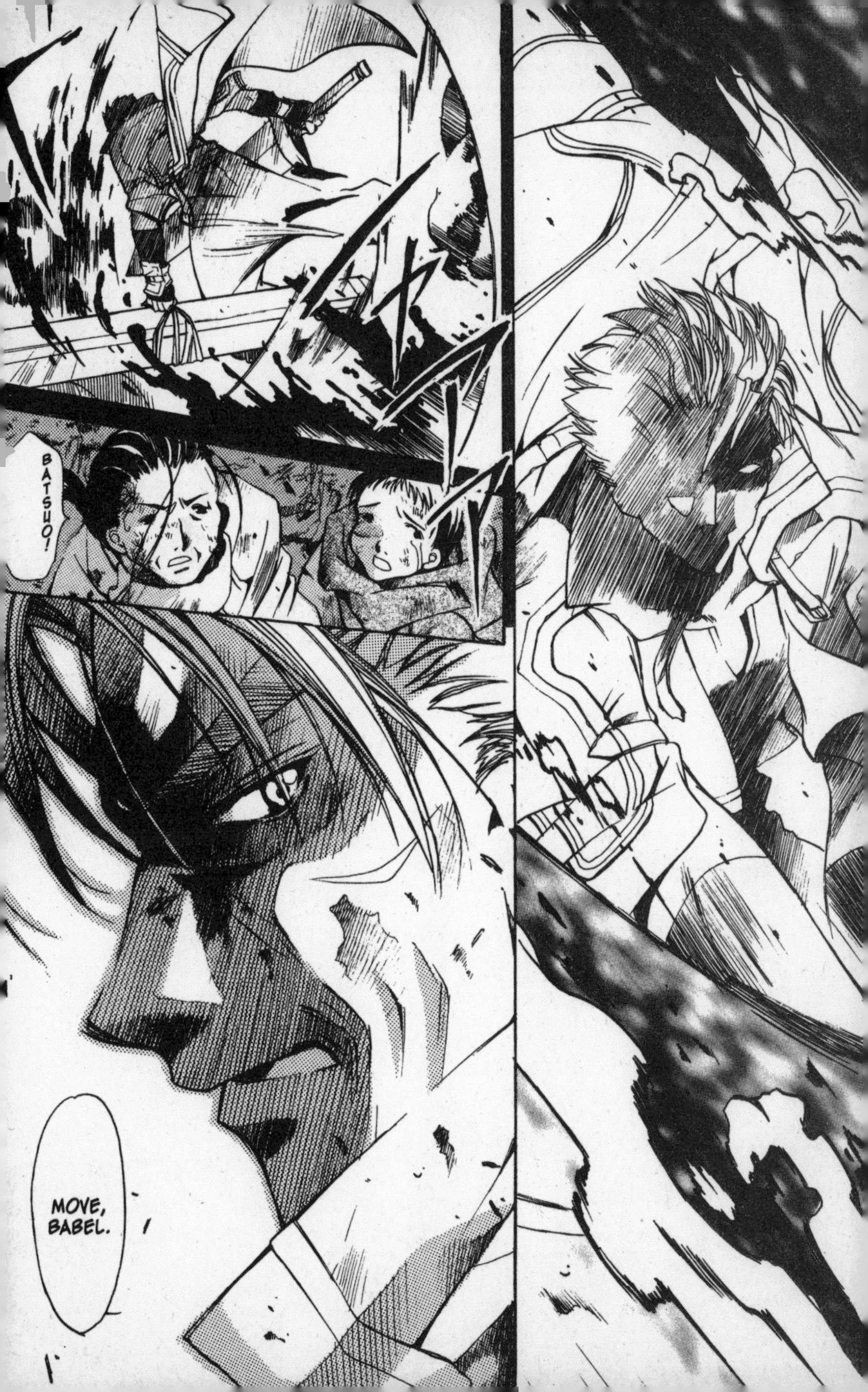
BATSUO!
MOVE, BABEL.

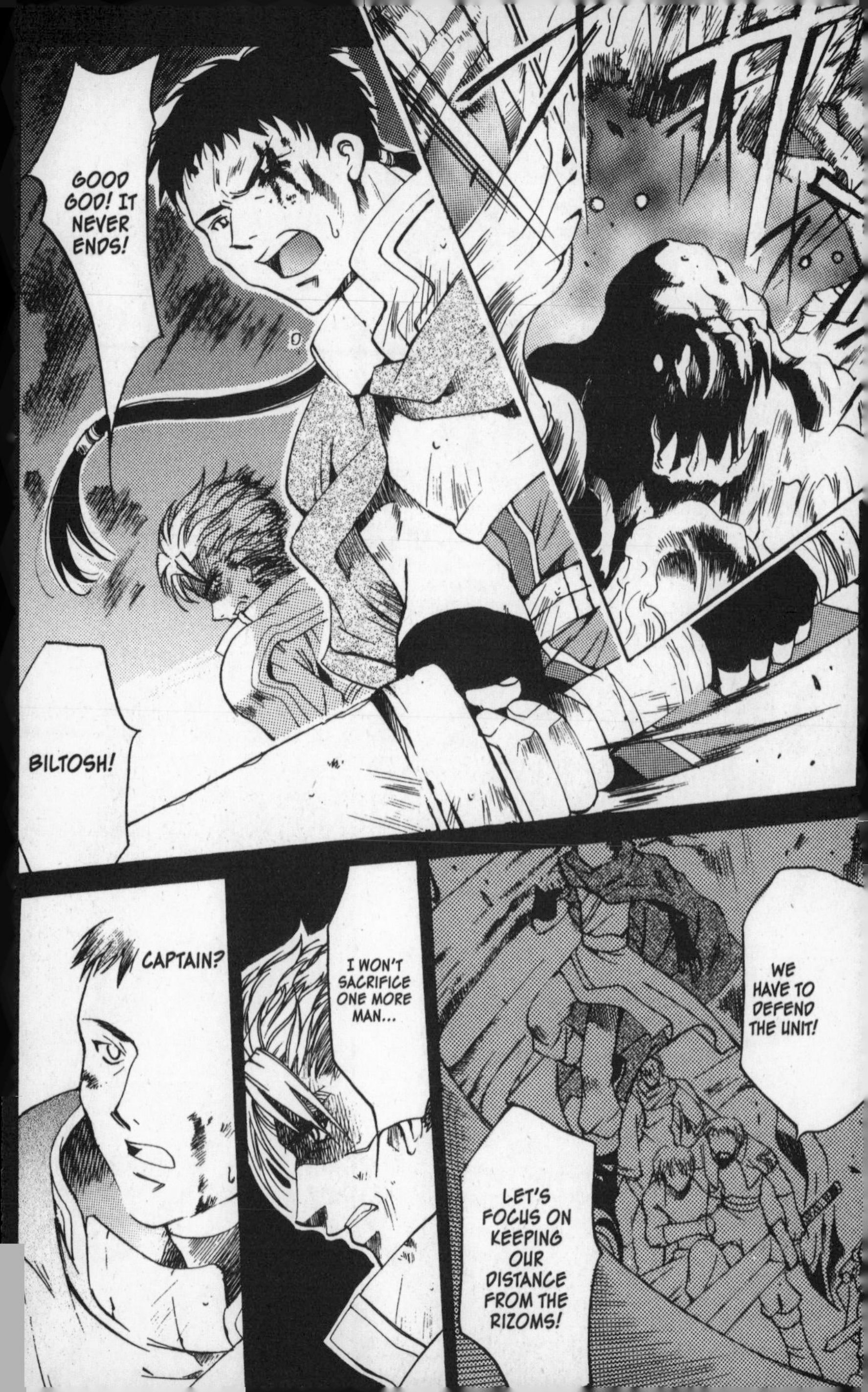
GOOD GOD! IT NEVER ENDS!
BILTOSH!
WE HAVE TO DEFEND THE UNIT!
LET'S FOCUS ON KEEPING OUR DISTANCE FROM THE RIZOMS!
I WON'T SACRIFICE ONE MORE MAN...
CAPTAIN?

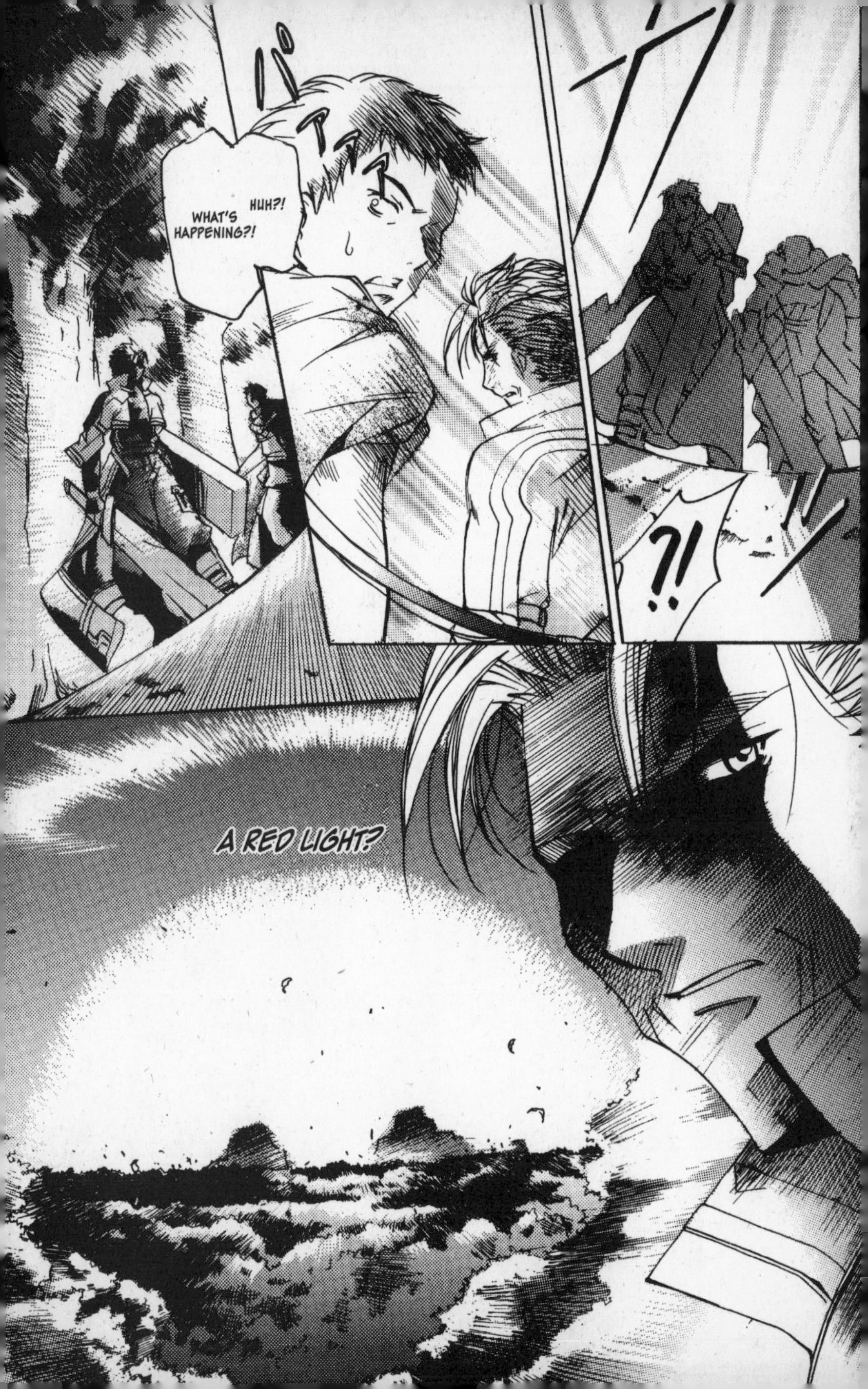
?!
HUH?! WHAT'S HAPPENING?!
A RED LIGHT?

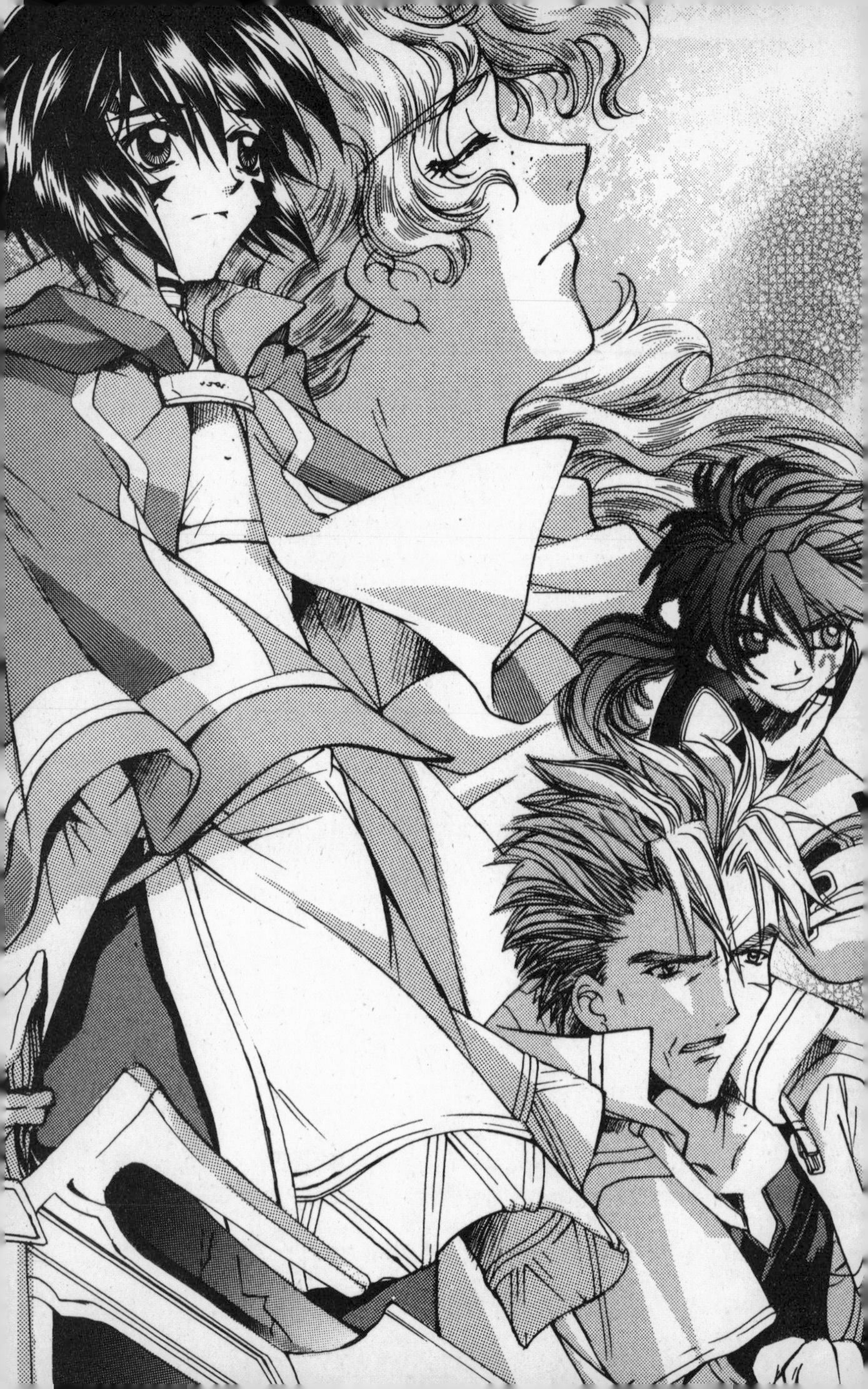

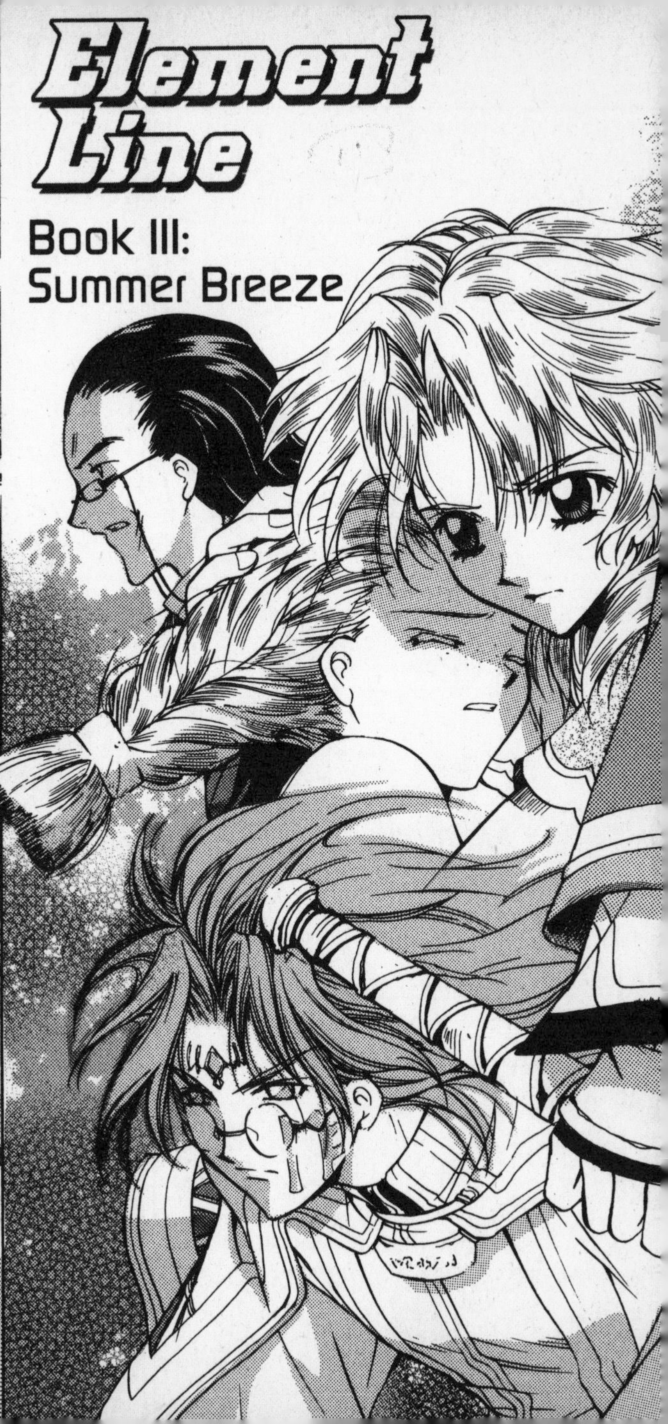
Element Line
Book III:
Summer Breeze
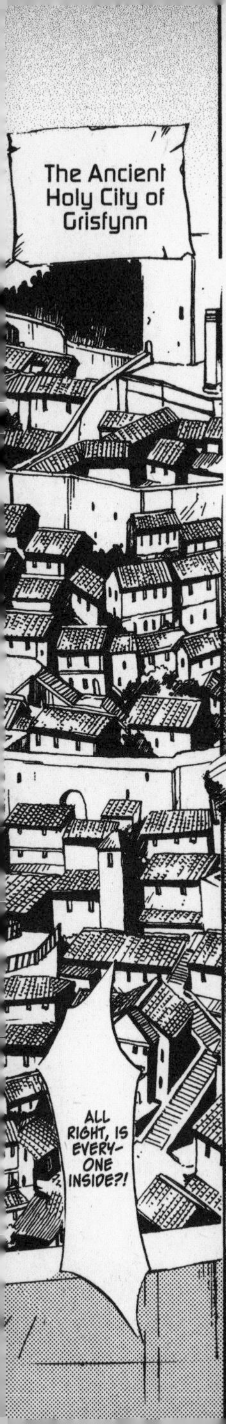
The Ancient Holy City of Grisfynn
ALL RIGHT, IS EVERY-ONE INSIDE?!

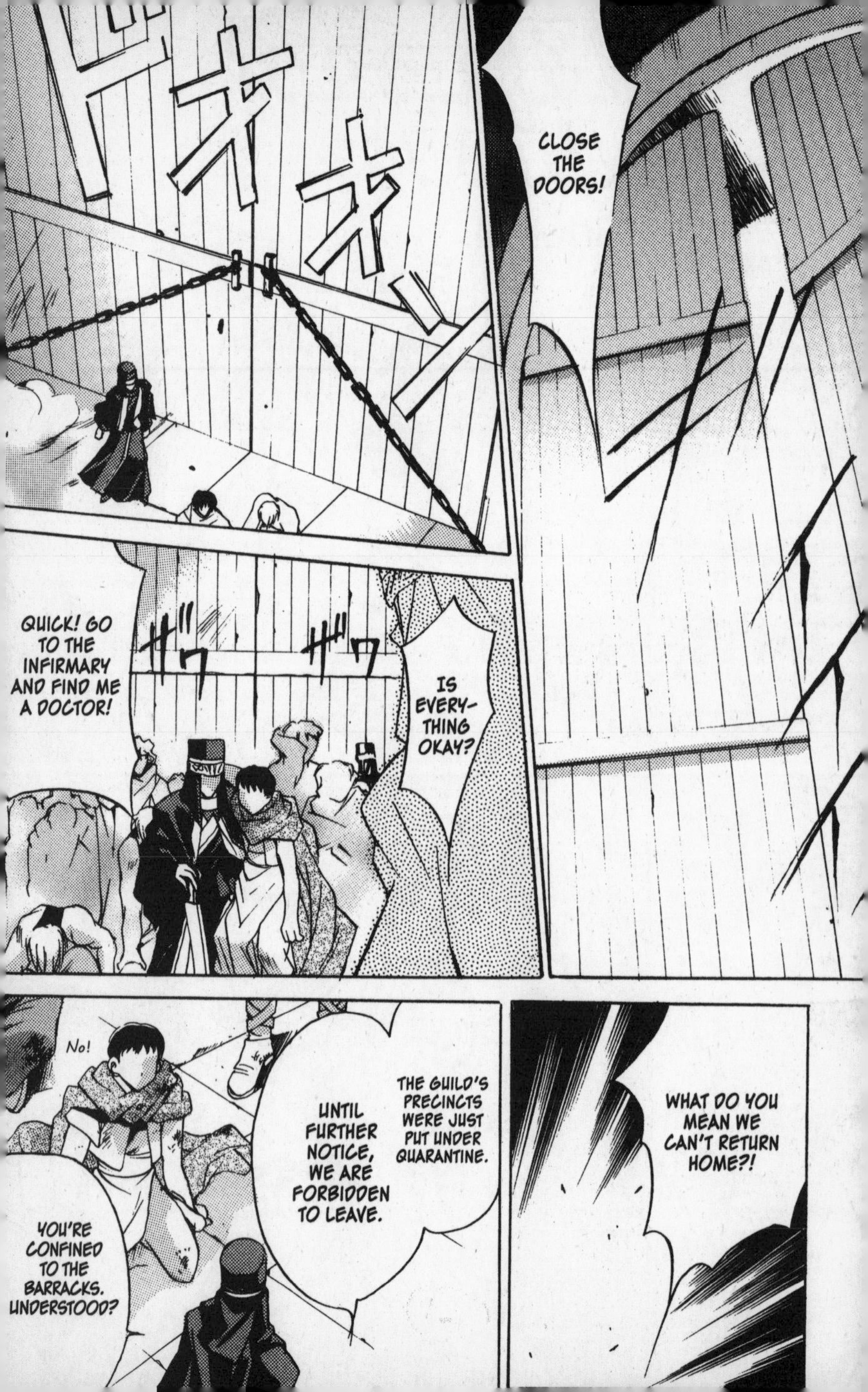
CLOSE THE DOORS!
ドオオン
IS EVERYTHING OKAY?
ザワ ザワ
QUICK! GO TO THE INFIRMARY AND FIND ME A DOCTOR!
WHAT DO YOU MEAN WE CAN'T RETURN HOME?!
THE GUILD'S PRECINCTS WERE JUST PUT UNDER QUARANTINE.
UNTIL FURTHER NOTICE, WE ARE FORBIDDEN TO LEAVE.
No!
YOU'RE CONFINED TO THE BARRACKS. UNDERSTOOD?

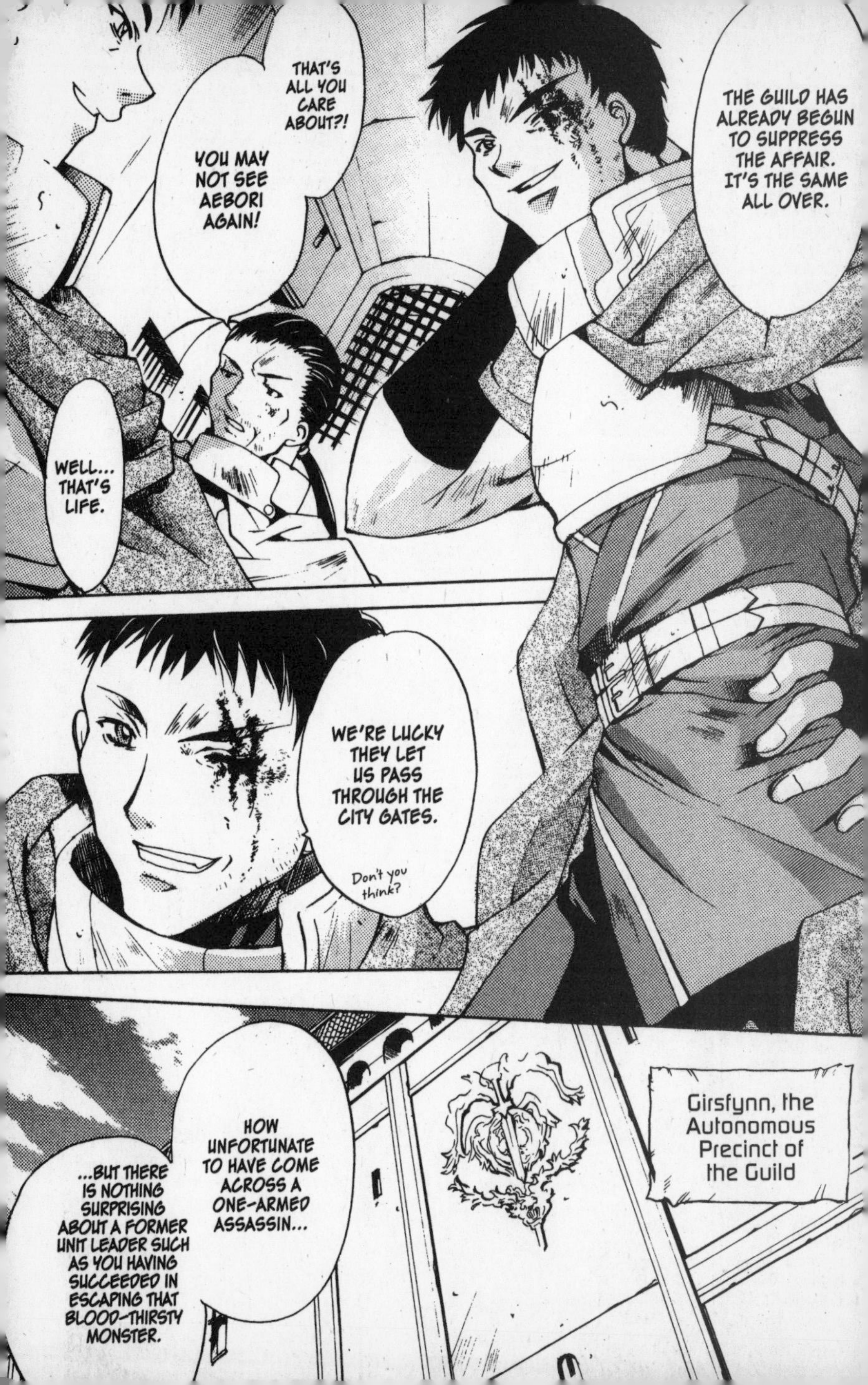
THE GUILD HAS ALREADY BEGUN TO SUPPRESS THE AFFAIR. IT'S THE SAME ALL OVER.
THAT'S ALL YOU CARE ABOUT?!
YOU MAY NOT SEE AEBORI AGAIN!
WELL... THAT'S LIFE.
WE'RE LUCKY THEY LET US PASS THROUGH THE CITY GATES.
Don't you think?
Girsfynn, the Autonomous Precinct of the Guild
HOW UNFORTUNATE TO HAVE COME ACROSS A ONE-ARMED ASSASSIN...
...BUT THERE IS NOTHING SURPRISING ABOUT A FORMER UNIT LEADER SUCH AS YOU HAVING SUCCEEDED IN ESCAPING THAT BLOOD-THIRSTY MONSTER.

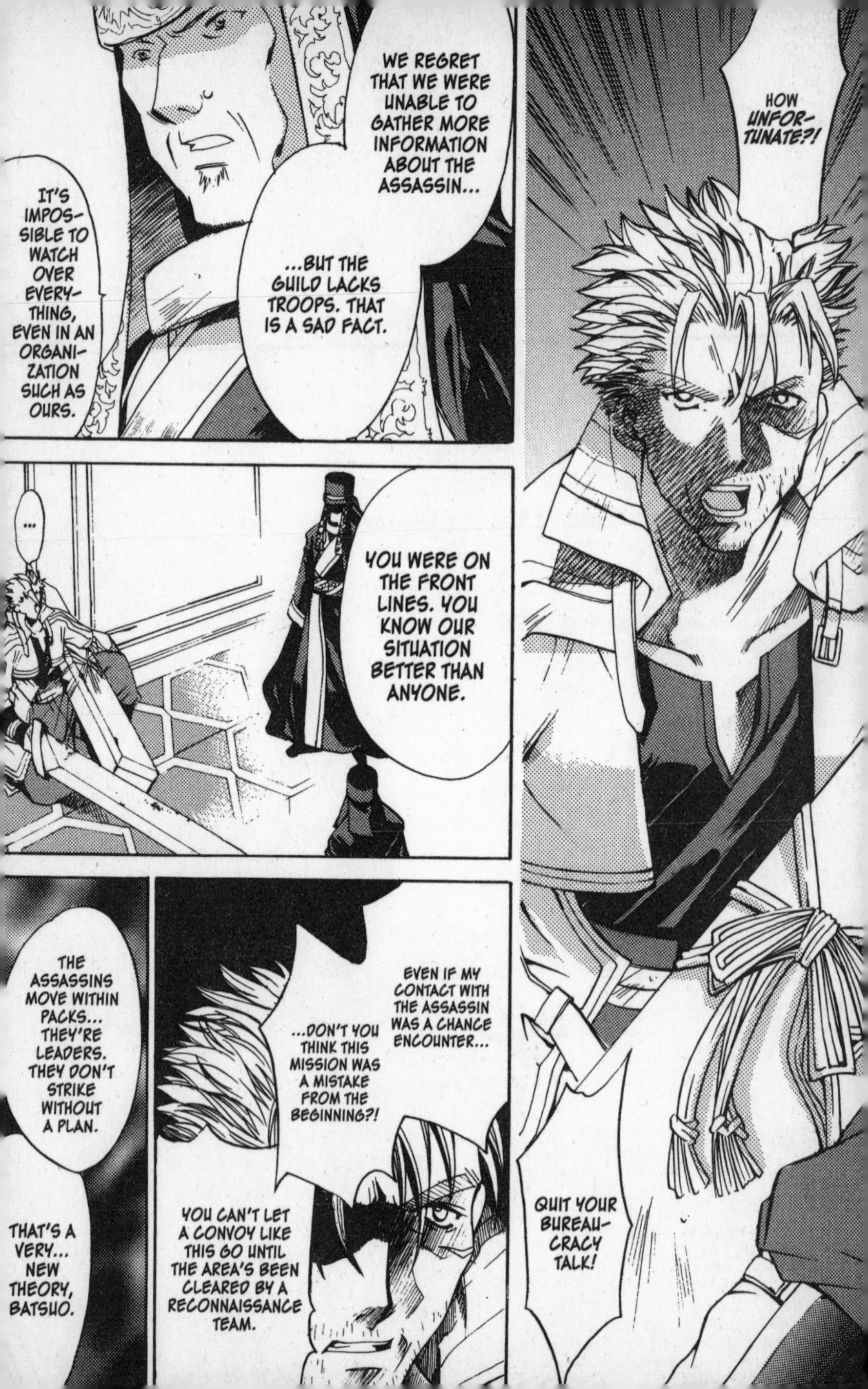
HOW UNFOR-TUNATE?!
QUIT YOUR BUREAU-CRACY TALK!
WE REGRET THAT WE WERE UNABLE TO GATHER MORE INFORMATION ABOUT THE ASSASSIN...
...BUT THE GUILD LACKS TROOPS. THAT IS A SAD FACT.
IT'S IMPOS-SIBLE TO WATCH OVER EVERY-THING, EVEN IN AN ORGANI-ZATION SUCH AS OURS.
YOU WERE ON THE FRONT LINES. YOU KNOW OUR SITUATION BETTER THAN ANYONE.
...
EVEN IF MY CONTACT WITH THE ASSASSIN WAS A CHANCE ENCOUNTER...
...DON'T YOU THINK THIS MISSION WAS A MISTAKE FROM THE BEGINNING?!
YOU CAN'T LET A CONVOY LIKE THIS GO UNTIL THE AREA'S BEEN CLEARED BY A RECONNAISSANCE TEAM.
THE ASSASSINS MOVE WITHIN PACKS... THEY'RE LEADERS. THEY DON'T STRIKE WITHOUT A PLAN.
THAT'S A VERY... NEW THEORY, BATSUO.

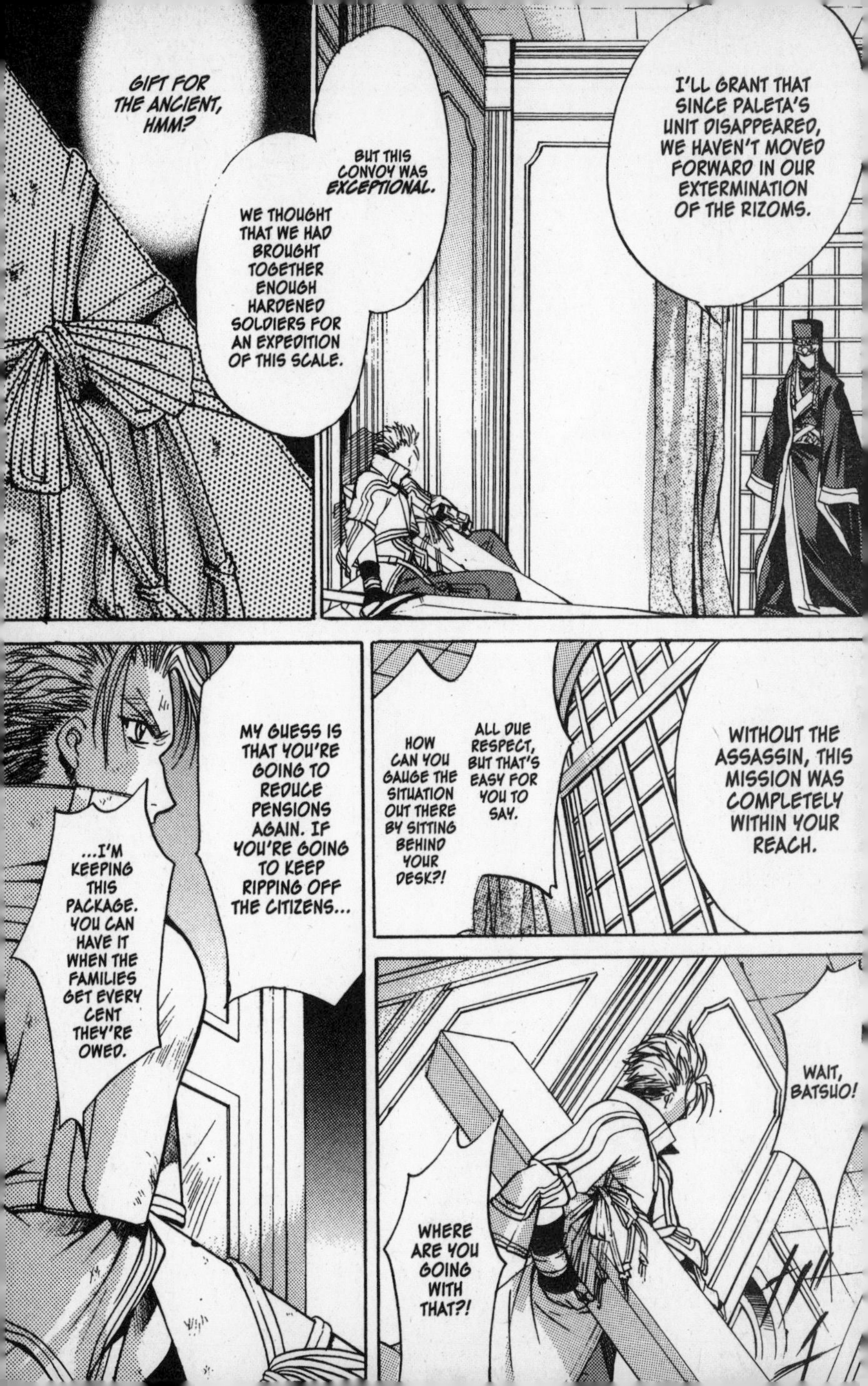
I'LL GRANT THAT SINCE PALETA'S UNIT DISAPPEARED, WE HAVEN'T MOVED FORWARD IN OUR EXTERMINATION OF THE RIZOMS.
BUT THIS CONVOY WAS *EXCEPTIONAL.*
WE THOUGHT THAT WE HAD BROUGHT TOGETHER ENOUGH HARDENED SOLDIERS FOR AN EXPEDITION OF THIS SCALE.
GIFT FOR THE ANCIENT, HMM?
WITHOUT THE ASSASSIN, THIS MISSION WAS COMPLETELY WITHIN YOUR REACH.
ALL DUE RESPECT, BUT THAT'S EASY FOR YOU TO SAY.
HOW CAN YOU GAUGE THE SITUATION OUT THERE BY SITTING BEHIND YOUR DESK?!
WAIT, BATSUO!
WHERE ARE YOU GOING WITH THAT?!
MY GUESS IS THAT YOU'RE GOING TO REDUCE PENSIONS AGAIN. IF YOU'RE GOING TO KEEP RIPPING OFF THE CITIZENS...
...I'M KEEPING THIS PACKAGE. YOU CAN HAVE IT WHEN THE FAMILIES GET EVERY CENT THEY'RE OWED.

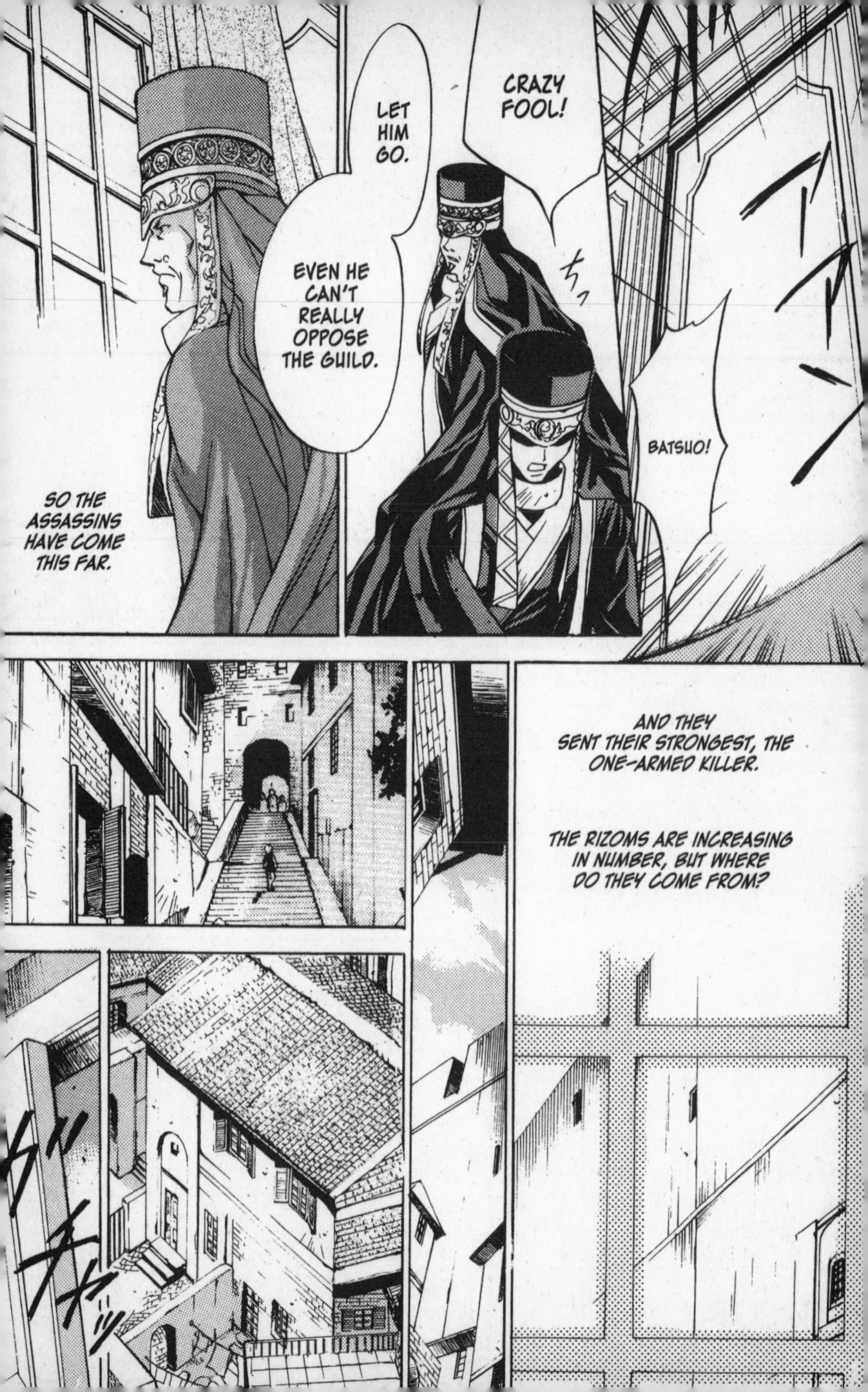
CRAZY FOOL!
BATSUO!
LET HIM GO.
EVEN HE CAN'T REALLY OPPOSE THE GUILD.
SO THE ASSASSINS HAVE COME THIS FAR.
AND THEY SENT THEIR STRONGEST, THE ONE-ARMED KILLER.
THE RIZOMS ARE INCREASING IN NUMBER, BUT WHERE DO THEY COME FROM?

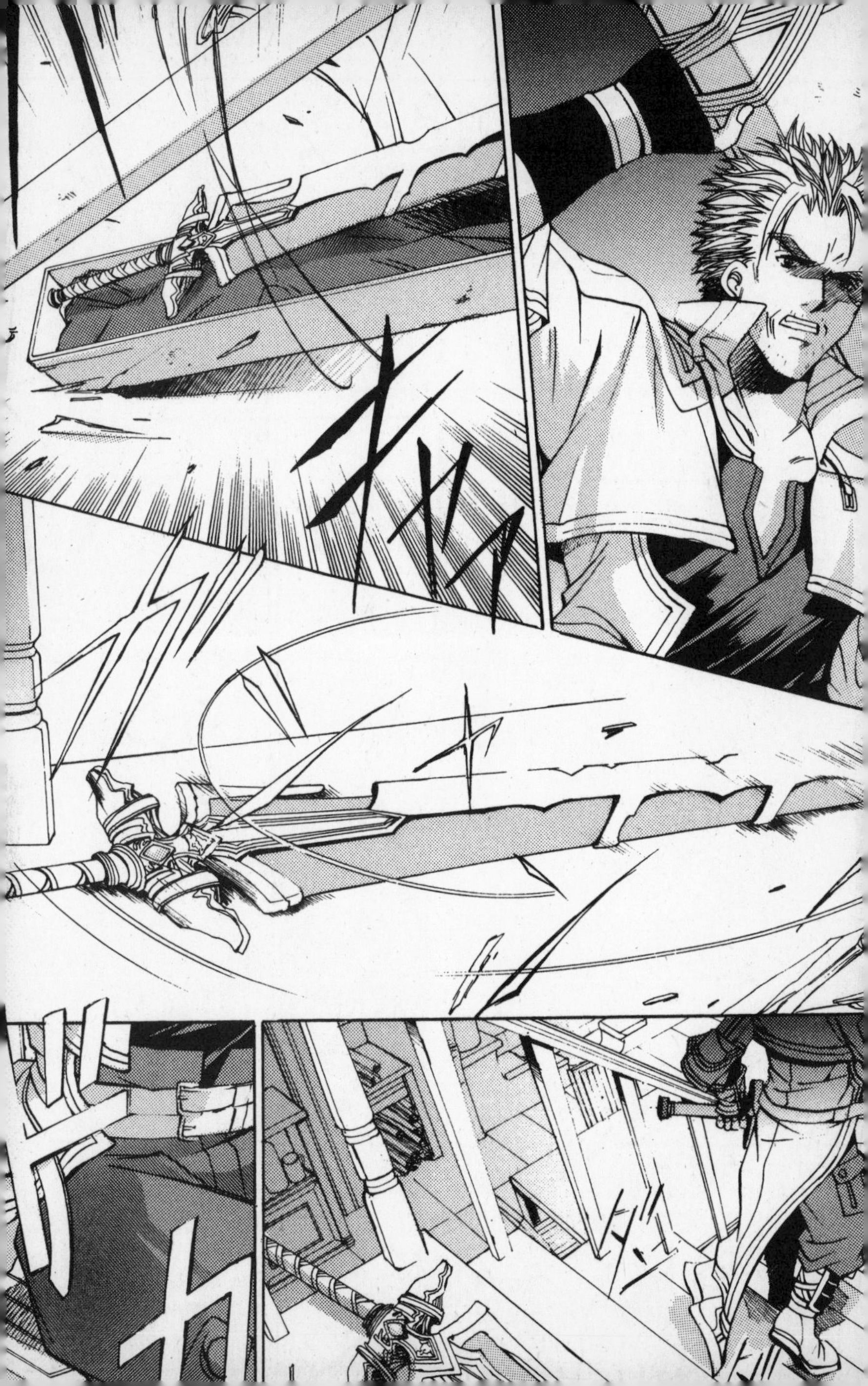

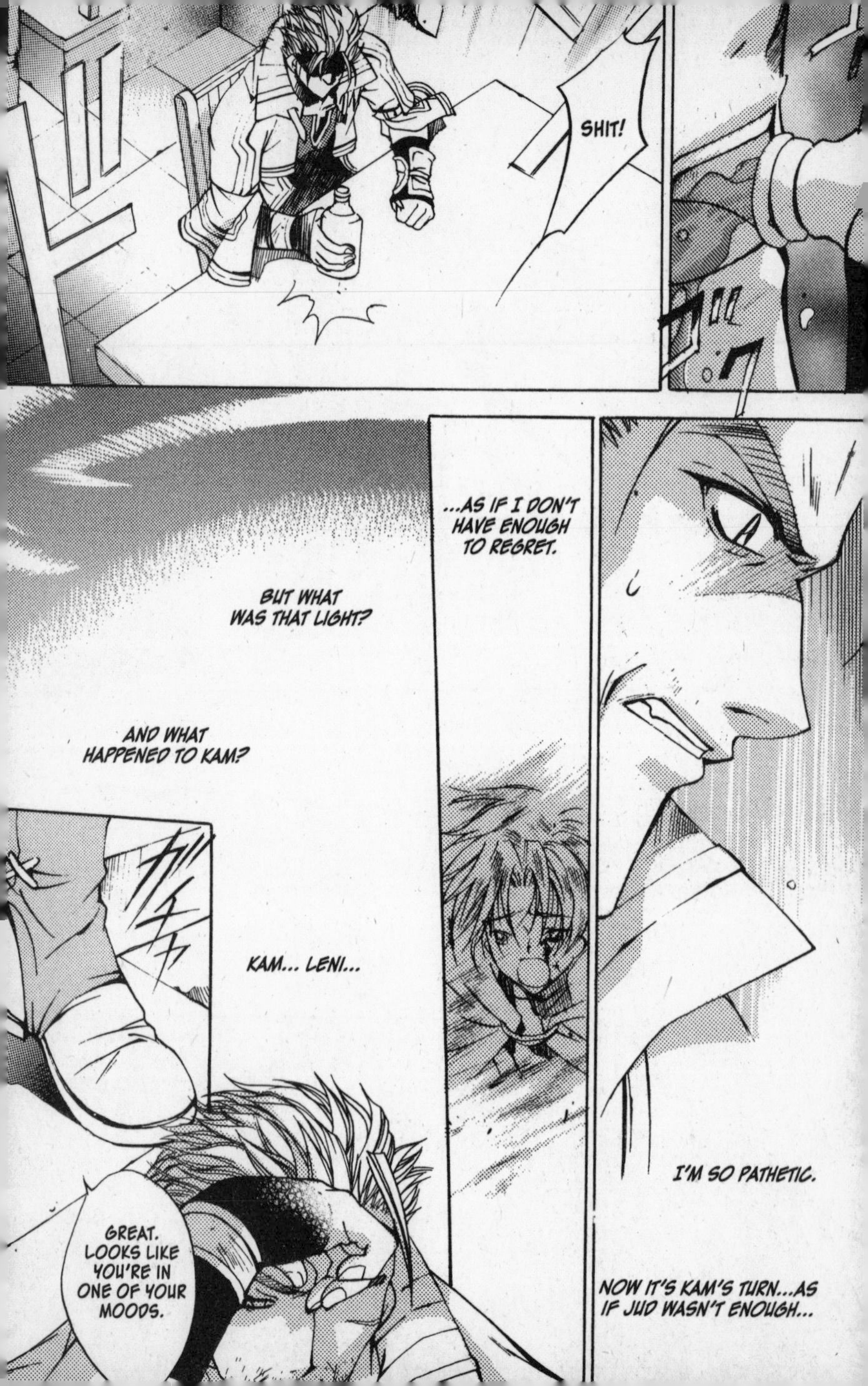
SHIT!
I'M SO PATHETIC.
NOW IT'S KAM'S TURN...AS IF JUD WASN'T ENOUGH...
...AS IF I DON'T HAVE ENOUGH TO REGRET.
BUT WHAT WAS THAT LIGHT?
AND WHAT HAPPENED TO KAM?
KAM... LENI...
GREAT. LOOKS LIKE YOU'RE IN ONE OF YOUR MOODS.

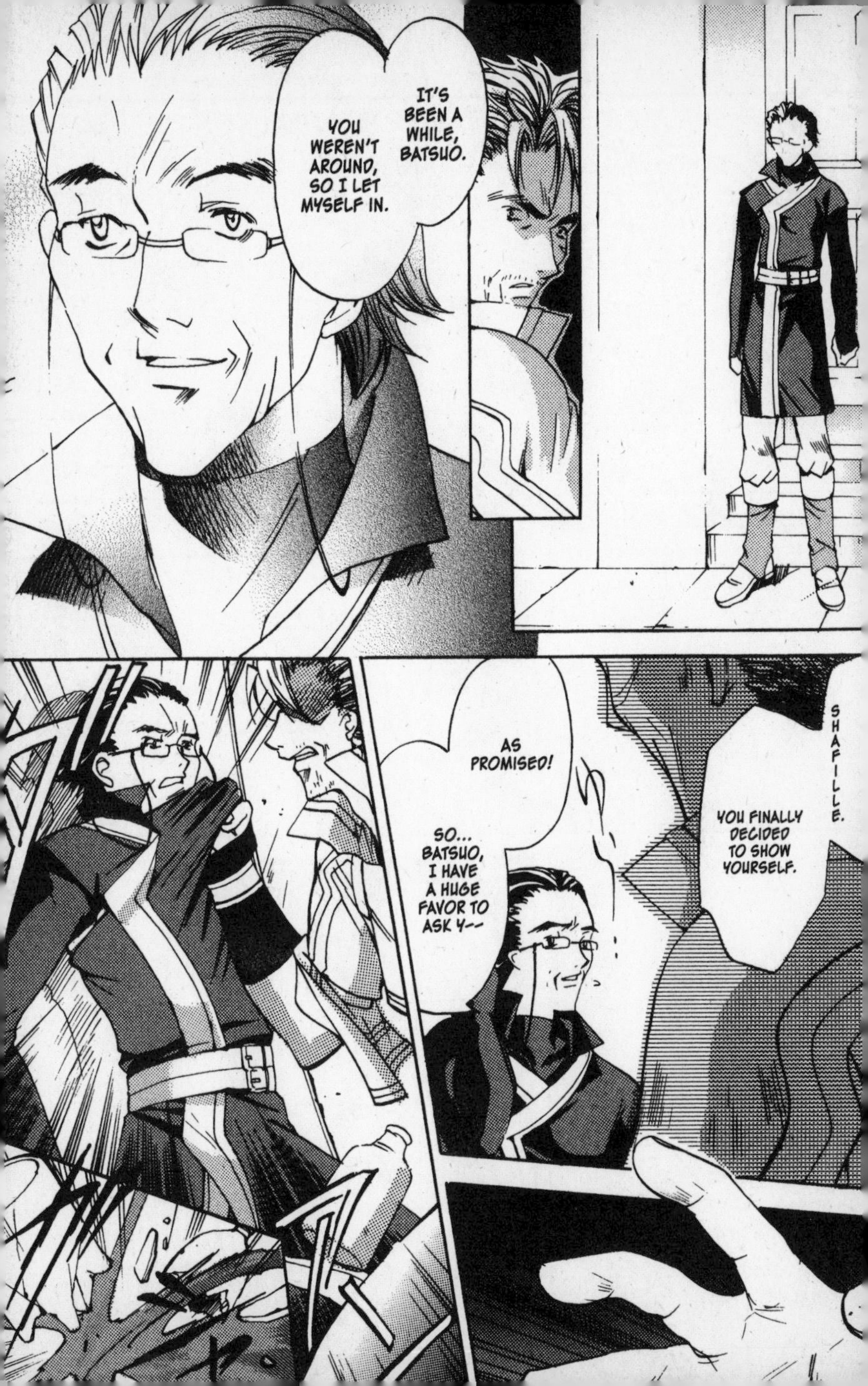
IT'S BEEN A WHILE, BATSUO.
YOU WEREN'T AROUND, SO I LET MYSELF IN.
SHAFILLE.
YOU FINALLY DECIDED TO SHOW YOURSELF.
AS PROMISED!
SO... BATSUO, I HAVE A HUGE FAVOR TO ASK Y--

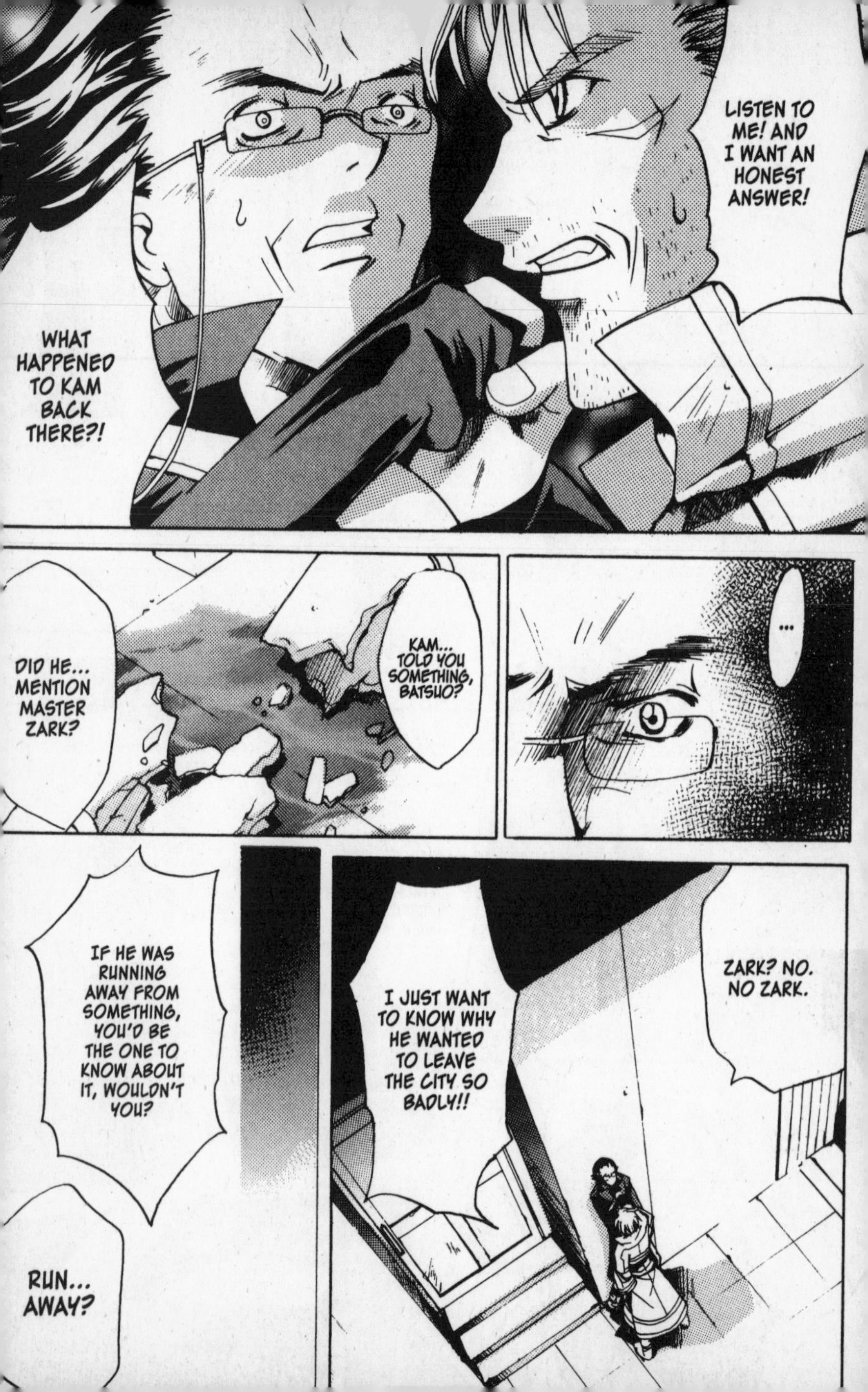
LISTEN TO ME! AND I WANT AN HONEST ANSWER!
WHAT HAPPENED TO KAM BACK THERE?!
...
KAM... TOLD YOU SOMETHING, BATSUO?
DID HE... MENTION MASTER ZARK?
ZARK? NO. NO ZARK.
I JUST WANT TO KNOW WHY HE WANTED TO LEAVE THE CITY SO BADLY!!
IF HE WAS RUNNING AWAY FROM SOMETHING, YOU'D BE THE ONE TO KNOW ABOUT IT, WOULDN'T YOU?
RUN... AWAY?

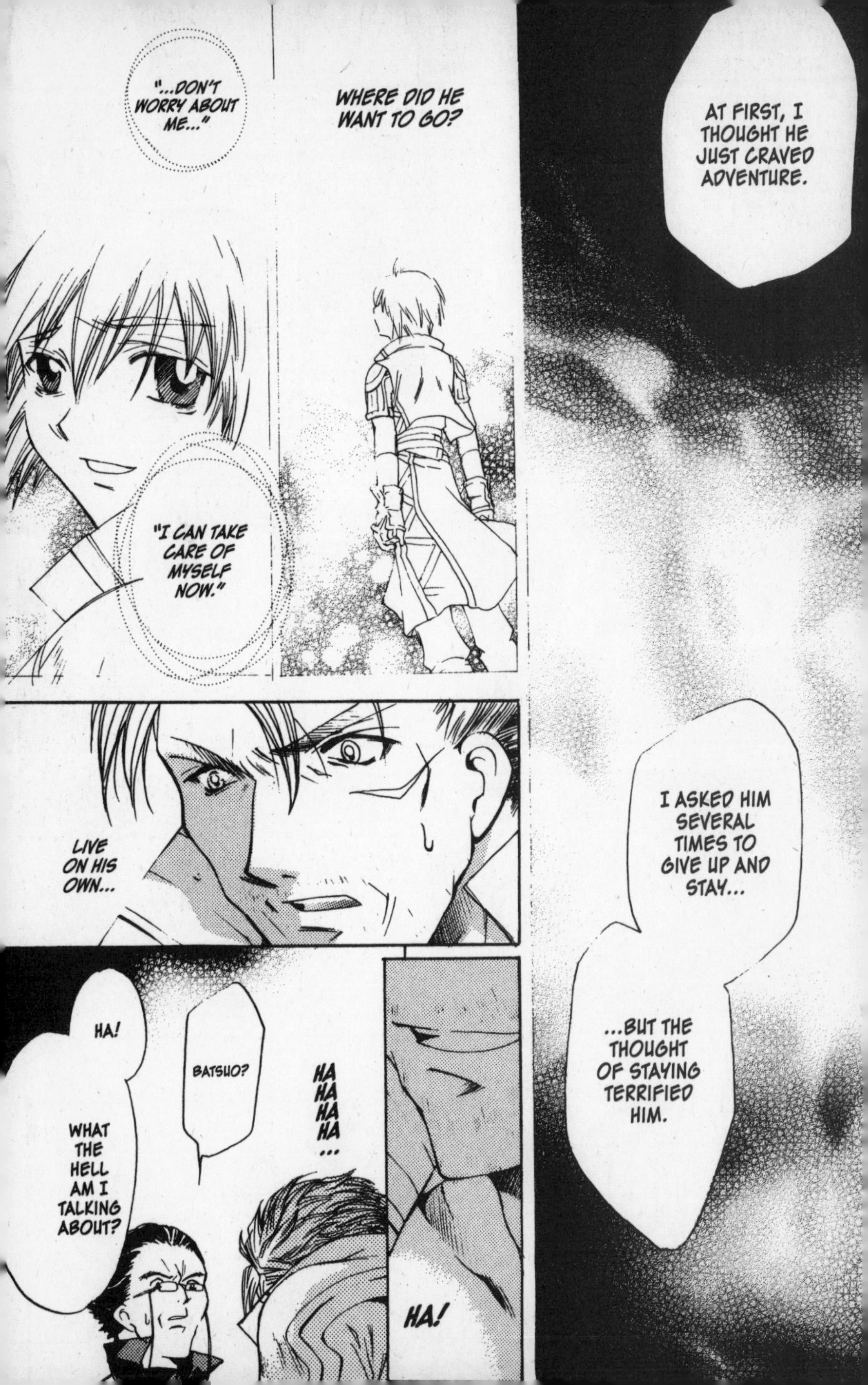
AT FIRST, I THOUGHT HE JUST CRAVED ADVENTURE.
I ASKED HIM SEVERAL TIMES TO GIVE UP AND STAY...
...BUT THE THOUGHT OF STAYING TERRIFIED HIM.
WHERE DID HE WANT TO GO?
"...DON'T WORRY ABOUT ME..."
"I CAN TAKE CARE OF MYSELF NOW."
LIVE ON HIS OWN...
HA!
HA HA HA HA...
BATSUO?
HA!
WHAT THE HELL AM I TALKING ABOUT?

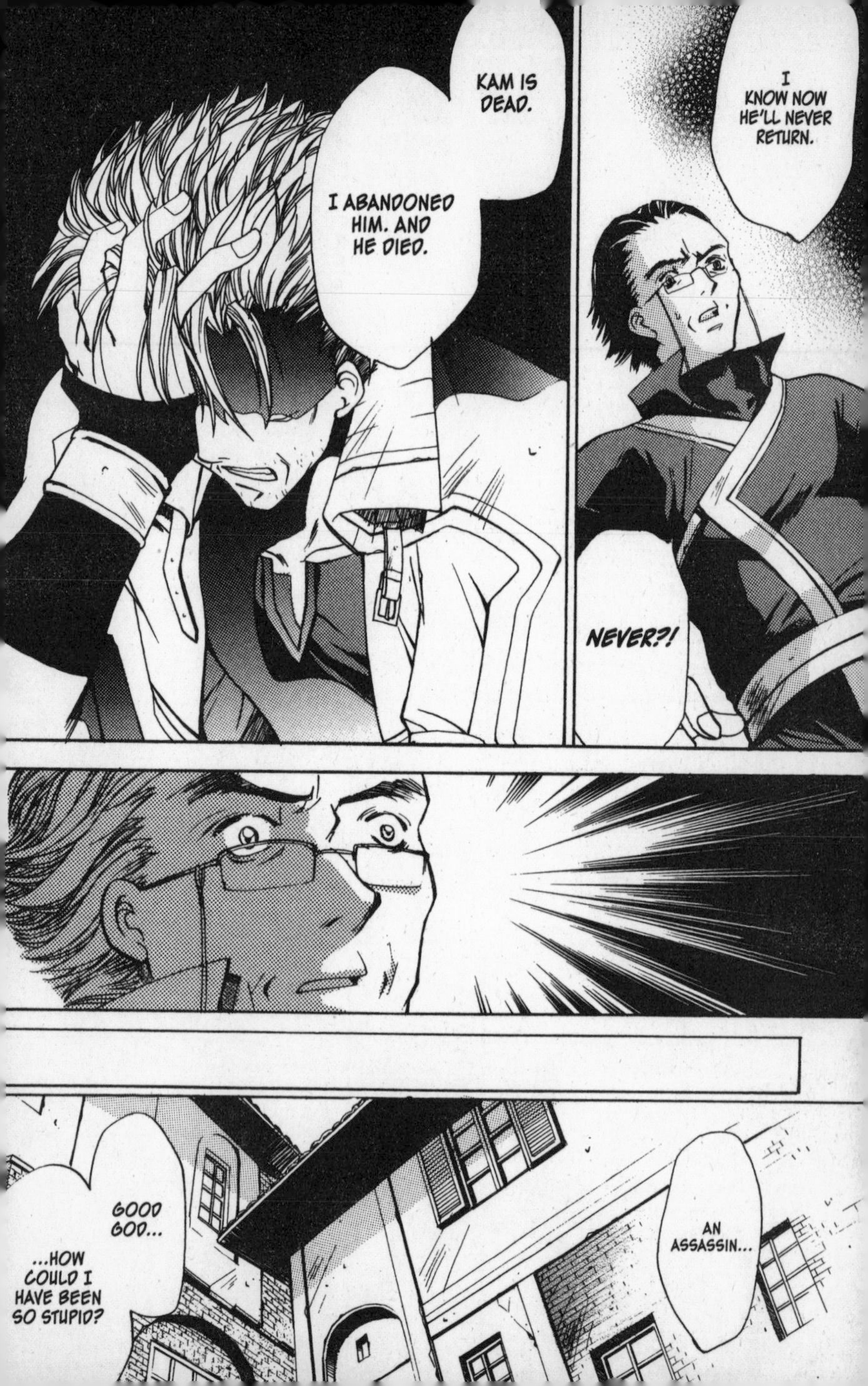
I KNOW NOW HE'LL NEVER RETURN.
NEVER?!
KAM IS DEAD.
I ABANDONED HIM. AND HE DIED.
AN ASSASSIN...
GOOD GOD...
...HOW COULD I HAVE BEEN SO STUPID?

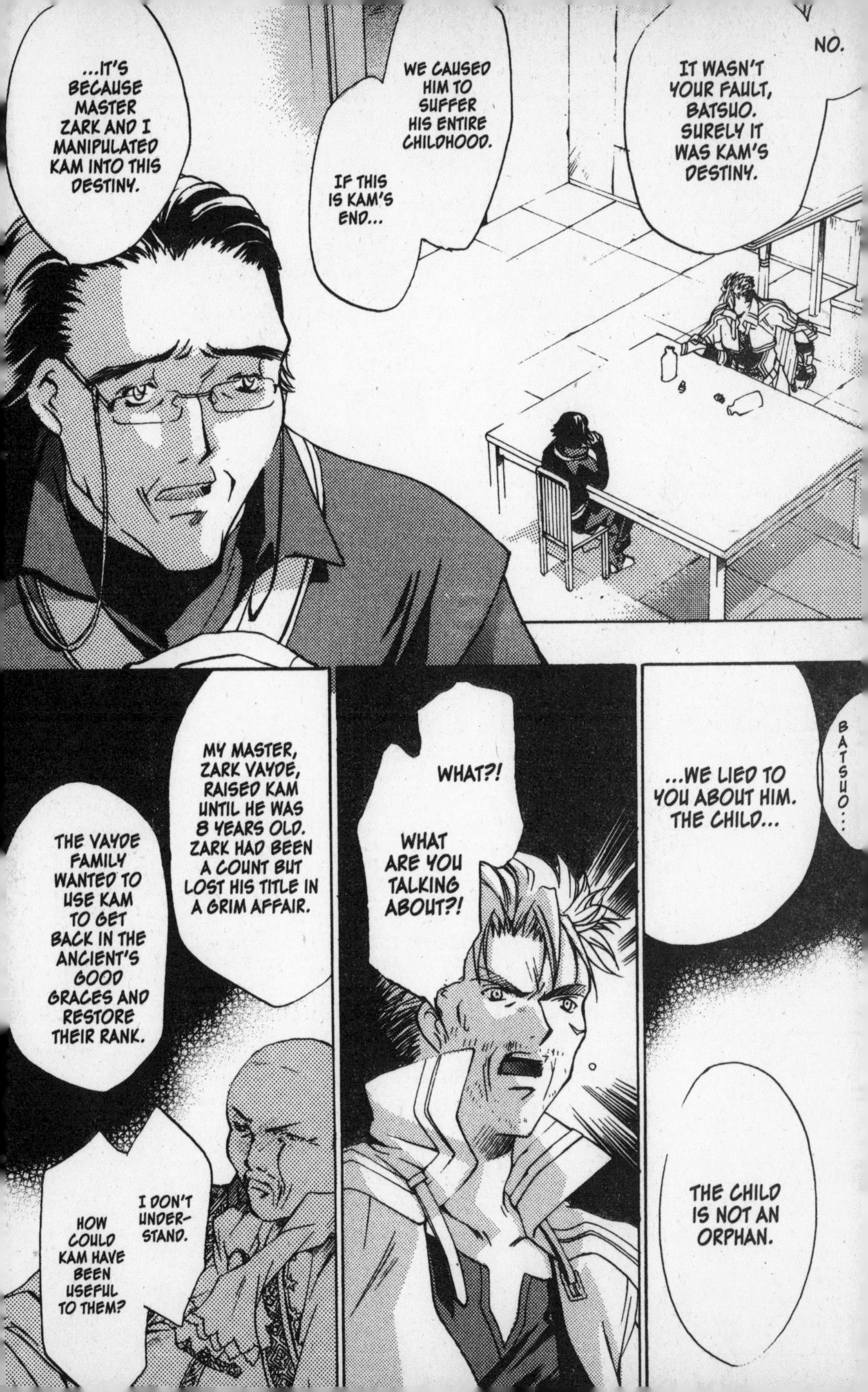
NO.
IT WASN'T YOUR FAULT, BATSUO. SURELY IT WAS KAM'S DESTINY.
WE CAUSED HIM TO SUFFER HIS ENTIRE CHILDHOOD.
IF THIS IS KAM'S END...
...IT'S BECAUSE MASTER ZARK AND I MANIPULATED KAM INTO THIS DESTINY.
BATSUO...
...WE LIED TO YOU ABOUT HIM. THE CHILD...
THE CHILD IS NOT AN ORPHAN.
WHAT?!
WHAT ARE YOU TALKING ABOUT?!
MY MASTER, ZARK VAYDE, RAISED KAM UNTIL HE WAS 8 YEARS OLD. ZARK HAD BEEN A COUNT BUT LOST HIS TITLE IN A GRIM AFFAIR.
THE VAYDE FAMILY WANTED TO USE KAM TO GET BACK IN THE ANCIENT'S GOOD GRACES AND RESTORE THEIR RANK.
I DON'T UNDER-STAND.
HOW COULD KAM HAVE BEEN USEFUL TO THEM?

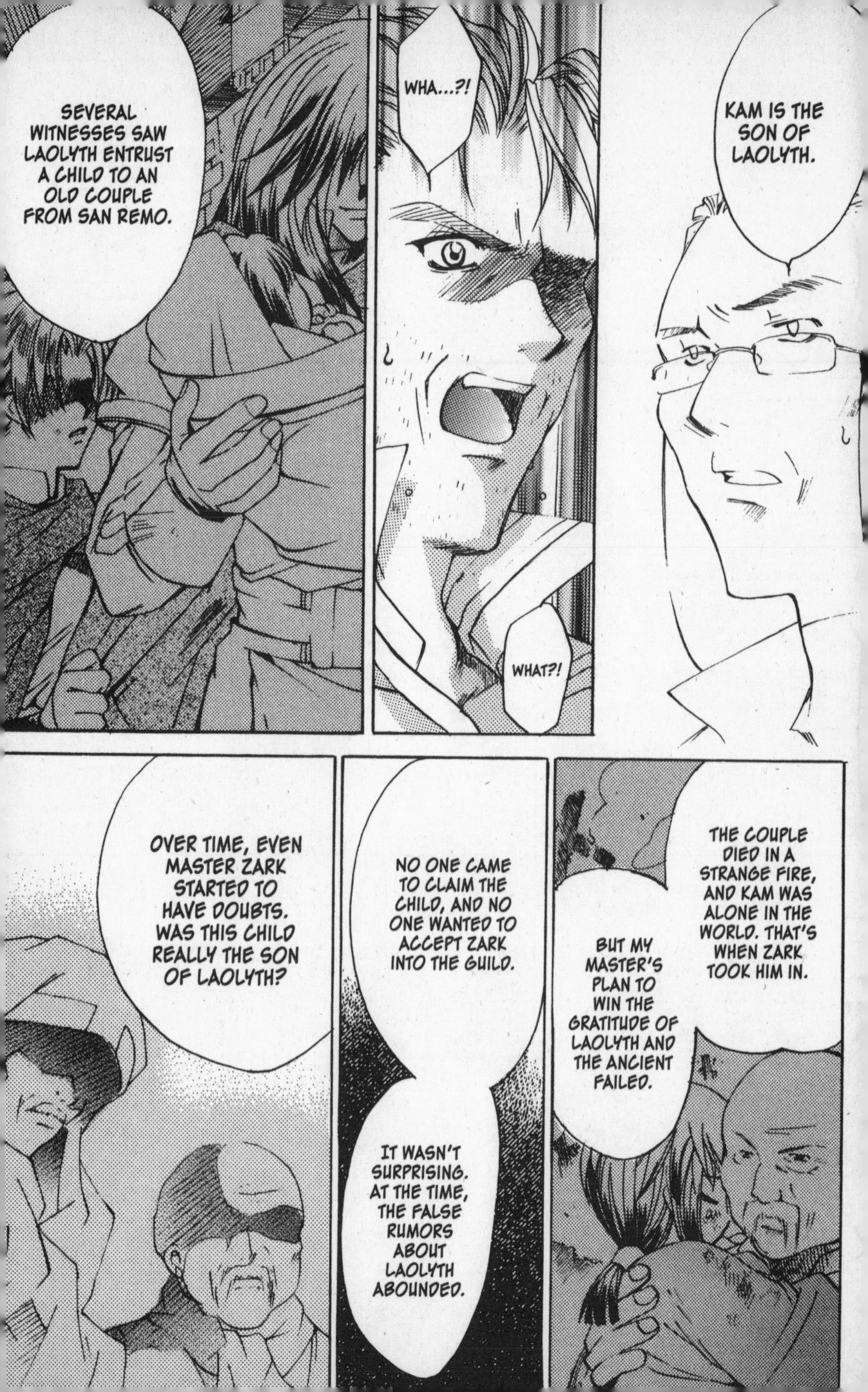
KAM IS THE SON OF LAOLYTH.
WHA...?!
WHAT?!
SEVERAL WITNESSES SAW LAOLYTH ENTRUST A CHILD TO AN OLD COUPLE FROM SAN REMO.
THE COUPLE DIED IN A STRANGE FIRE, AND KAM WAS ALONE IN THE WORLD. THAT'S WHEN ZARK TOOK HIM IN.
BUT MY MASTER'S PLAN TO WIN THE GRATITUDE OF LAOLYTH AND THE ANCIENT FAILED.
NO ONE CAME TO CLAIM THE CHILD, AND NO ONE WANTED TO ACCEPT ZARK INTO THE GUILD.
IT WASN'T SURPRISING. AT THE TIME, THE FALSE RUMORS ABOUT LAOLYTH ABOUNDED.
OVER TIME, EVEN MASTER ZARK STARTED TO HAVE DOUBTS. WAS THIS CHILD REALLY THE SON OF LAOLYTH?

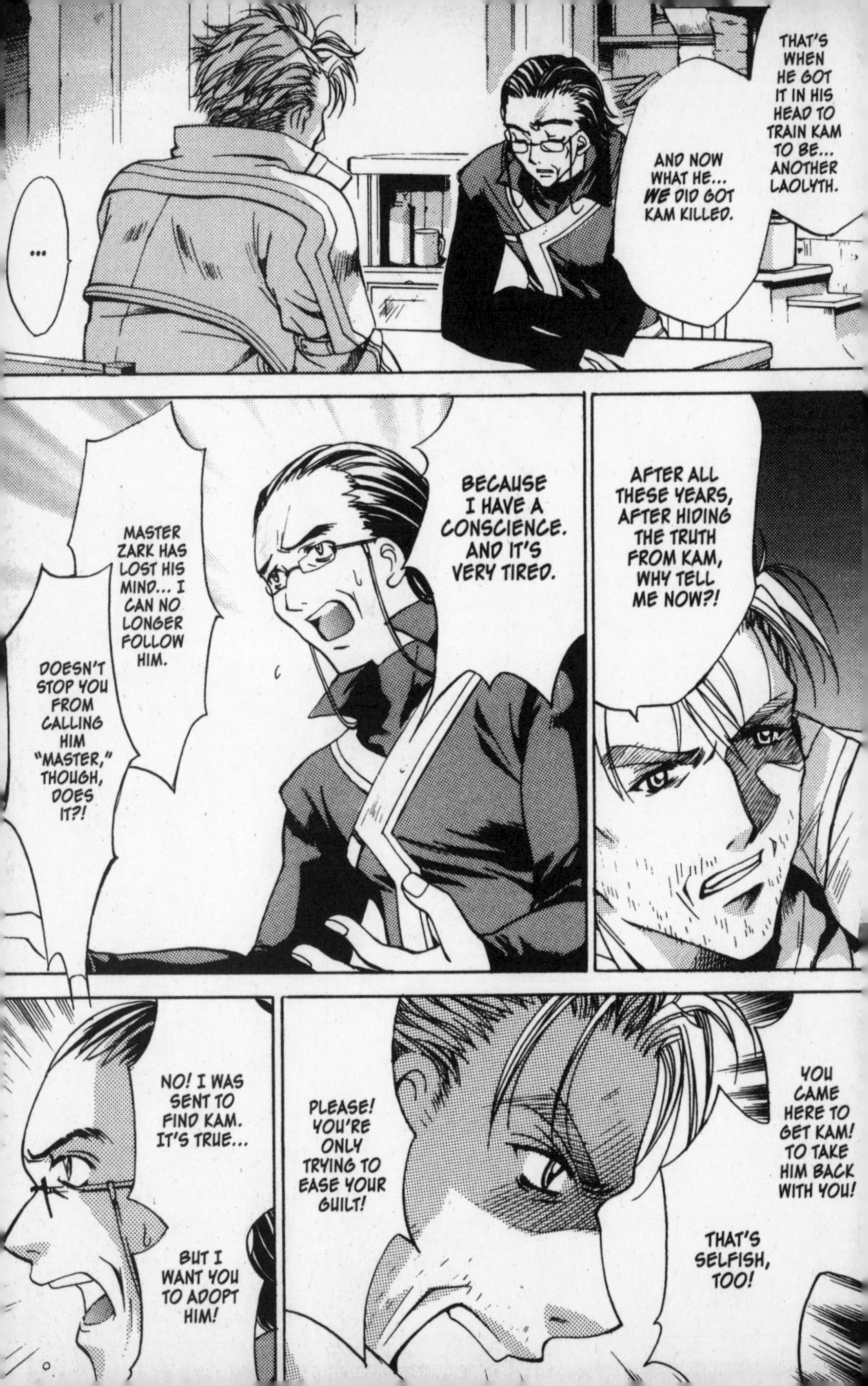
THAT'S WHEN HE GOT IT IN HIS HEAD TO TRAIN KAM TO BE... ANOTHER LAOLYTH.
AND NOW WHAT HE... *WE* DID GOT KAM KILLED.
...
AFTER ALL THESE YEARS, AFTER HIDING THE TRUTH FROM KAM, WHY TELL ME NOW?!
BECAUSE I HAVE A CONSCIENCE. AND IT'S VERY TIRED.
MASTER ZARK HAS LOST HIS MIND... I CAN NO LONGER FOLLOW HIM.
DOESN'T STOP YOU FROM CALLING HIM "MASTER," THOUGH, DOES IT?!
YOU CAME HERE TO GET KAM! TO TAKE HIM BACK WITH YOU!
THAT'S SELFISH, TOO!
PLEASE! YOU'RE ONLY TRYING TO EASE YOUR GUILT!
NO! I WAS SENT TO FIND KAM. IT'S TRUE...
BUT I WANT YOU TO ADOPT HIM!

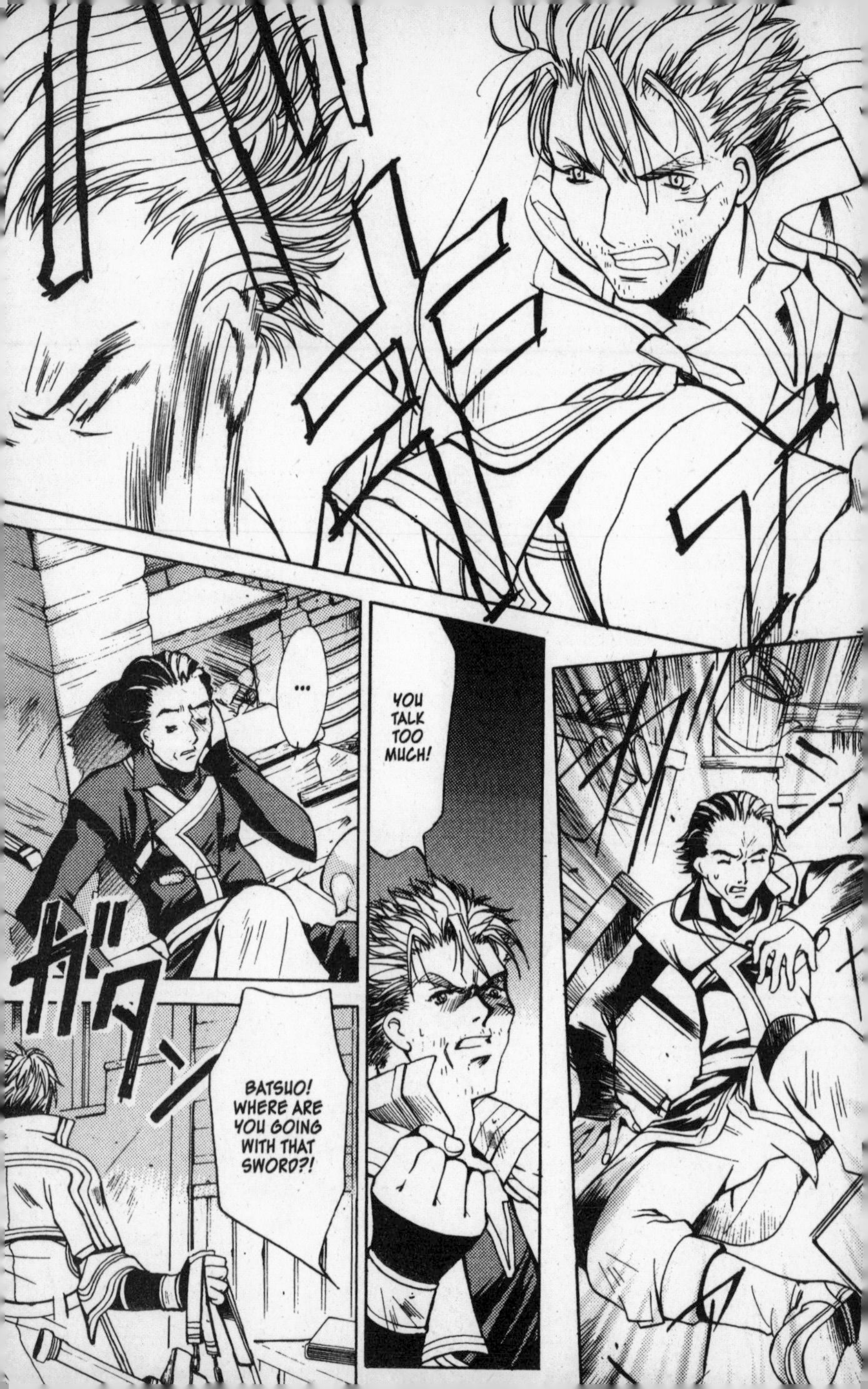
YOU TALK TOO MUCH!
...
BATSUO! WHERE ARE YOU GOING WITH THAT SWORD?!

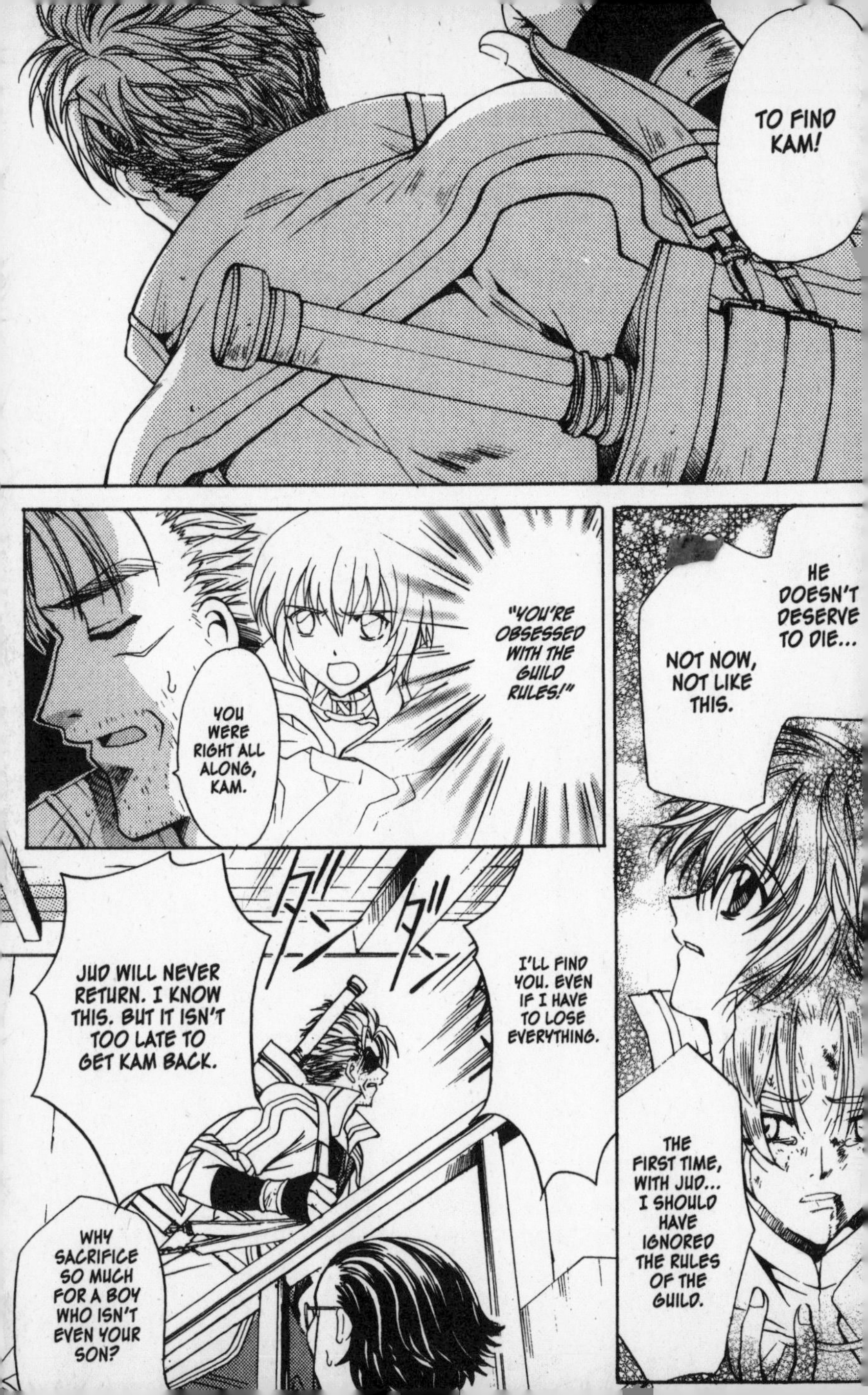

TO FIND KAM!
HE DOESN'T DESERVE TO DIE...
NOT NOW, NOT LIKE THIS.
THE FIRST TIME, WITH JUD... I SHOULD HAVE IGNORED THE RULES OF THE GUILD.
"YOU'RE OBSESSED WITH THE GUILD RULES!"
YOU WERE RIGHT ALL ALONG, KAM.
ダッ
ダッ
I'LL FIND YOU. EVEN IF I HAVE TO LOSE EVERYTHING.
JUD WILL NEVER RETURN. I KNOW THIS. BUT IT ISN'T TOO LATE TO GET KAM BACK.
WHY SACRIFICE SO MUCH FOR A BOY WHO ISN'T EVEN YOUR SON?

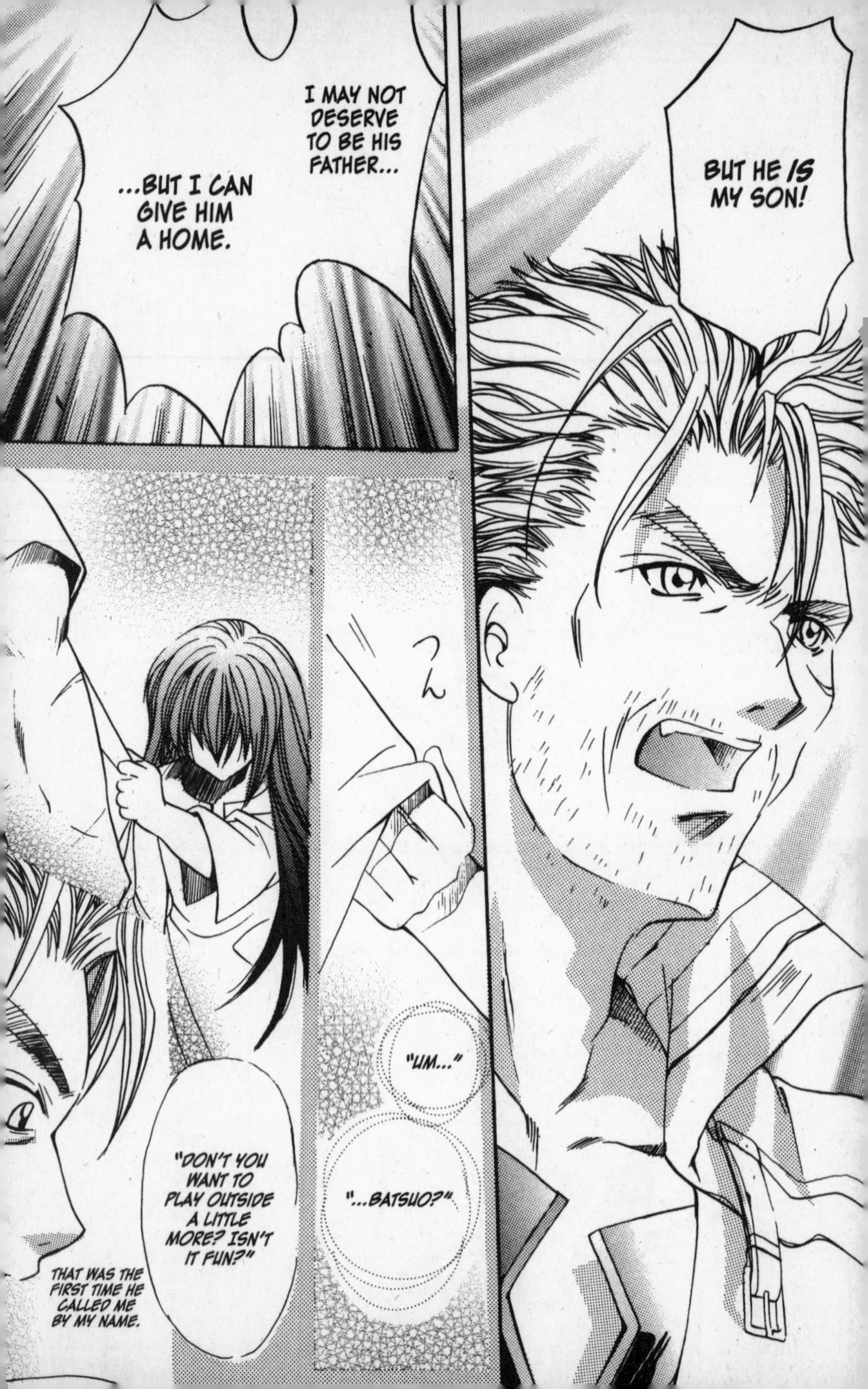
BUT HE IS MY SON!
I MAY NOT DESERVE TO BE HIS FATHER...
...BUT I CAN GIVE HIM A HOME.
"UM..."
"...BATSUO?"
"DON'T YOU WANT TO PLAY OUTSIDE A LITTLE MORE? ISN'T IT FUN?"
THAT WAS THE FIRST TIME HE CALLED ME BY MY NAME.

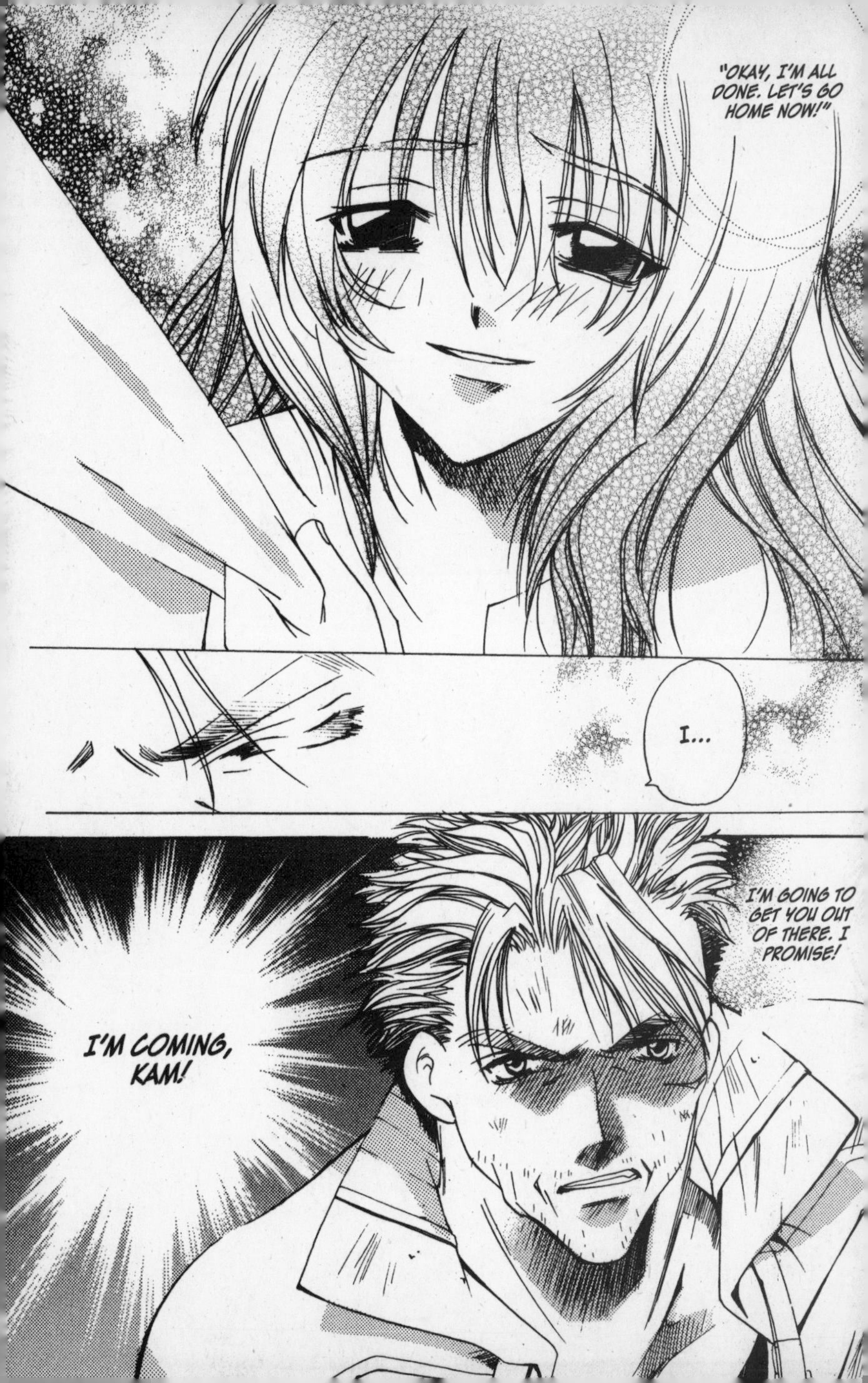
"OKAY, I'M ALL DONE. LET'S GO HOME NOW!"
I...
I'M GOING TO GET YOU OUT OF THERE. I PROMISE!
I'M COMING, KAM!

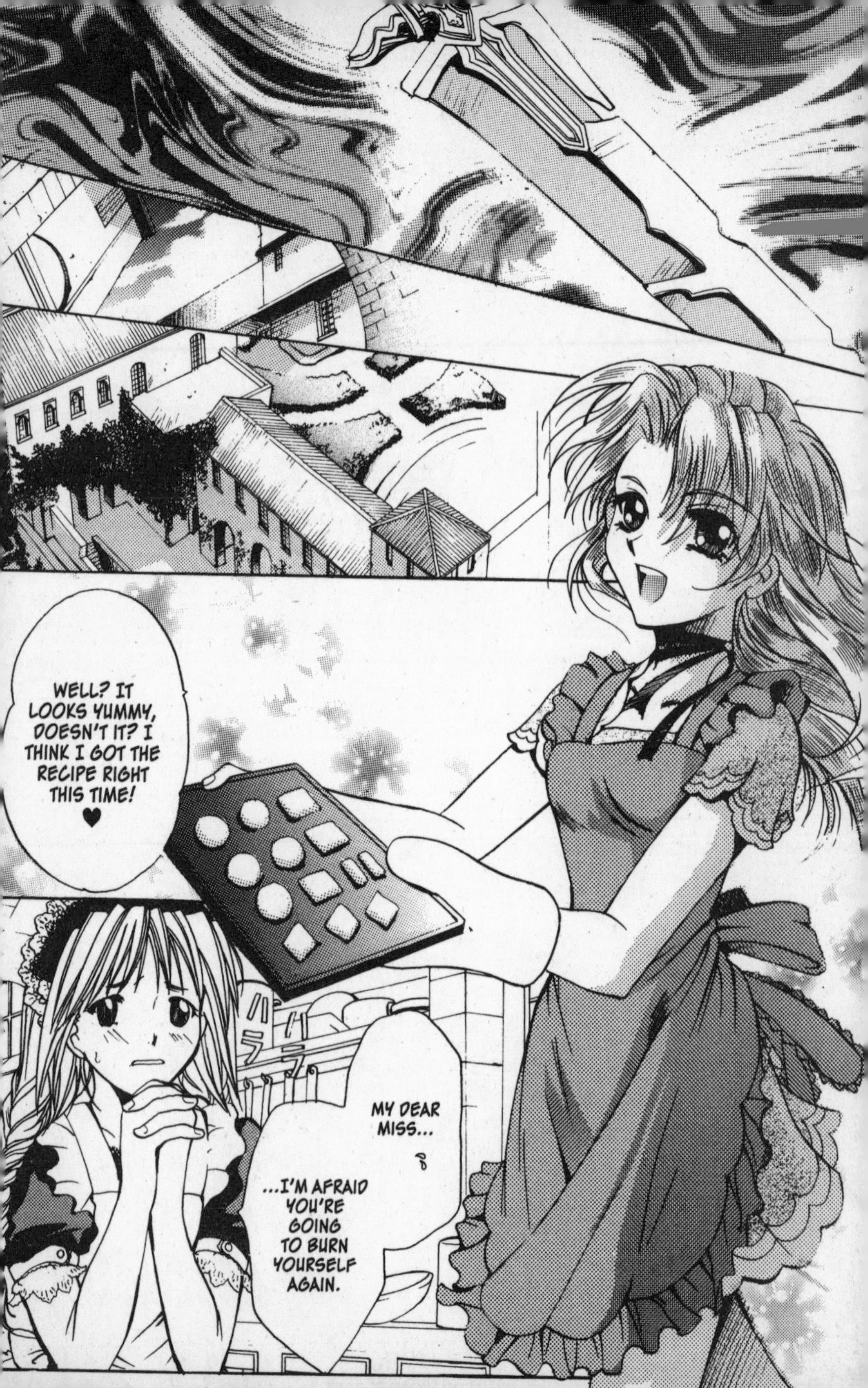
WELL? IT LOOKS YUMMY, DOESN'T IT? I THINK I GOT THE RECIPE RIGHT THIS TIME! ♥
MY DEAR MISS...
...I'M AFRAID YOU'RE GOING TO BURN YOURSELF AGAIN.

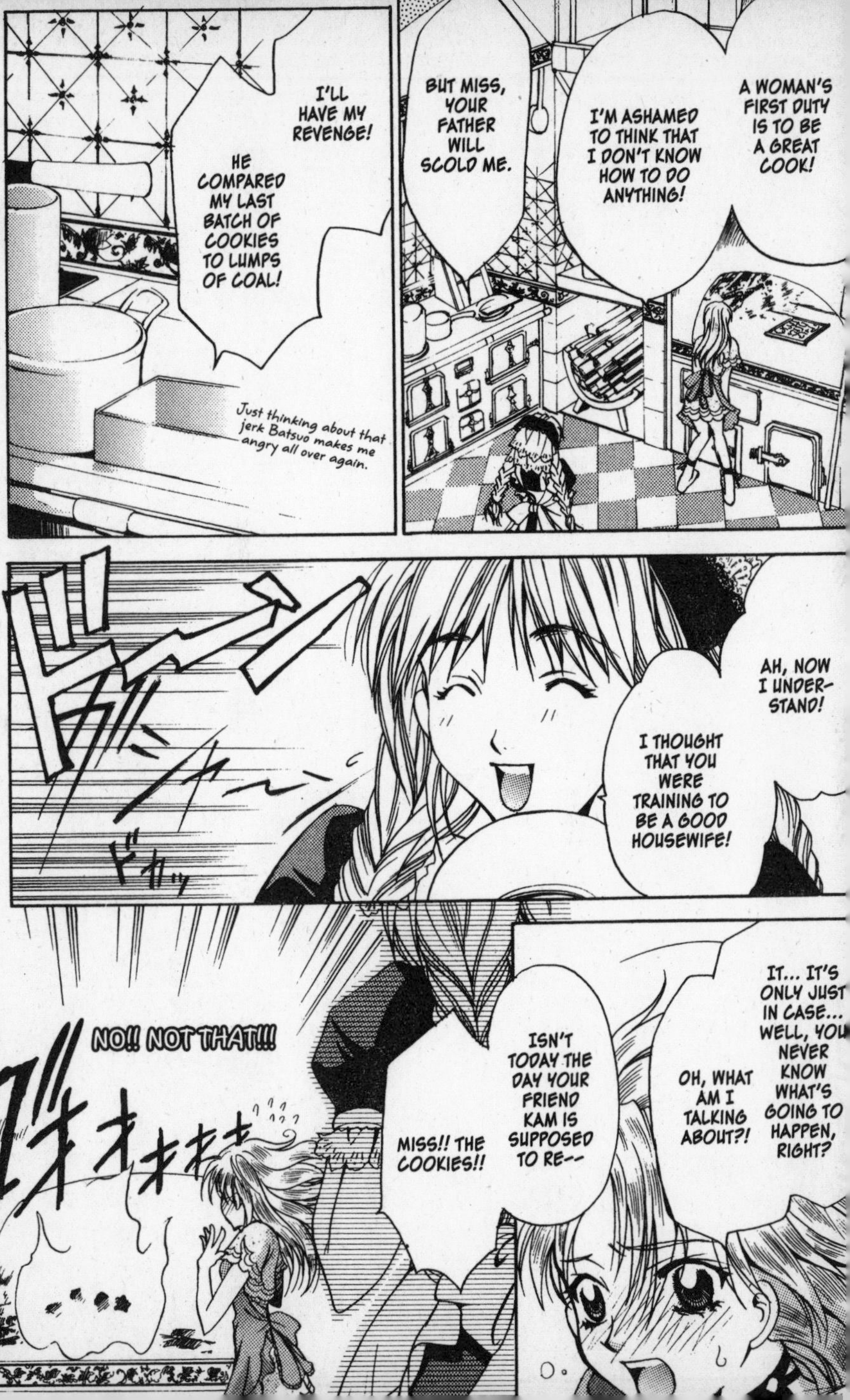
A WOMAN'S FIRST DUTY IS TO BE A GREAT COOK!
I'M ASHAMED TO THINK THAT I DON'T KNOW HOW TO DO ANYTHING!
BUT MISS, YOUR FATHER WILL SCOLD ME.
I'LL HAVE MY REVENGE!
HE COMPARED MY LAST BATCH OF COOKIES TO LUMPS OF COAL!
Just thinking about that jerk Batsuo makes me angry all over again.
AH, NOW I UNDERSTAND!
I THOUGHT THAT YOU WERE TRAINING TO BE A GOOD HOUSEWIFE!
IT... IT'S ONLY JUST IN CASE... WELL, YOU NEVER KNOW WHAT'S GOING TO HAPPEN, RIGHT?
OH, WHAT AM I TALKING ABOUT?!
ISN'T TODAY THE DAY YOUR FRIEND KAM IS SUPPOSED TO RE--
MISS!! THE COOKIES!!
NO!! NOT THAT!!!

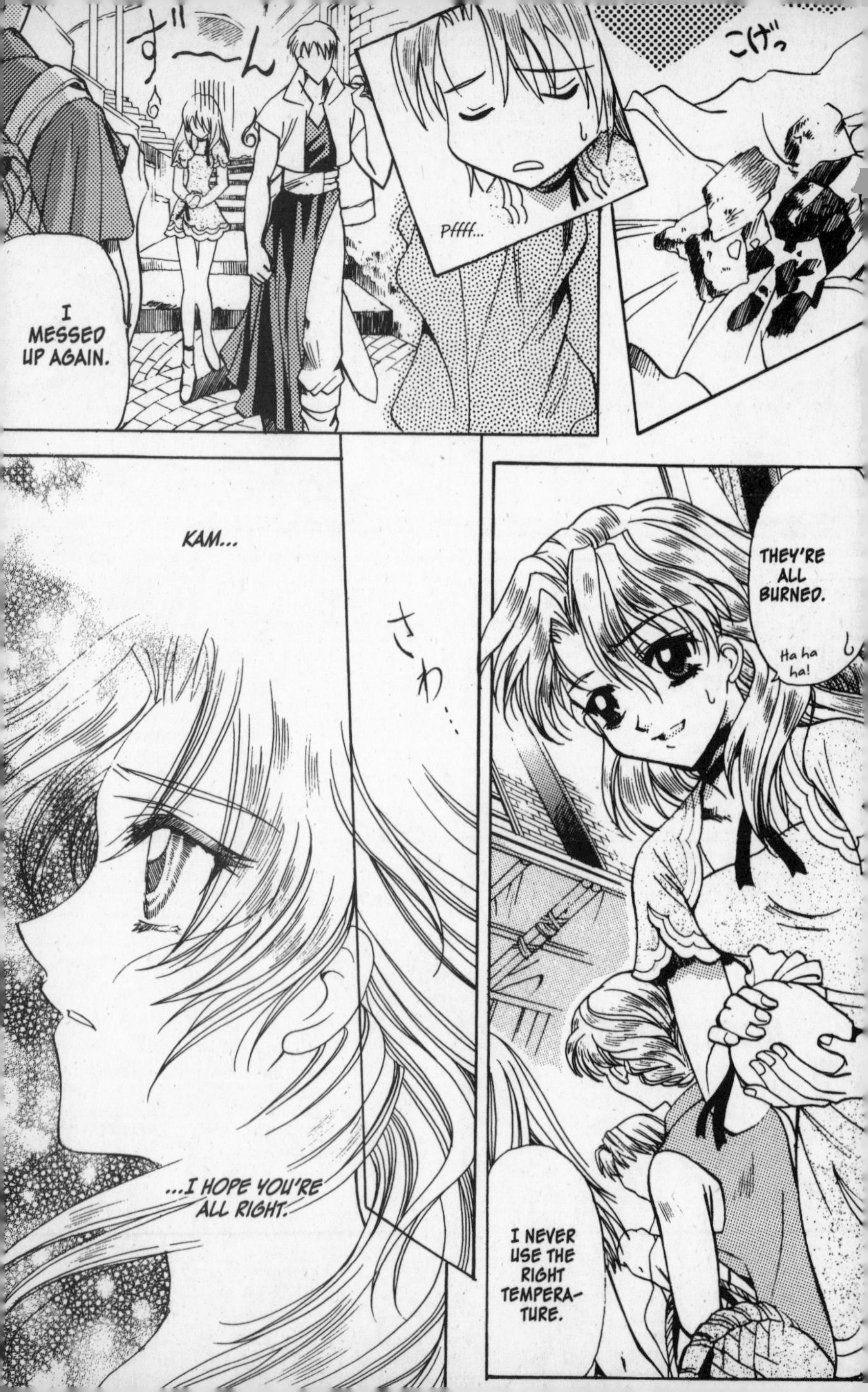
こげっ
Pffff...
ず〜ん
I MESSED UP AGAIN.
THEY'RE ALL BURNED.
Ha ha ha!
I NEVER USE THE RIGHT TEMPERATURE.
さわ…
KAM...
...I HOPE YOU'RE ALL RIGHT.

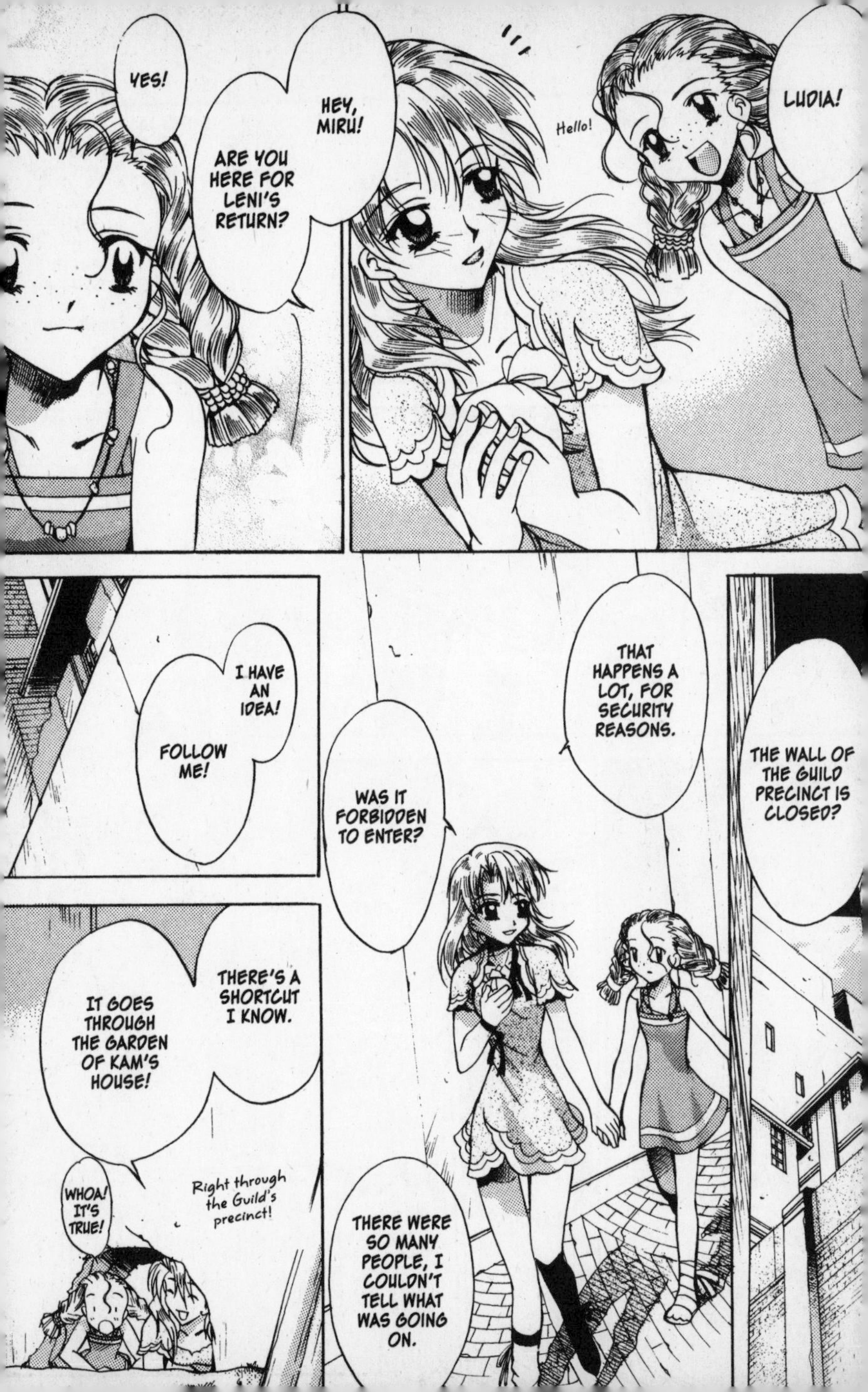
LUDIA!
Hello!
HEY, MIRU!
ARE YOU HERE FOR LENI'S RETURN?
YES!
THE WALL OF THE GUILD PRECINCT IS CLOSED?
THAT HAPPENS A LOT, FOR SECURITY REASONS.
WAS IT FORBIDDEN TO ENTER?
THERE WERE SO MANY PEOPLE, I COULDN'T TELL WHAT WAS GOING ON.
I HAVE AN IDEA!
FOLLOW ME!
THERE'S A SHORTCUT I KNOW.
IT GOES THROUGH THE GARDEN OF KAM'S HOUSE!
Right through the Guild's precinct!
WHOA! IT'S TRUE!

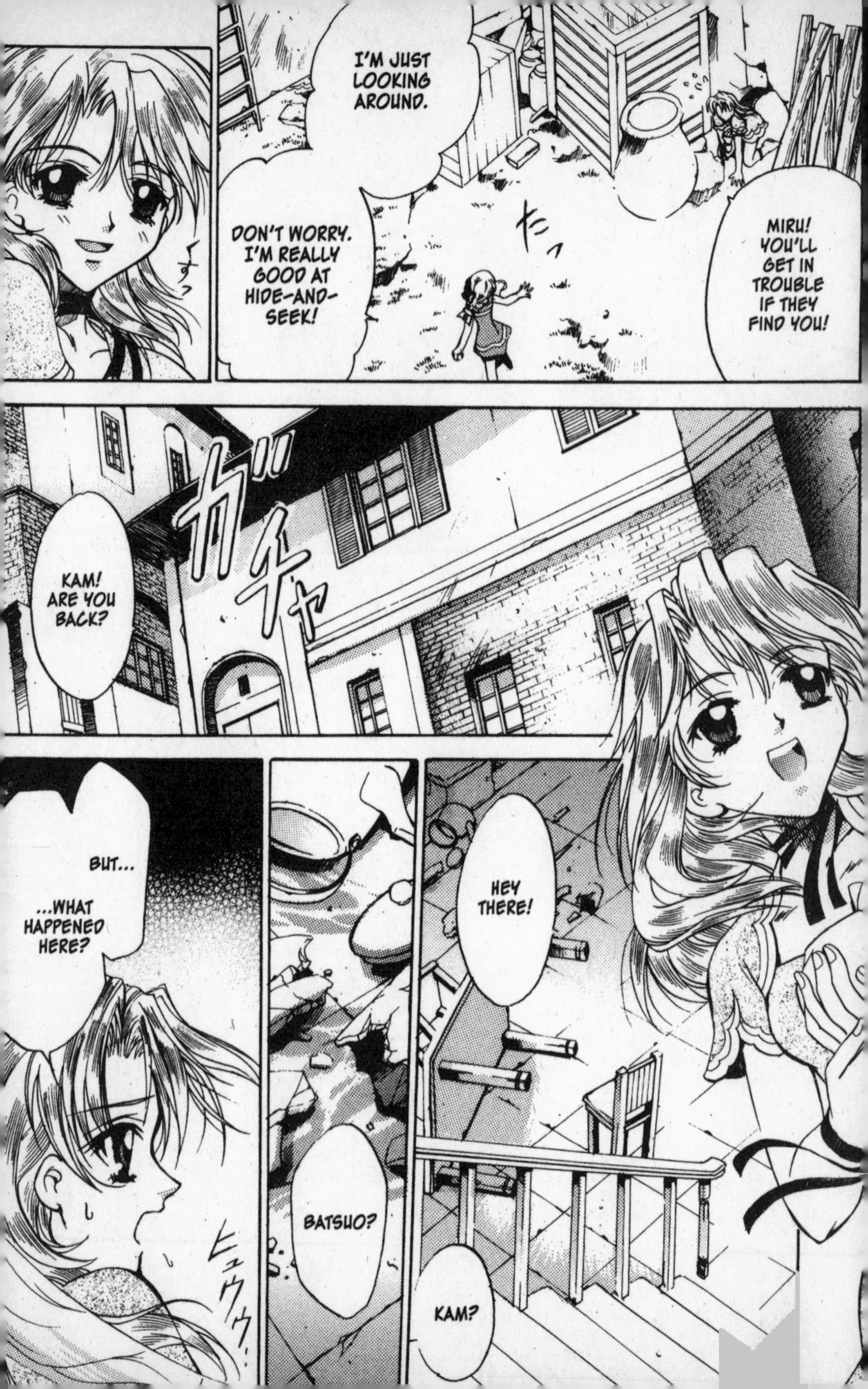
MIRU! YOU'LL GET IN TROUBLE IF THEY FIND YOU!
I'M JUST LOOKING AROUND.
DON'T WORRY. I'M REALLY GOOD AT HIDE-AND-SEEK!
ガチャ
KAM! ARE YOU BACK?
HEY THERE!
KAM?
BATSUO?
BUT...
...WHAT HAPPENED HERE?

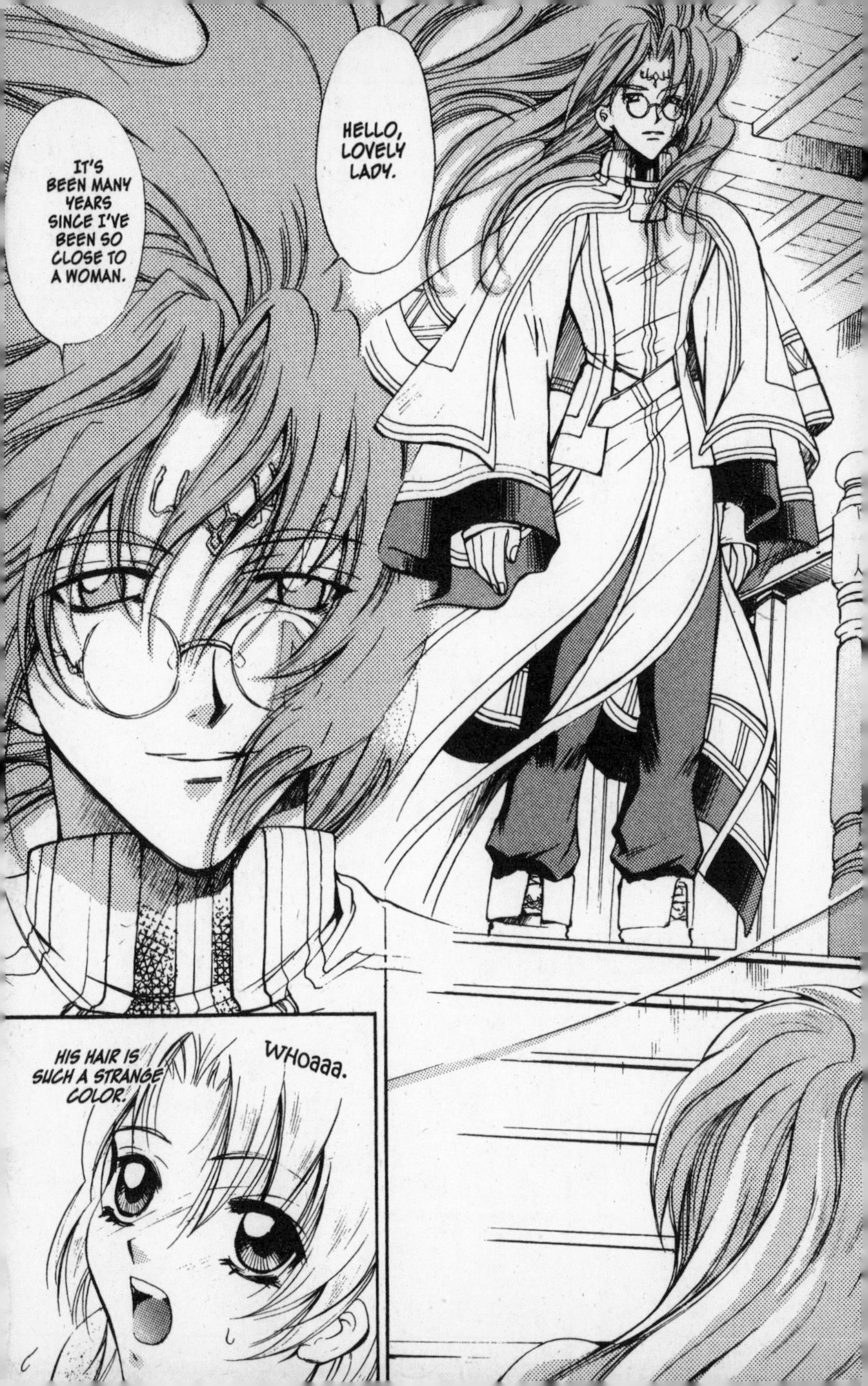
HELLO, LOVELY LADY.
IT'S BEEN MANY YEARS SINCE I'VE BEEN SO CLOSE TO A WOMAN.
WHOAAA.
HIS HAIR IS SUCH A STRANGE COLOR.

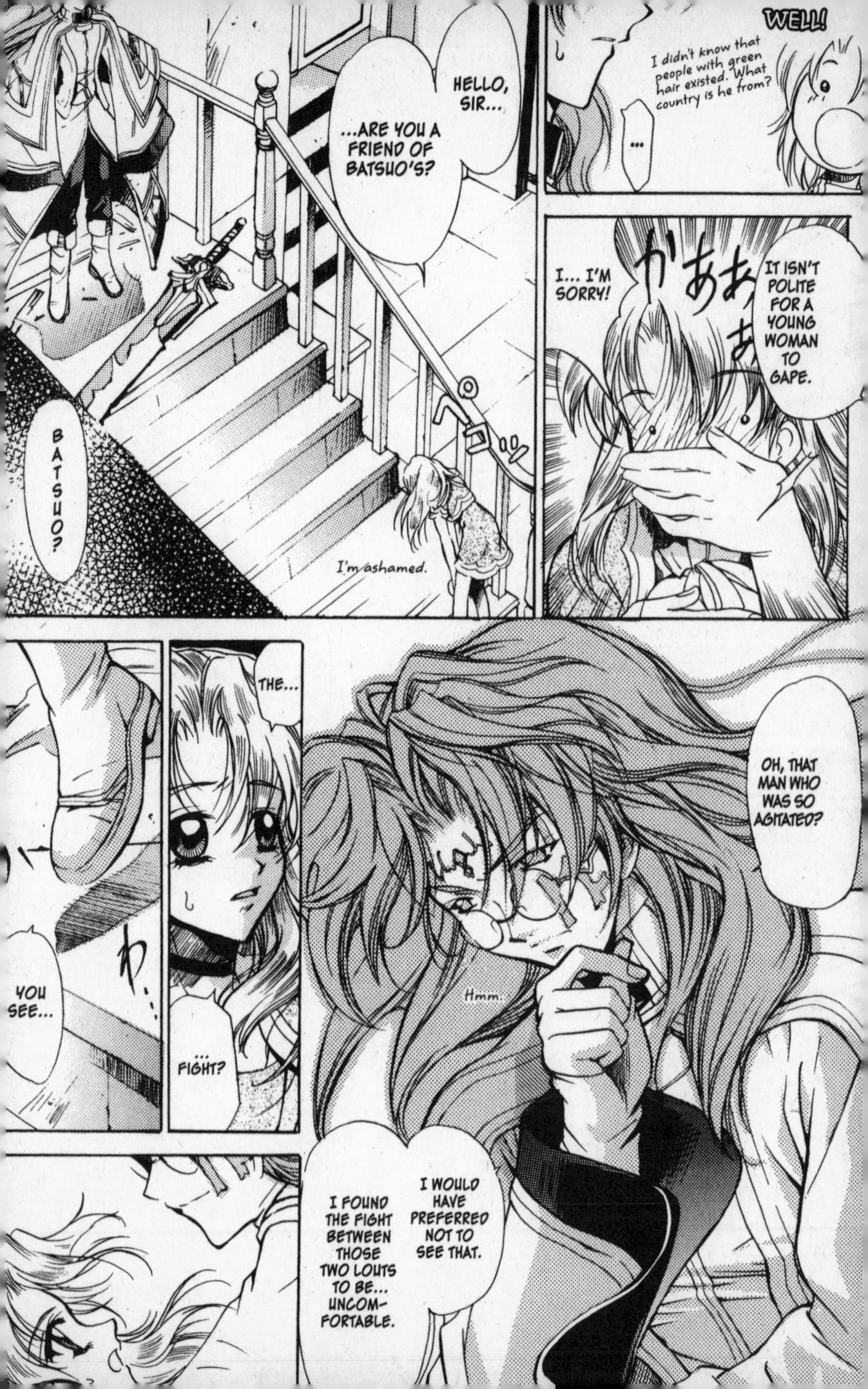
WELL!
I didn't know that people with green hair existed. What country is he from?
...
IT ISN'T POLITE FOR A YOUNG WOMAN TO GAPE.
I... I'M SORRY!
かああ
HELLO, SIR...
...ARE YOU A FRIEND OF BATSUO'S?
I'm ashamed.
BATSUO?
OH, THAT MAN WHO WAS SO AGITATED?
Hmm.
I WOULD HAVE PREFERRED NOT TO SEE THAT.
I FOUND THE FIGHT BETWEEN THOSE TWO LOUTS TO BE... UNCOMFORTABLE.
THE...
...FIGHT?
わ
YOU SEE...

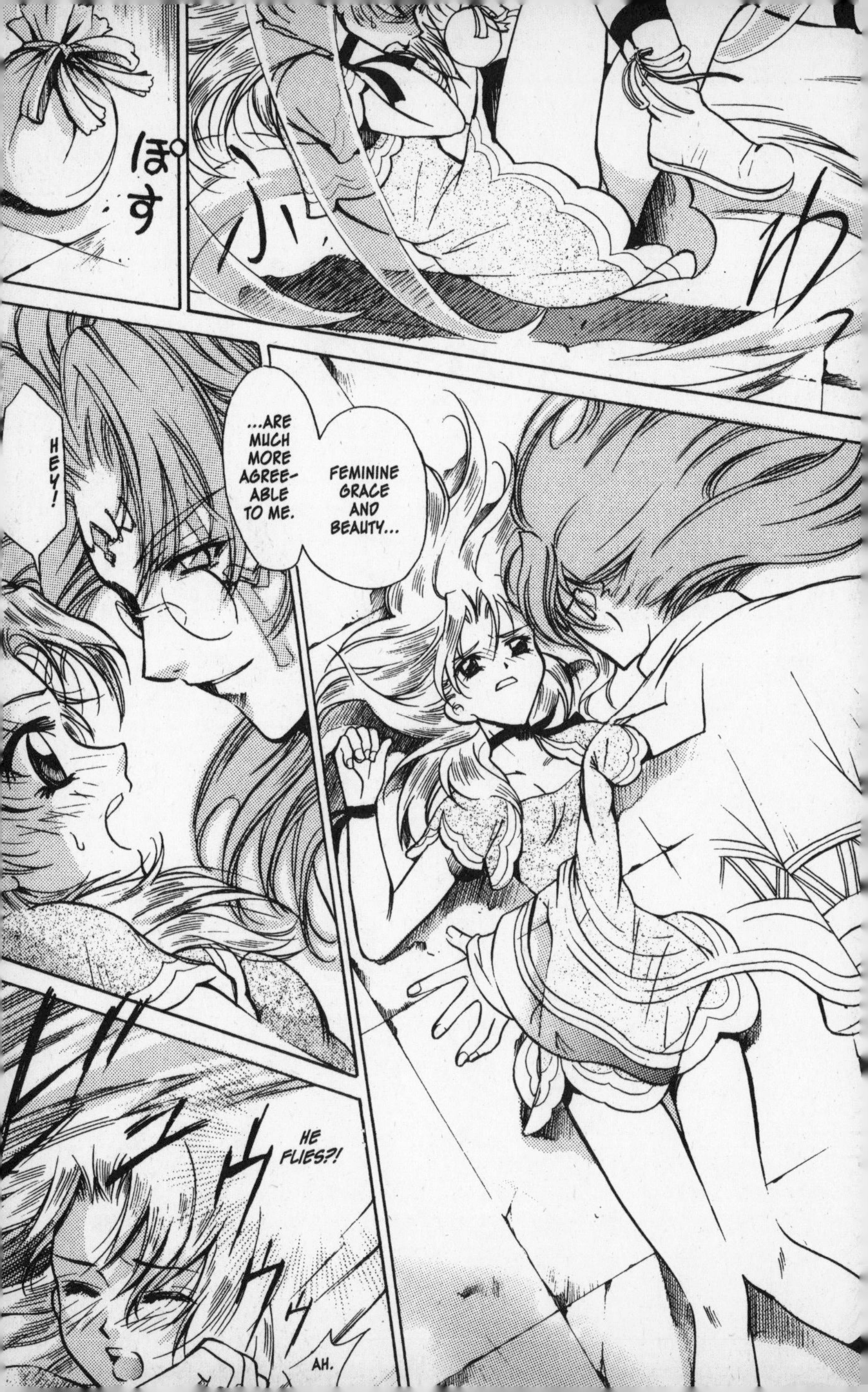
わ
ふ
ぽす
FEMININE GRACE AND BEAUTY...
...ARE MUCH MORE AGREE-ABLE TO ME.
HEY!
HE FLIES?!
AH.

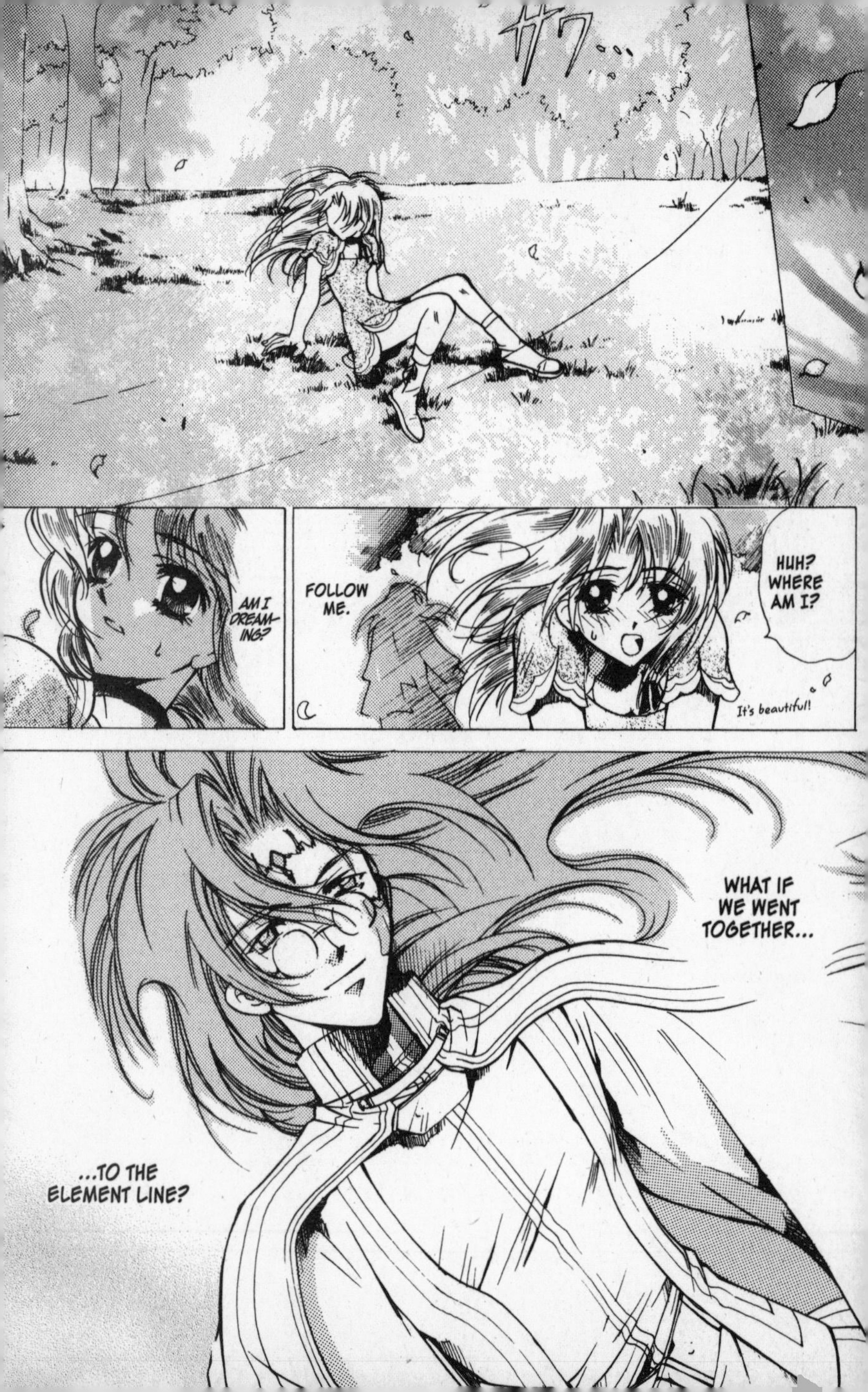
サワ…
HUH? WHERE AM I?
It's beautiful!
FOLLOW ME.
AM I DREAMING?
WHAT IF WE WENT TOGETHER...
...TO THE ELEMENT LINE?

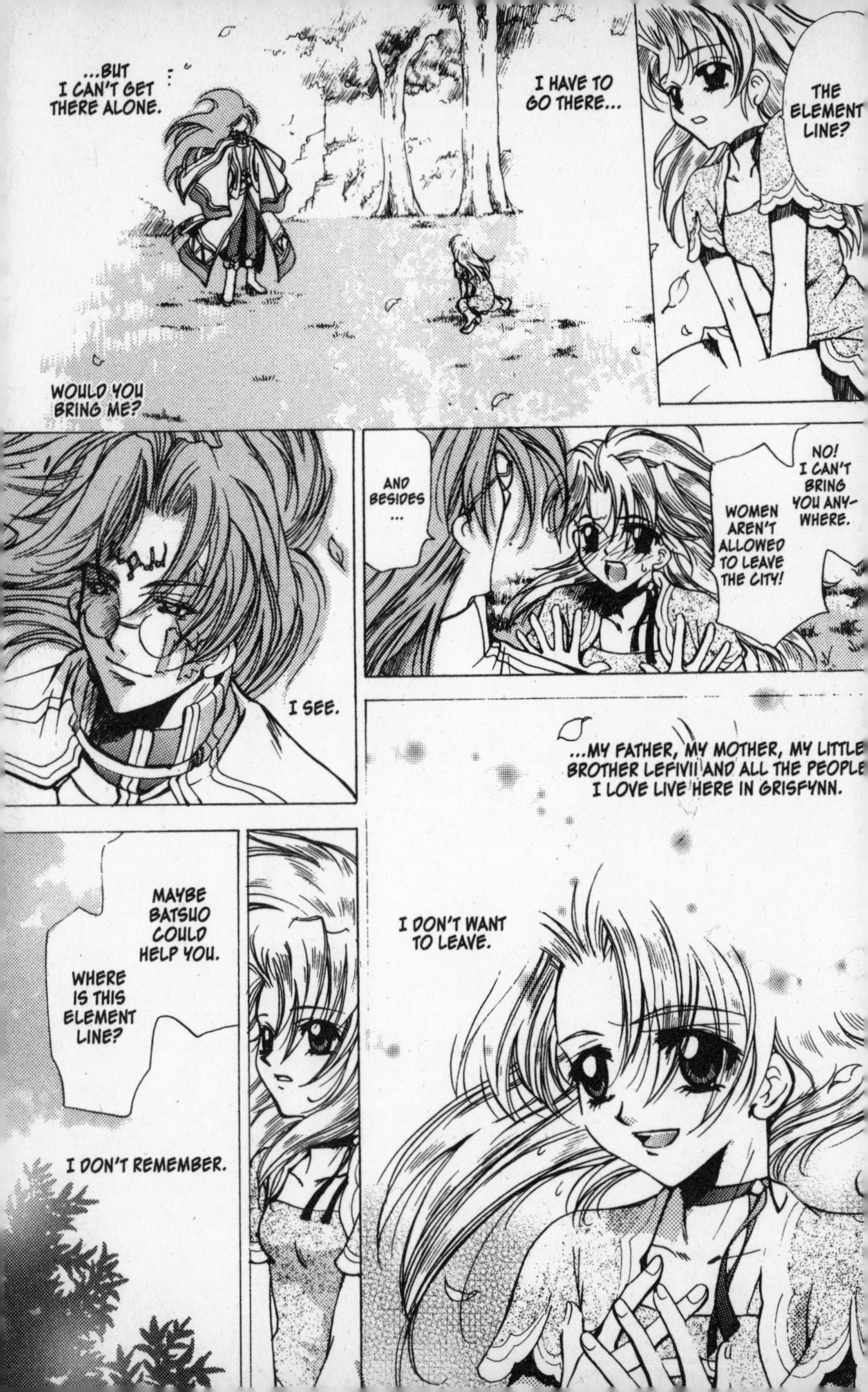
THE ELEMENT LINE?
I HAVE TO GO THERE...
...BUT I CAN'T GET THERE ALONE.
WOULD YOU BRING ME?
NO! I CAN'T BRING YOU ANY-WHERE.
WOMEN AREN'T ALLOWED TO LEAVE THE CITY!
AND BESIDES ...
...MY FATHER, MY MOTHER, MY LITTLE BROTHER LEFIVII AND ALL THE PEOPLE I LOVE LIVE HERE IN GRISFYNN.
I DON'T WANT TO LEAVE.
I SEE.
MAYBE BATSUO COULD HELP YOU.
WHERE IS THIS ELEMENT LINE?
I DON'T REMEMBER.

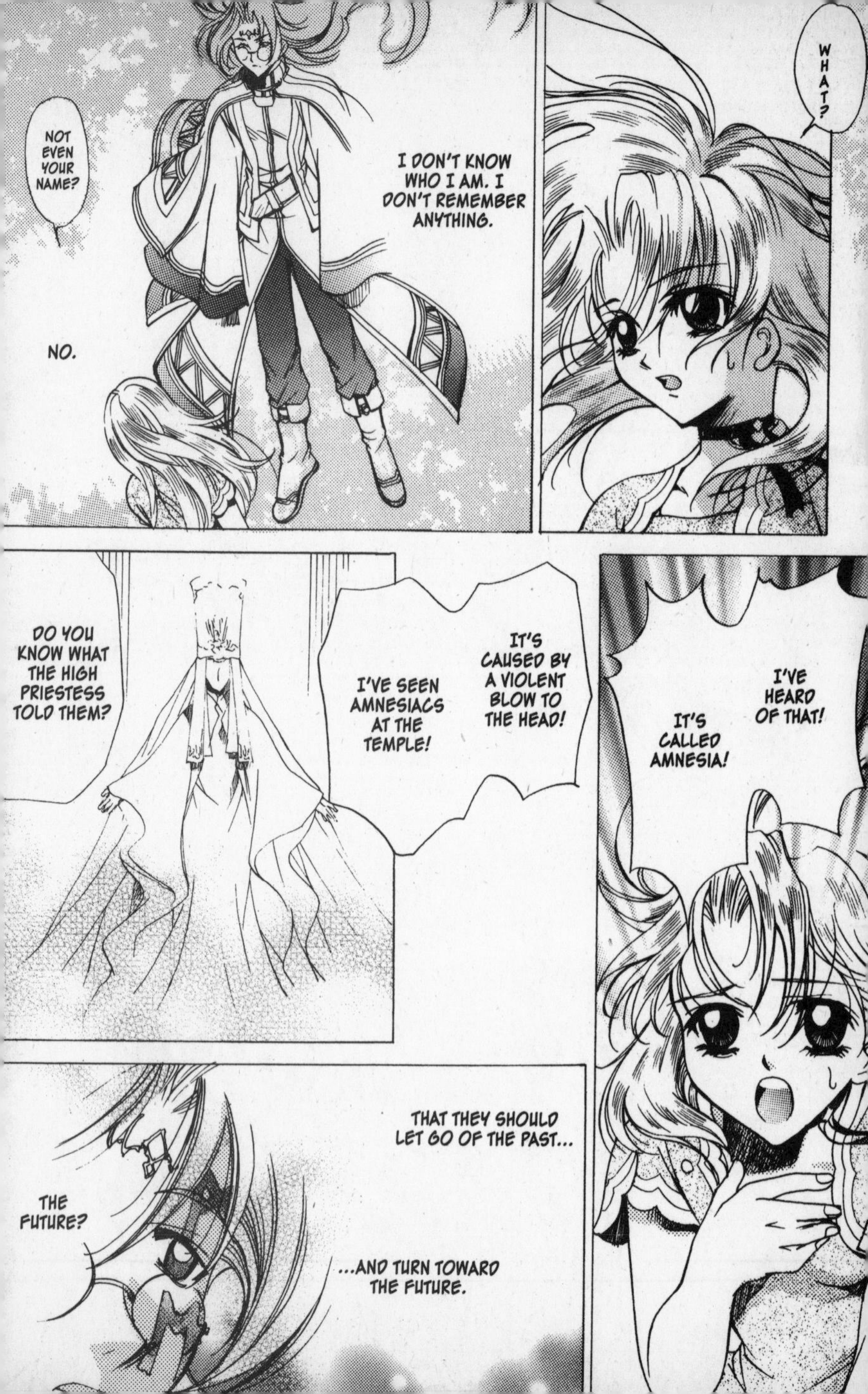
WHAT?
I DON'T KNOW WHO I AM. I DON'T REMEMBER ANYTHING.
NOT EVEN YOUR NAME?
NO.
I'VE HEARD OF THAT!
IT'S CALLED AMNESIA!
IT'S CAUSED BY A VIOLENT BLOW TO THE HEAD!
I'VE SEEN AMNESIACS AT THE TEMPLE!
DO YOU KNOW WHAT THE HIGH PRIESTESS TOLD THEM?
THAT THEY SHOULD LET GO OF THE PAST...
...AND TURN TOWARD THE FUTURE.
THE FUTURE?

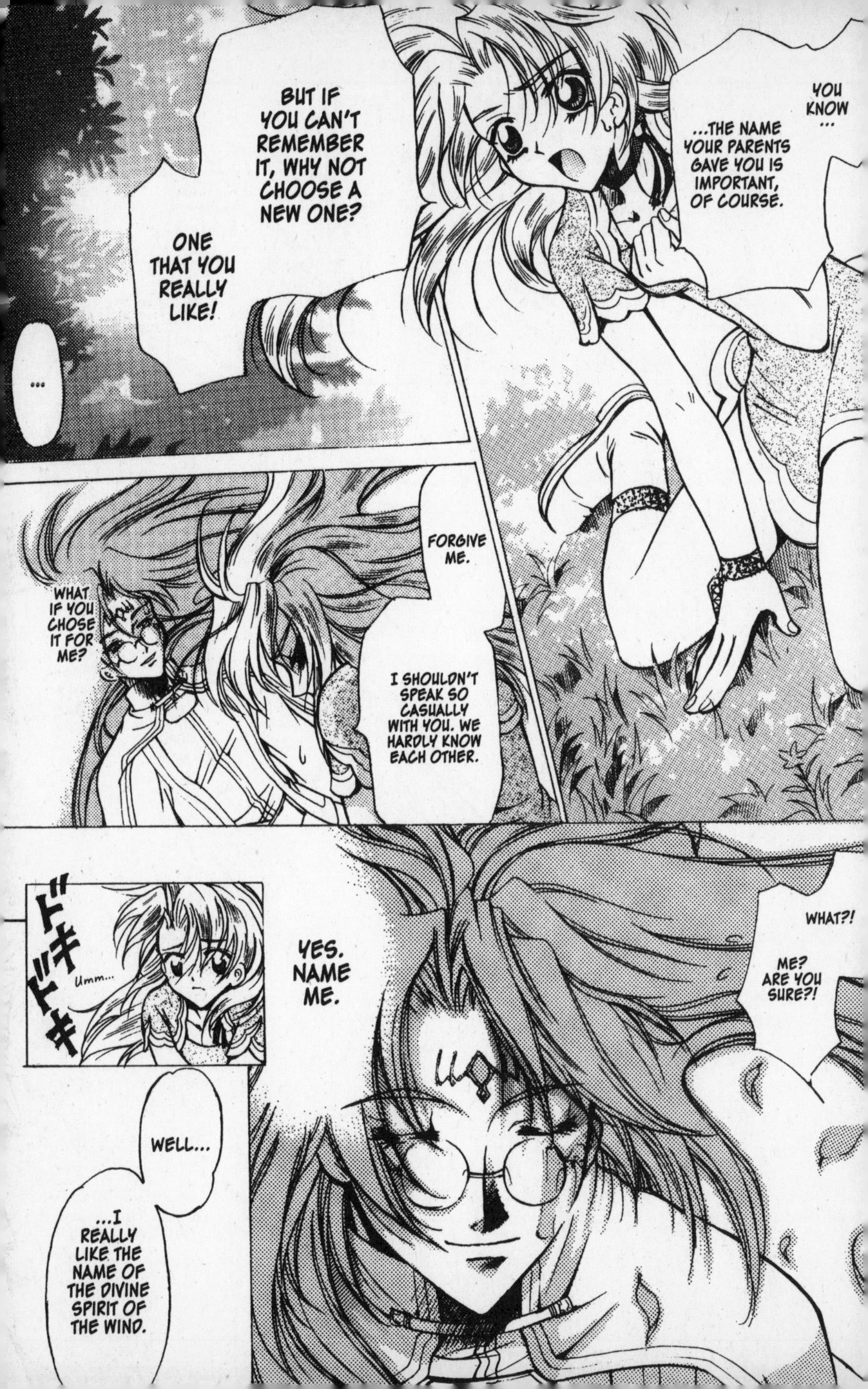
YOU KNOW ...
...THE NAME YOUR PARENTS GAVE YOU IS IMPORTANT, OF COURSE.
BUT IF YOU CAN'T REMEMBER IT, WHY NOT CHOOSE A NEW ONE?
ONE THAT YOU REALLY LIKE!
...
FORGIVE ME.
I SHOULDN'T SPEAK SO CASUALLY WITH YOU. WE HARDLY KNOW EACH OTHER.
WHAT IF YOU CHOSE IT FOR ME?
WHAT?!
ME? ARE YOU SURE?!
YES. NAME ME.
ドキドキ
Umm...
WELL...
...I REALLY LIKE THE NAME OF THE DIVINE SPIRIT OF THE WIND.

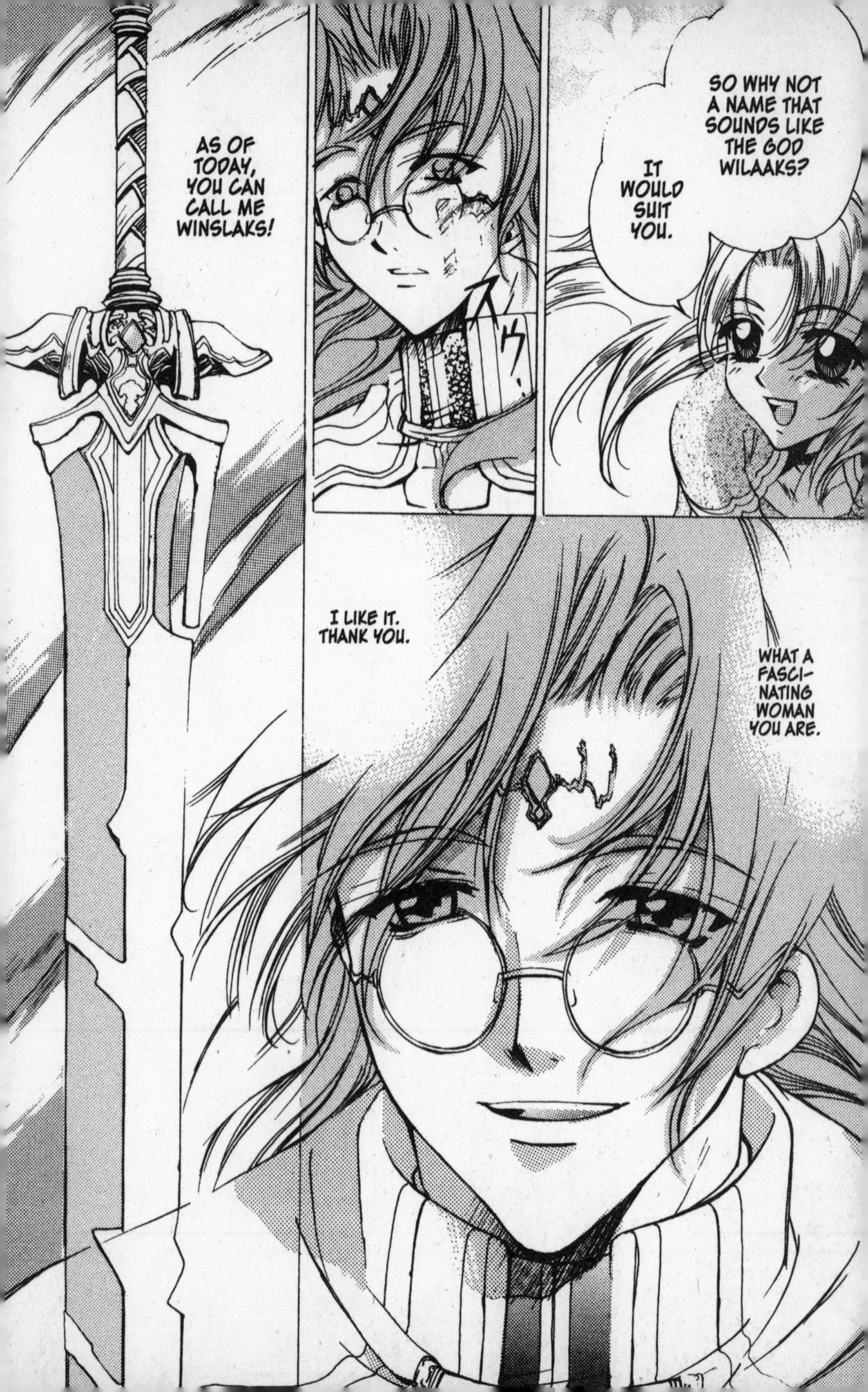
SO WHY NOT A NAME THAT SOUNDS LIKE THE GOD WILAAKS?
IT WOULD SUIT YOU.
スウ
I LIKE IT. THANK YOU.
WHAT A FASCI- NATING WOMAN YOU ARE.
AS OF TODAY, YOU CAN CALL ME WINSLAKS!

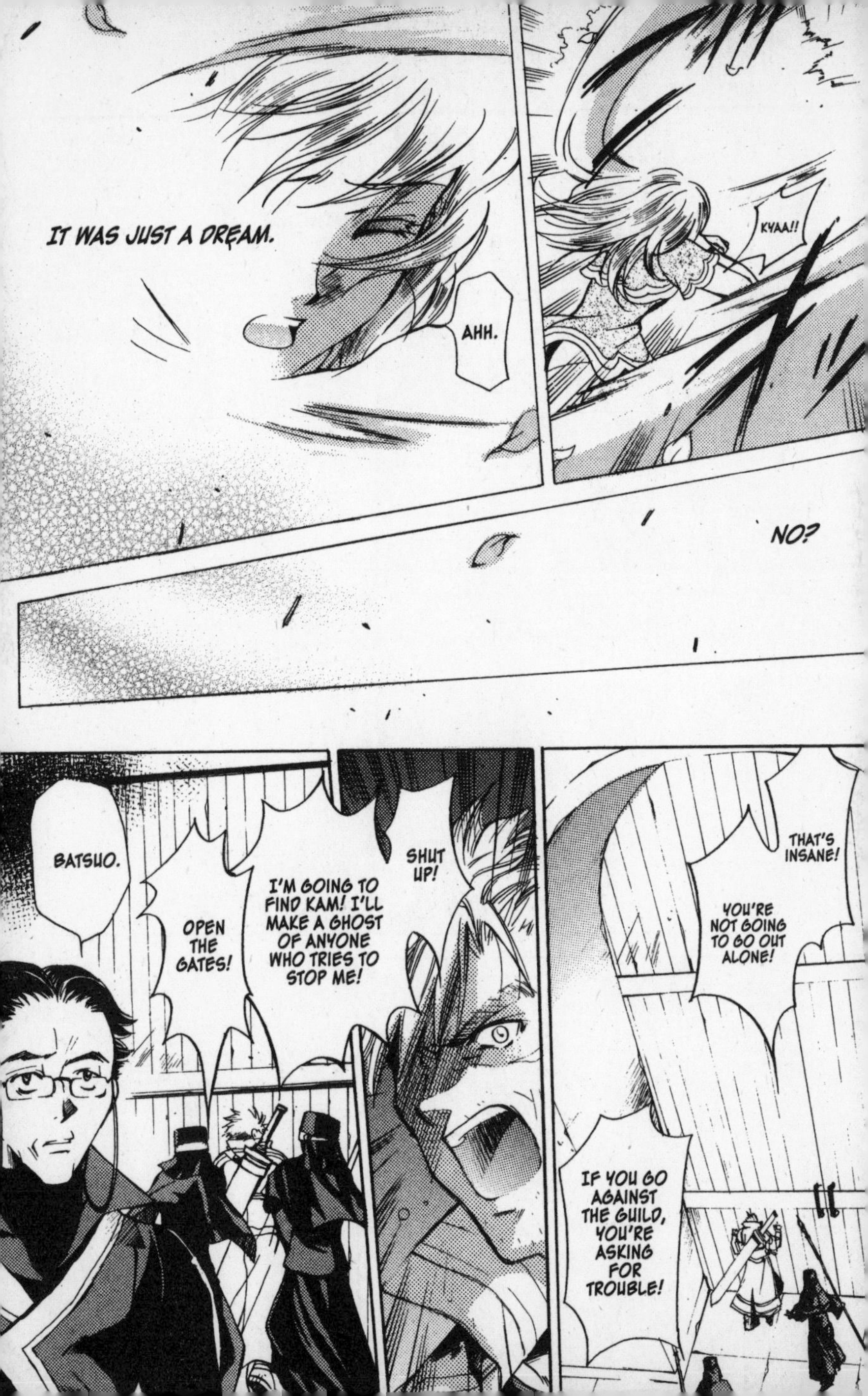
KYAA!!
AHH.
IT WAS JUST A DREAM.
NO?
THAT'S INSANE!
YOU'RE NOT GOING TO GO OUT ALONE!
IF YOU GO AGAINST THE GUILD, YOU'RE ASKING FOR TROUBLE!
SHUT UP!
I'M GOING TO FIND KAM! I'LL MAKE A GHOST OF ANYONE WHO TRIES TO STOP ME!
OPEN THE GATES!
BATSUO.

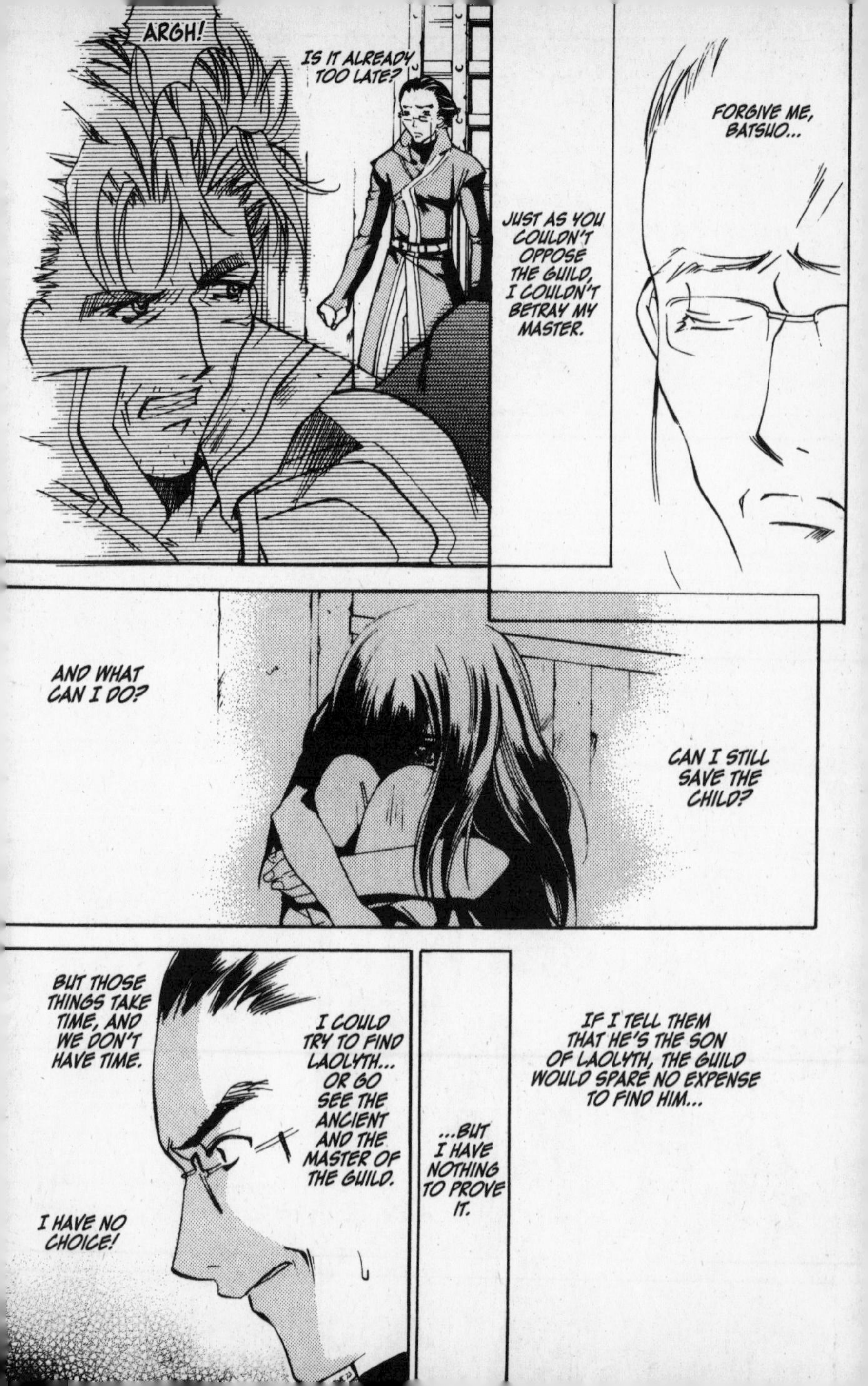
FORGIVE ME, BATSUO...
JUST AS YOU COULDN'T OPPOSE THE GUILD, I COULDN'T BETRAY MY MASTER.
IS IT ALREADY TOO LATE?
ARGH!
CAN I STILL SAVE THE CHILD?
AND WHAT CAN I DO?
IF I TELL THEM THAT HE'S THE SON OF LAOLYTH, THE GUILD WOULD SPARE NO EXPENSE TO FIND HIM...
...BUT I HAVE NOTHING TO PROVE IT.
I COULD TRY TO FIND LAOLYTH... OR GO SEE THE ANCIENT AND THE MASTER OF THE GUILD.
BUT THOSE THINGS TAKE TIME, AND WE DON'T HAVE TIME.
I HAVE NO CHOICE!

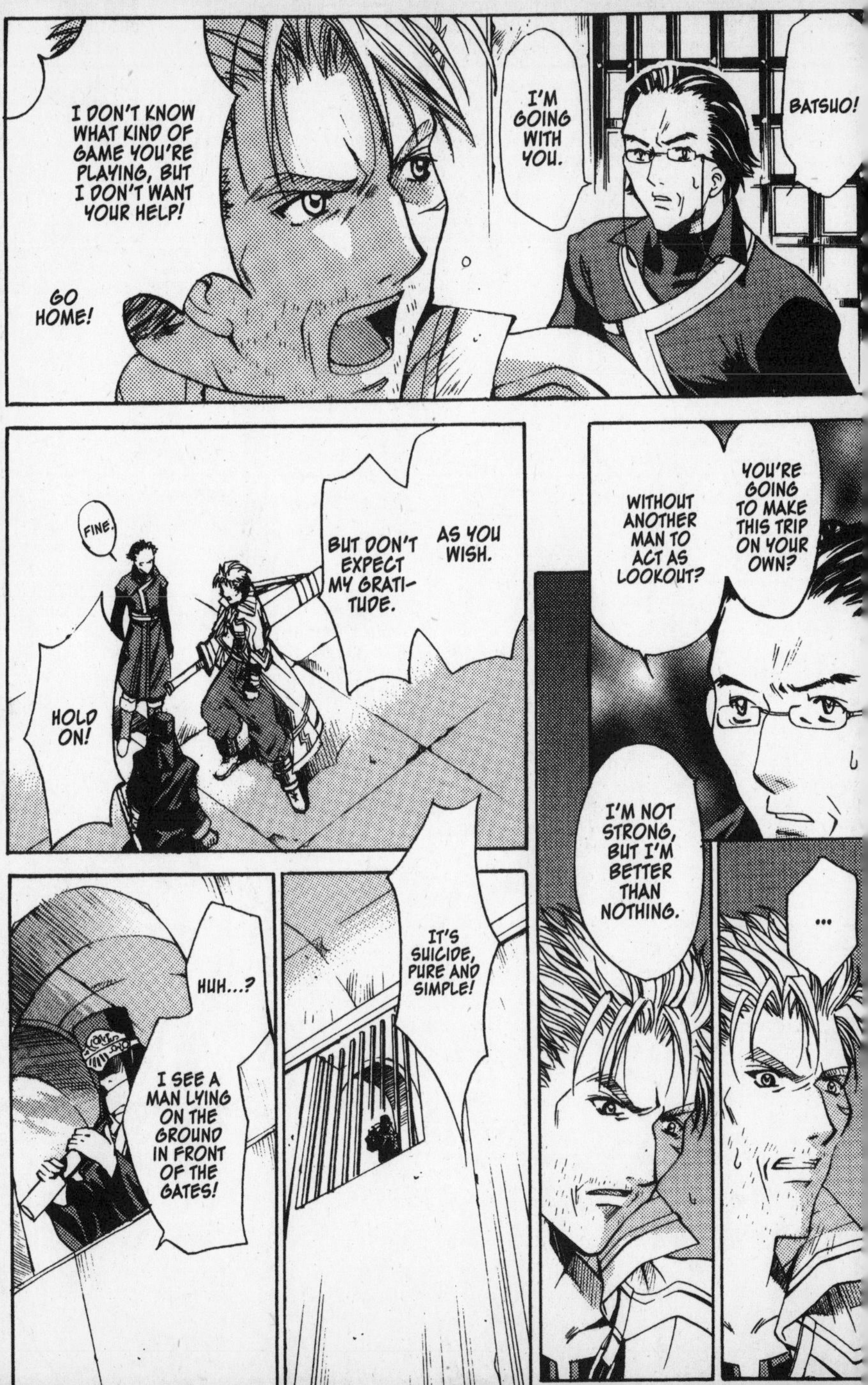
BATSUO!
I'M GOING WITH YOU.
I DON'T KNOW WHAT KIND OF GAME YOU'RE PLAYING, BUT I DON'T WANT YOUR HELP!
GO HOME!
YOU'RE GOING TO MAKE THIS TRIP ON YOUR OWN?
WITHOUT ANOTHER MAN TO ACT AS LOOKOUT?
I'M NOT STRONG, BUT I'M BETTER THAN NOTHING.
...
AS YOU WISH.
BUT DON'T EXPECT MY GRATITUDE.
FINE.
HOLD ON!
IT'S SUICIDE, PURE AND SIMPLE!
HUH...?
I SEE A MAN LYING ON THE GROUND IN FRONT OF THE GATES!

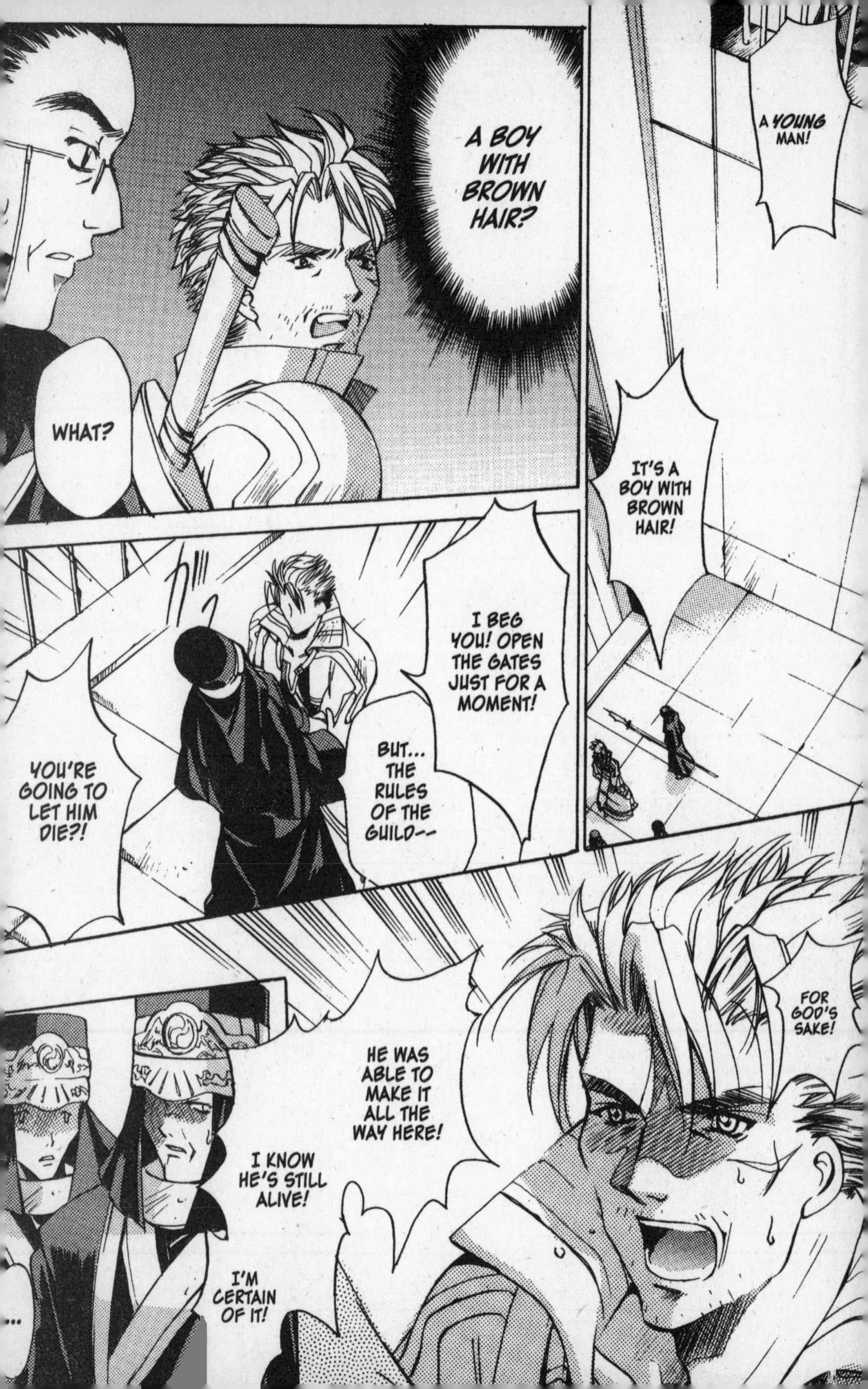
A YOUNG MAN!
IT'S A BOY WITH BROWN HAIR!
A BOY WITH BROWN HAIR?
WHAT?
I BEG YOU! OPEN THE GATES JUST FOR A MOMENT!
BUT... THE RULES OF THE GUILD--
YOU'RE GOING TO LET HIM DIE?!
FOR GOD'S SAKE!
HE WAS ABLE TO MAKE IT ALL THE WAY HERE!
I KNOW HE'S STILL ALIVE!
I'M CERTAIN OF IT!
...

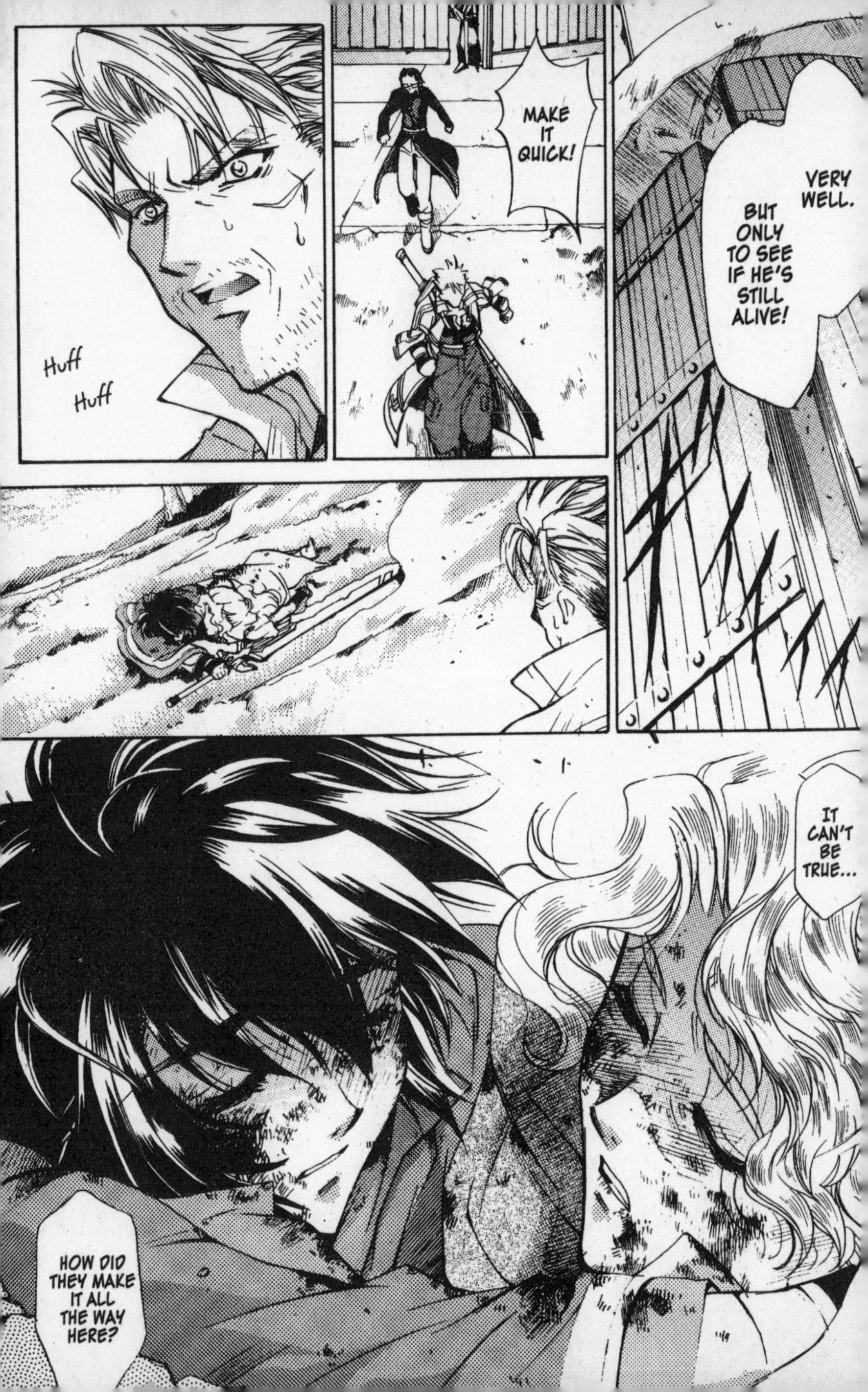
VERY WELL. BUT ONLY TO SEE IF HE'S STILL ALIVE!
MAKE IT QUICK!
Huff
Huff
IT CAN'T BE TRUE...
HOW DID THEY MAKE IT ALL THE WAY HERE?

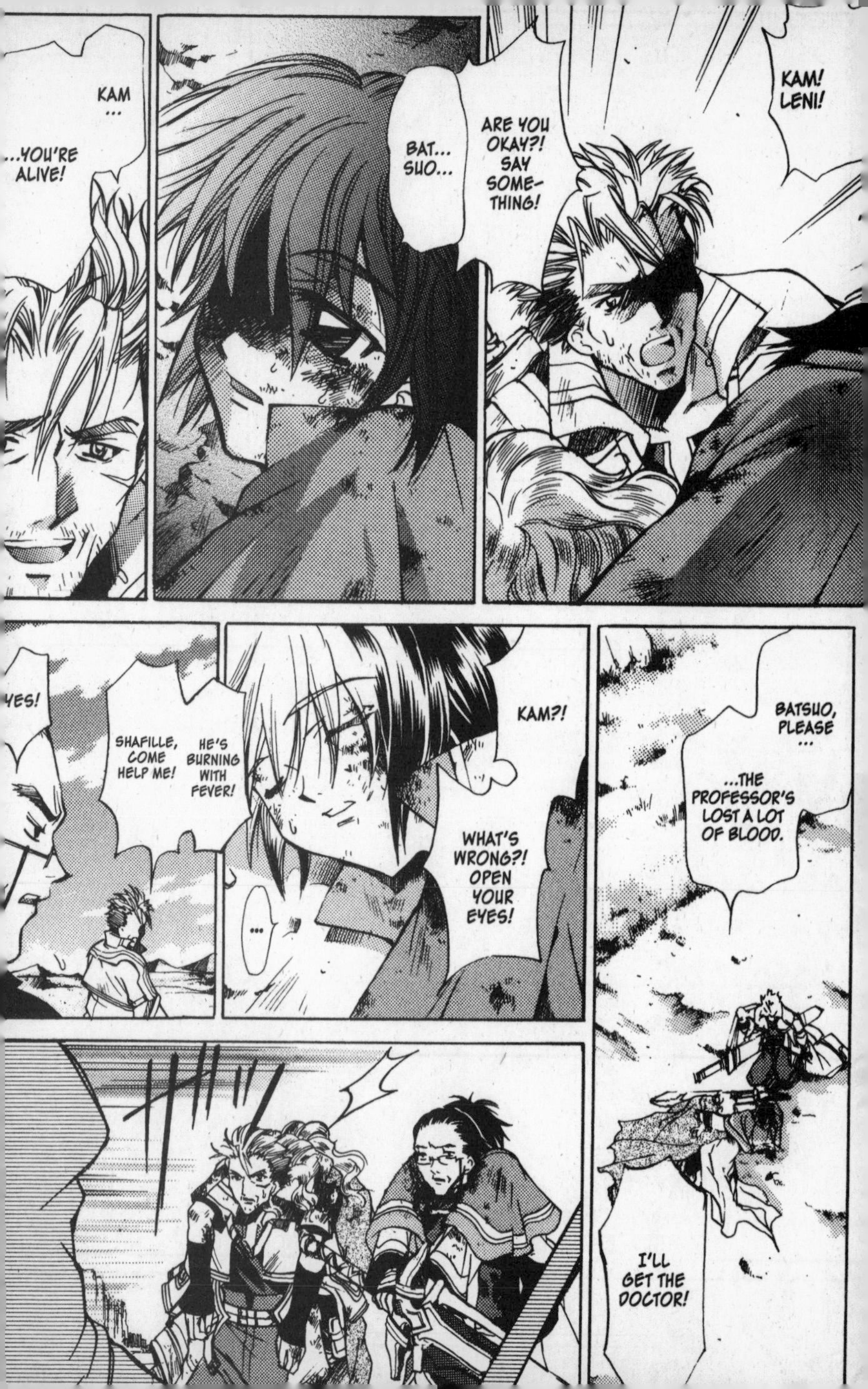
KAM! LENI!
ARE YOU OKAY?! SAY SOME-THING!
BAT... SUO...
KAM ...
...YOU'RE ALIVE!
BATSUO, PLEASE ...
...THE PROFESSOR'S LOST A LOT OF BLOOD.
I'LL GET THE DOCTOR!
KAM?!
WHAT'S WRONG?! OPEN YOUR EYES!
...
HE'S BURNING WITH FEVER!
SHAFILLE, COME HELP ME!
YES!

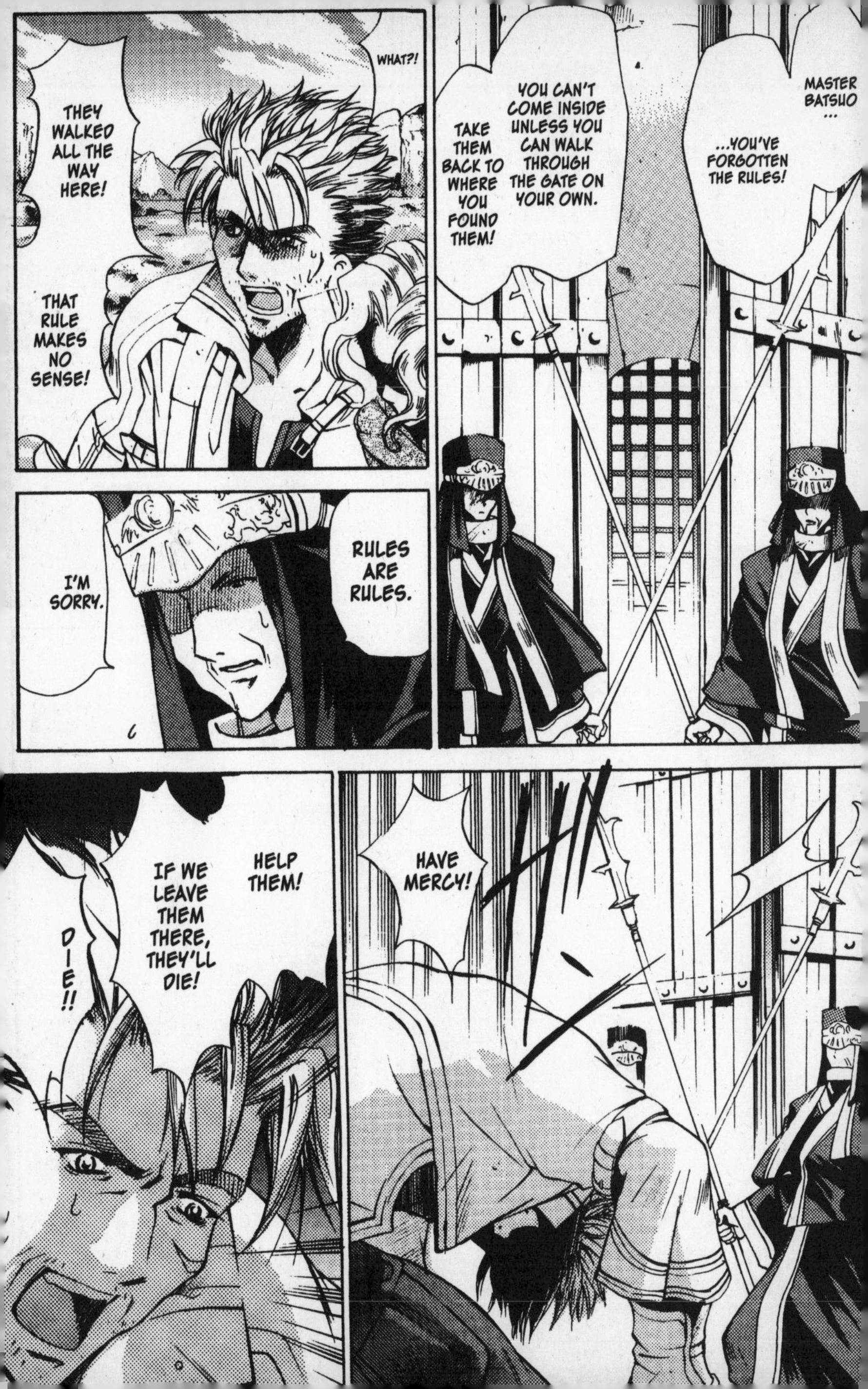
MASTER BATSUO ...
...YOU'VE FORGOTTEN THE RULES!
YOU CAN'T COME INSIDE UNLESS YOU CAN WALK THROUGH THE GATE ON YOUR OWN.
TAKE THEM BACK TO WHERE YOU FOUND THEM!
WHAT?!
THEY WALKED ALL THE WAY HERE!
THAT RULE MAKES NO SENSE!
RULES ARE RULES.
I'M SORRY.
HAVE MERCY!
HELP THEM!
IF WE LEAVE THEM THERE, THEY'LL DIE!
DIE!!

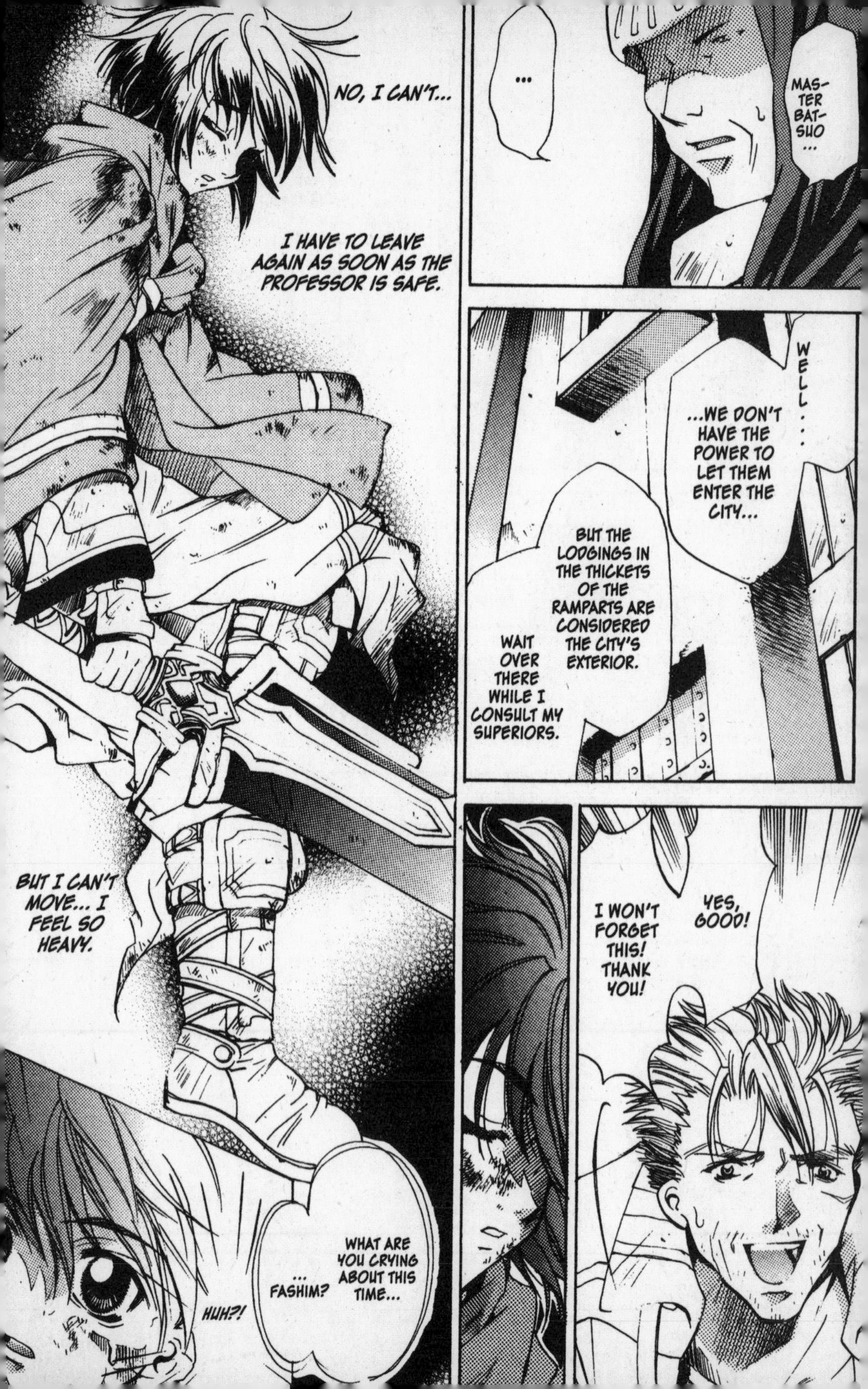
MASTER BATSUO...
...
WELL...
...WE DON'T HAVE THE POWER TO LET THEM ENTER THE CITY...
BUT THE LODGINGS IN THE THICKETS OF THE RAMPARTS ARE CONSIDERED THE CITY'S EXTERIOR.
WAIT OVER THERE WHILE I CONSULT MY SUPERIORS.
YES, GOOD!
I WON'T FORGET THIS! THANK YOU!
NO, I CAN'T...
I HAVE TO LEAVE AGAIN AS SOON AS THE PROFESSOR IS SAFE.
BUT I CAN'T MOVE... I FEEL SO HEAVY.
WHAT ARE YOU CRYING ABOUT THIS TIME...
...FASHIM?
HUH?!

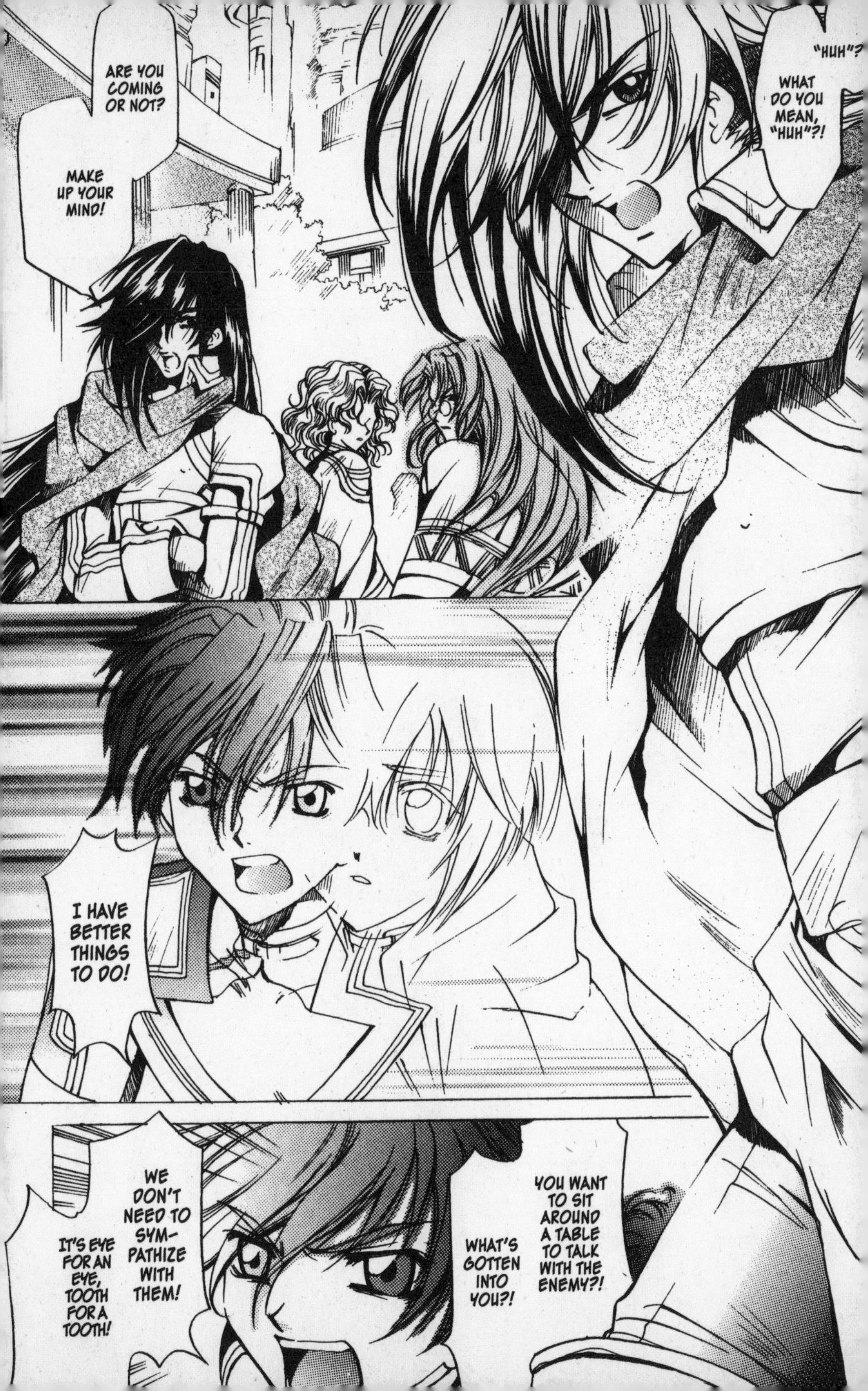
"HUH"?
WHAT DO YOU MEAN, "HUH"?!
ARE YOU COMING OR NOT?
MAKE UP YOUR MIND!
I HAVE BETTER THINGS TO DO!
YOU WANT TO SIT AROUND A TABLE TO TALK WITH THE ENEMY?!
WHAT'S GOTTEN INTO YOU?!
WE DON'T NEED TO SYM-PATHIZE WITH THEM!
IT'S EYE FOR AN EYE, TOOTH FOR A TOOTH!

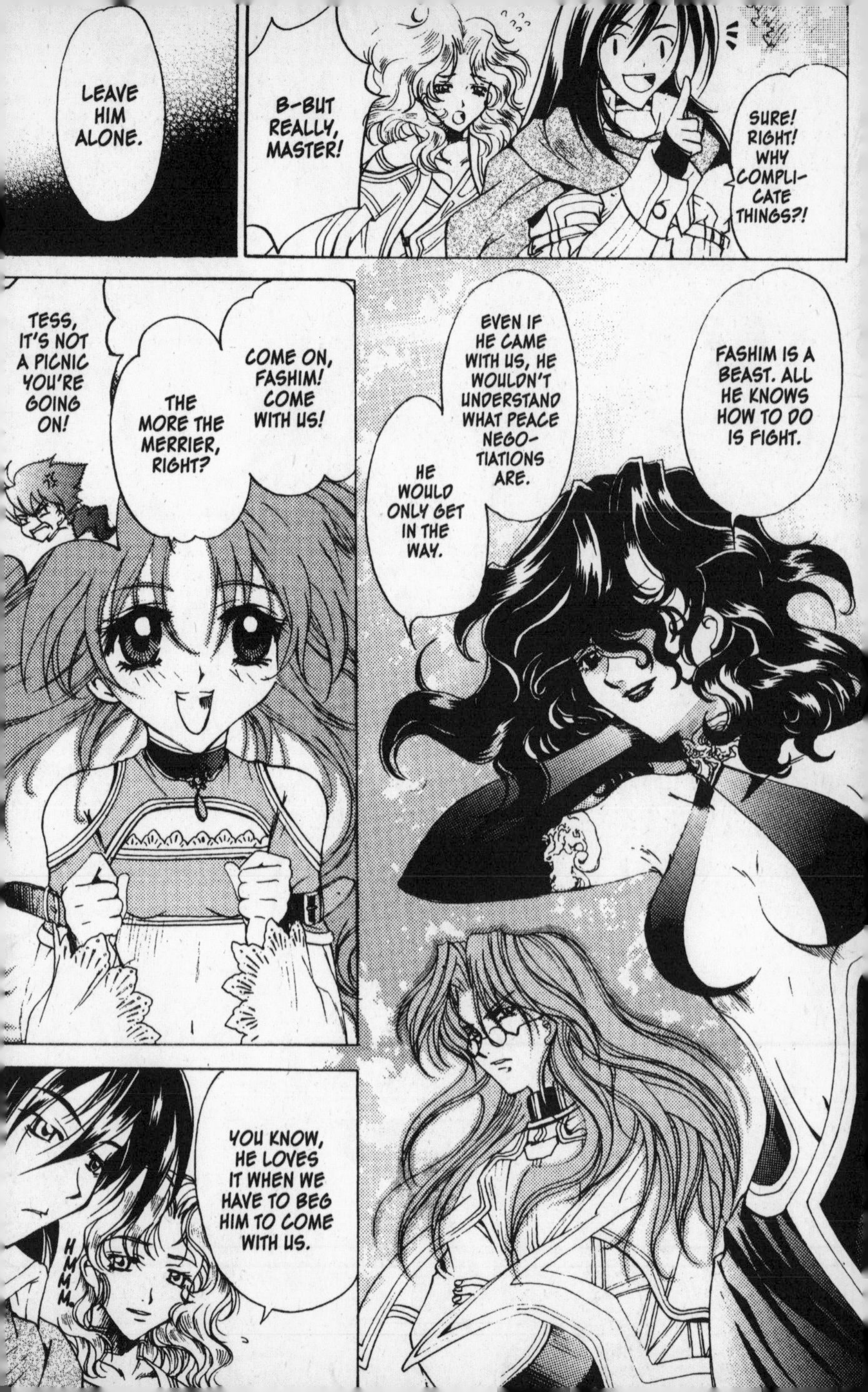
SURE! RIGHT! WHY COMPLICATE THINGS?!
B-BUT REALLY, MASTER!
LEAVE HIM ALONE.
FASHIM IS A BEAST. ALL HE KNOWS HOW TO DO IS FIGHT.
EVEN IF HE CAME WITH US, HE WOULDN'T UNDERSTAND WHAT PEACE NEGOTIATIONS ARE.
HE WOULD ONLY GET IN THE WAY.
COME ON, FASHIM! COME WITH US!
THE MORE THE MERRIER, RIGHT?
TESS, IT'S NOT A PICNIC YOU'RE GOING ON!
YOU KNOW, HE LOVES IT WHEN WE HAVE TO BEG HIM TO COME WITH US.
HMMM.

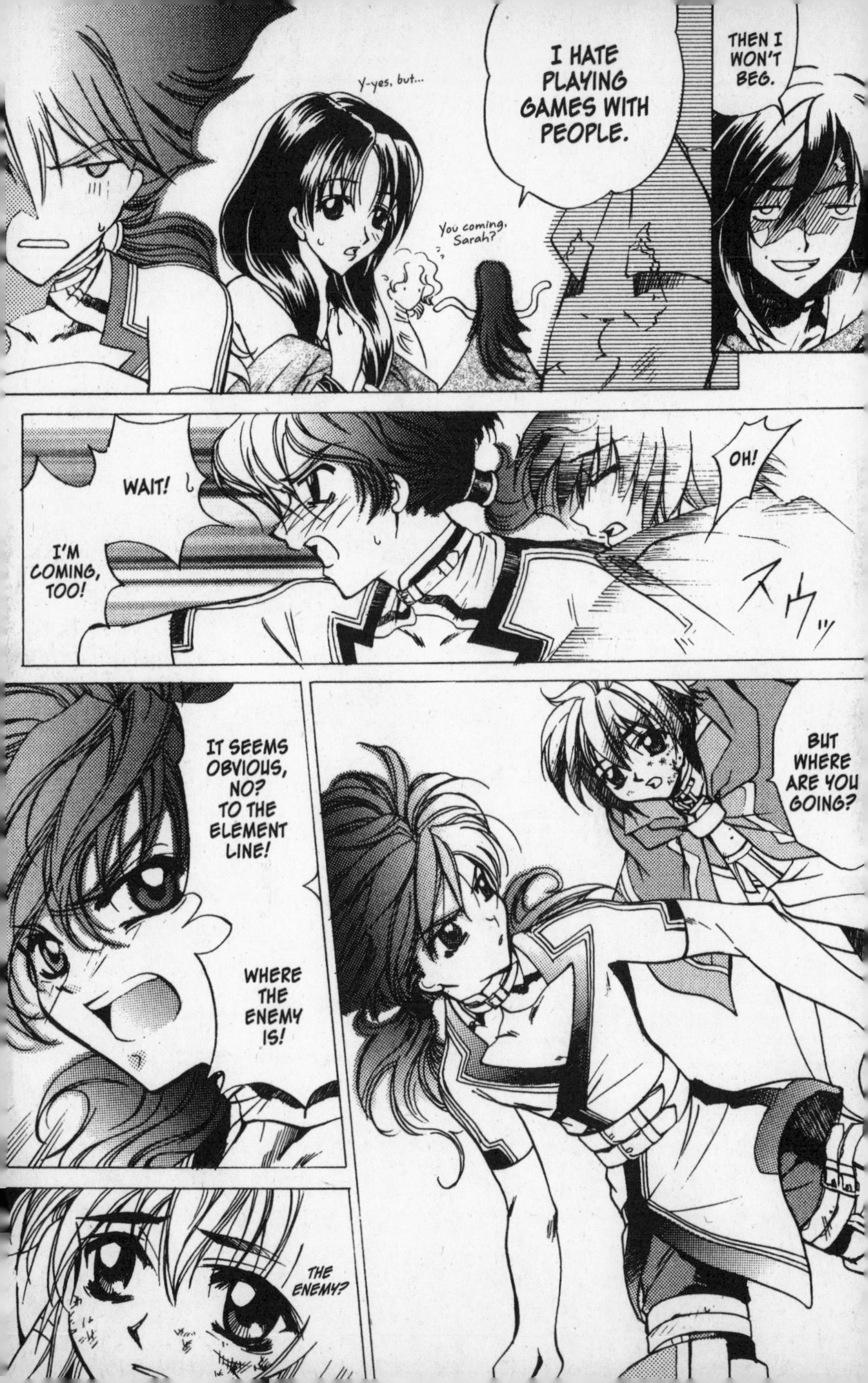
THEN I WON'T BEG.
I HATE PLAYING GAMES WITH PEOPLE.
You coming, Sarah?
Y-yes, but...
OH!
WAIT!
I'M COMING, TOO!
BUT WHERE ARE YOU GOING?
IT SEEMS OBVIOUS, NO? TO THE ELEMENT LINE!
WHERE THE ENEMY IS!
THE ENEMY?

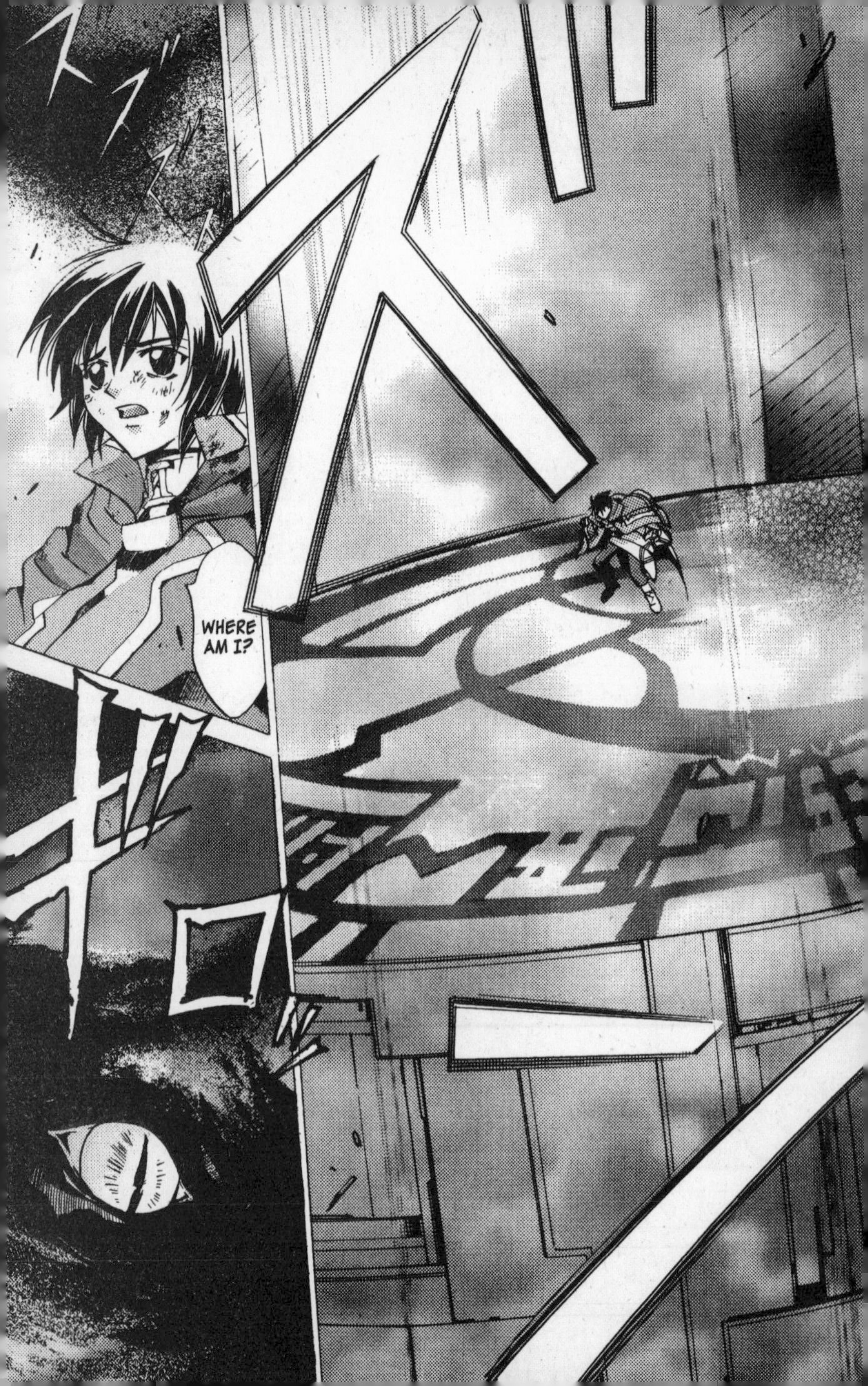
WHERE AM I?

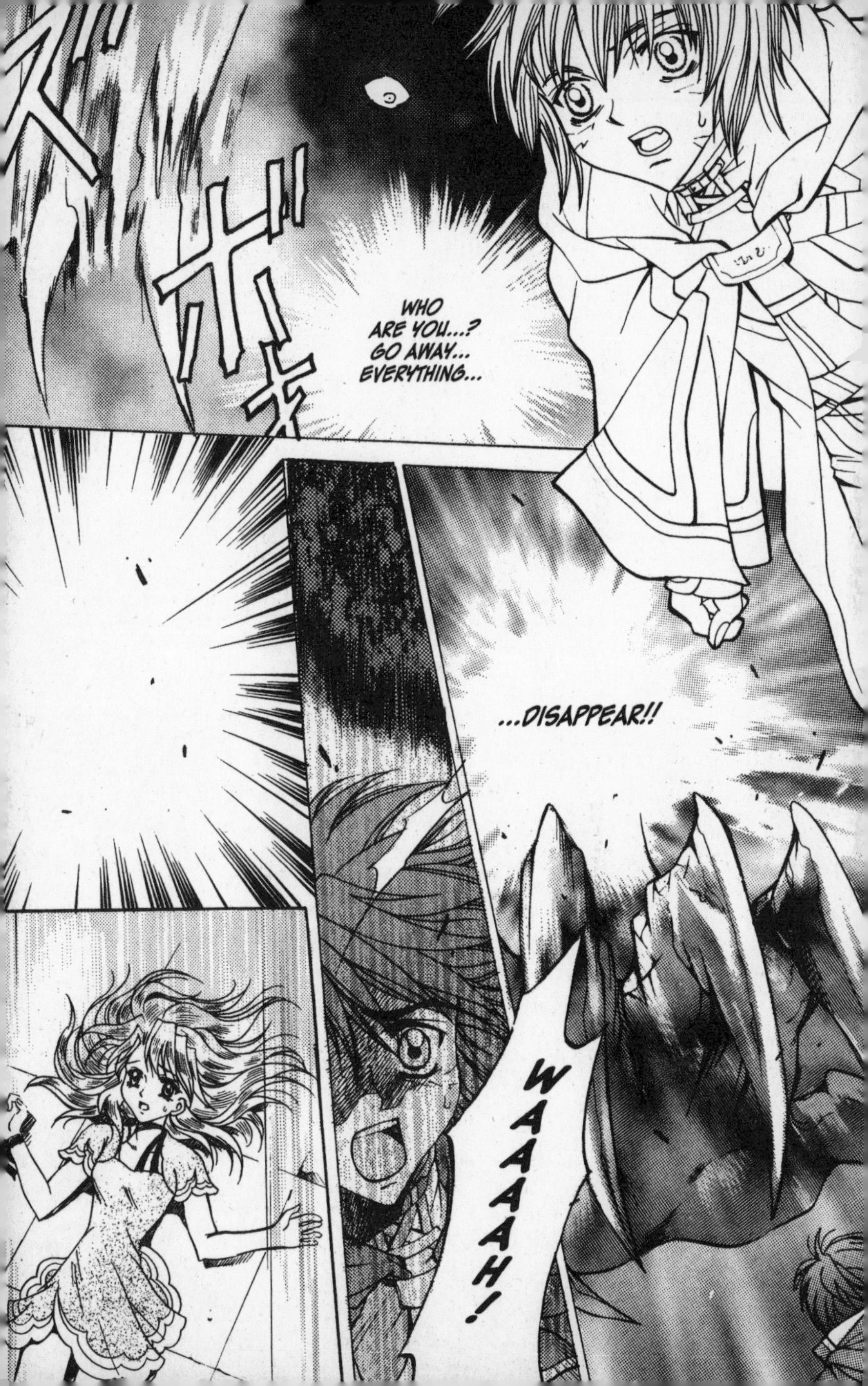
WHO ARE YOU...? GO AWAY... EVERYTHING...
...DISAPPEAR!!
WAAAAAH!

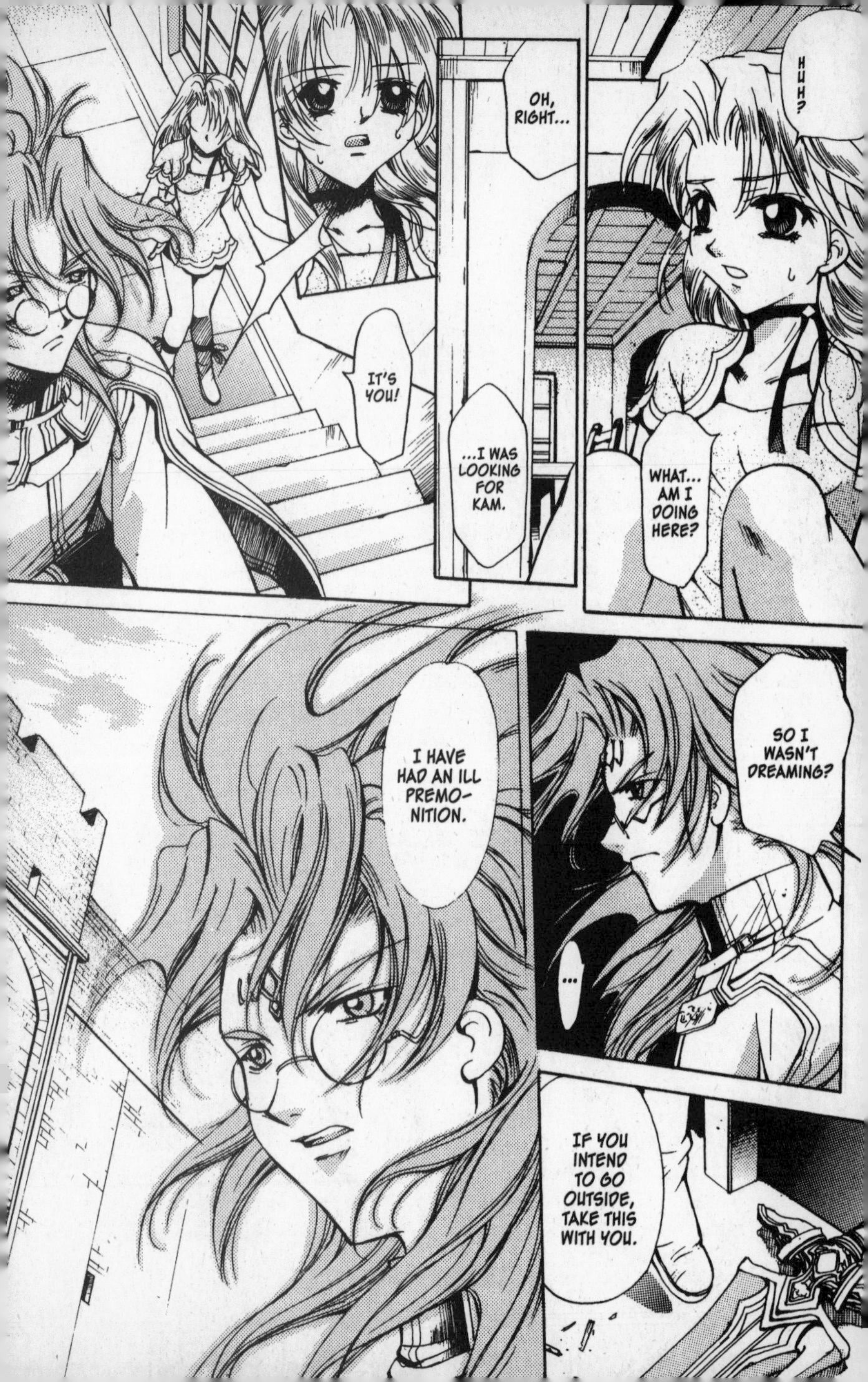
HUH?
WHAT... AM I DOING HERE?
OH, RIGHT...
...I WAS LOOKING FOR KAM.
IT'S YOU!
SO I WASN'T DREAMING?
...
IF YOU INTEND TO GO OUTSIDE, TAKE THIS WITH YOU.
I HAVE HAD AN ILL PREMONITION.

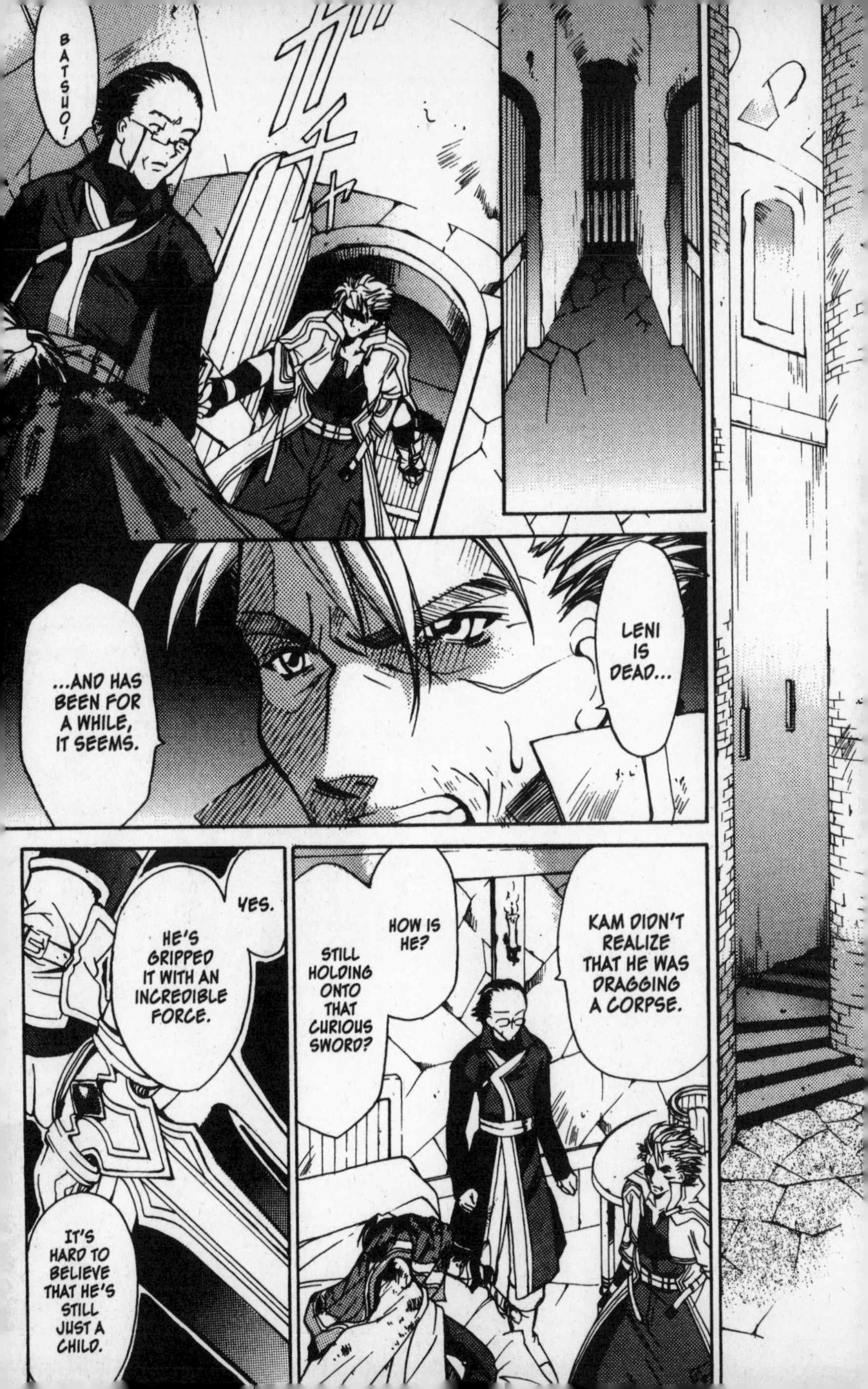
BATSUO!
LENI IS DEAD...
...AND HAS BEEN FOR A WHILE, IT SEEMS.
KAM DIDN'T REALIZE THAT HE WAS DRAGGING A CORPSE.
HOW IS HE?
STILL HOLDING ONTO THAT CURIOUS SWORD?
YES.
HE'S GRIPPED IT WITH AN INCREDIBLE FORCE.
IT'S HARD TO BELIEVE THAT HE'S STILL JUST A CHILD.

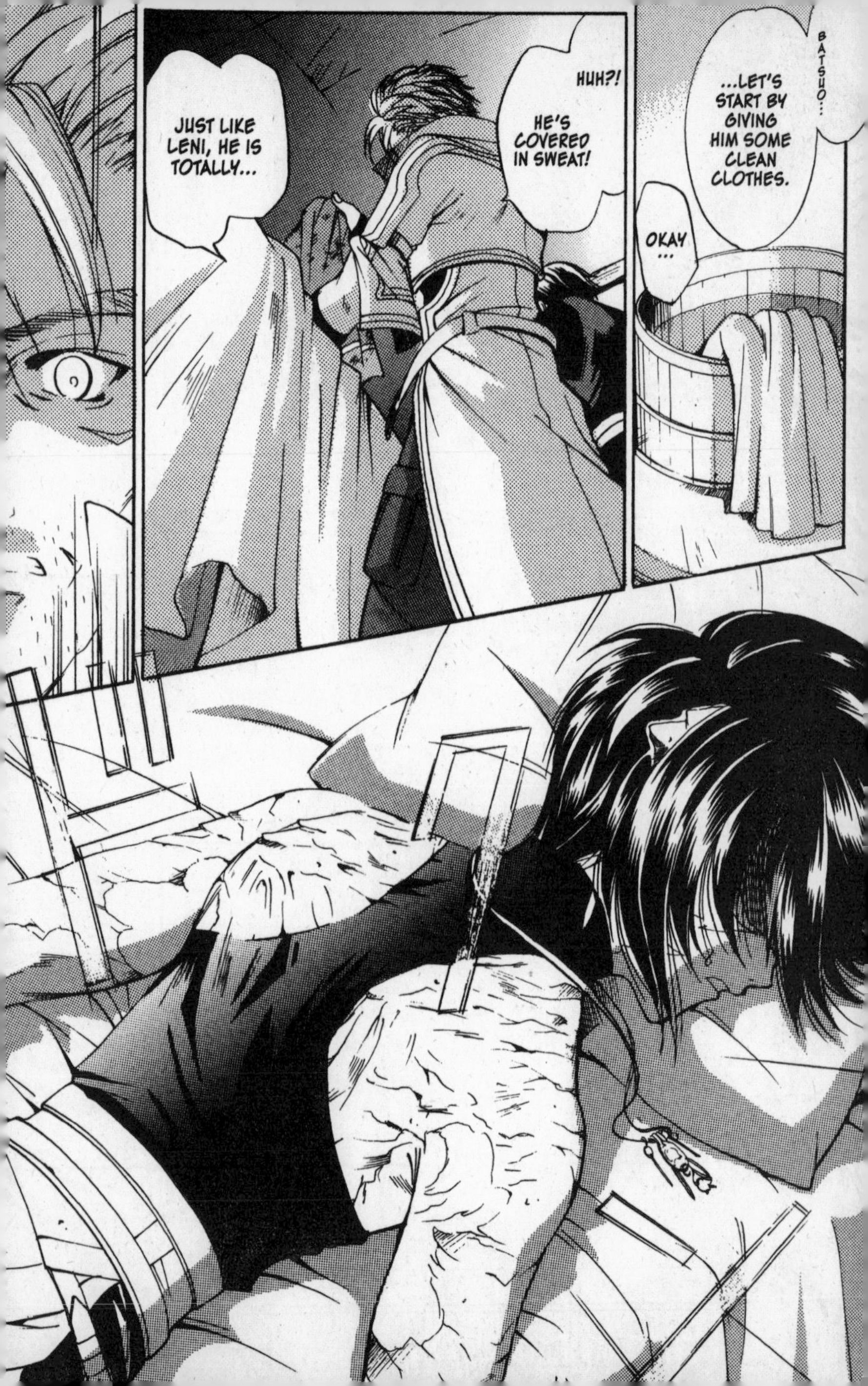
BATSUO...
...LET'S START BY GIVING HIM SOME CLEAN CLOTHES.
OKAY...
HUH?!
HE'S COVERED IN SWEAT!
JUST LIKE LENI, HE IS TOTALLY...

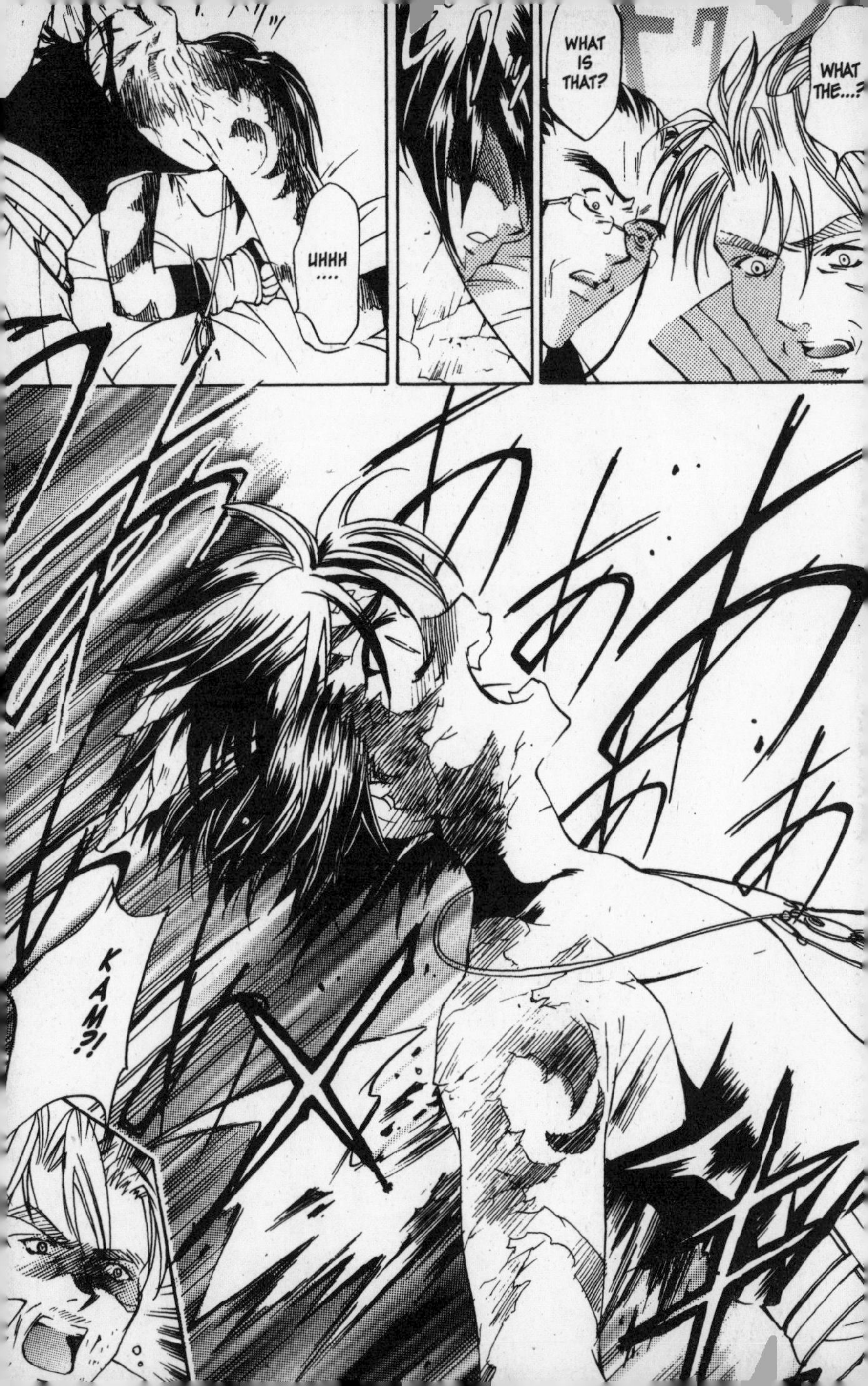
WHAT THE...?
WHAT IS THAT?
UHHH ....
ああああ
KAMI?!

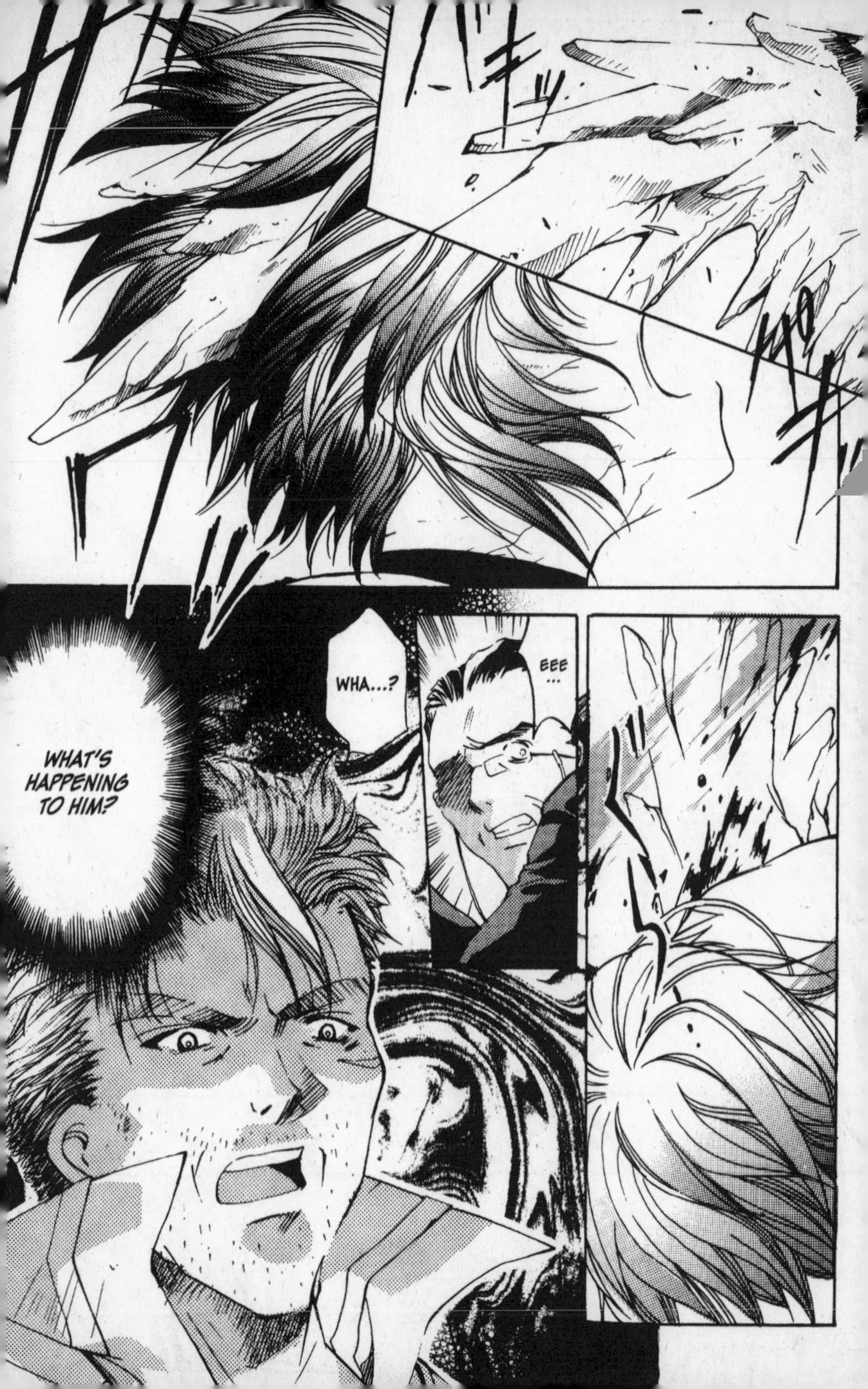
バキッ
EEE ...
WHA...?
WHAT'S HAPPENING TO HIM?

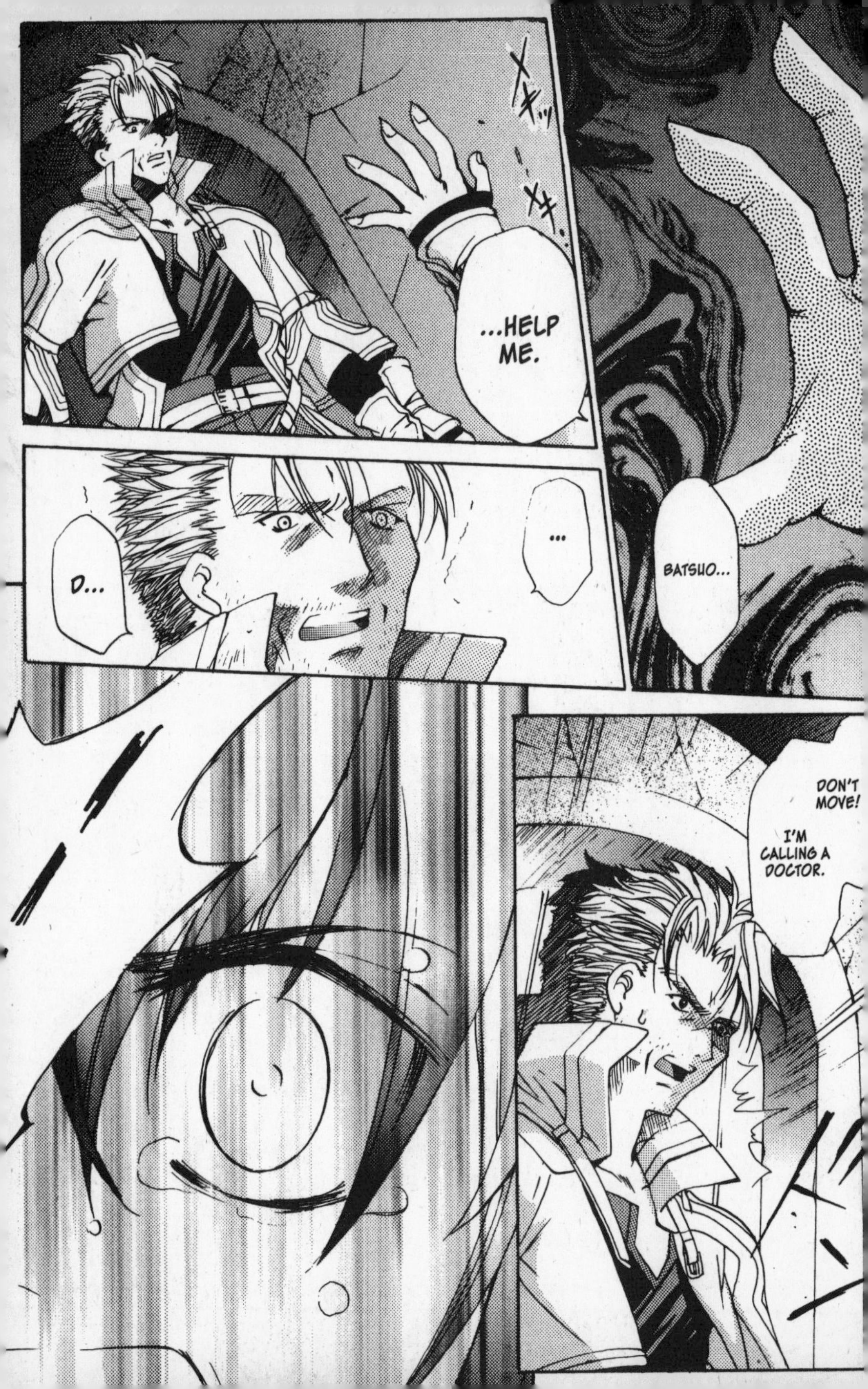
BATSUO...
...HELP ME.
...
D...
DON'T MOVE!
I'M CALLING A DOCTOR.

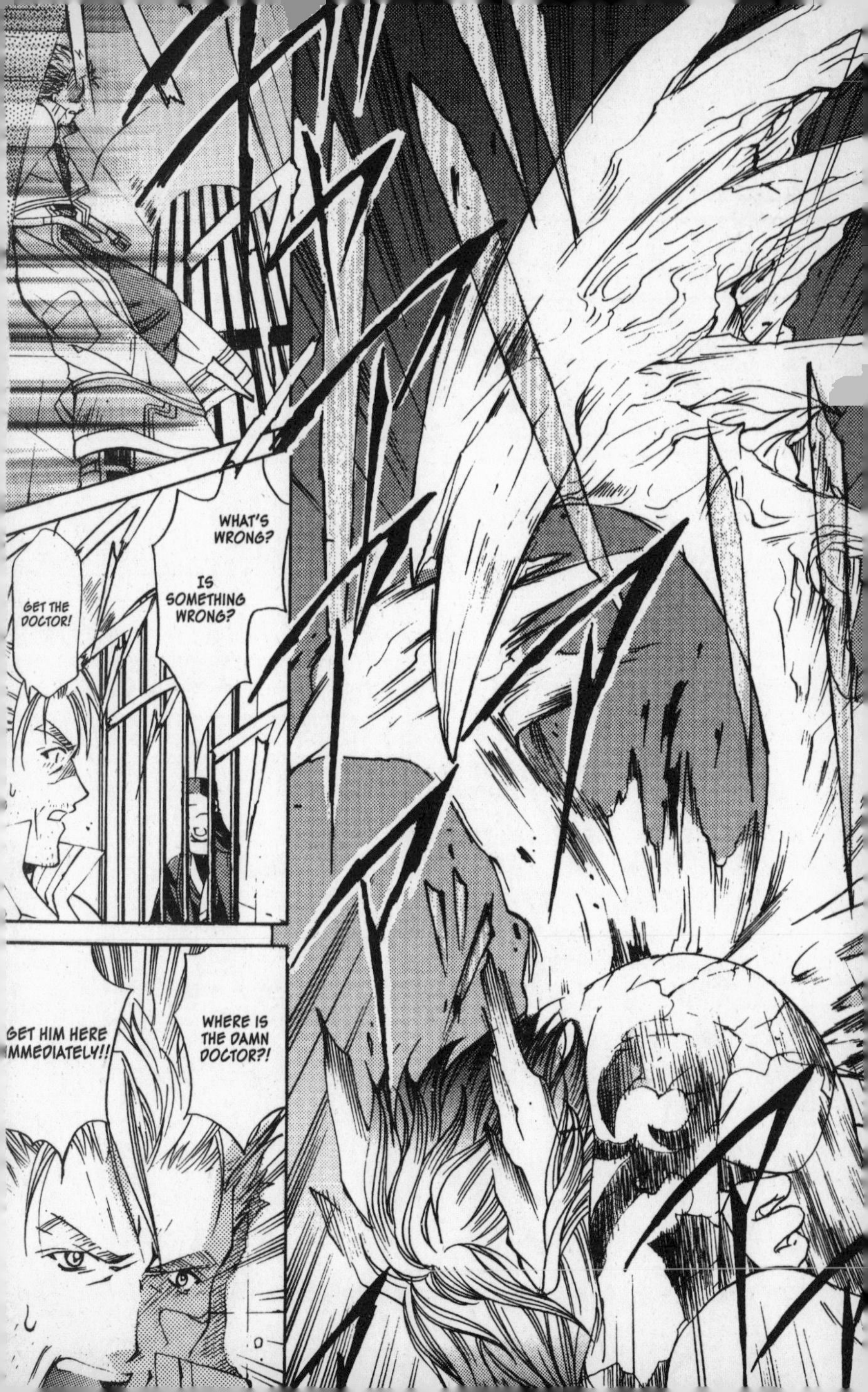
WHAT'S WRONG?
IS SOMETHING WRONG?
GET THE DOCTOR!
WHERE IS THE DAMN DOCTOR?!
GET HIM HERE IMMEDIATELY!!

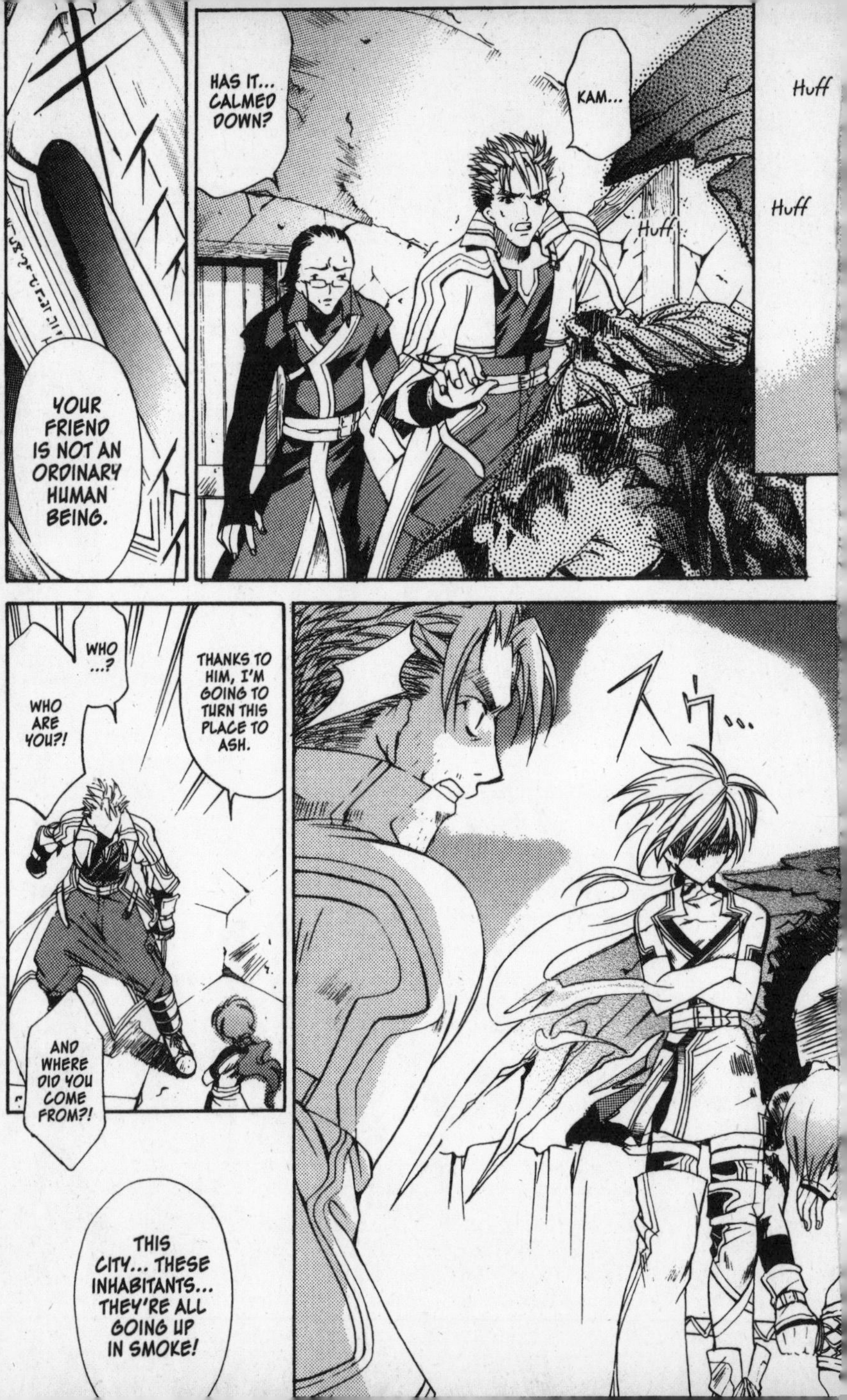
Huff
Huff
Huff
KAM...
HAS IT... CALMED DOWN?
YOUR FRIEND IS NOT AN ORDINARY HUMAN BEING.
THIS CITY... THESE INHABITANTS... THEY'RE ALL GOING UP IN SMOKE!
THANKS TO HIM, I'M GOING TO TURN THIS PLACE TO ASH.
WHO ...?
WHO ARE YOU?!
AND WHERE DID YOU COME FROM?!

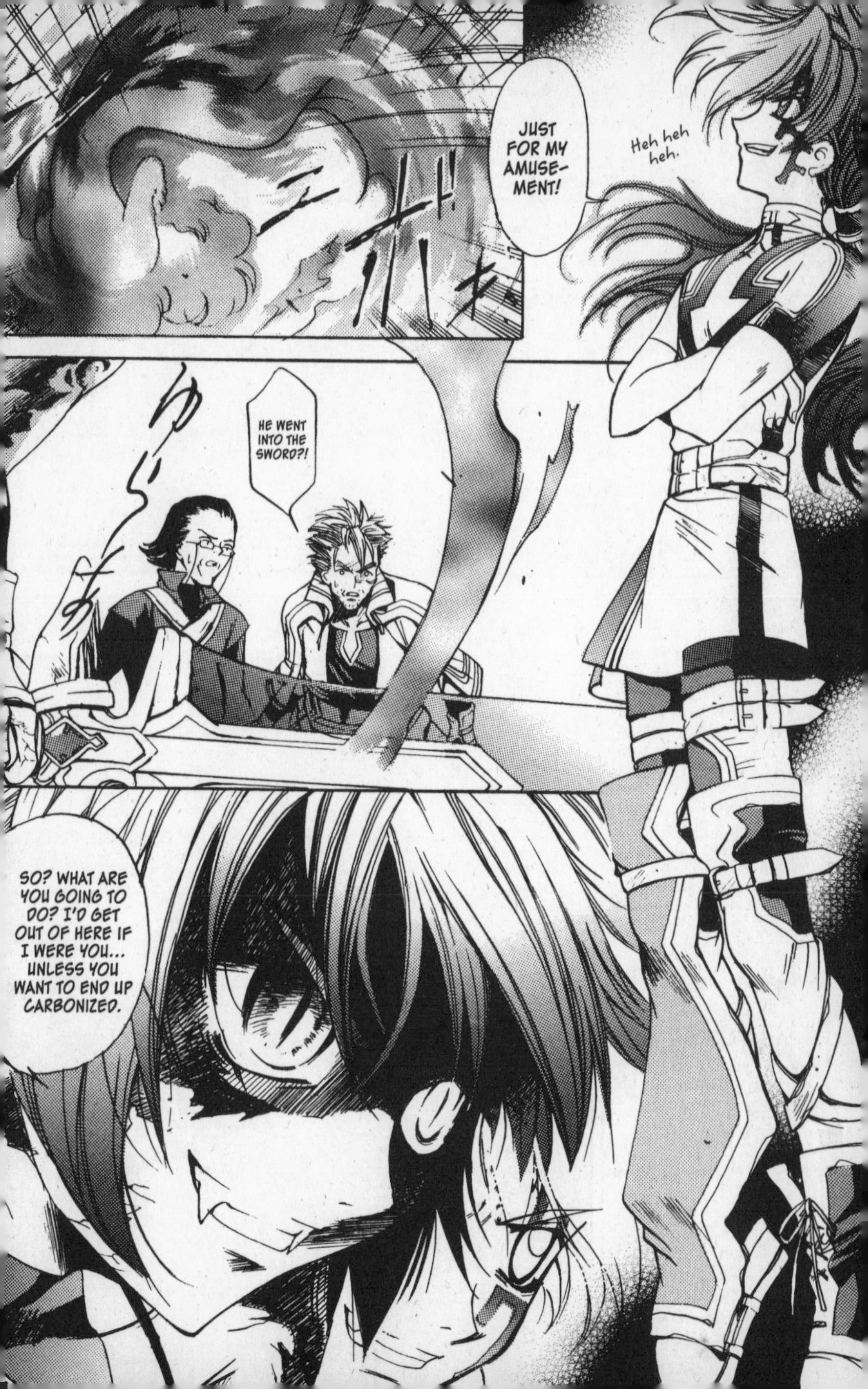
Heh heh heh.
JUST FOR MY AMUSEMENT!
HE WENT INTO THE SWORD?!
SO? WHAT ARE YOU GOING TO DO? I'D GET OUT OF HERE IF I WERE YOU... UNLESS YOU WANT TO END UP CARBONIZED.

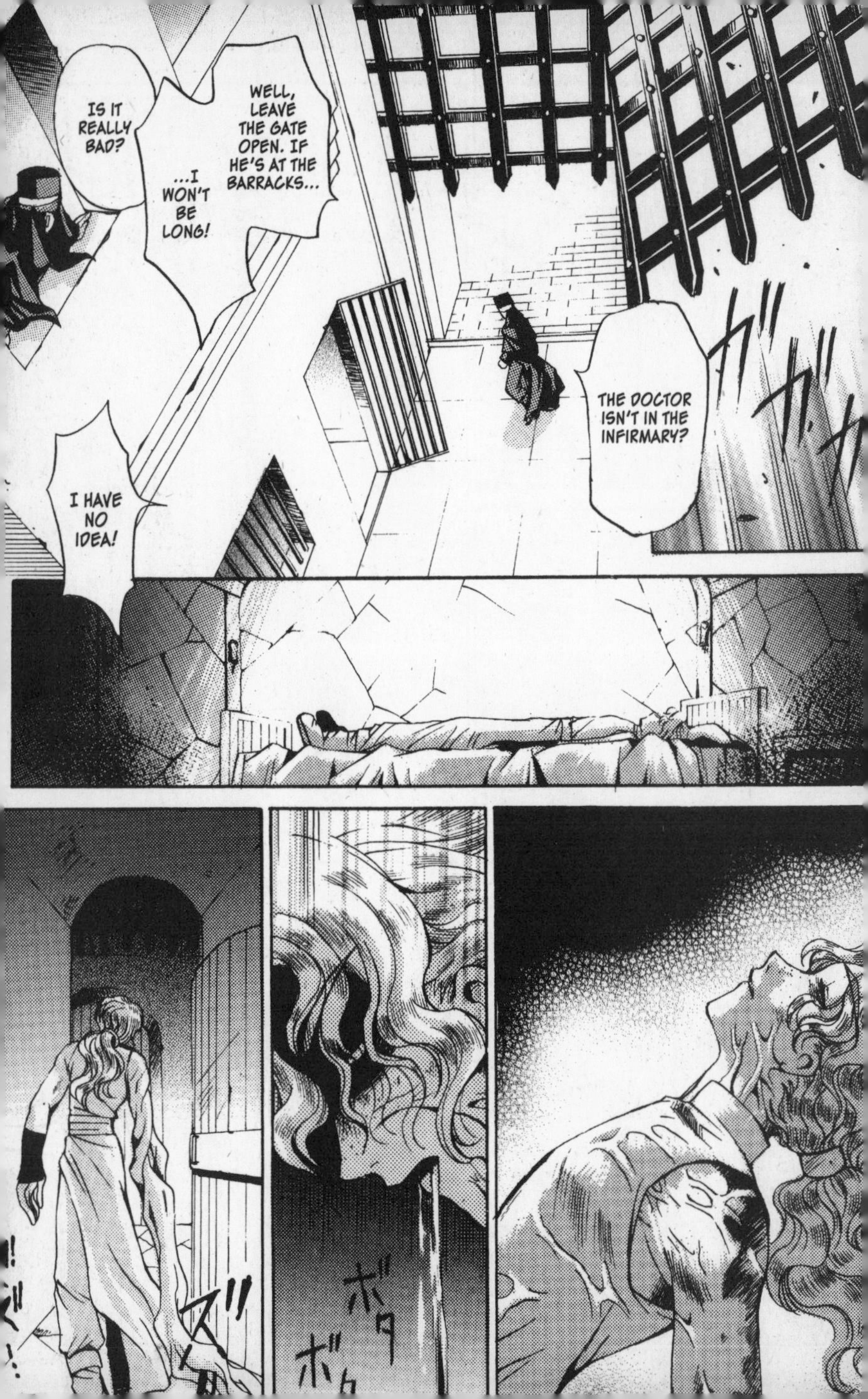
THE DOCTOR ISN'T IN THE INFIRMARY?
WELL, LEAVE THE GATE OPEN. IF HE'S AT THE BARRACKS...
...I WON'T BE LONG!
IS IT REALLY BAD?
I HAVE NO IDEA!

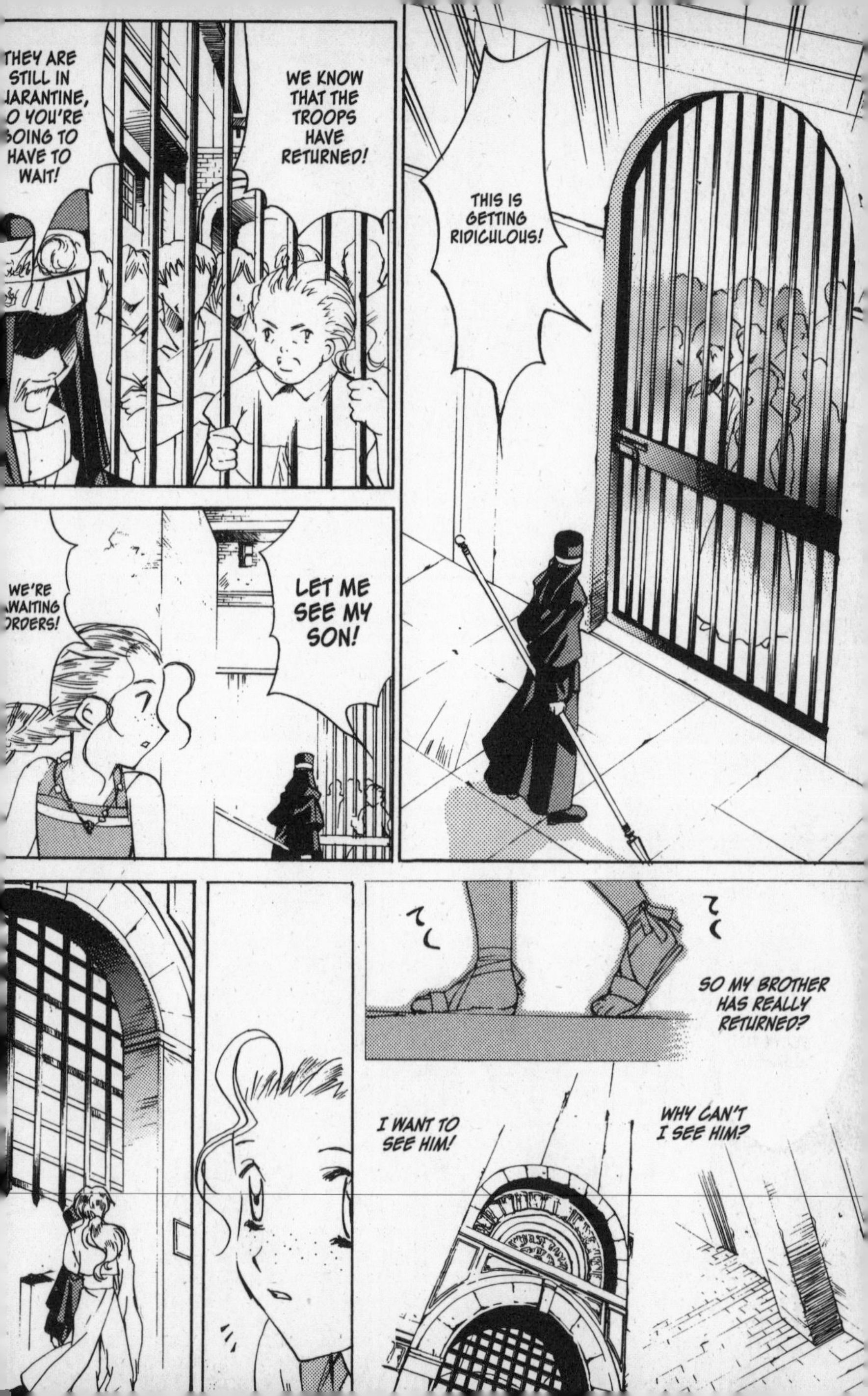
THIS IS GETTING RIDICULOUS!
WE KNOW THAT THE TROOPS HAVE RETURNED!
THEY ARE STILL IN UARANTINE, O YOU'RE OING TO HAVE TO WAIT!
LET ME SEE MY SON!
WE'RE WAITING RDERS!
SO MY BROTHER HAS REALLY RETURNED?
WHY CAN'T I SEE HIM?
I WANT TO SEE HIM!

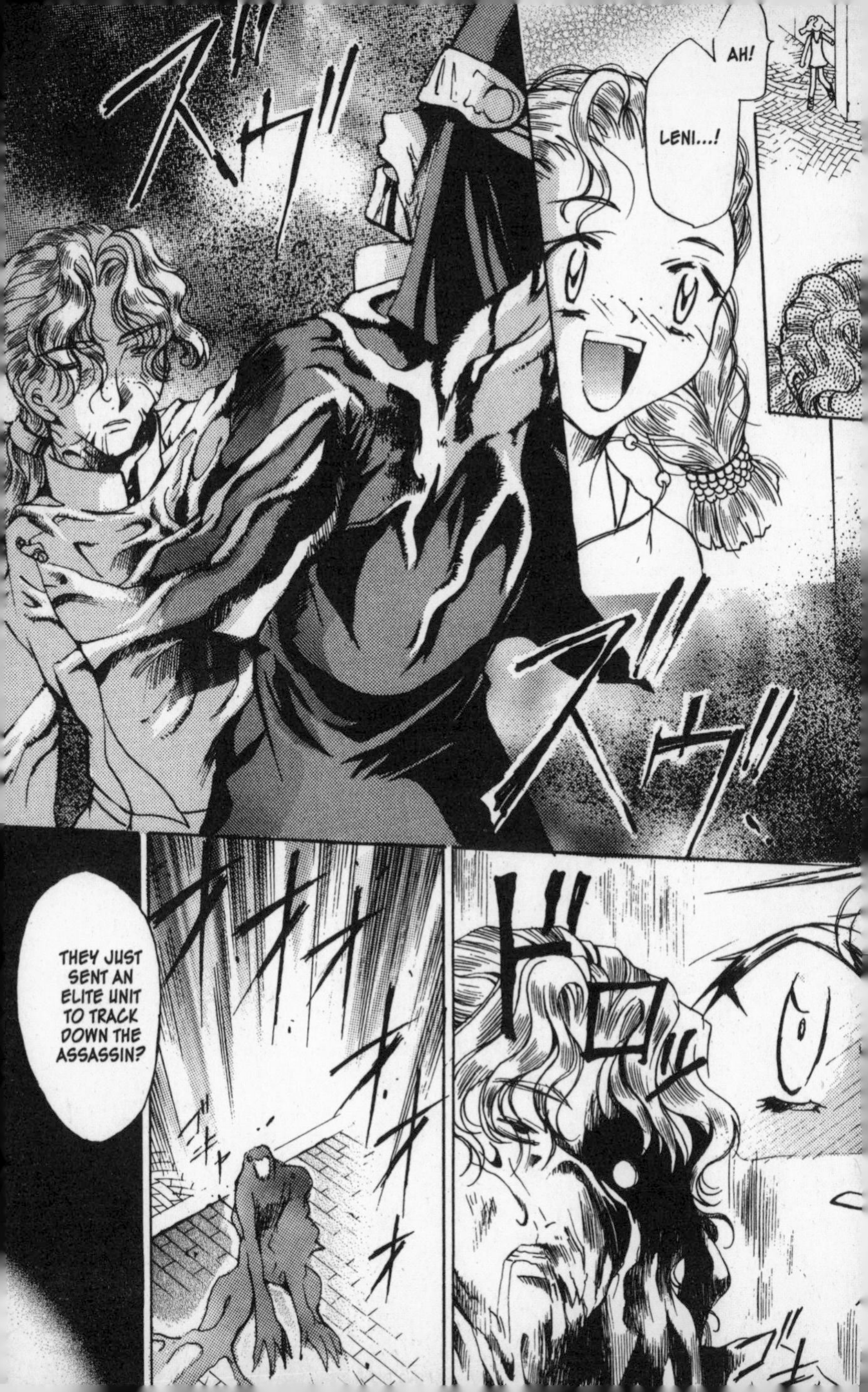
AH!
LENI...!
THEY JUST SENT AN ELITE UNIT TO TRACK DOWN THE ASSASSIN?

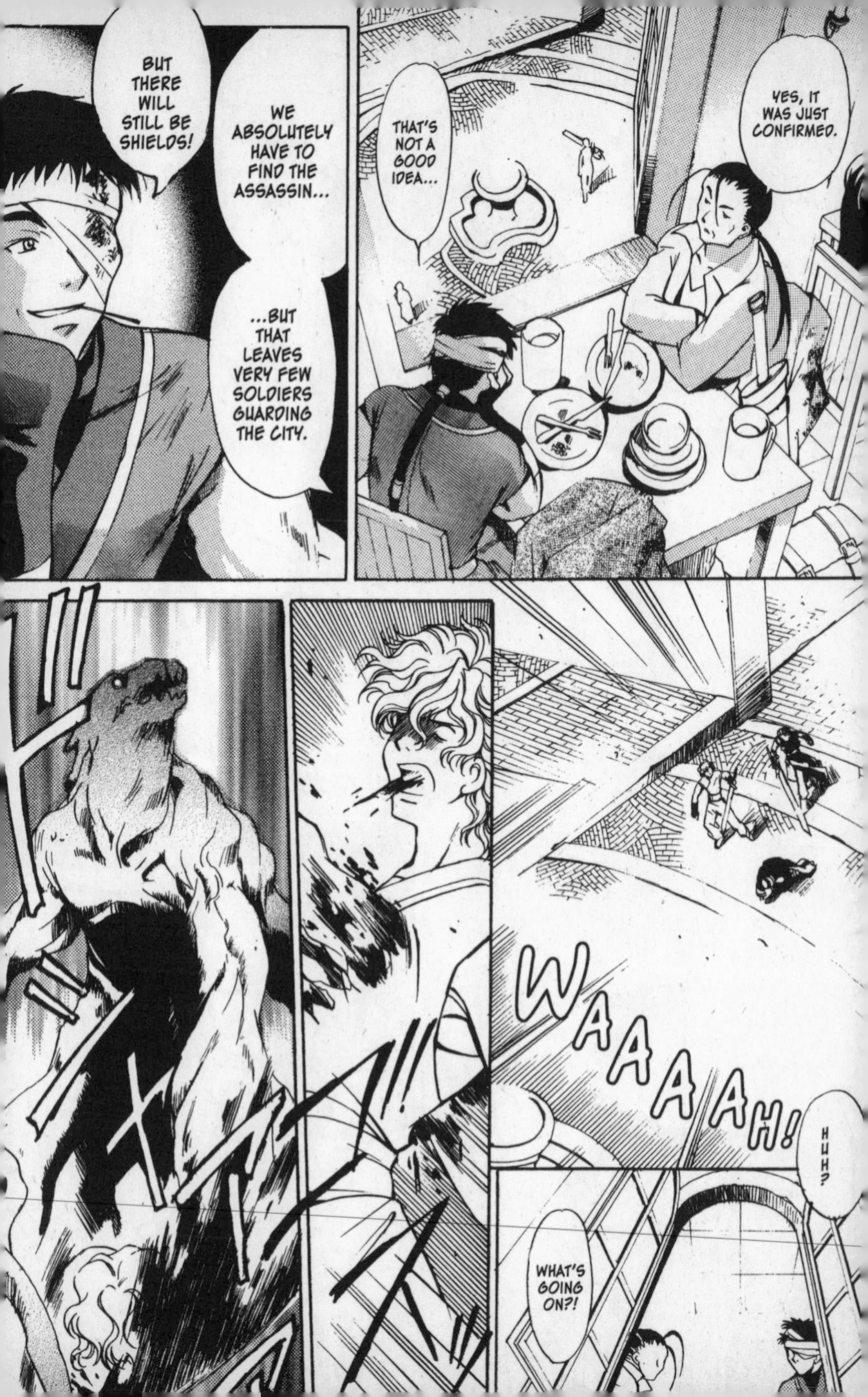
YES, IT WAS JUST CONFIRMED.
THAT'S NOT A GOOD IDEA...
WE ABSOLUTELY HAVE TO FIND THE ASSASSIN...
...BUT THAT LEAVES VERY FEW SOLDIERS GUARDING THE CITY.
BUT THERE WILL STILL BE SHIELDS!
WAAAAAH!
HUH?
WHAT'S GOING ON?!

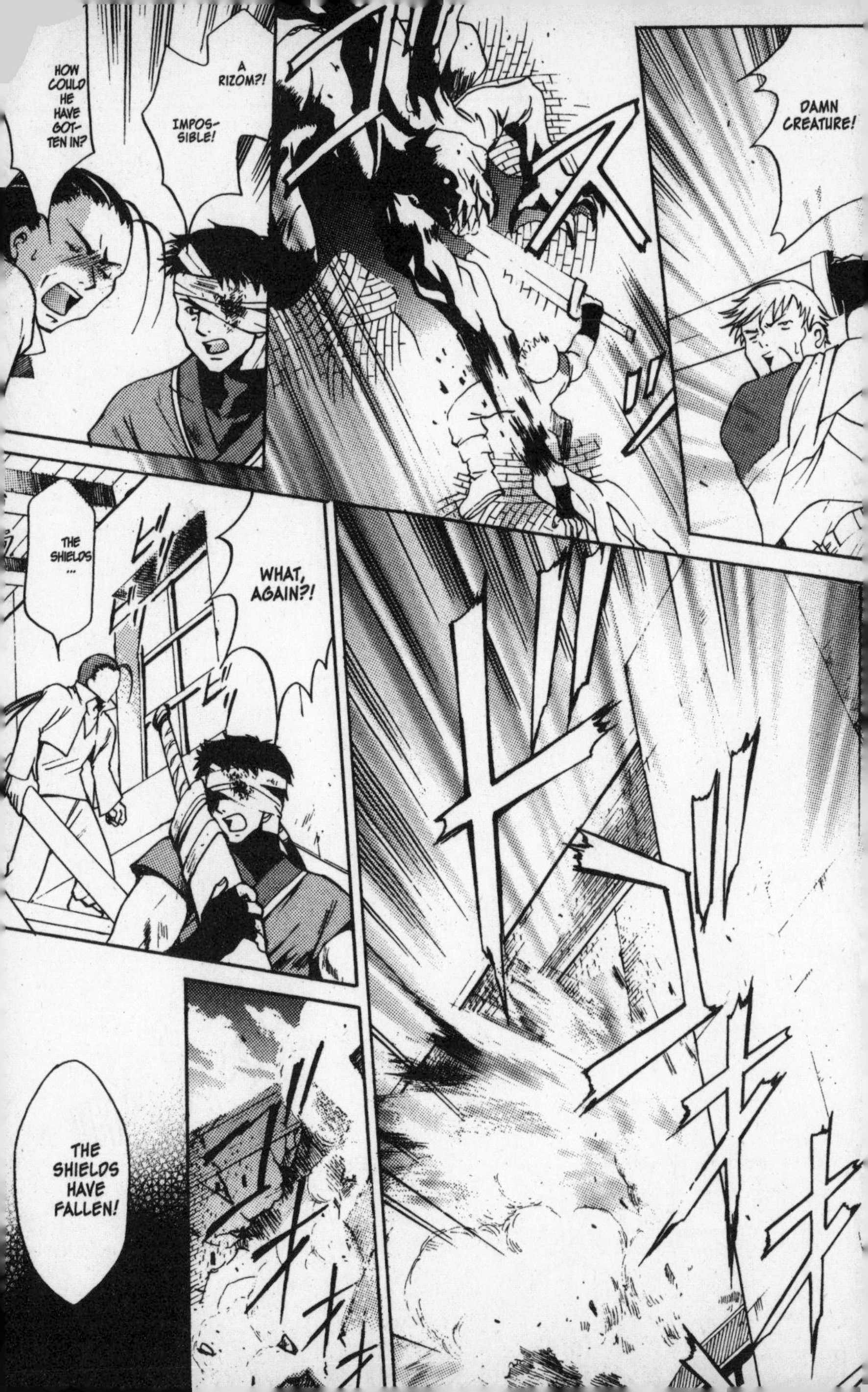
DAMN CREATURE!
A RIZOM?!
IMPOS-SIBLE!
HOW COULD HE HAVE GOT-TEN IN?
WHAT, AGAIN?!
THE SHIELDS ...
THE SHIELDS HAVE FALLEN!

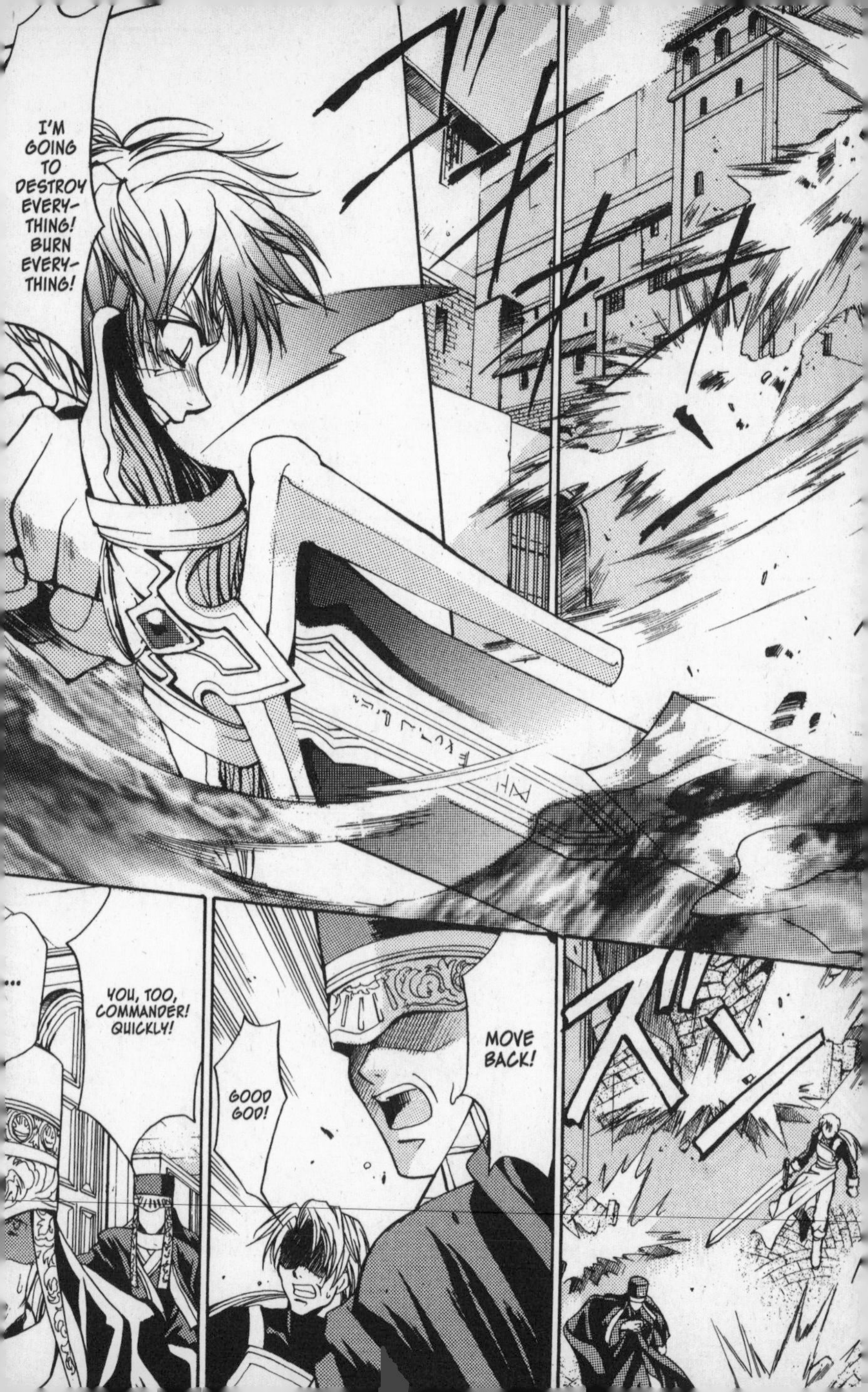
I'M GOING TO DESTROY EVERY-THING! BURN EVERY-THING!
MOVE BACK!
GOOD GOD!
YOU, TOO, COMMANDER! QUICKLY!
...

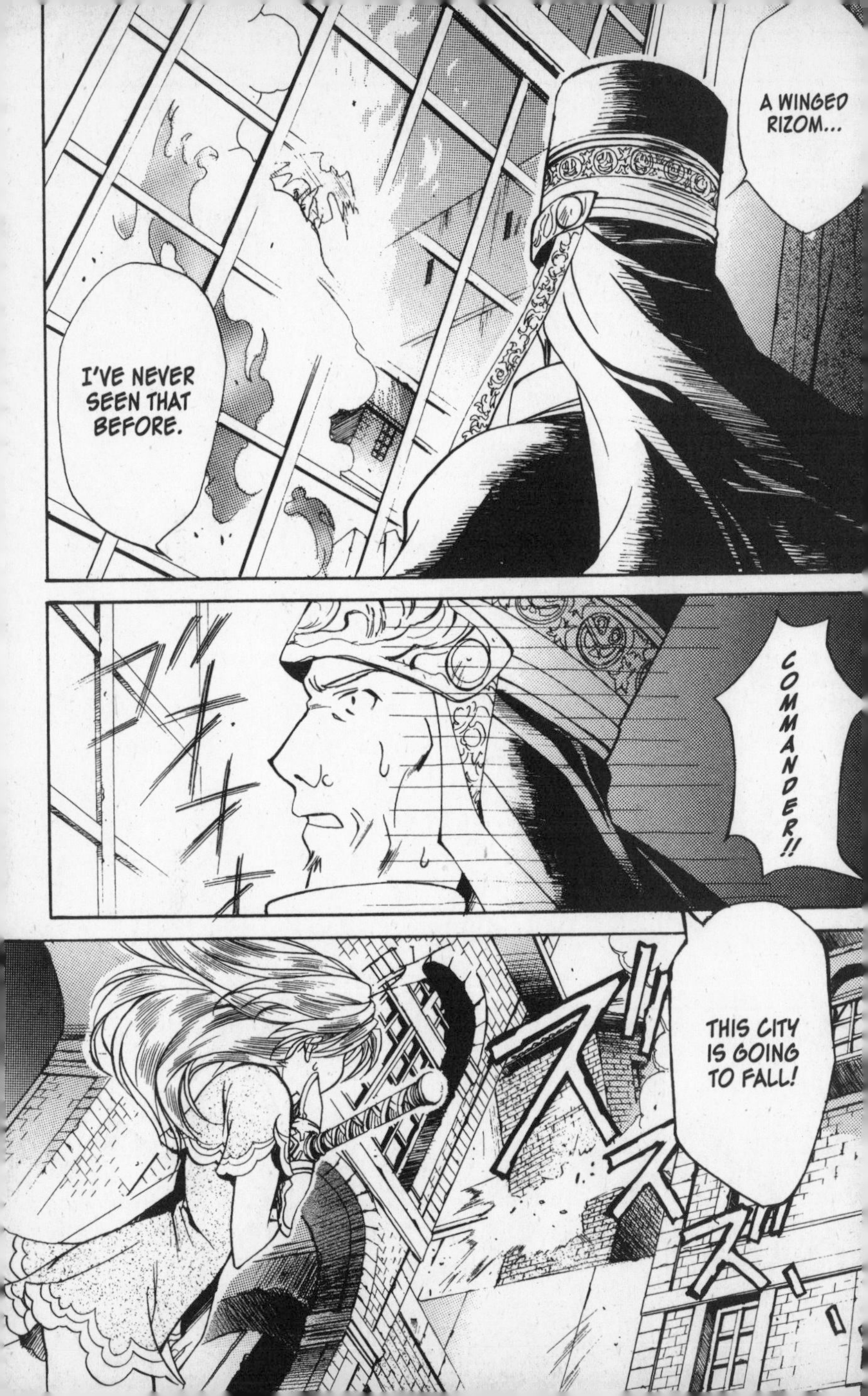
A WINGED RIZOM...
I'VE NEVER SEEN THAT BEFORE.
COMMANDER!!
THIS CITY IS GOING TO FALL!

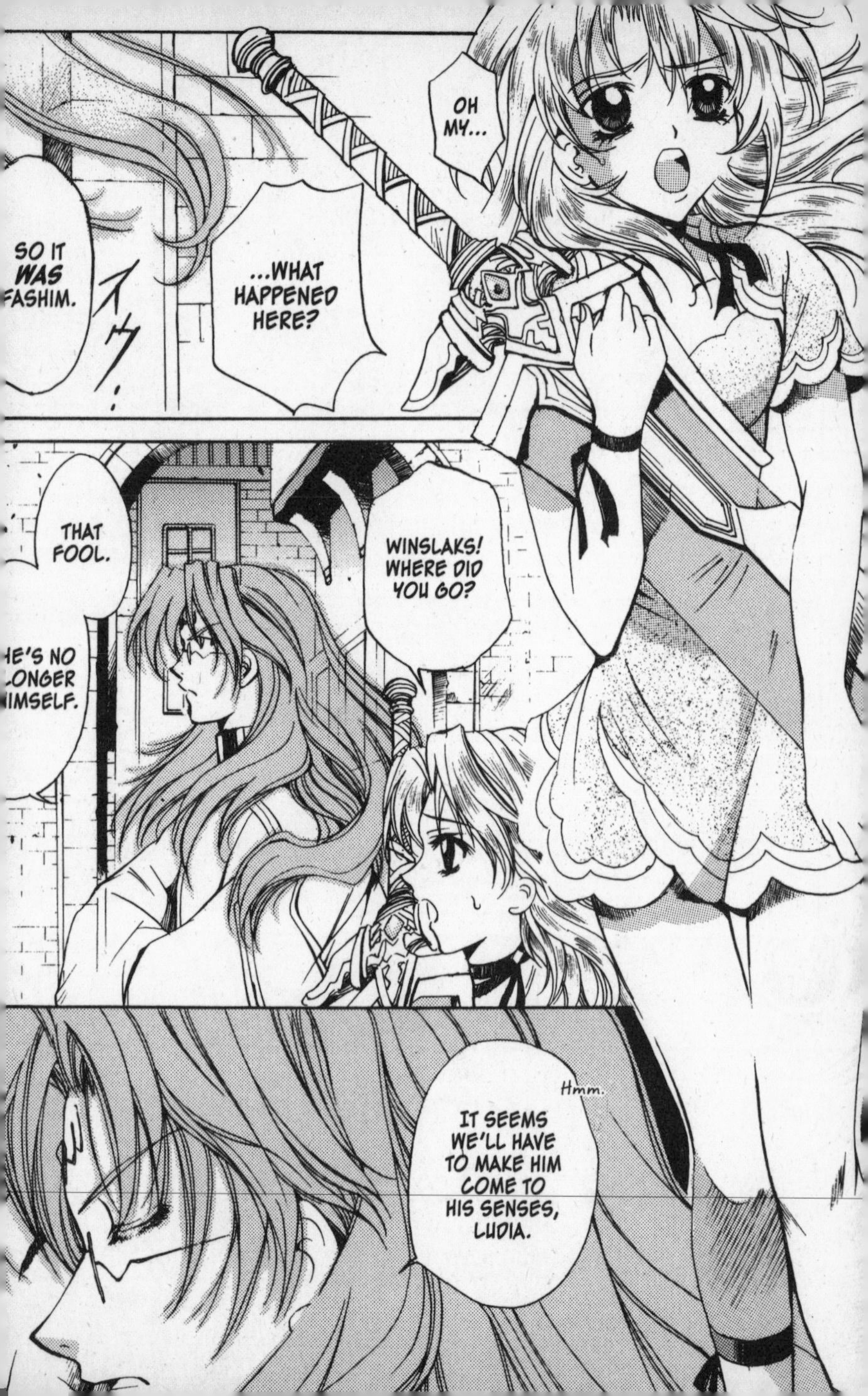
OH MY...
...WHAT HAPPENED HERE?
SO IT WAS FASHIM.
WINSLAKS! WHERE DID YOU GO?
THAT FOOL.
E'S NO LONGER IMSELF.
Hmm.
IT SEEMS WE'LL HAVE TO MAKE HIM COME TO HIS SENSES, LUDIA.

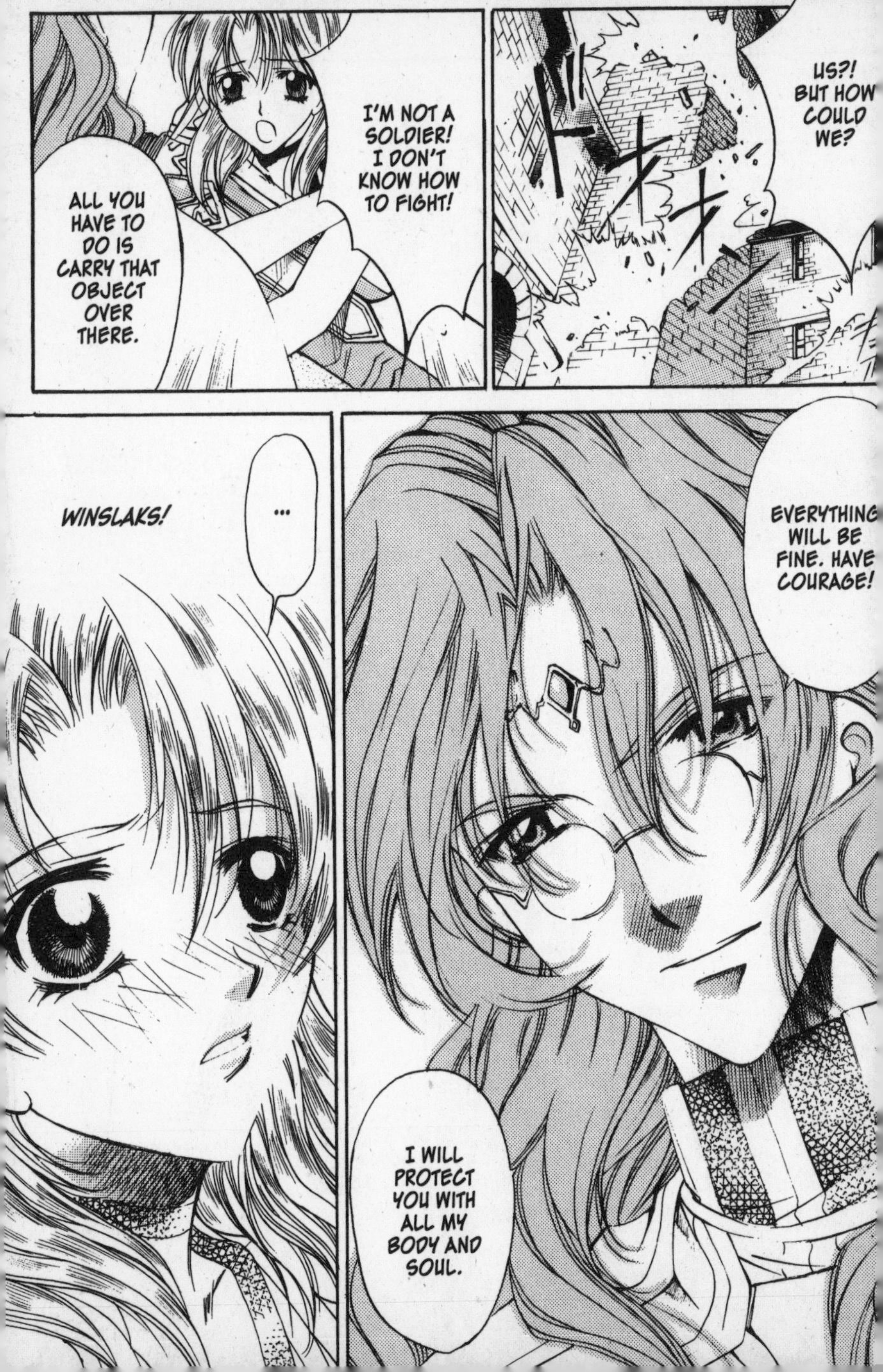
US?! BUT HOW COULD WE?
I'M NOT A SOLDIER! I DON'T KNOW HOW TO FIGHT!
ALL YOU HAVE TO DO IS CARRY THAT OBJECT OVER THERE.
EVERYTHING WILL BE FINE. HAVE COURAGE!
I WILL PROTECT YOU WITH ALL MY BODY AND SOUL.
...
WINSLAKS!

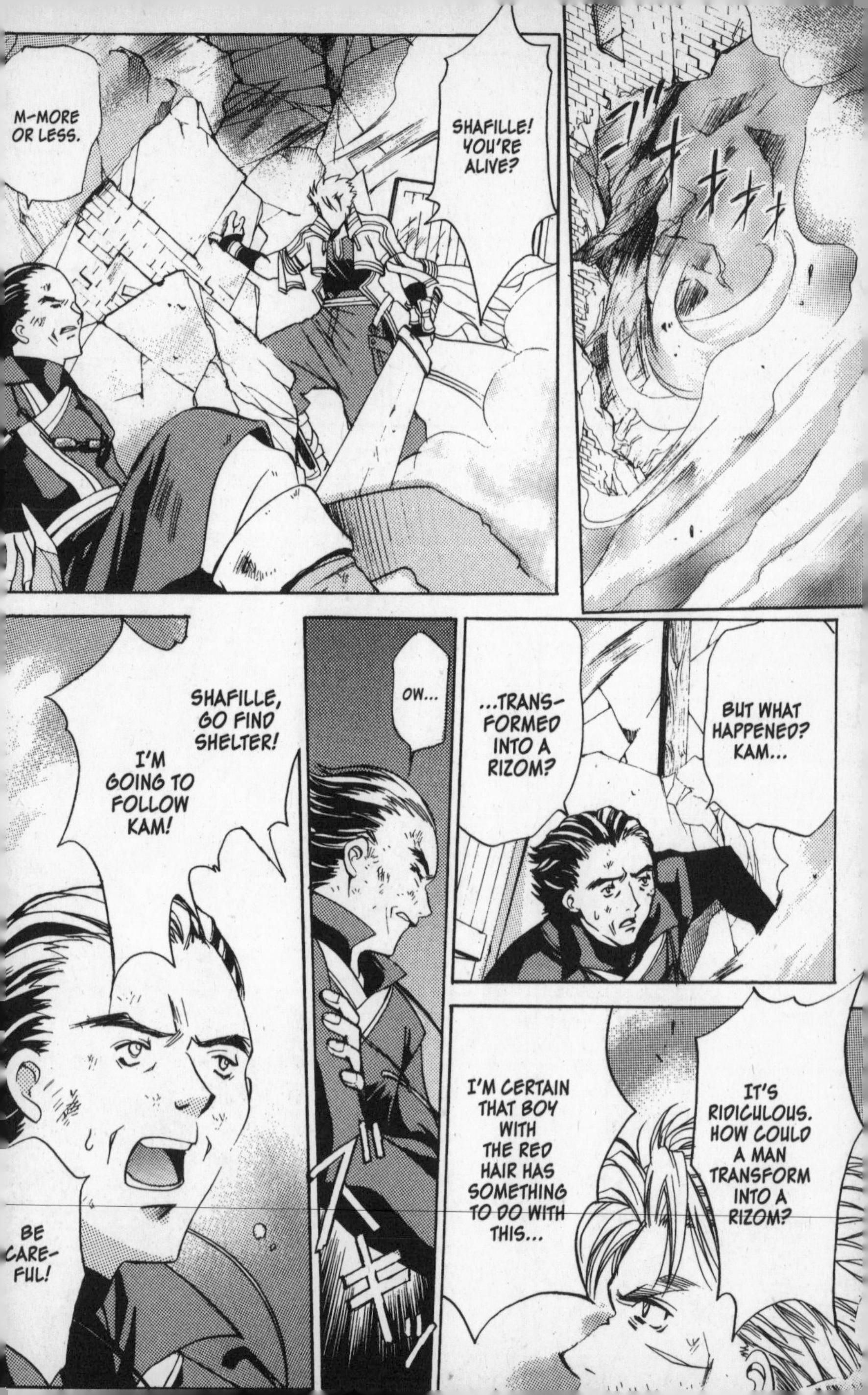
SHAFILLE! YOU'RE ALIVE?
M-MORE OR LESS.
BUT WHAT HAPPENED? KAM...
...TRANS-FORMED INTO A RIZOM?
IT'S RIDICULOUS. HOW COULD A MAN TRANSFORM INTO A RIZOM?
I'M CERTAIN THAT BOY WITH THE RED HAIR HAS SOMETHING TO DO WITH THIS...
OW...
SHAFILLE, GO FIND SHELTER!
I'M GOING TO FOLLOW KAM!
BE CARE-FUL!

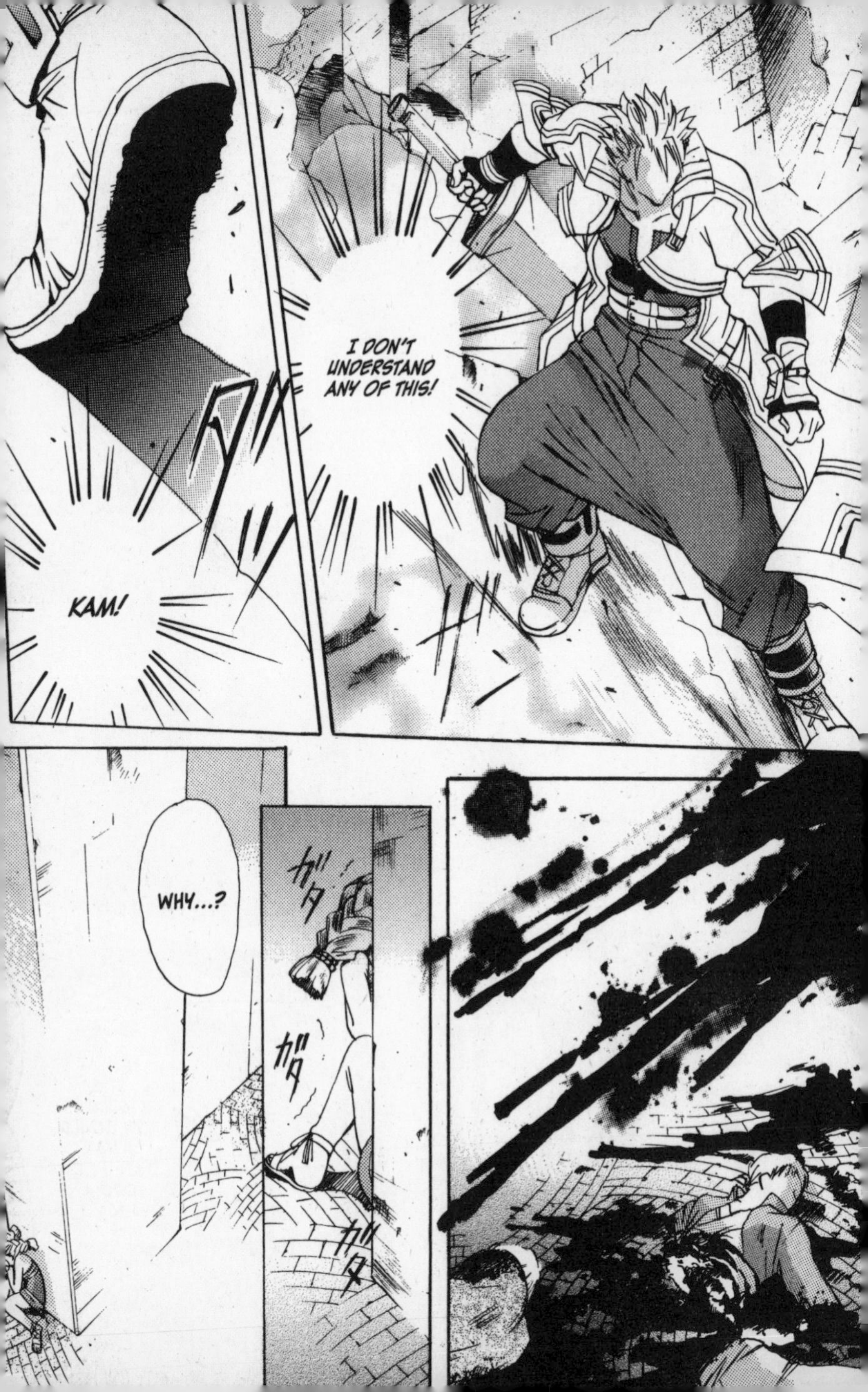
I DON'T UNDERSTAND ANY OF THIS!
KAM!
ガタ
ガタ
ガタ
WHY...?

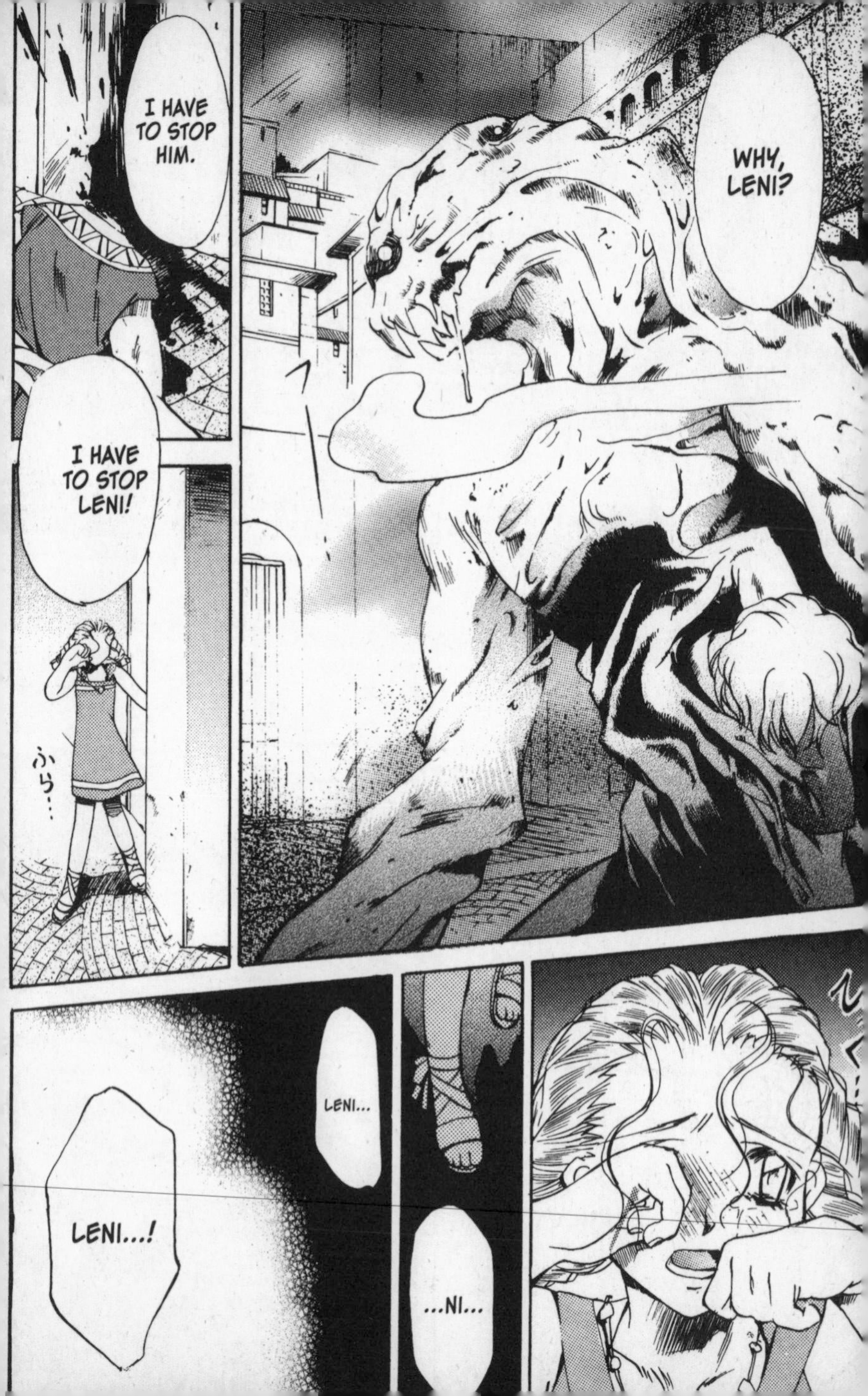
WHY, LENI?
I HAVE TO STOP HIM.
I HAVE TO STOP LENI!
ふら…
LENI...
...NI...
LENI...!

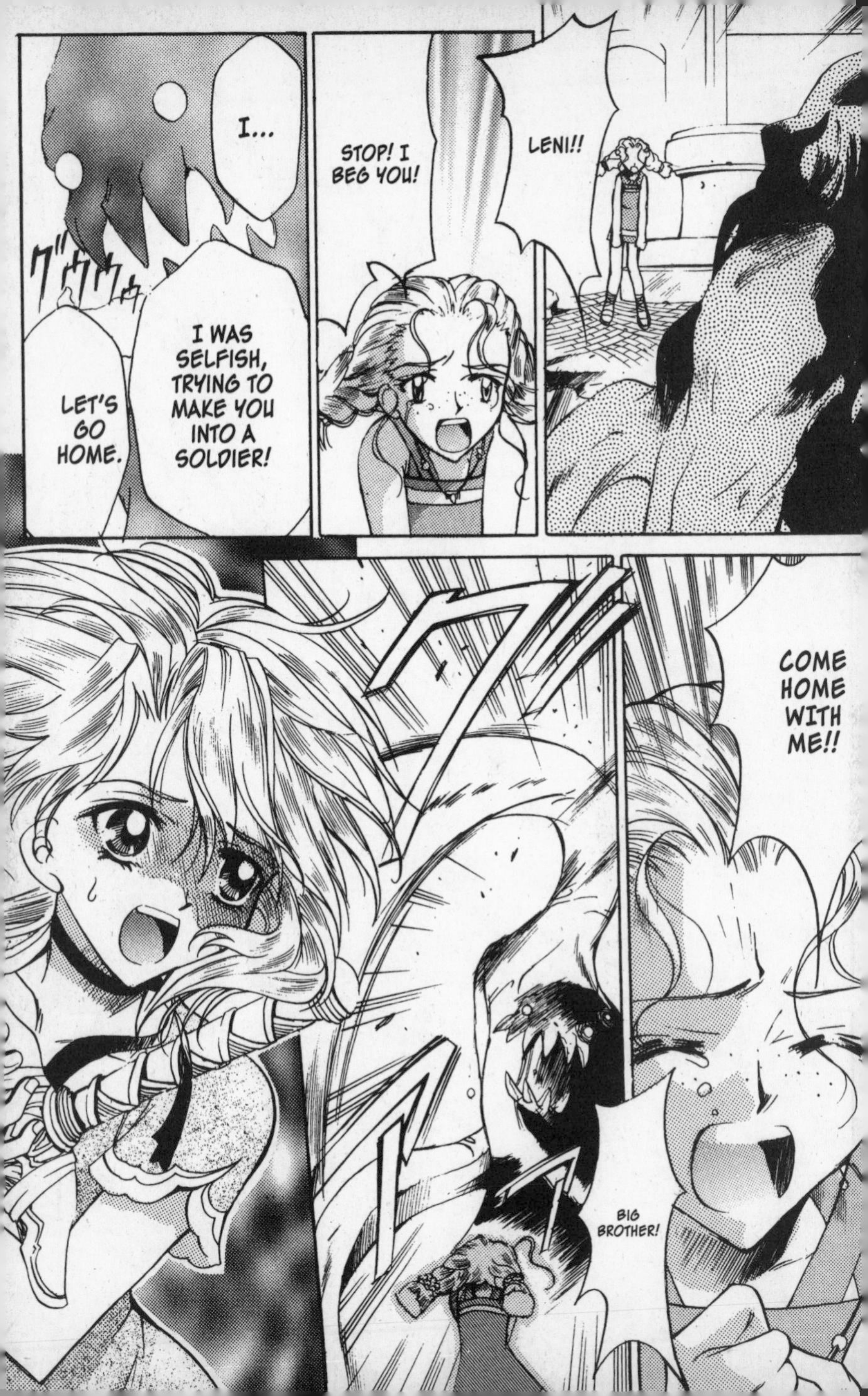
LENI!!
STOP! I BEG YOU!
I...
I WAS SELFISH, TRYING TO MAKE YOU INTO A SOLDIER!
LET'S GO HOME.
COME HOME WITH ME!!
BIG BROTHER!

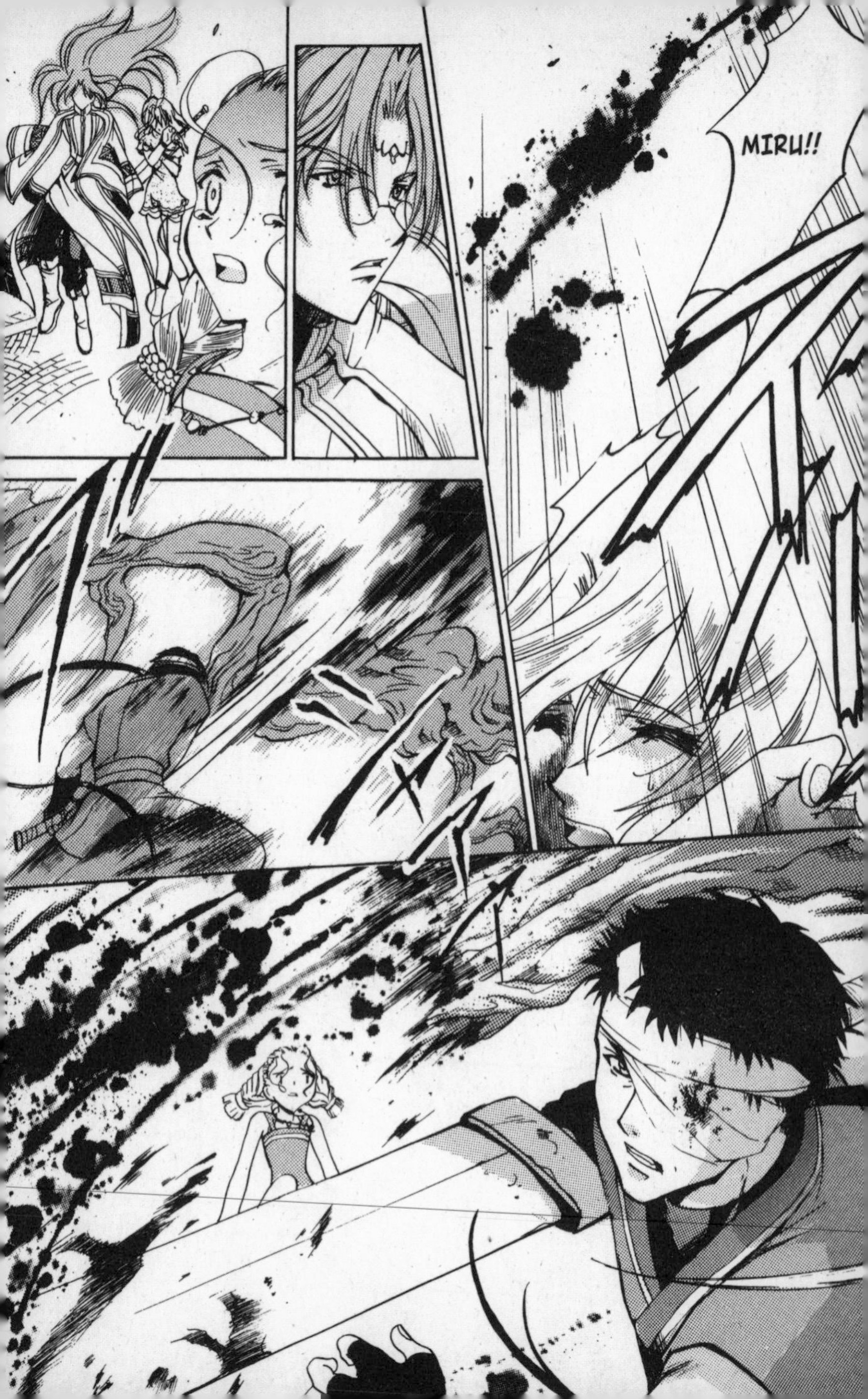
MIRU!!

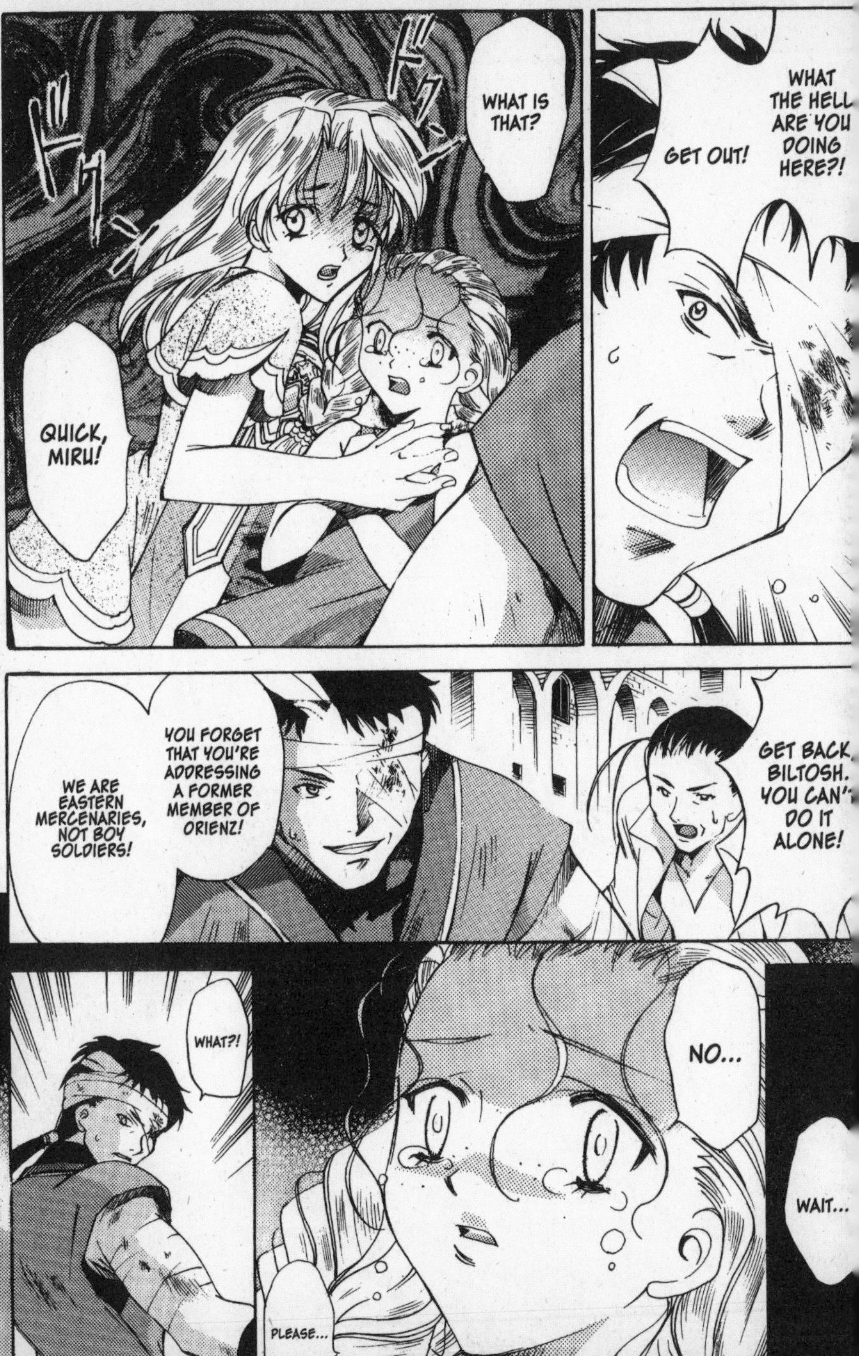
WHAT THE HELL ARE YOU DOING HERE?!
GET OUT!
WHAT IS THAT?
QUICK, MIRU!
GET BACK, BILTOSH. YOU CAN'T DO IT ALONE!
YOU FORGET THAT YOU'RE ADDRESSING A FORMER MEMBER OF ORIENZ!
WE ARE EASTERN MERCENARIES, NOT BOY SOLDIERS!
NO...
WAIT...
PLEASE...
WHAT?!

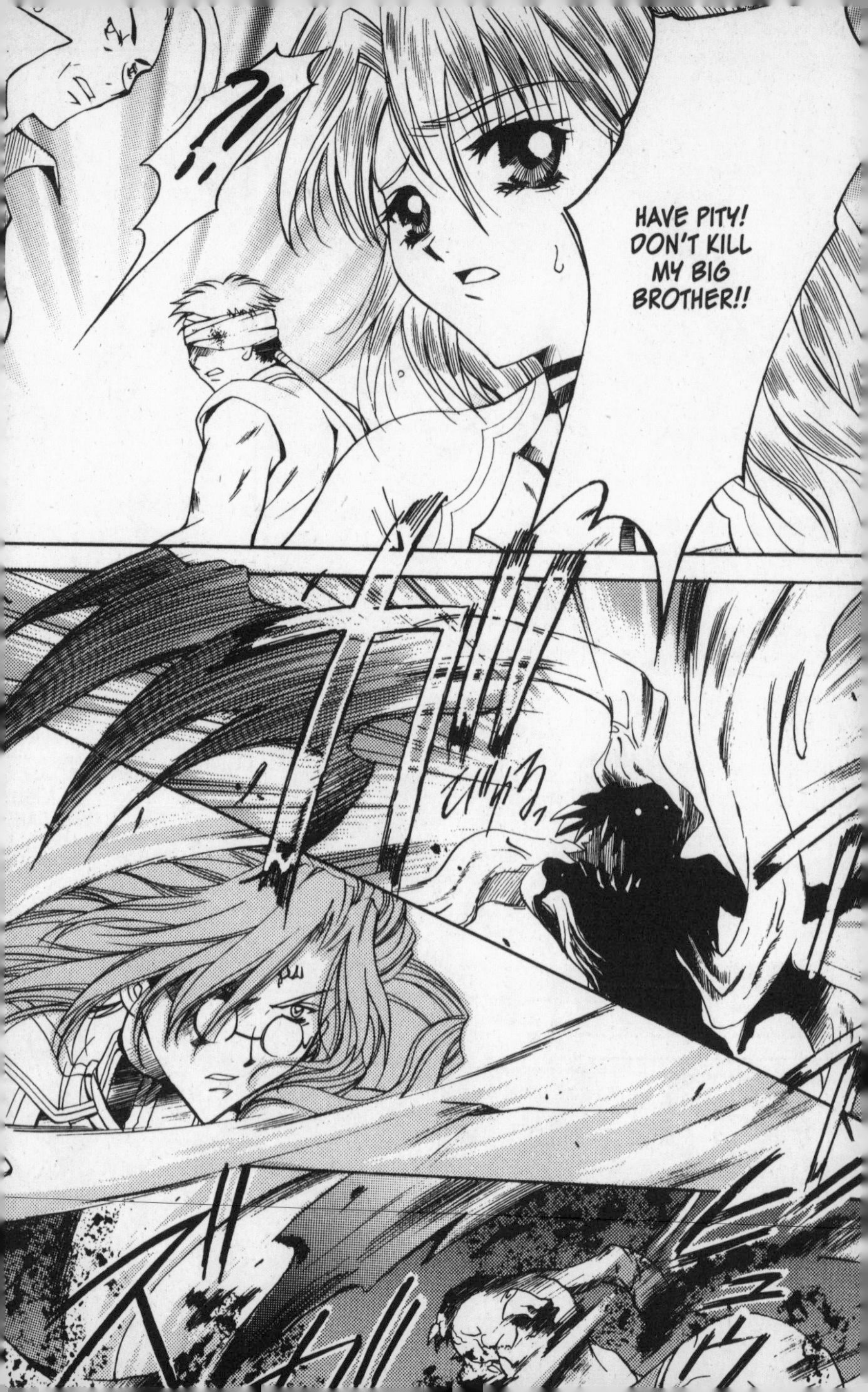
HAVE PITY! DON'T KILL MY BIG BROTHER!!

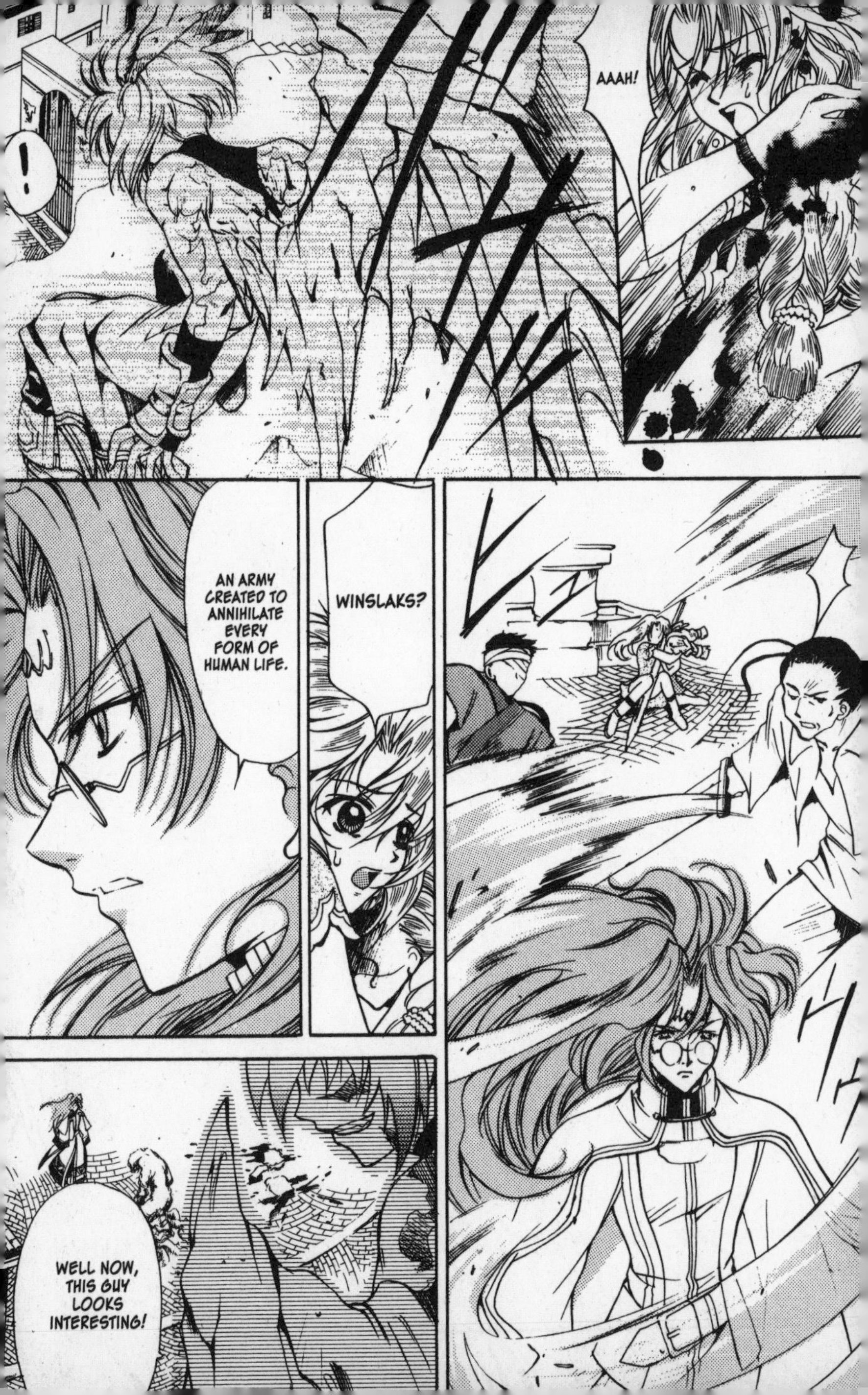

AAAH!
!
WINSLAKS?
AN ARMY CREATED TO ANNIHILATE EVERY FORM OF HUMAN LIFE.
WELL NOW, THIS GUY LOOKS INTERESTING!

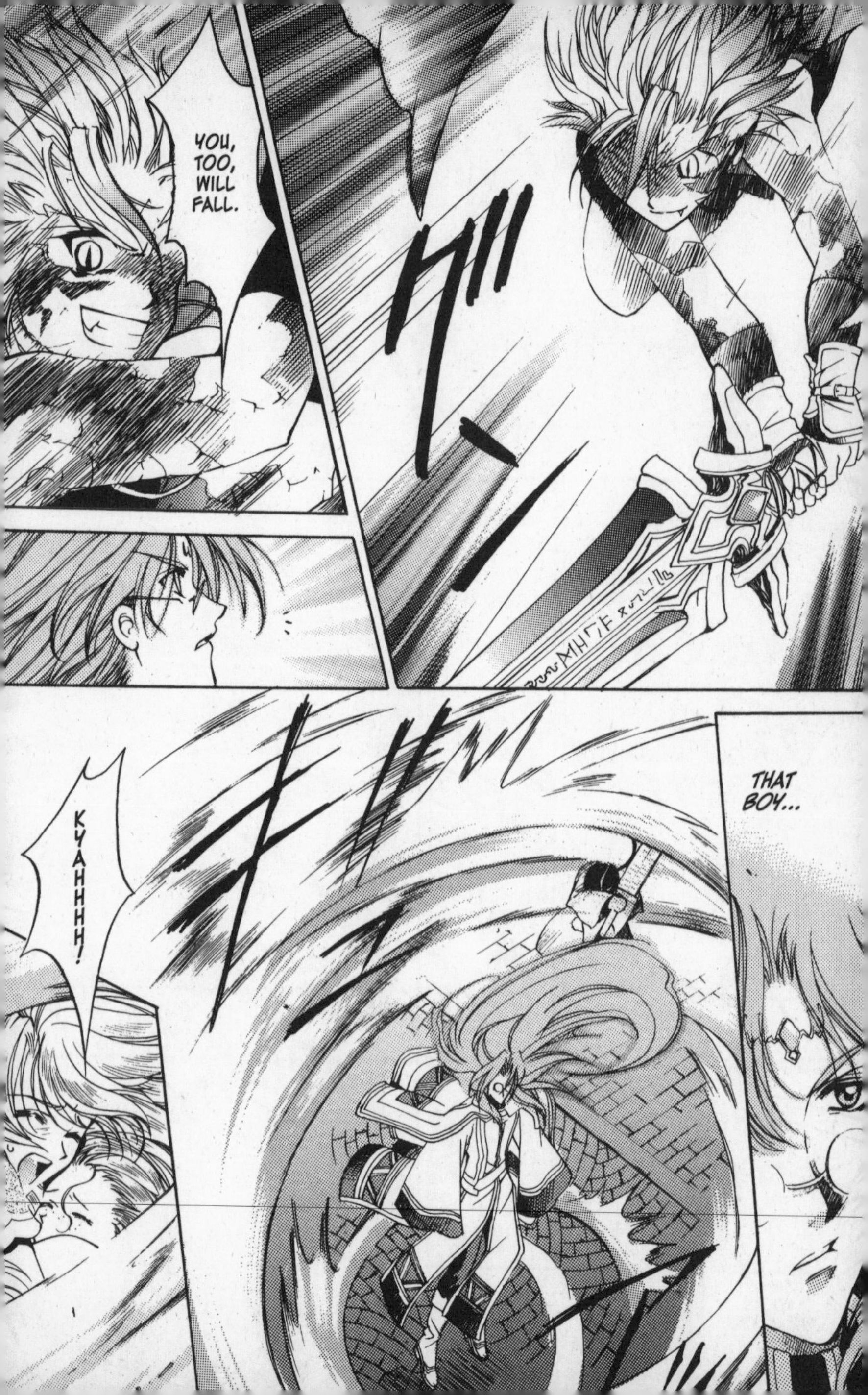
YOU, TOO, WILL FALL.
THAT BOY...
KYAHHHH!

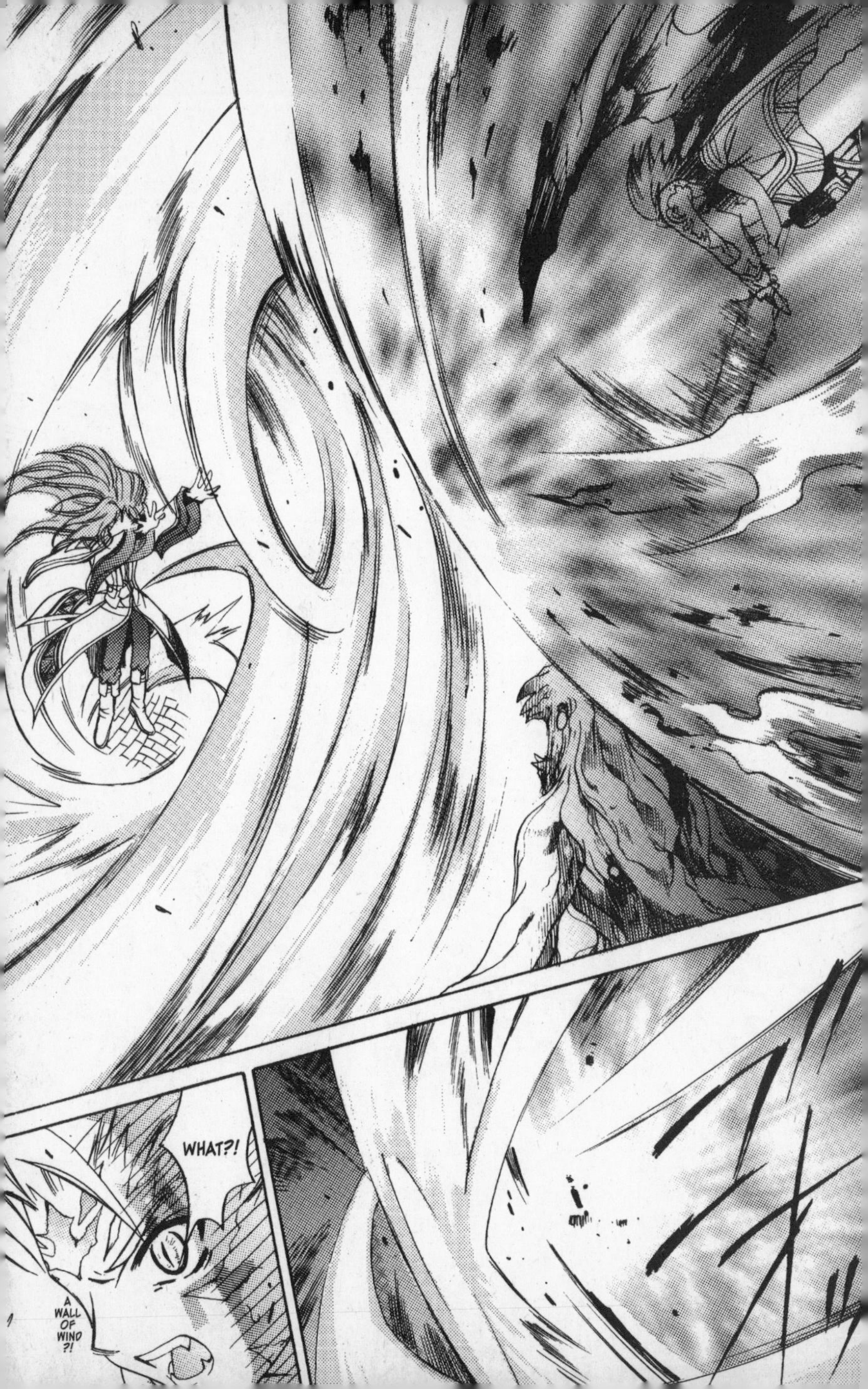
WHAT?!
A WALL OF WIND ?!

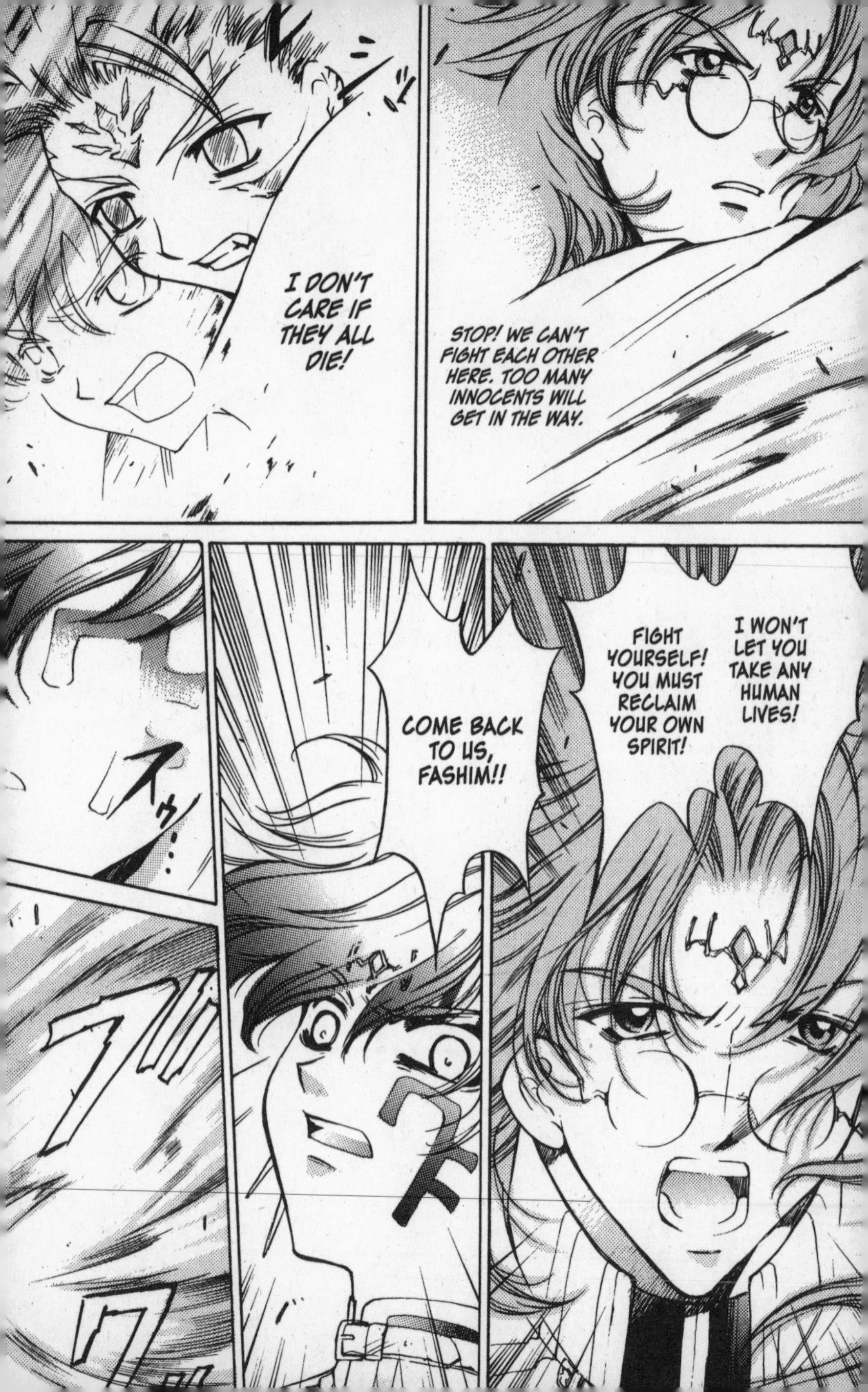

STOP! WE CAN'T FIGHT EACH OTHER HERE. TOO MANY INNOCENTS WILL GET IN THE WAY.
I DON'T CARE IF THEY ALL DIE!
I WON'T LET YOU TAKE ANY HUMAN LIVES!
FIGHT YOURSELF! YOU MUST RECLAIM YOUR OWN SPIRIT!
COME BACK TO US, FASHIM!!

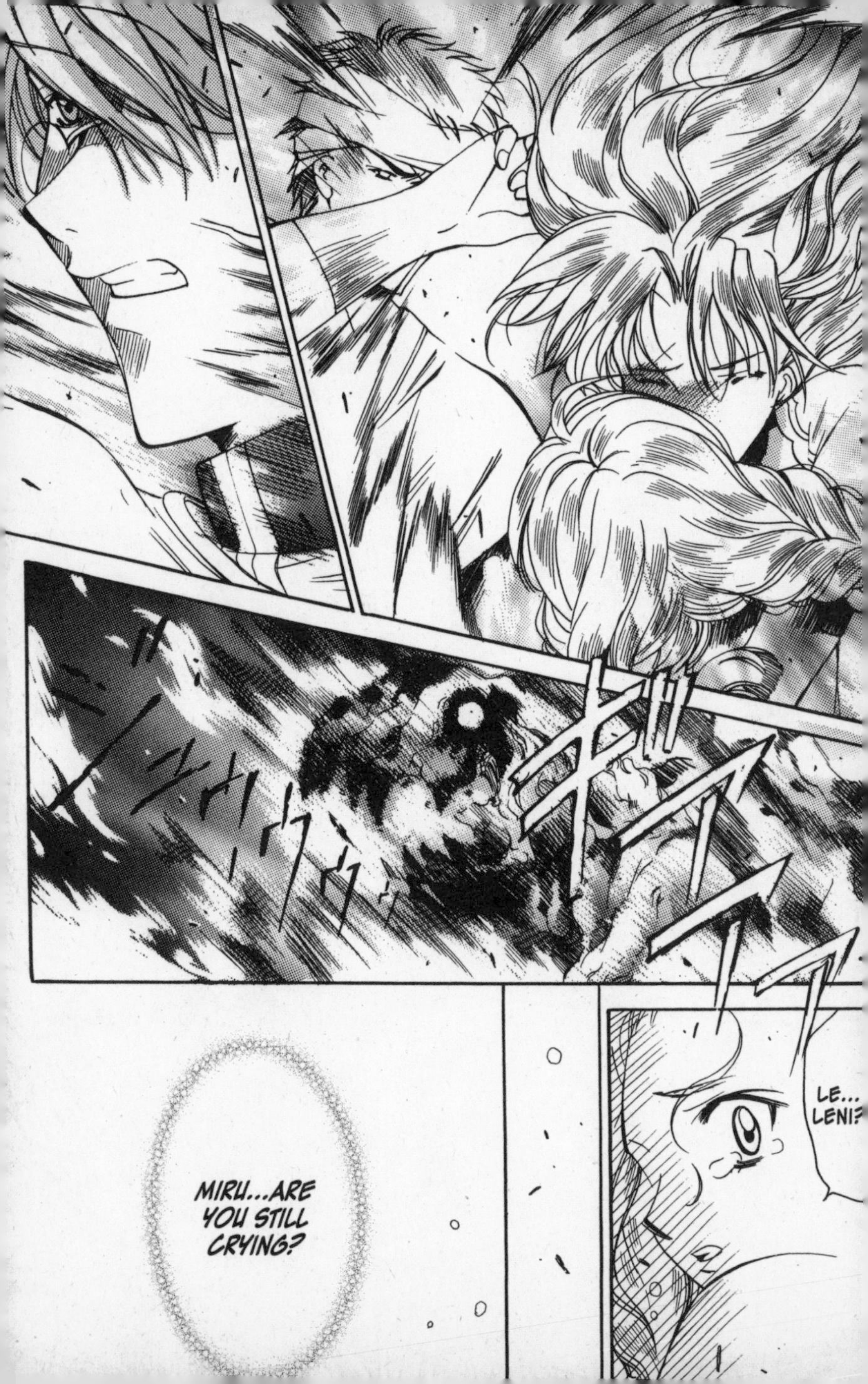
LE... LENI!?
MIRU...ARE YOU STILL CRYING?

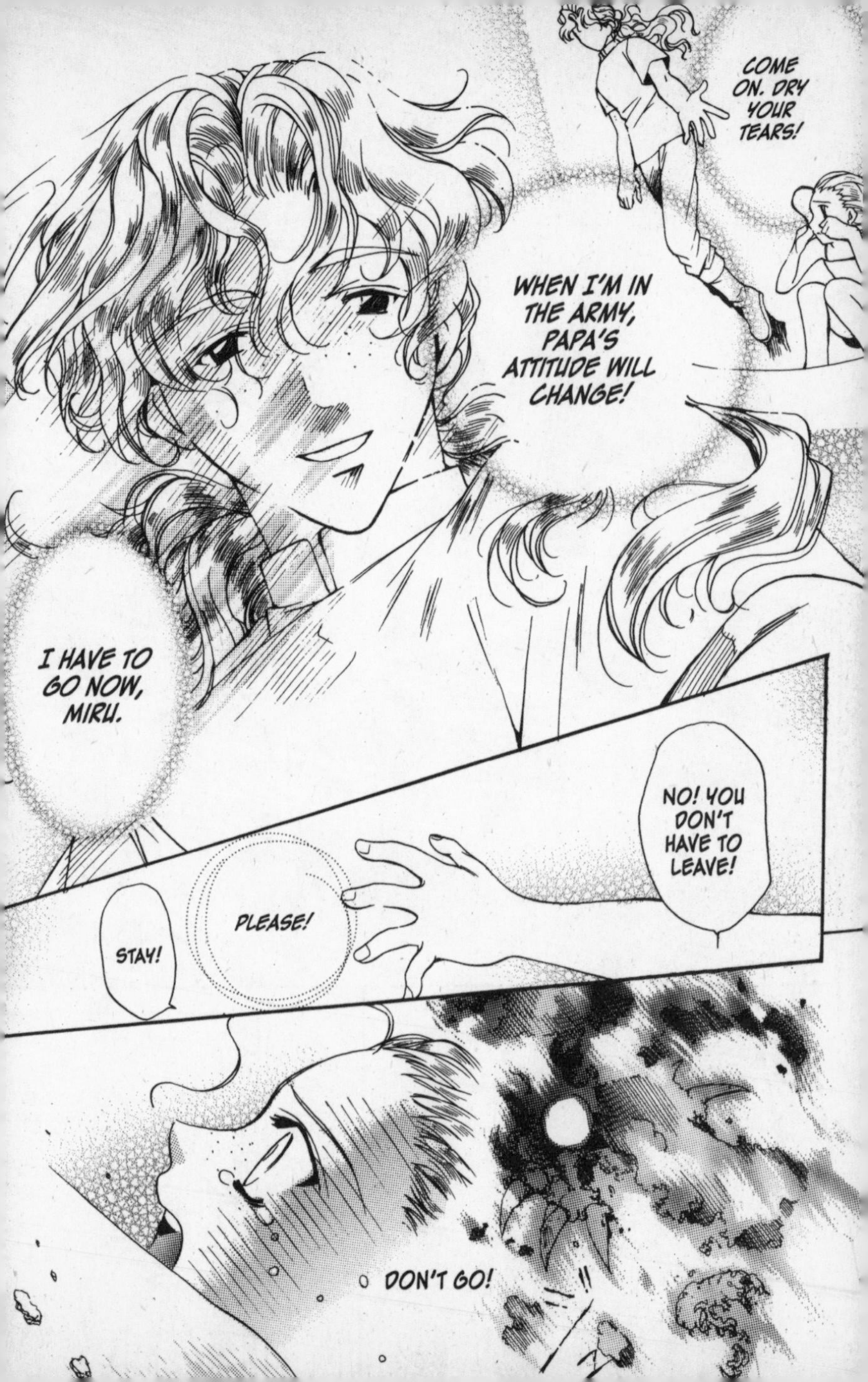
COME ON. DRY YOUR TEARS!
WHEN I'M IN THE ARMY, PAPA'S ATTITUDE WILL CHANGE!
I HAVE TO GO NOW, MIRU.
NO! YOU DON'T HAVE TO LEAVE!
PLEASE!
STAY!
!!
DON'T GO!

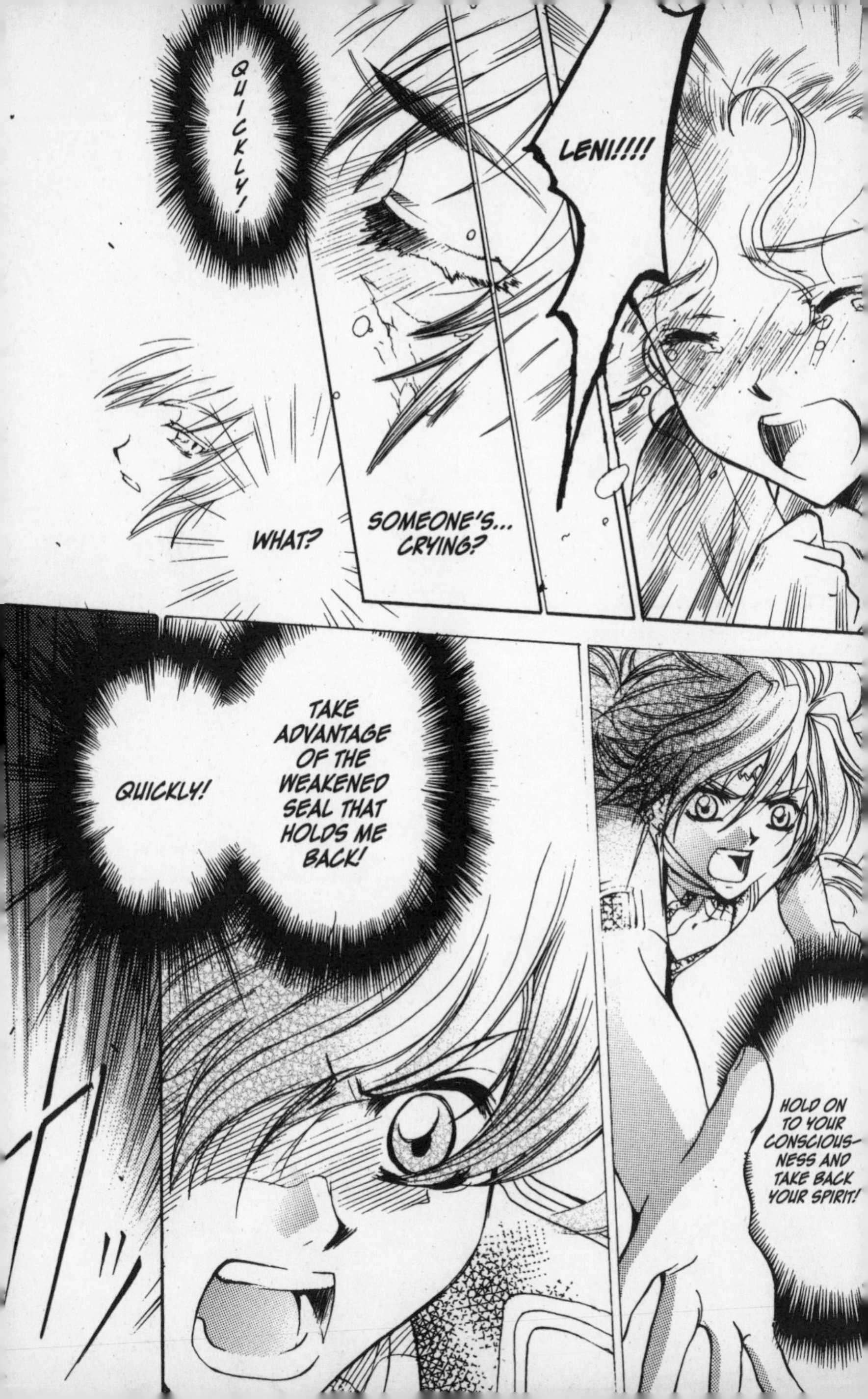
LENI!!!!
SOMEONE'S... CRYING?
QUICKLY!
WHAT?
HOLD ON TO YOUR CONSCIOUS-NESS AND TAKE BACK YOUR SPIRIT!
TAKE ADVANTAGE OF THE WEAKENED SEAL THAT HOLDS ME BACK!
QUICKLY!

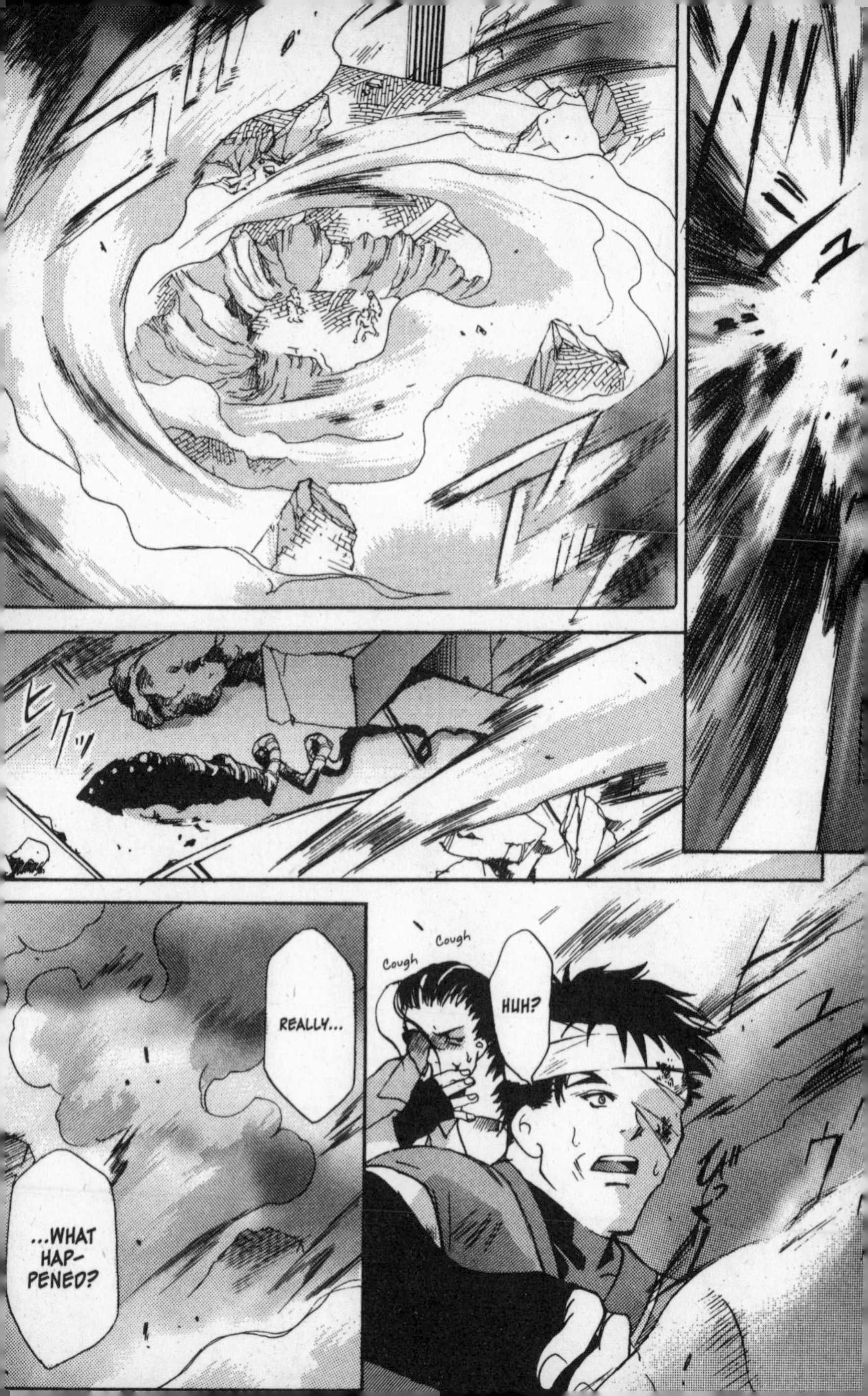
Cough
Cough
HUH?
REALLY...
...WHAT HAP-PENED?

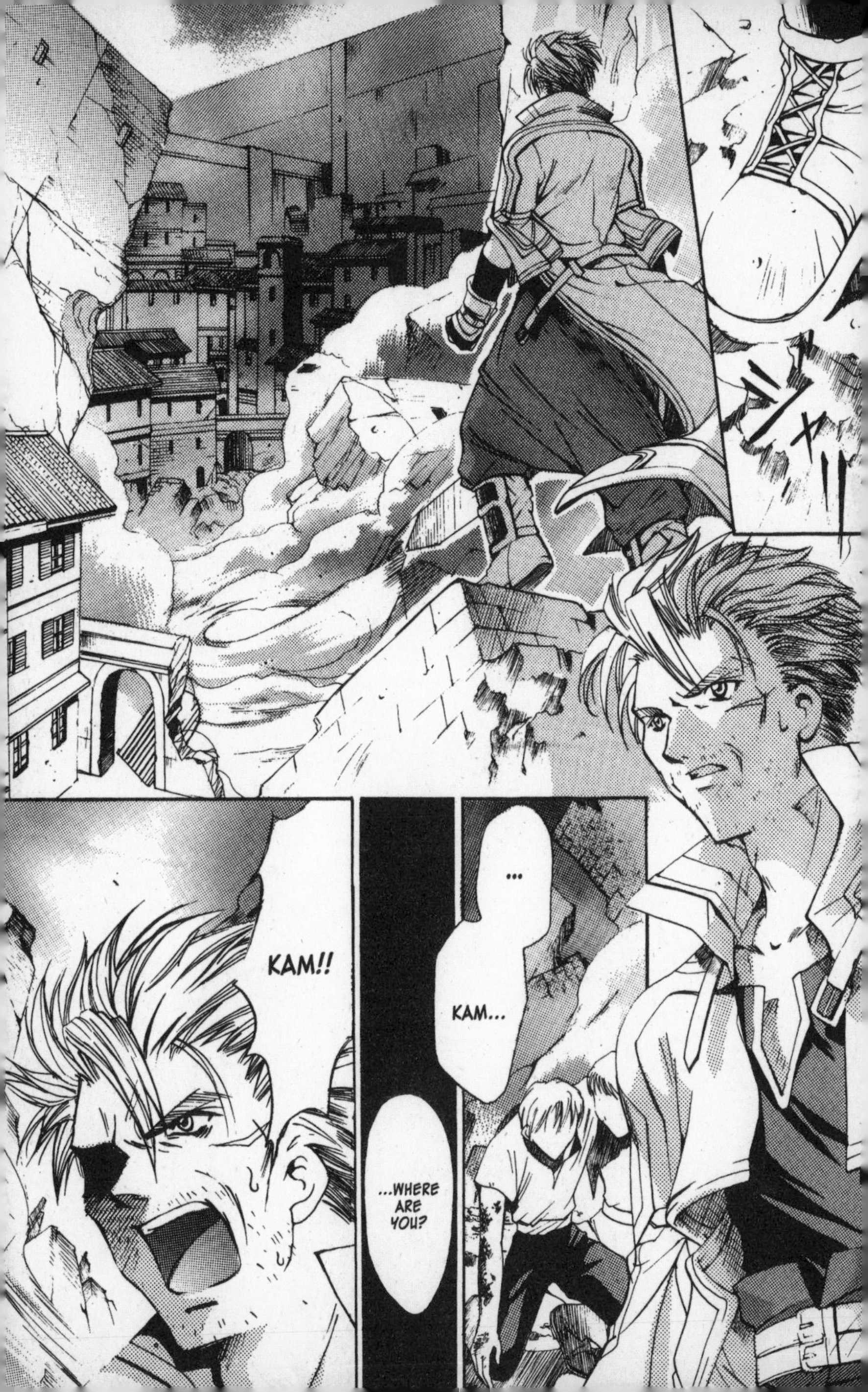
...
KAM...
...WHERE ARE YOU?
KAM!!

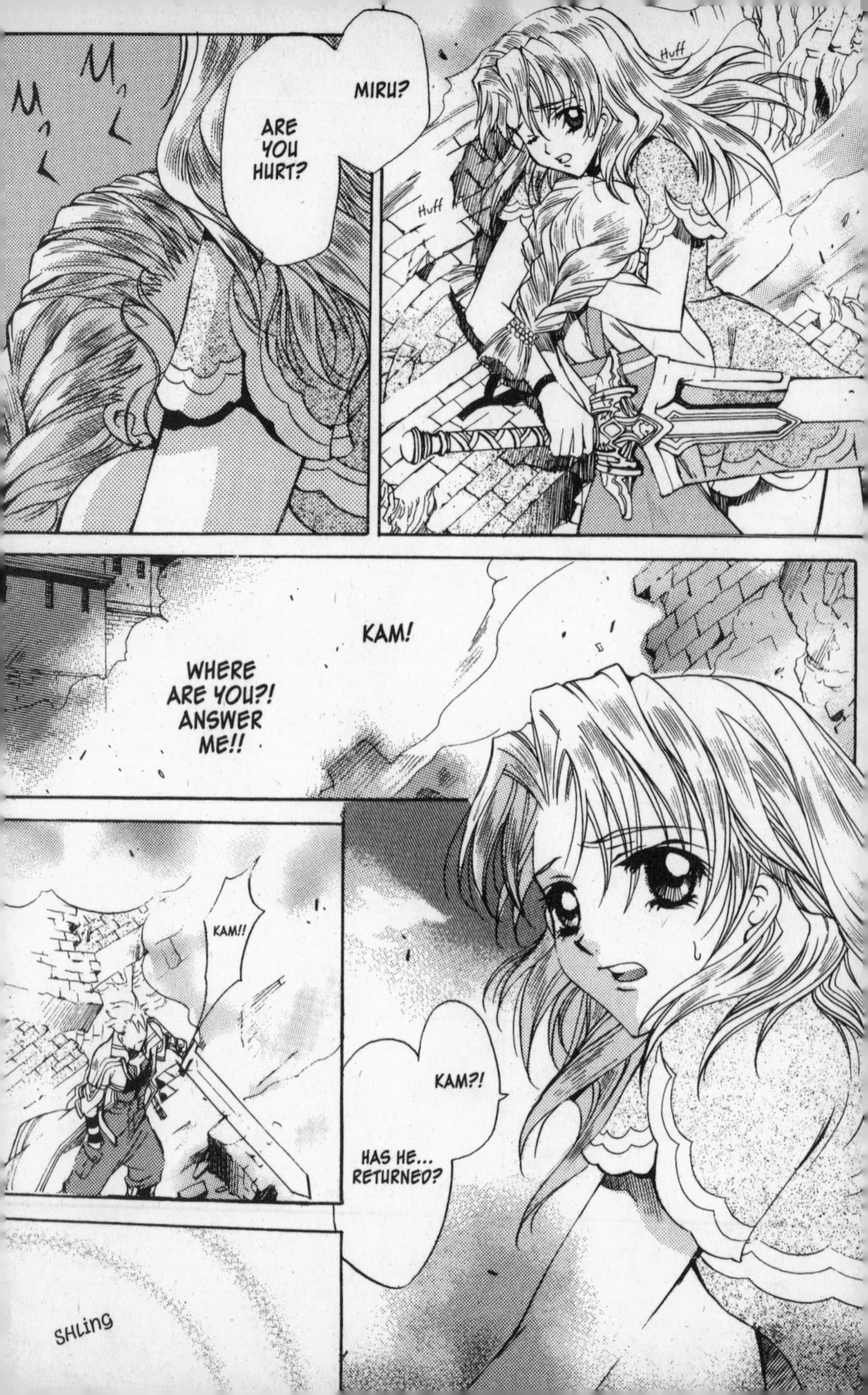
Huff
Huff
MIRU?
ARE YOU HURT?
KAM!
WHERE ARE YOU?! ANSWER ME!!
KAM?!
HAS HE... RETURNED?
KAM!!
SHLing

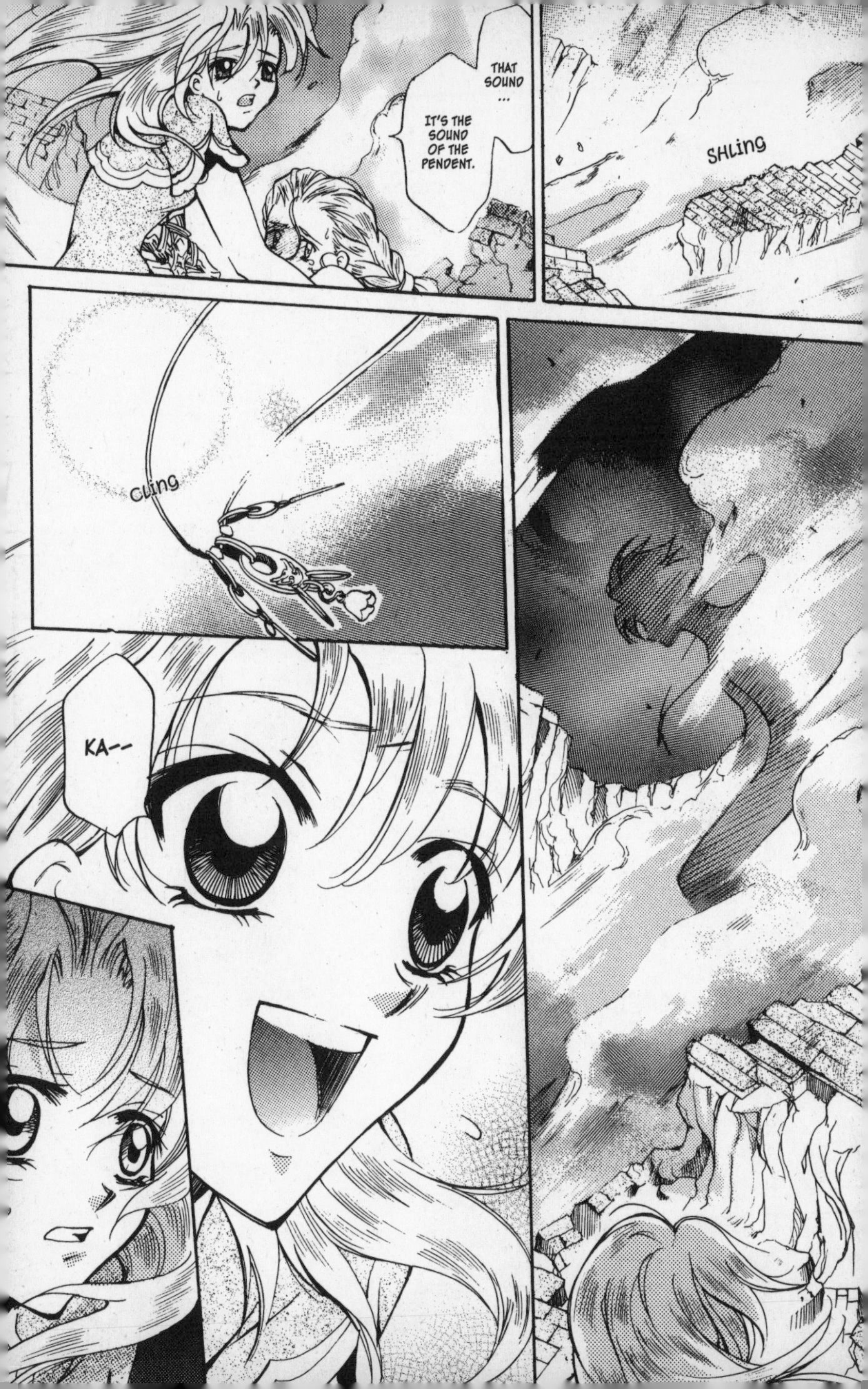
SHLing
THAT SOUND ...
IT'S THE SOUND OF THE PENDENT.
CLing
KA--

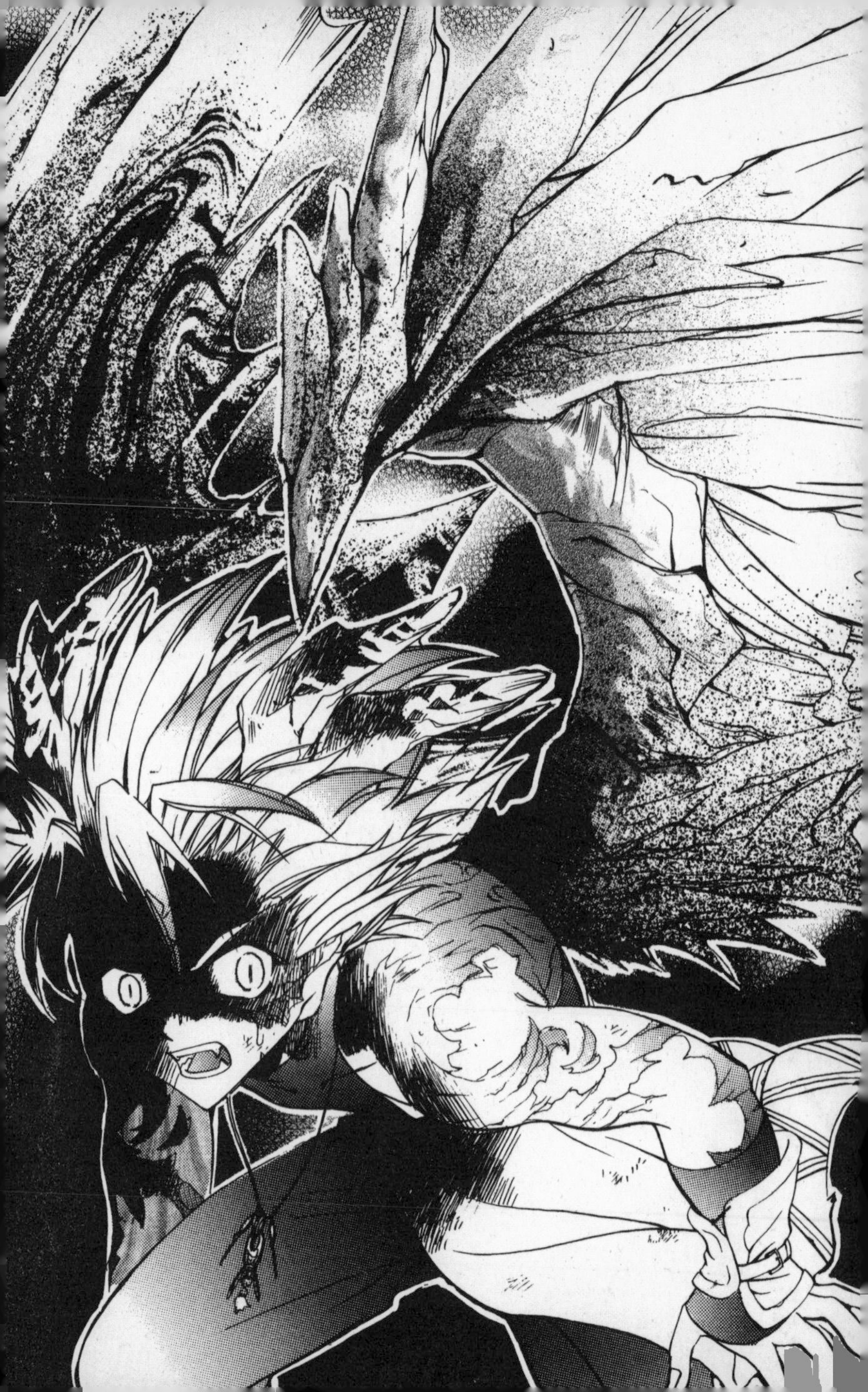

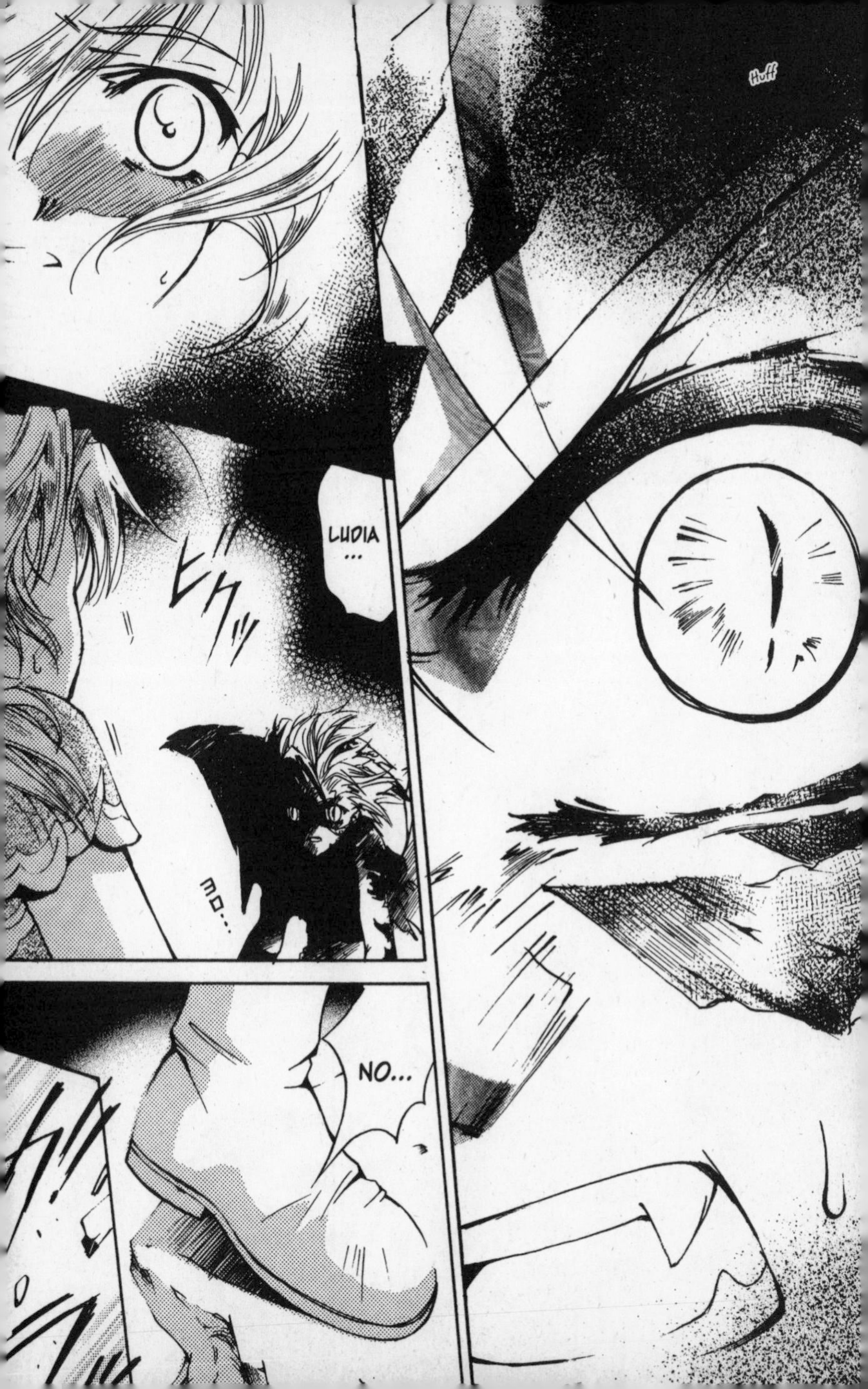
Huff
Huff
LUDIA ...
ビクッ
ヨロ…
NO...

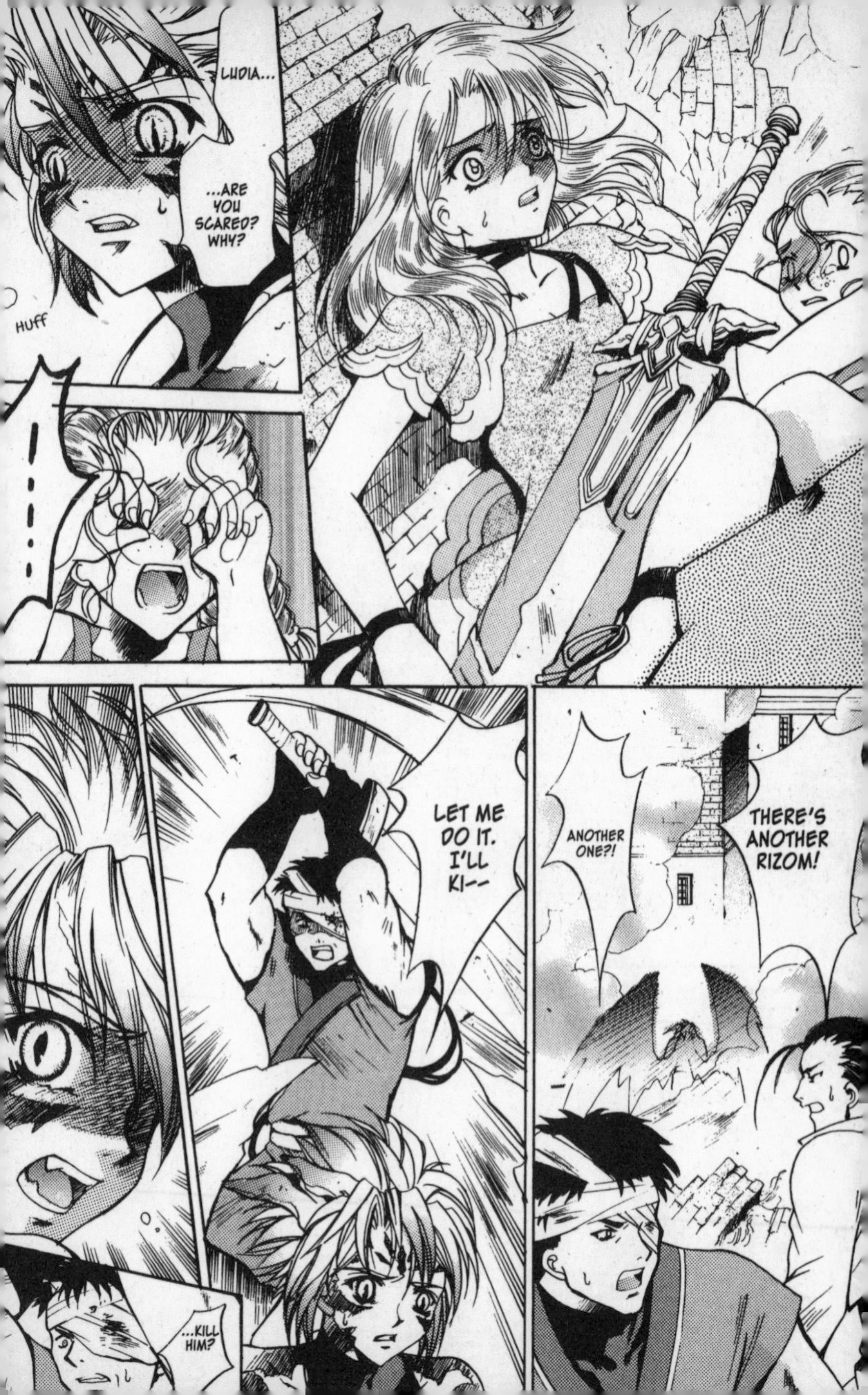
LUDIA...
...ARE YOU SCARED? WHY?
HUFF
!...
THERE'S ANOTHER RIZOM!
ANOTHER ONE?!
LET ME DO IT. I'LL KI--
...KILL HIM?

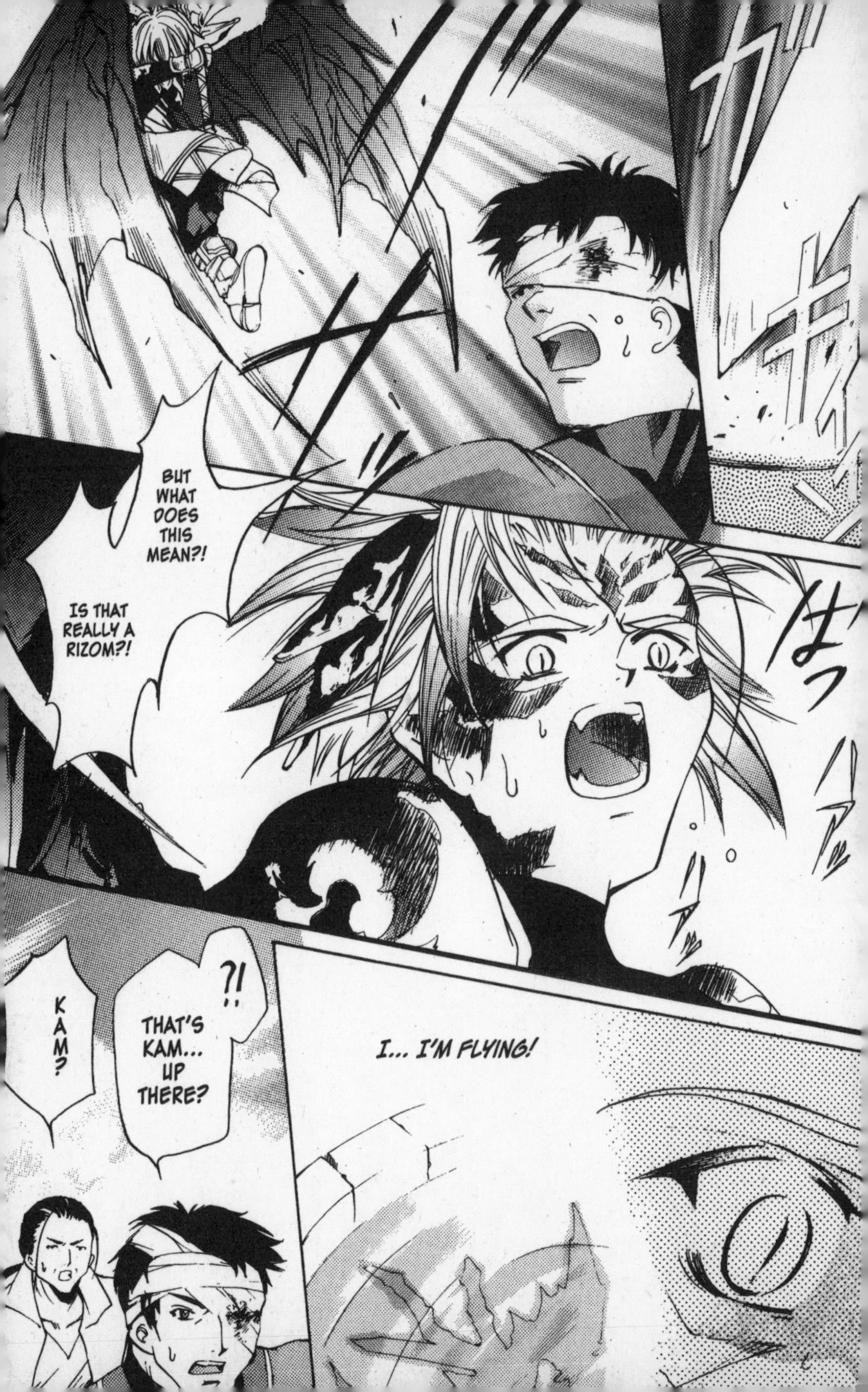

はっ
BUT WHAT DOES THIS MEAN?!
IS THAT REALLY A RIZOM?!
I... I'M FLYING!
?!
THAT'S KAM... UP THERE?
KAM?

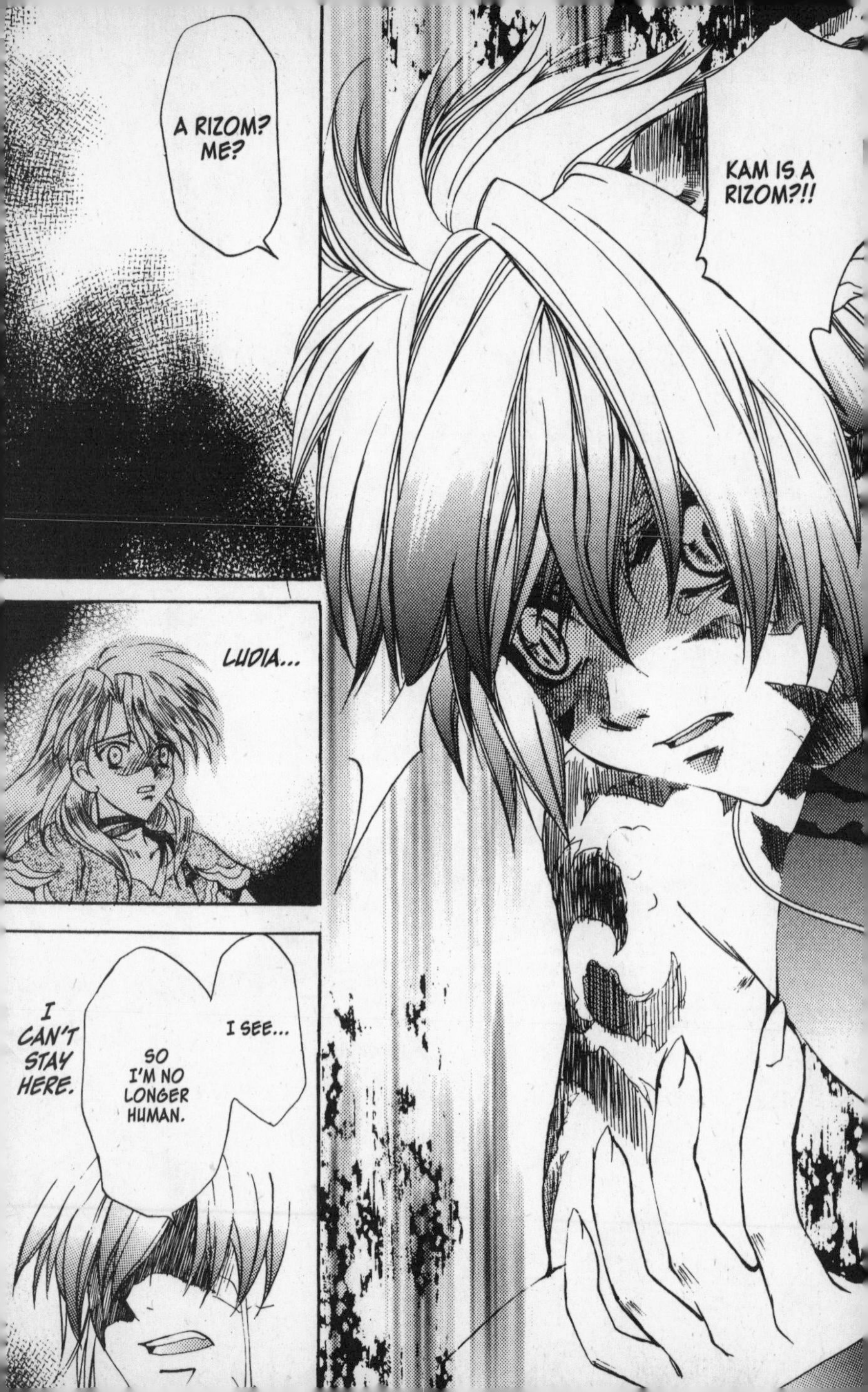
KAM IS A RIZOM?!!
A RIZOM? ME?
LUDIA...
I SEE... SO I'M NO LONGER HUMAN.
I CAN'T STAY HERE.

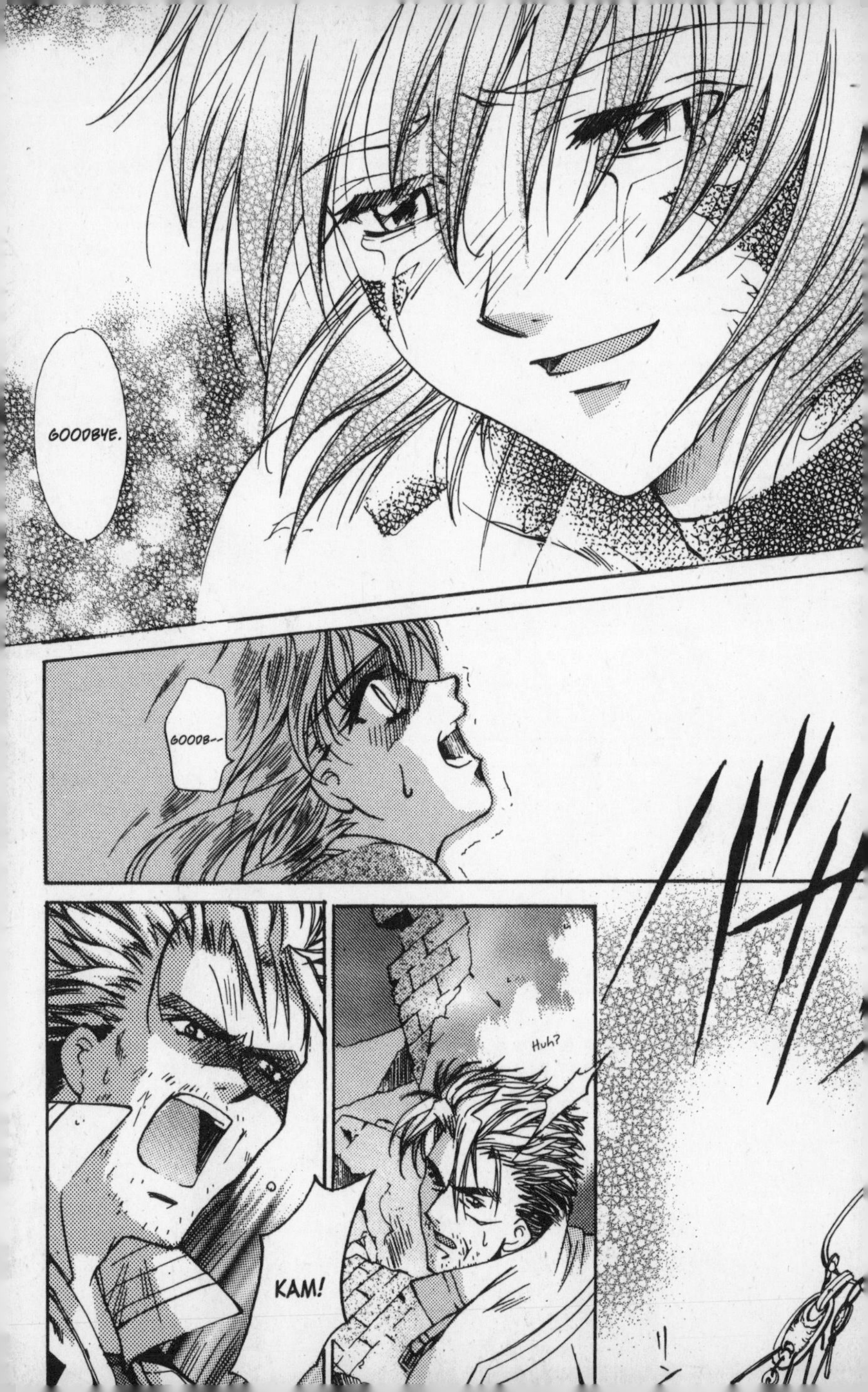
GOODBYE.
GOODB--
Huh?
KAM!

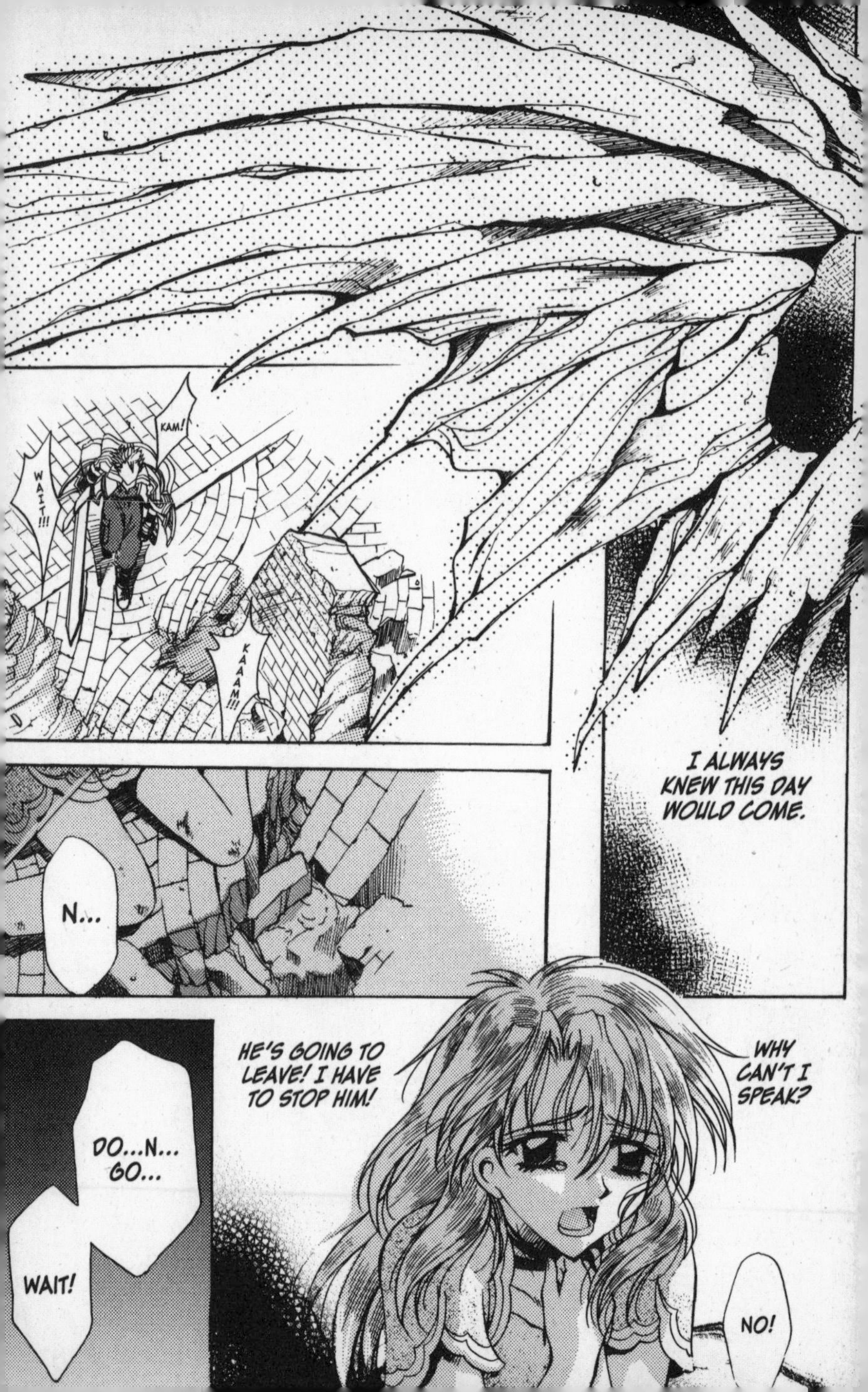
I ALWAYS KNEW THIS DAY WOULD COME.
KAM!
WAIT!!!
KAAAM!!!
N...
WHY CAN'T I SPEAK?
HE'S GOING TO LEAVE! I HAVE TO STOP HIM!
NO!
DO...N... GO...
WAIT!

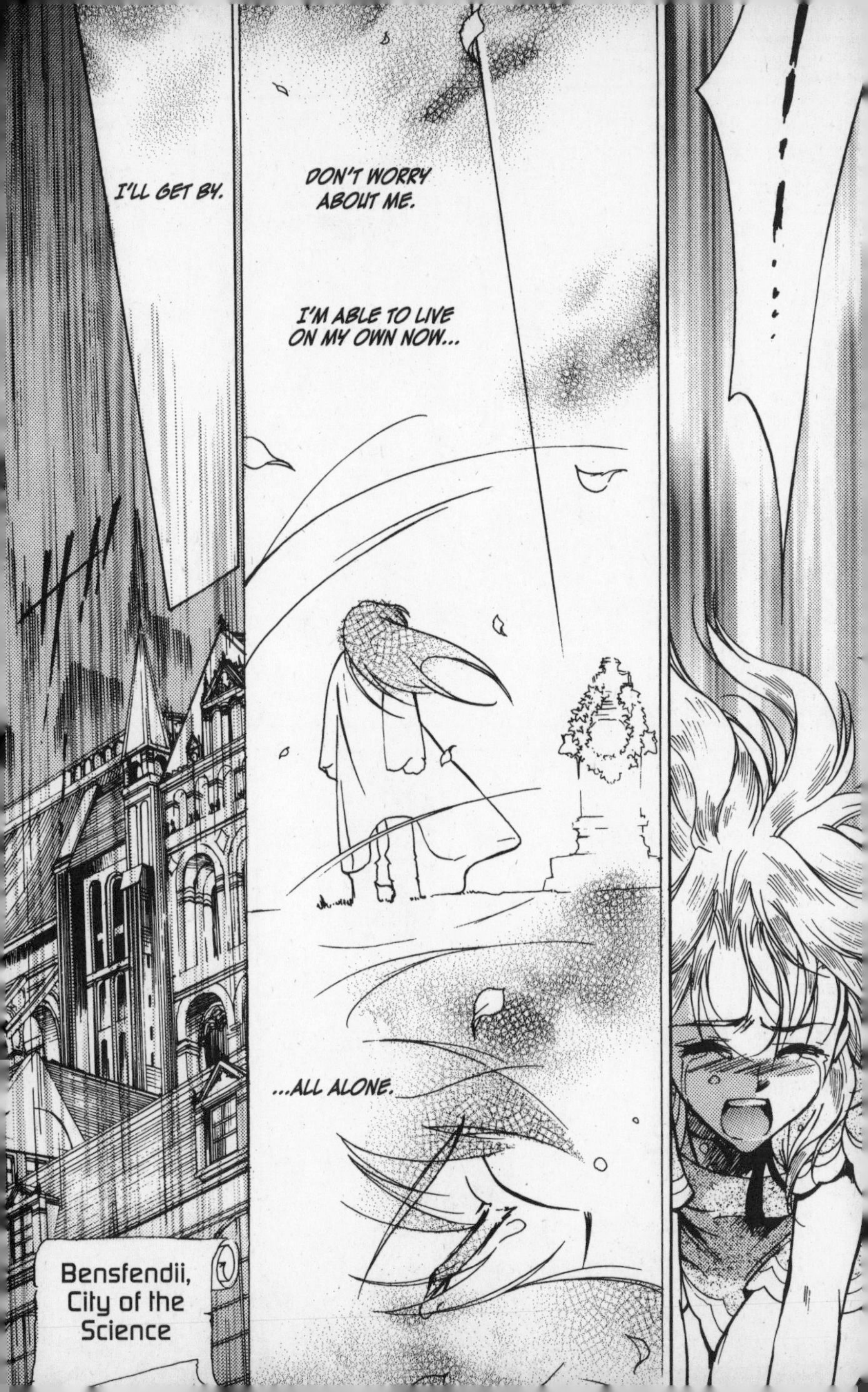
DON'T WORRY ABOUT ME.
I'M ABLE TO LIVE ON MY OWN NOW...
...ALL ALONE.
I'LL GET BY.
Bensfendii, City of the Science

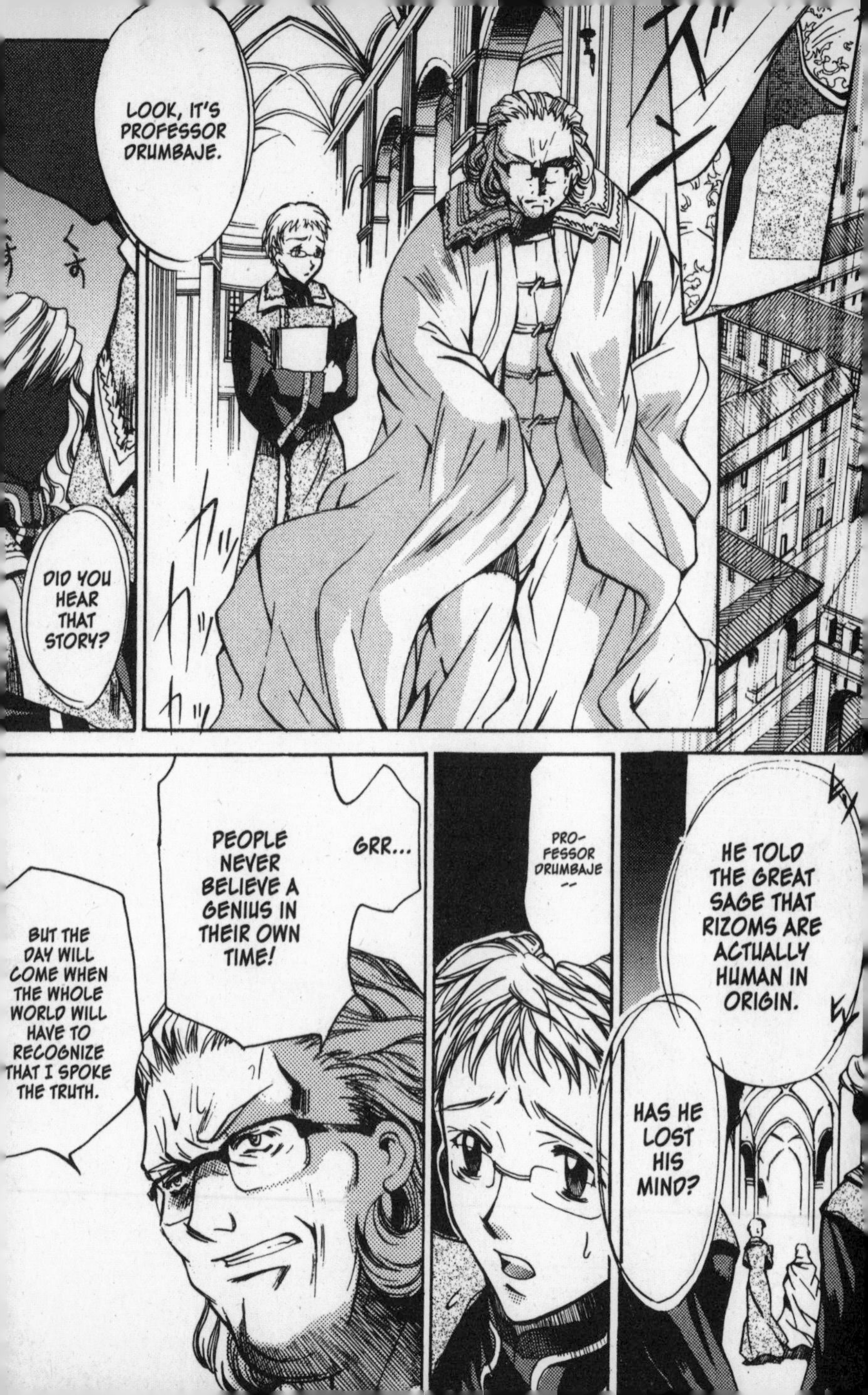
LOOK, IT'S PROFESSOR DRUMBAJE.
DID YOU HEAR THAT STORY?
HE TOLD THE GREAT SAGE THAT RIZOMS ARE ACTUALLY HUMAN IN ORIGIN.
HAS HE LOST HIS MIND?
PRO-FESSOR DRUMBAJE --
GRR...
PEOPLE NEVER BELIEVE A GENIUS IN THEIR OWN TIME!
BUT THE DAY WILL COME WHEN THE WHOLE WORLD WILL HAVE TO RECOGNIZE THAT I SPOKE THE TRUTH.

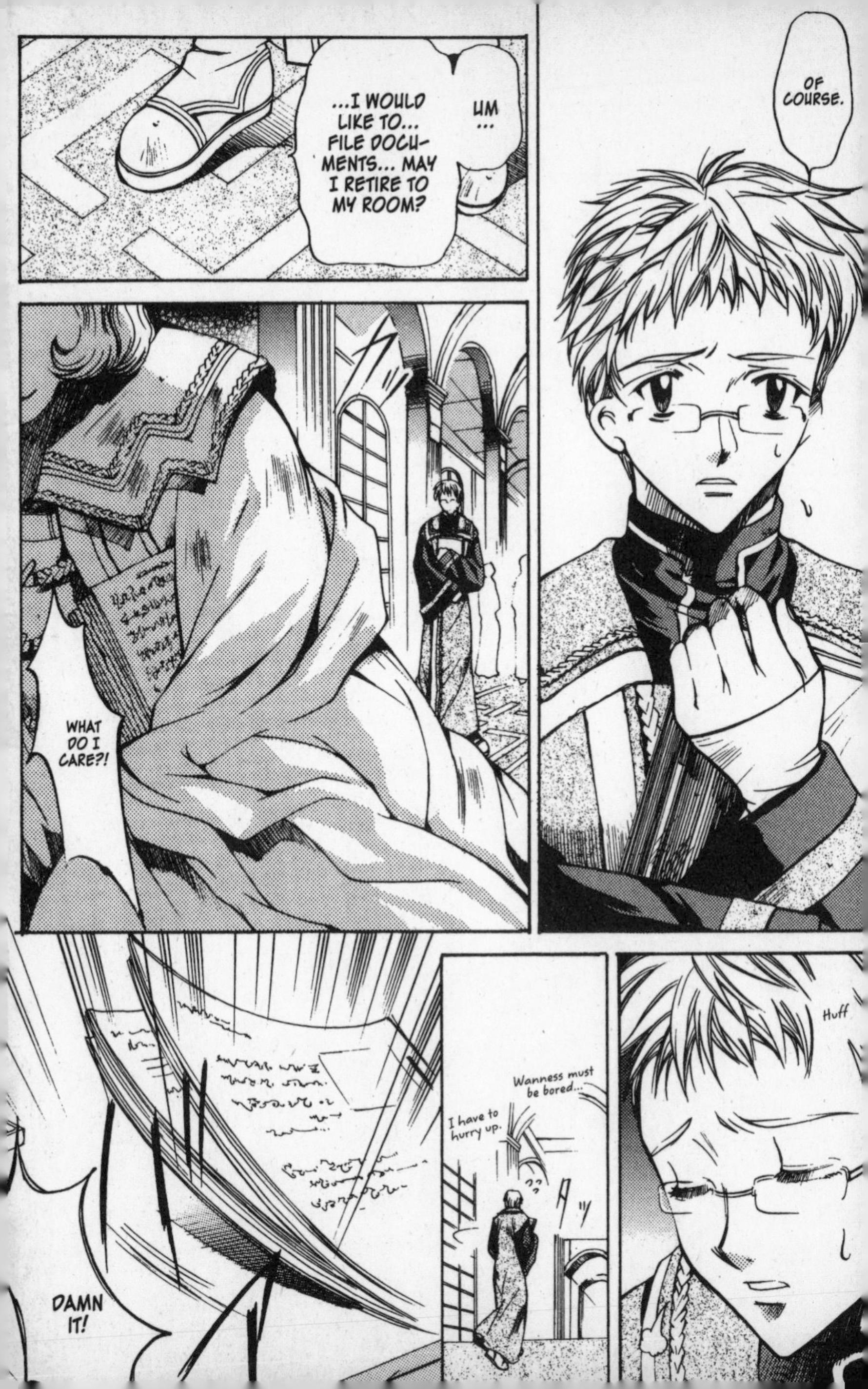

OF COURSE.
UM ...
...I WOULD LIKE TO... FILE DOCU-MENTS... MAY I RETIRE TO MY ROOM?
WHAT DO I CARE?!
Huff
Wanness must be bored...
I have to hurry up.
DAMN IT!

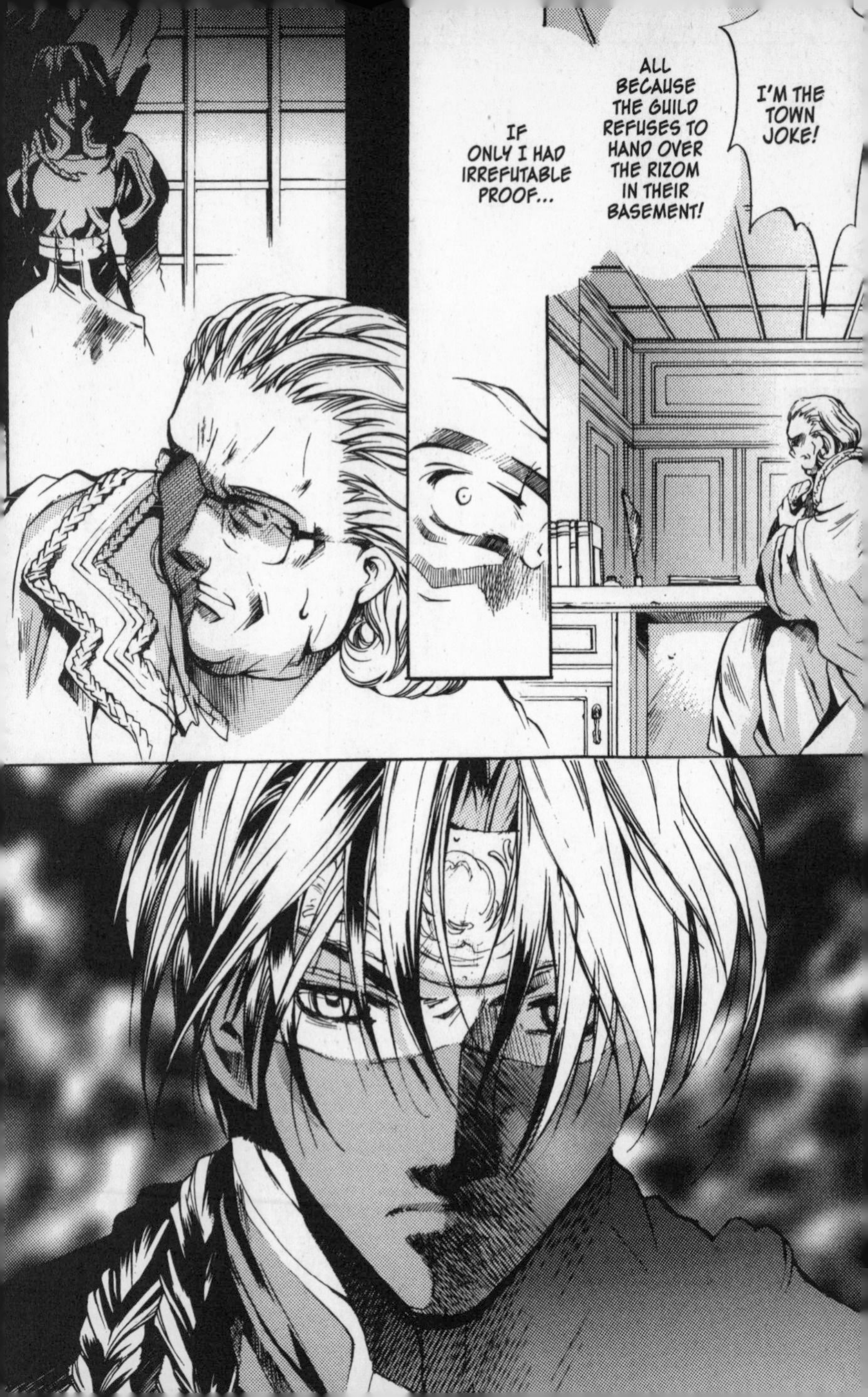
I'M THE TOWN JOKE!
ALL BECAUSE THE GUILD REFUSES TO HAND OVER THE RIZOM IN THEIR BASEMENT!
IF ONLY I HAD IRREFUTABLE PROOF...

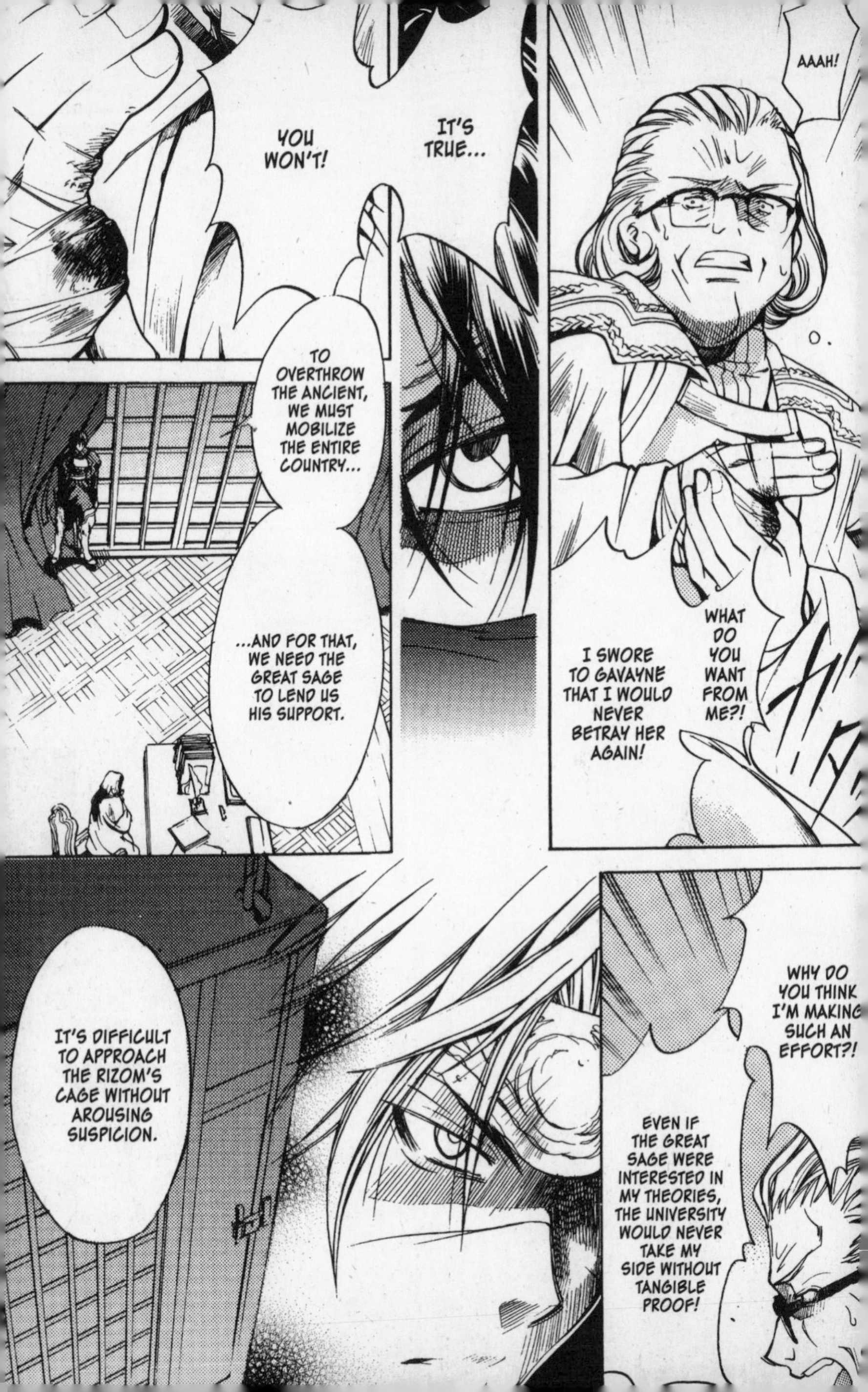
AAAH!
WHAT DO YOU WANT FROM ME?!
I SWORE TO GAVAYNE THAT I WOULD NEVER BETRAY HER AGAIN!
IT'S TRUE...
YOU WON'T!
TO OVERTHROW THE ANCIENT, WE MUST MOBILIZE THE ENTIRE COUNTRY...
...AND FOR THAT, WE NEED THE GREAT SAGE TO LEND US HIS SUPPORT.
WHY DO YOU THINK I'M MAKING SUCH AN EFFORT?!
EVEN IF THE GREAT SAGE WERE INTERESTED IN MY THEORIES, THE UNIVERSITY WOULD NEVER TAKE MY SIDE WITHOUT TANGIBLE PROOF!
IT'S DIFFICULT TO APPROACH THE RIZOM'S CAGE WITHOUT AROUSING SUSPICION.

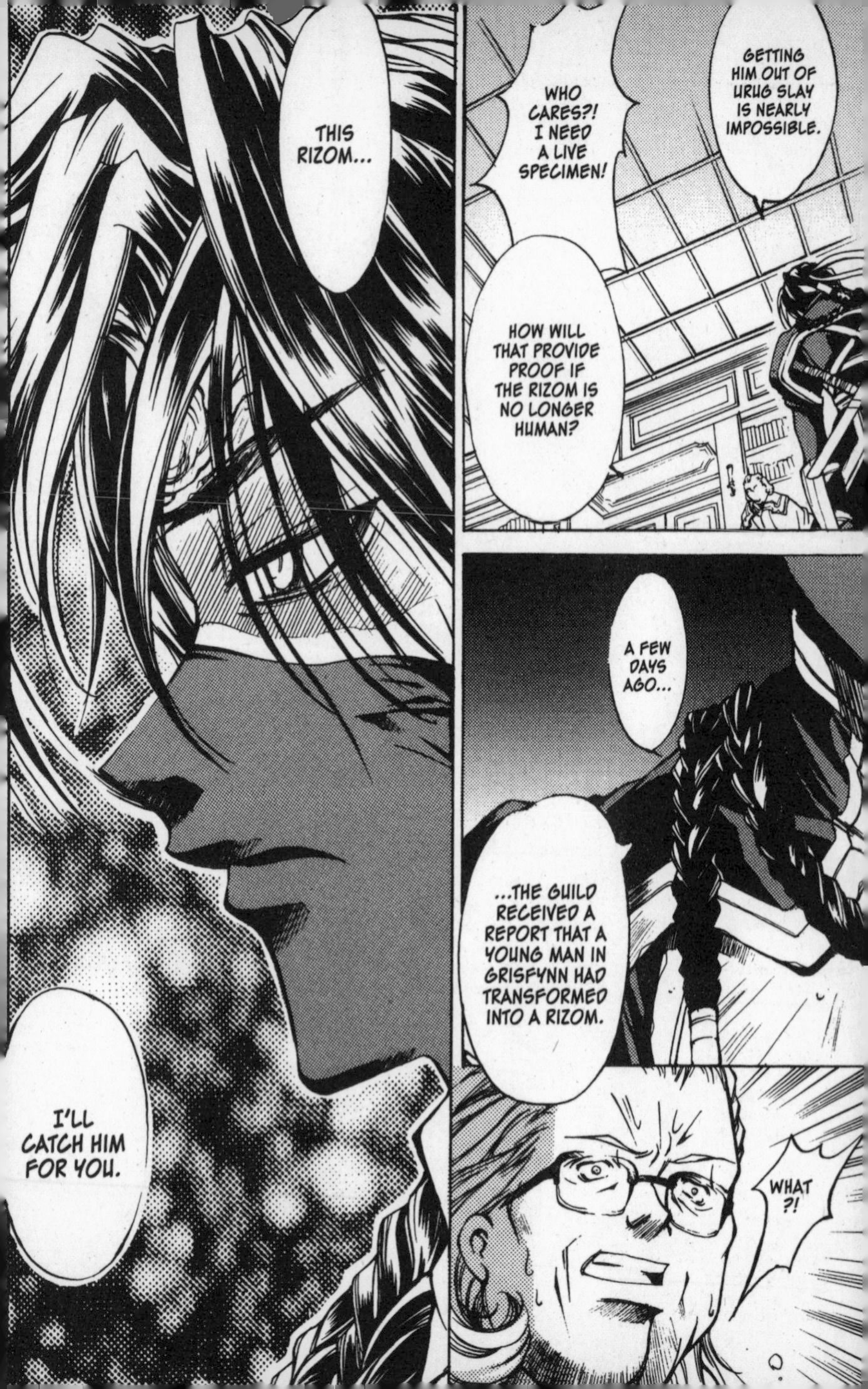
GETTING HIM OUT OF URUG SLAY IS NEARLY IMPOSSIBLE.
WHO CARES?! I NEED A LIVE SPECIMEN!
HOW WILL THAT PROVIDE PROOF IF THE RIZOM IS NO LONGER HUMAN?
A FEW DAYS AGO...
...THE GUILD RECEIVED A REPORT THAT A YOUNG MAN IN GRISFYNN HAD TRANSFORMED INTO A RIZOM.
WHAT?!
THIS RIZOM...
I'LL CATCH HIM FOR YOU.

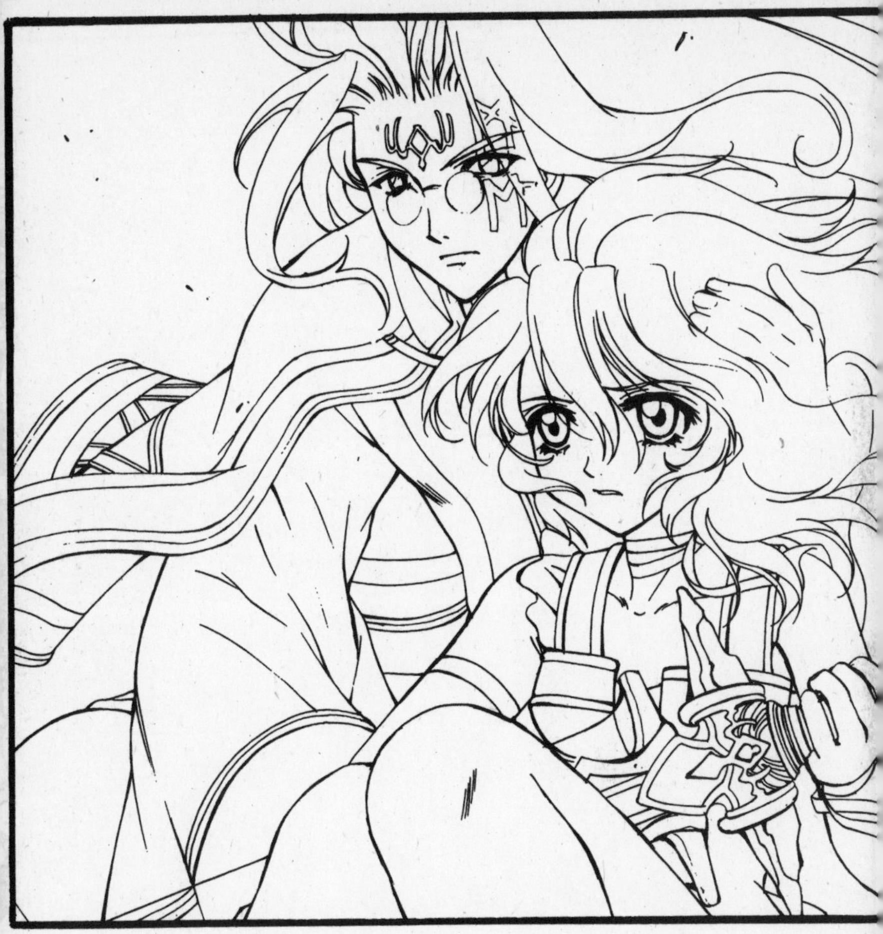

Element Line

Element
Line

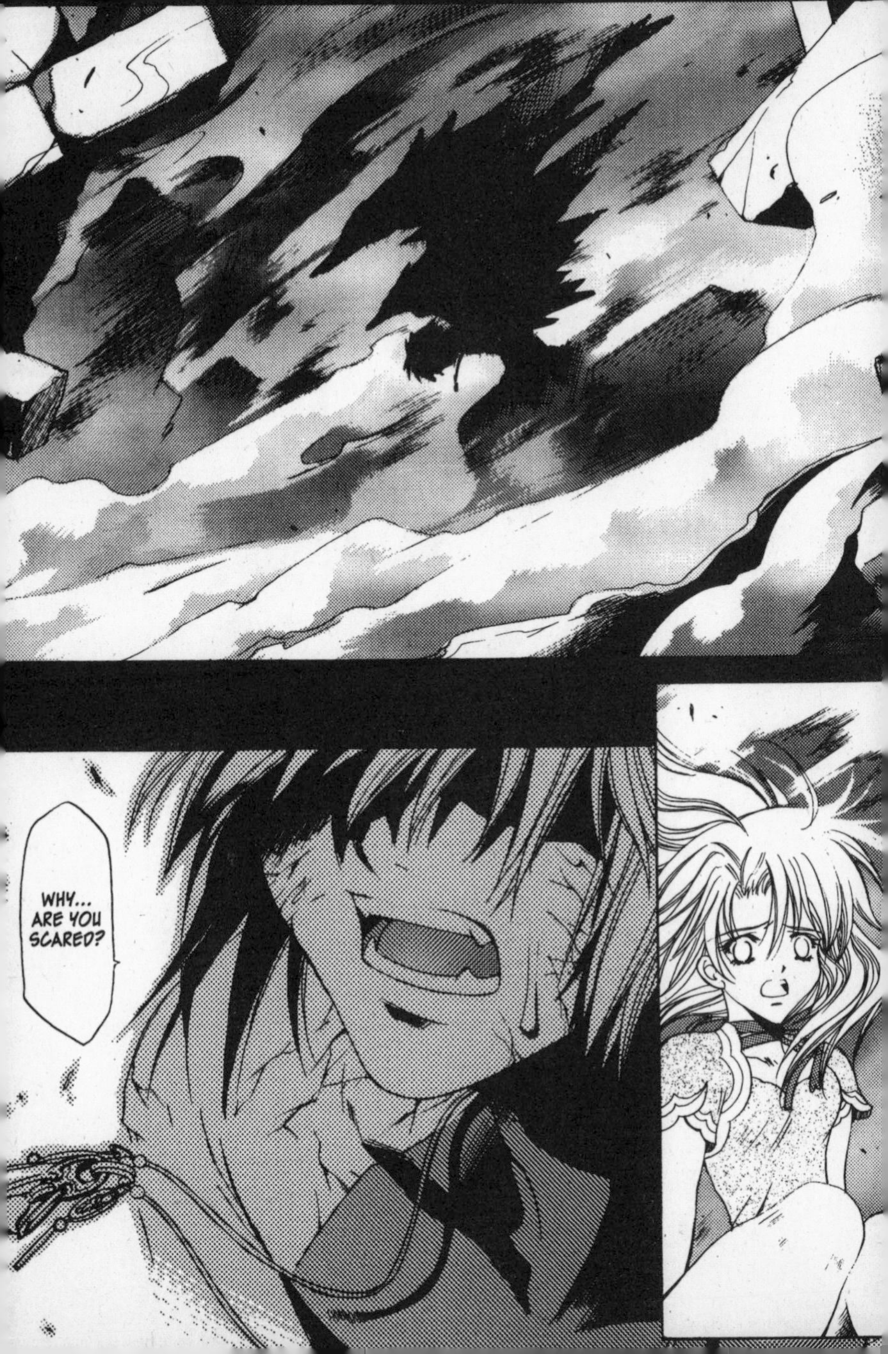
WHY... ARE YOU SCARED?

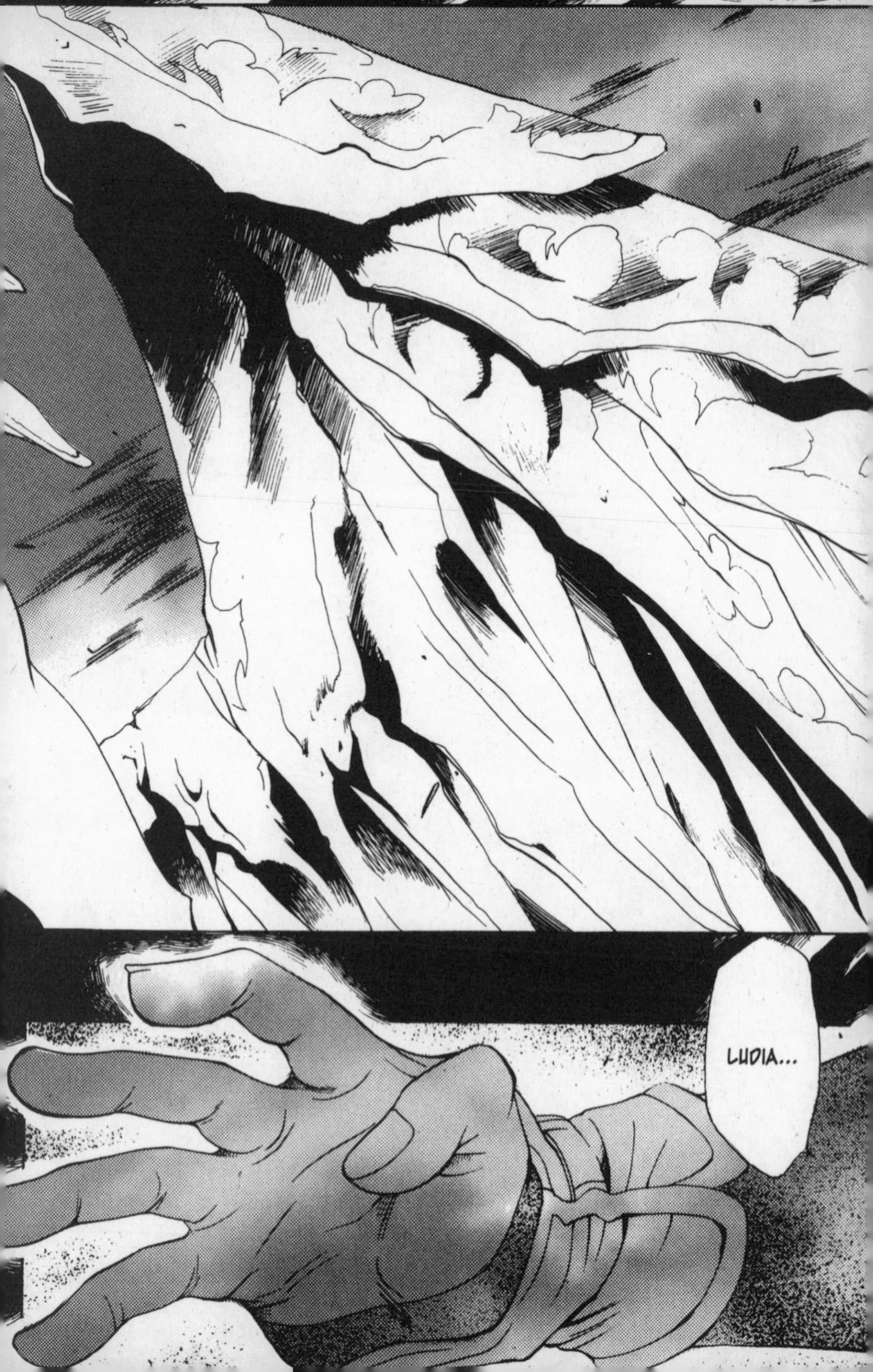
LUDIA...

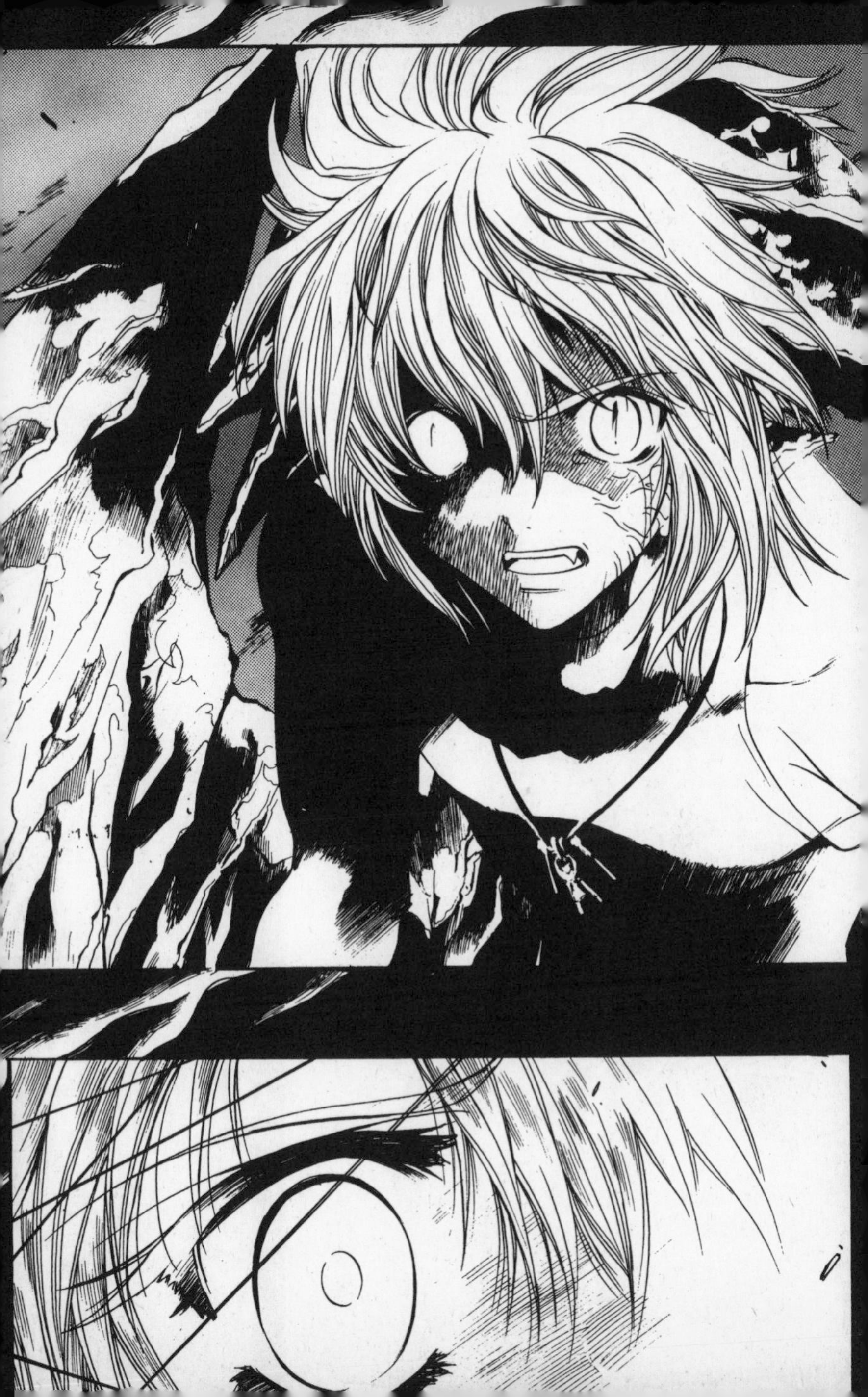

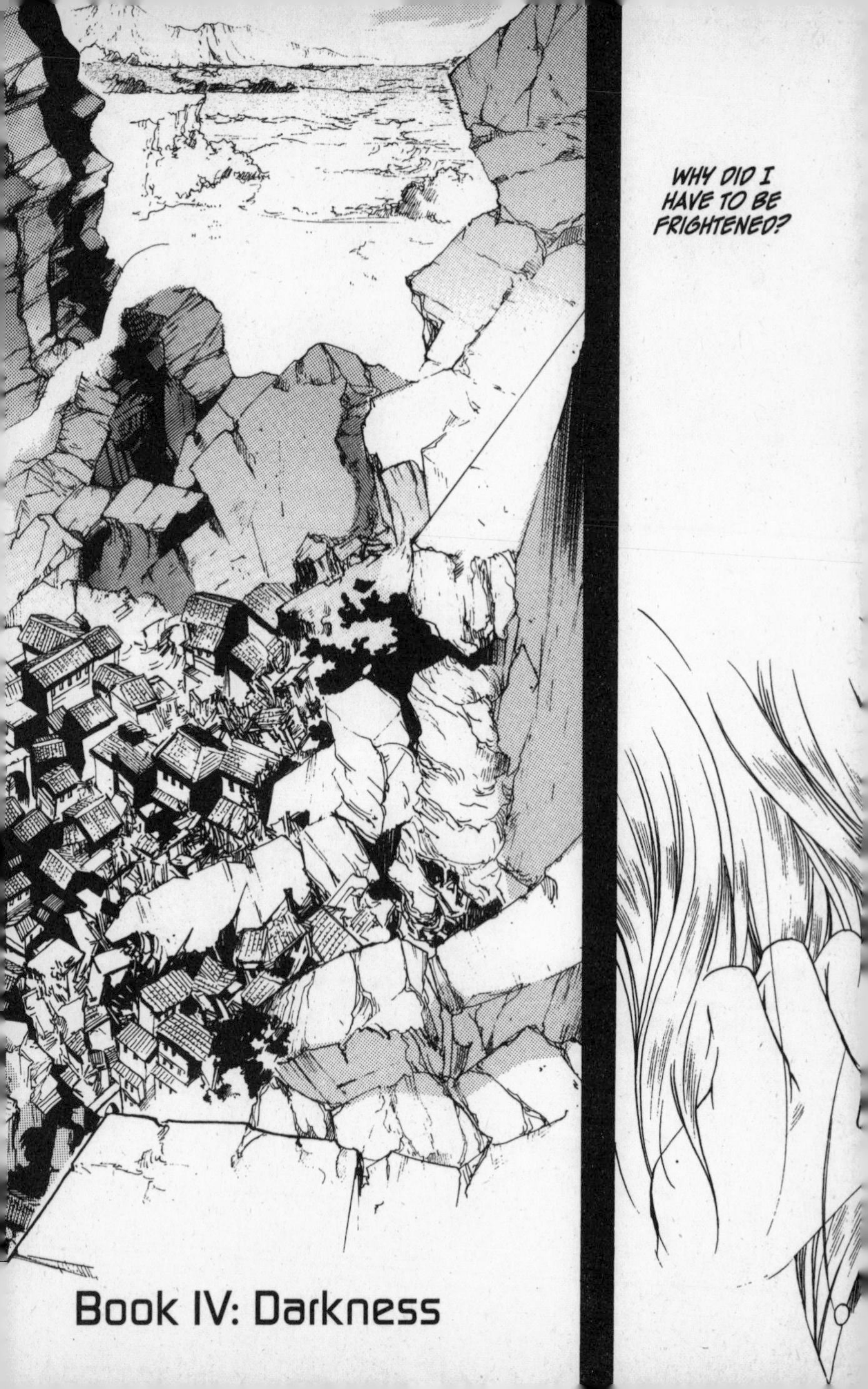
WHY DID I HAVE TO BE FRIGHTENED?
Book IV: Darkness

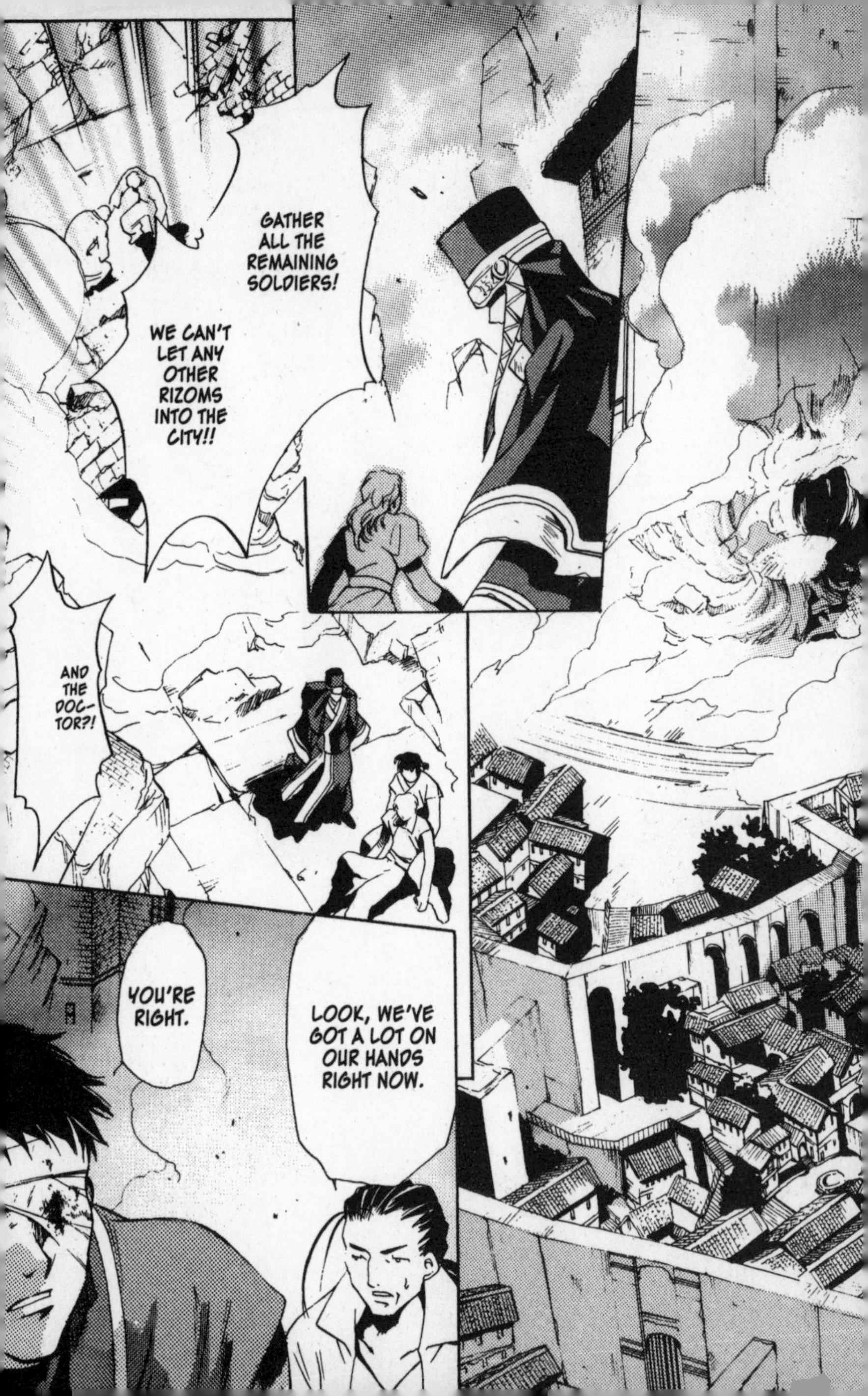
GATHER ALL THE REMAINING SOLDIERS!
WE CAN'T LET ANY OTHER RIZOMS INTO THE CITY!!
AND THE DOC-TOR?!
LOOK, WE'VE GOT A LOT ON OUR HANDS RIGHT NOW.
YOU'RE RIGHT.

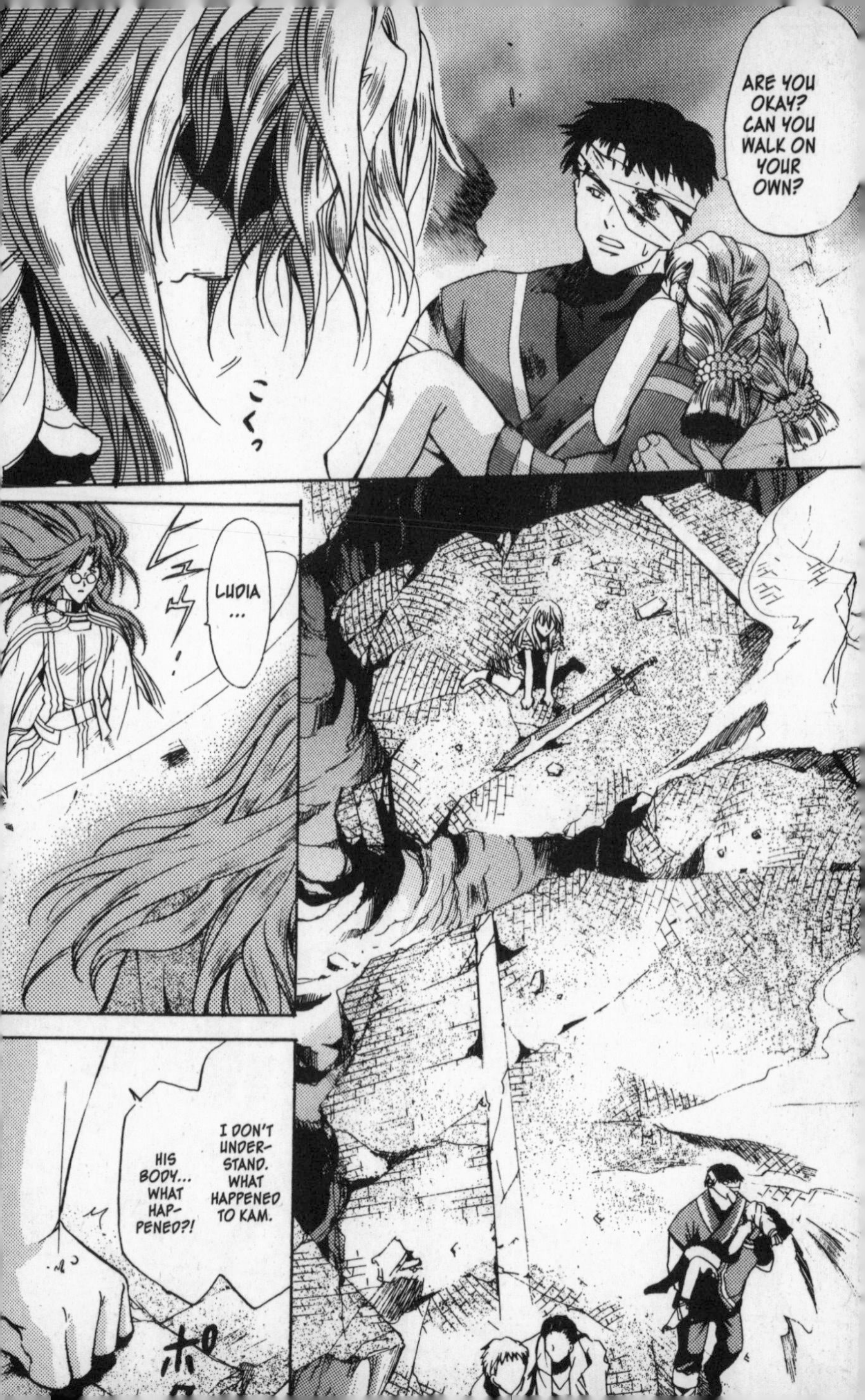
ARE YOU OKAY? CAN YOU WALK ON YOUR OWN?
こくっ
LUDIA ...
I DON'T UNDER-STAND. WHAT HAPPENED TO KAM.
HIS BODY... WHAT HAP-PENED?!

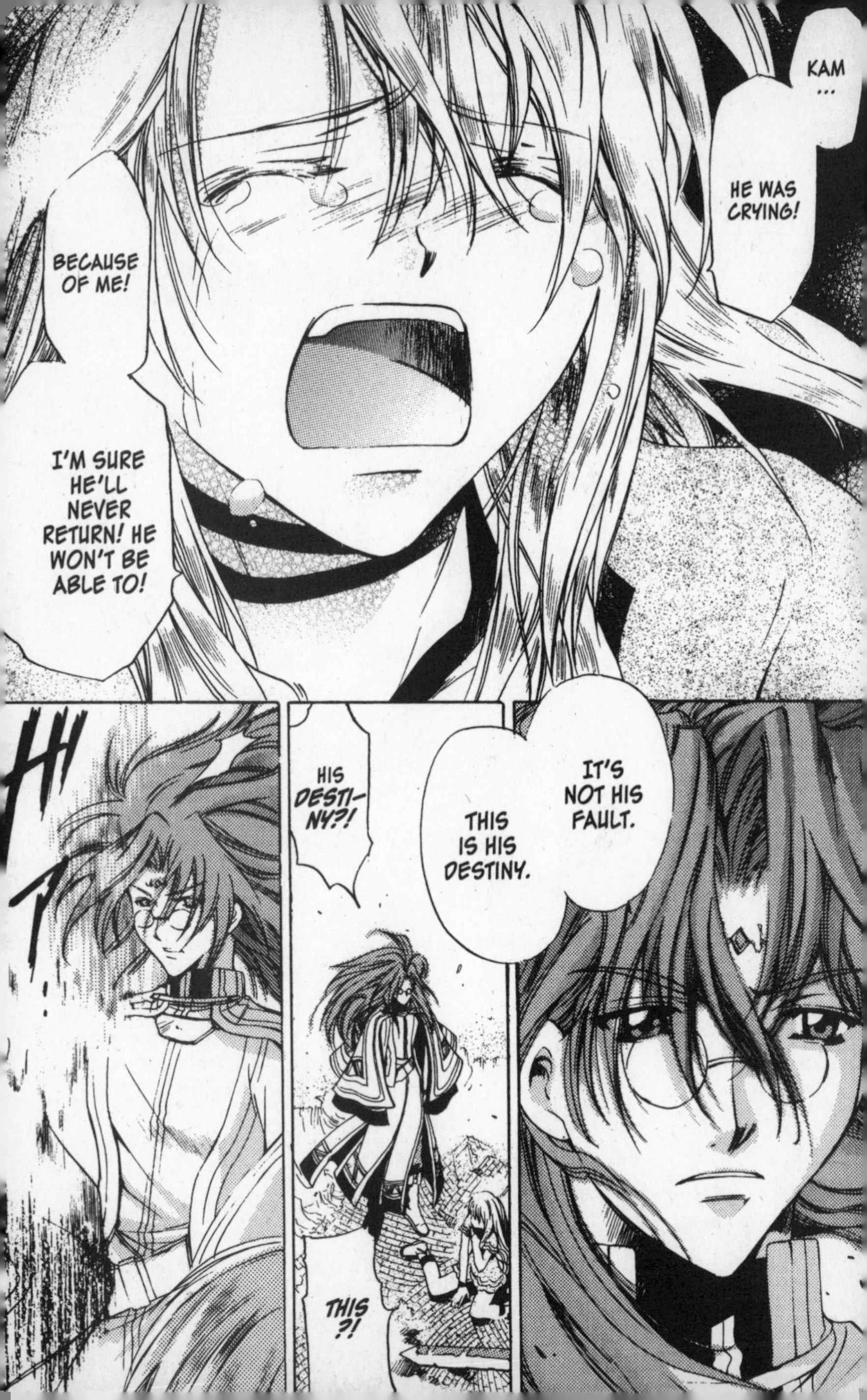
KAM ...
HE WAS CRYING!
BECAUSE OF ME!
I'M SURE HE'LL NEVER RETURN! HE WON'T BE ABLE TO!
IT'S NOT HIS FAULT.
THIS IS HIS DESTINY.
HIS DESTINY?!
THIS ?!

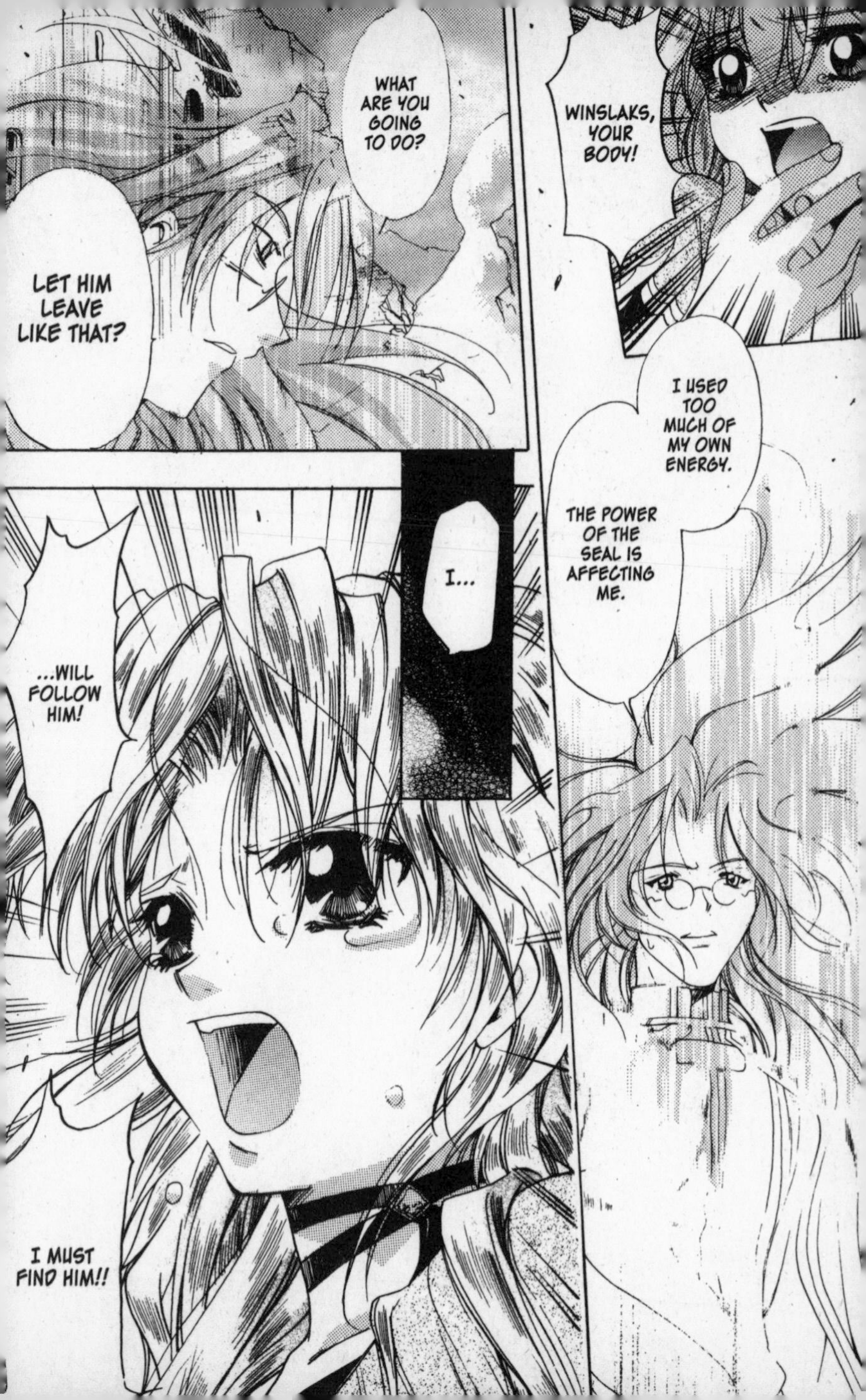
WINSLAKS, YOUR BODY!
I USED TOO MUCH OF MY OWN ENERGY.
THE POWER OF THE SEAL IS AFFECTING ME.
WHAT ARE YOU GOING TO DO?
LET HIM LEAVE LIKE THAT?
I...
...WILL FOLLOW HIM!
I MUST FIND HIM!!

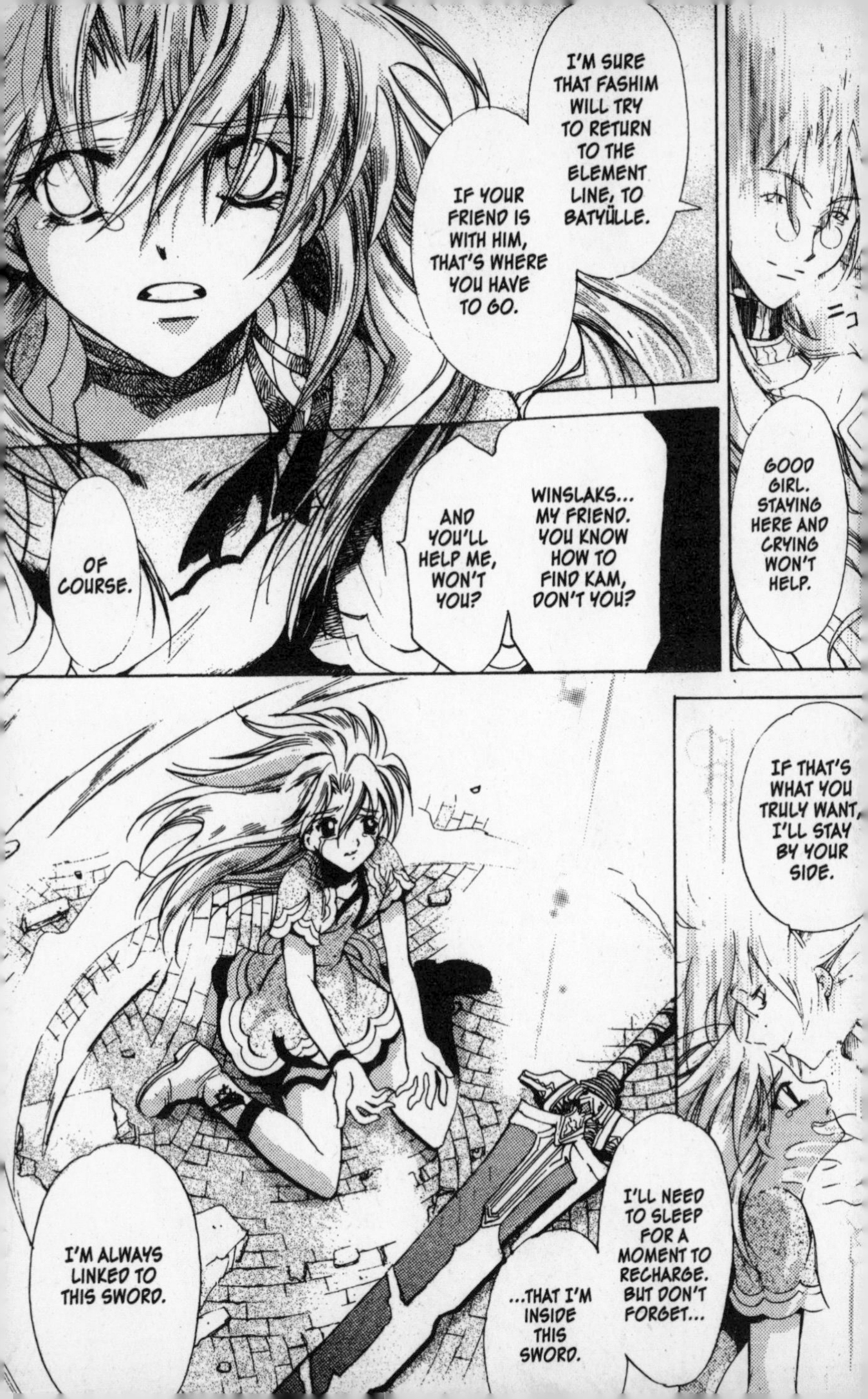
GOOD GIRL. STAYING HERE AND CRYING WON'T HELP.
I'M SURE THAT FASHIM WILL TRY TO RETURN TO THE ELEMENT LINE, TO BATYÜLLE.
IF YOUR FRIEND IS WITH HIM, THAT'S WHERE YOU HAVE TO GO.
WINSLAKS... MY FRIEND. YOU KNOW HOW TO FIND KAM, DON'T YOU?
AND YOU'LL HELP ME, WON'T YOU?
OF COURSE.
IF THAT'S WHAT YOU TRULY WANT, I'LL STAY BY YOUR SIDE.
I'LL NEED TO SLEEP FOR A MOMENT TO RECHARGE. BUT DON'T FORGET...
...THAT I'M INSIDE THIS SWORD.
I'M ALWAYS LINKED TO THIS SWORD.

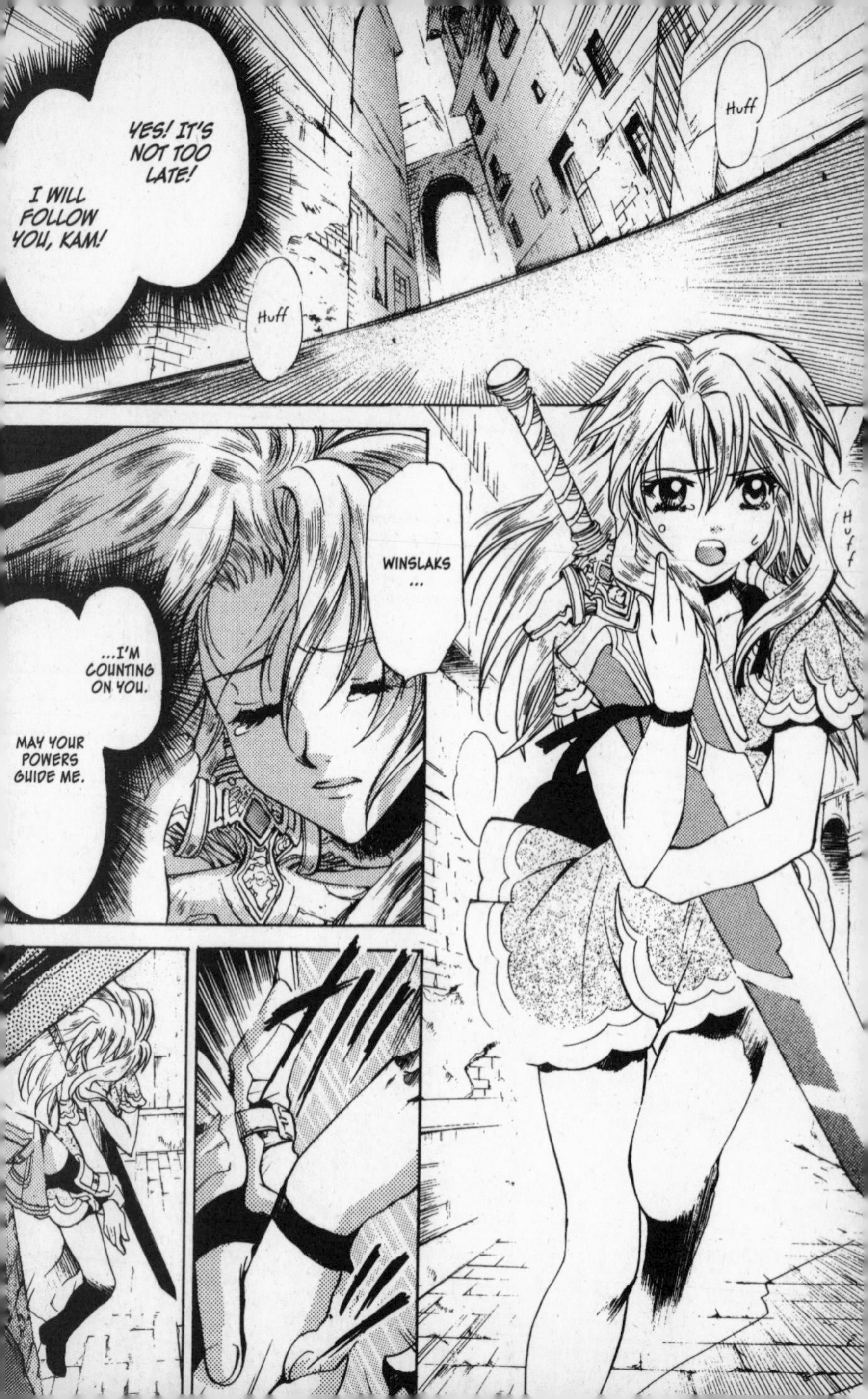
Huff
Huff
YES! IT'S NOT TOO LATE!
I WILL FOLLOW YOU, KAM!
Huff
WINSLAKS ...
...I'M COUNTING ON YOU.
MAY YOUR POWERS GUIDE ME.

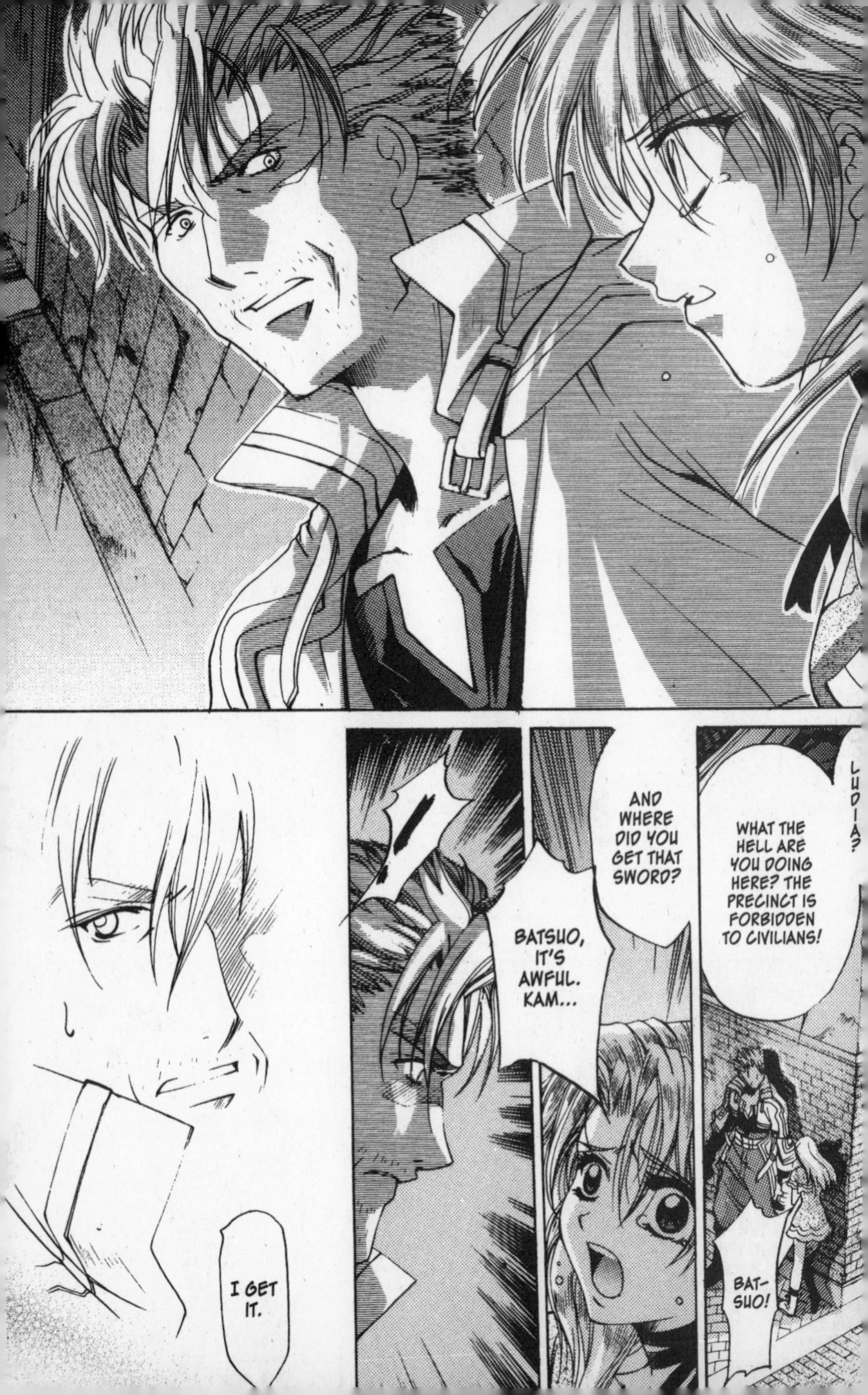
LUDIA?
WHAT THE HELL ARE YOU DOING HERE? THE PRECINCT IS FORBIDDEN TO CIVILIANS!
BAT-SUO!
AND WHERE DID YOU GET THAT SWORD?
BATSUO, IT'S AWFUL. KAM...
I GET IT.

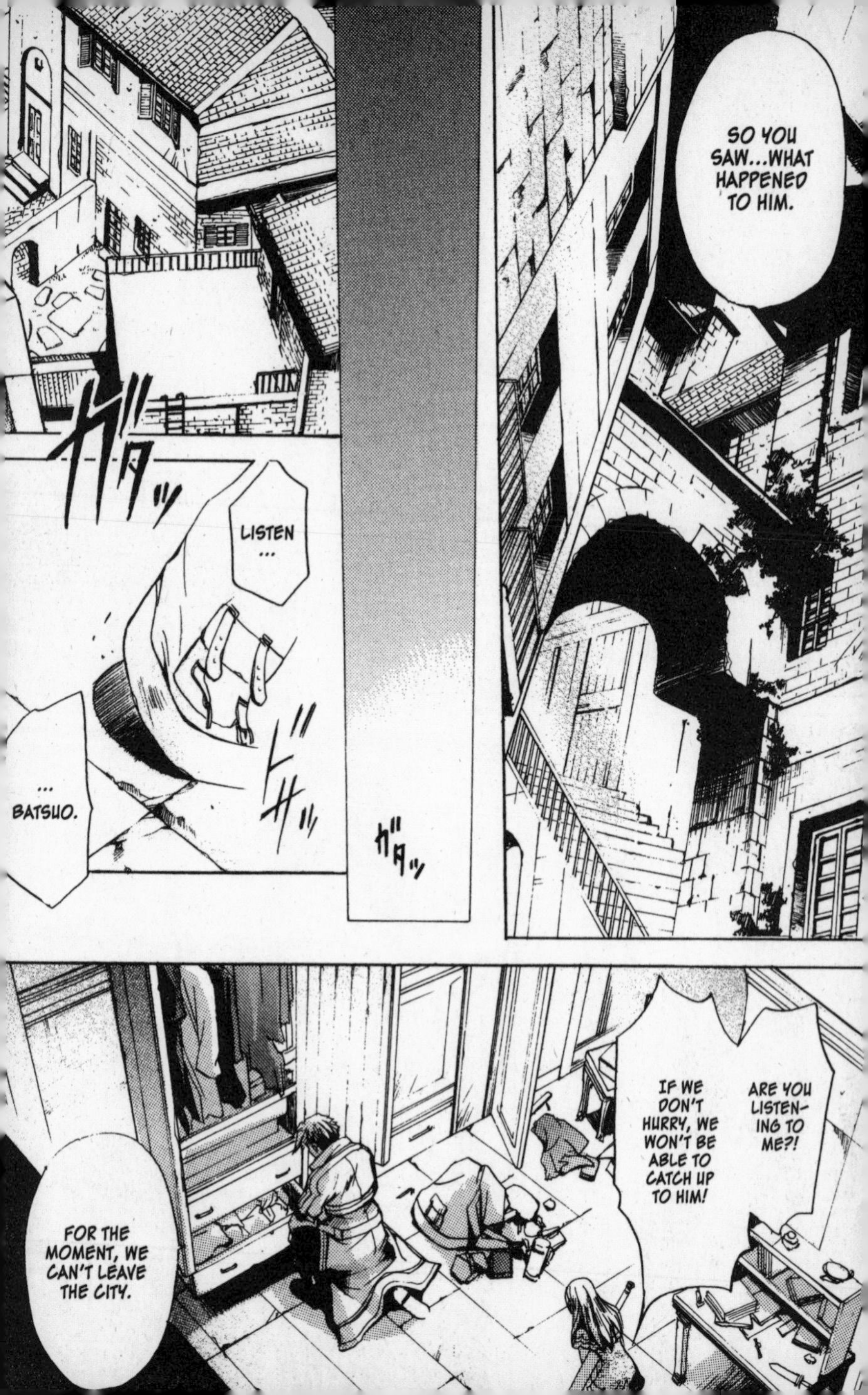
SO YOU SAW...WHAT HAPPENED TO HIM.
ガタッ
ガタッ
LISTEN ...
... BATSUO.
ARE YOU LISTENING TO ME?!
IF WE DON'T HURRY, WE WON'T BE ABLE TO CATCH UP TO HIM!
FOR THE MOMENT, WE CAN'T LEAVE THE CITY.

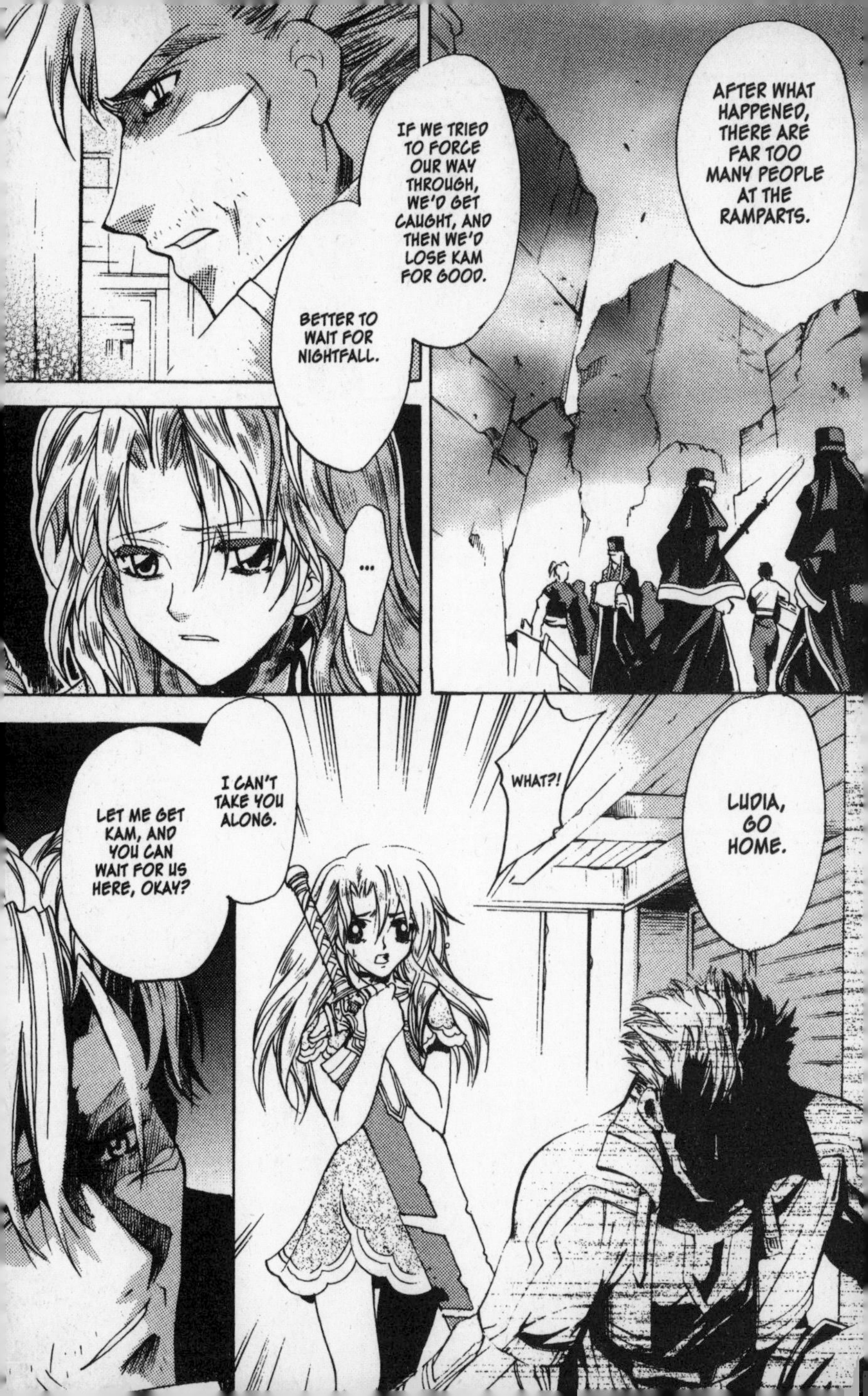
AFTER WHAT HAPPENED, THERE ARE FAR TOO MANY PEOPLE AT THE RAMPARTS.
IF WE TRIED TO FORCE OUR WAY THROUGH, WE'D GET CAUGHT, AND THEN WE'D LOSE KAM FOR GOOD.
BETTER TO WAIT FOR NIGHTFALL.
...
LUDIA, GO HOME.
WHAT?!
I CAN'T TAKE YOU ALONG.
LET ME GET KAM, AND YOU CAN WAIT FOR US HERE, OKAY?

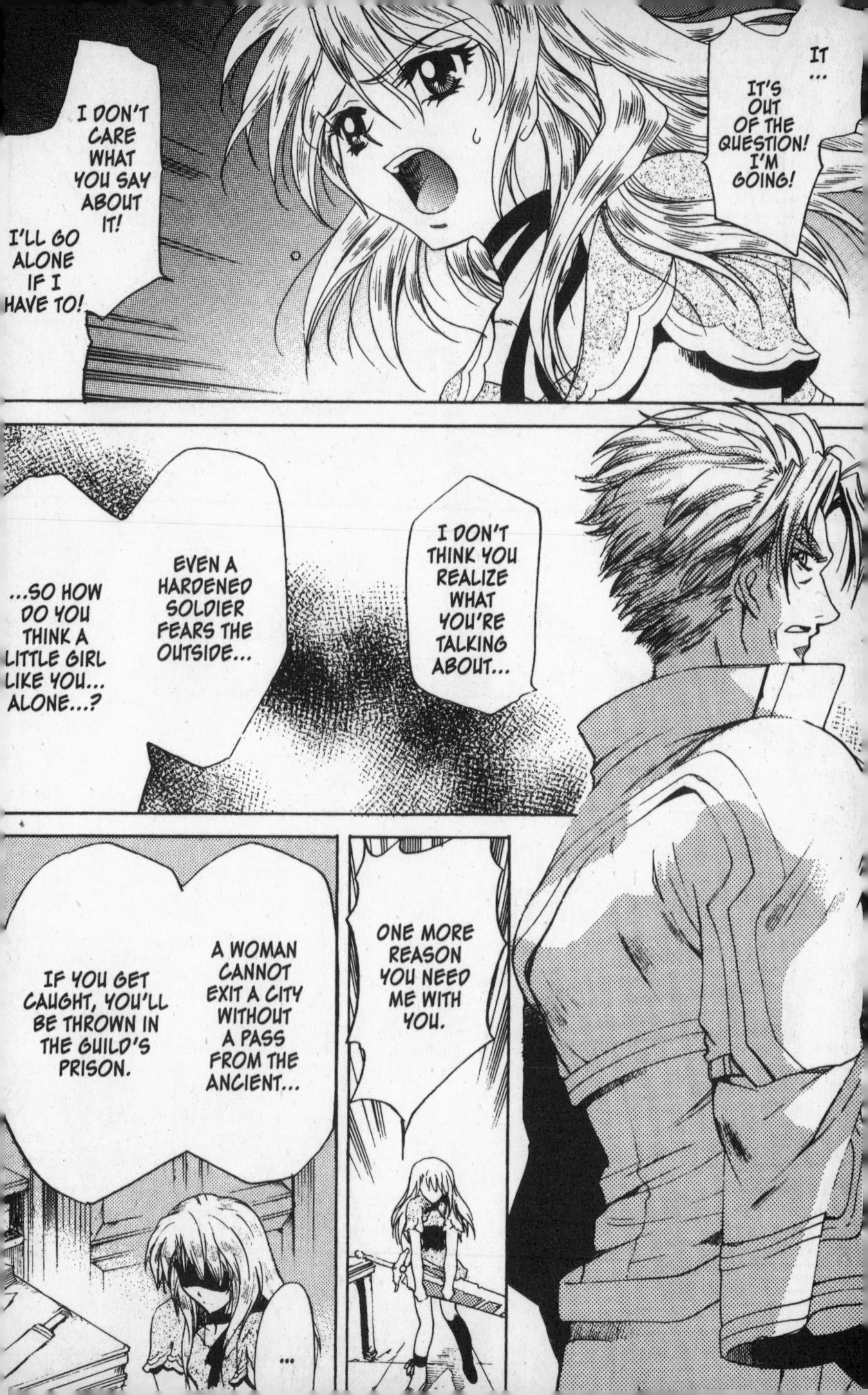
IT...
IT'S OUT OF THE QUESTION! I'M GOING!
I DON'T CARE WHAT YOU SAY ABOUT IT!
I'LL GO ALONE IF I HAVE TO!
I DON'T THINK YOU REALIZE WHAT YOU'RE TALKING ABOUT...
EVEN A HARDENED SOLDIER FEARS THE OUTSIDE...
...SO HOW DO YOU THINK A LITTLE GIRL LIKE YOU... ALONE...?
ONE MORE REASON YOU NEED ME WITH YOU.
A WOMAN CANNOT EXIT A CITY WITHOUT A PASS FROM THE ANCIENT...
IF YOU GET CAUGHT, YOU'LL BE THROWN IN THE GUILD'S PRISON.
...

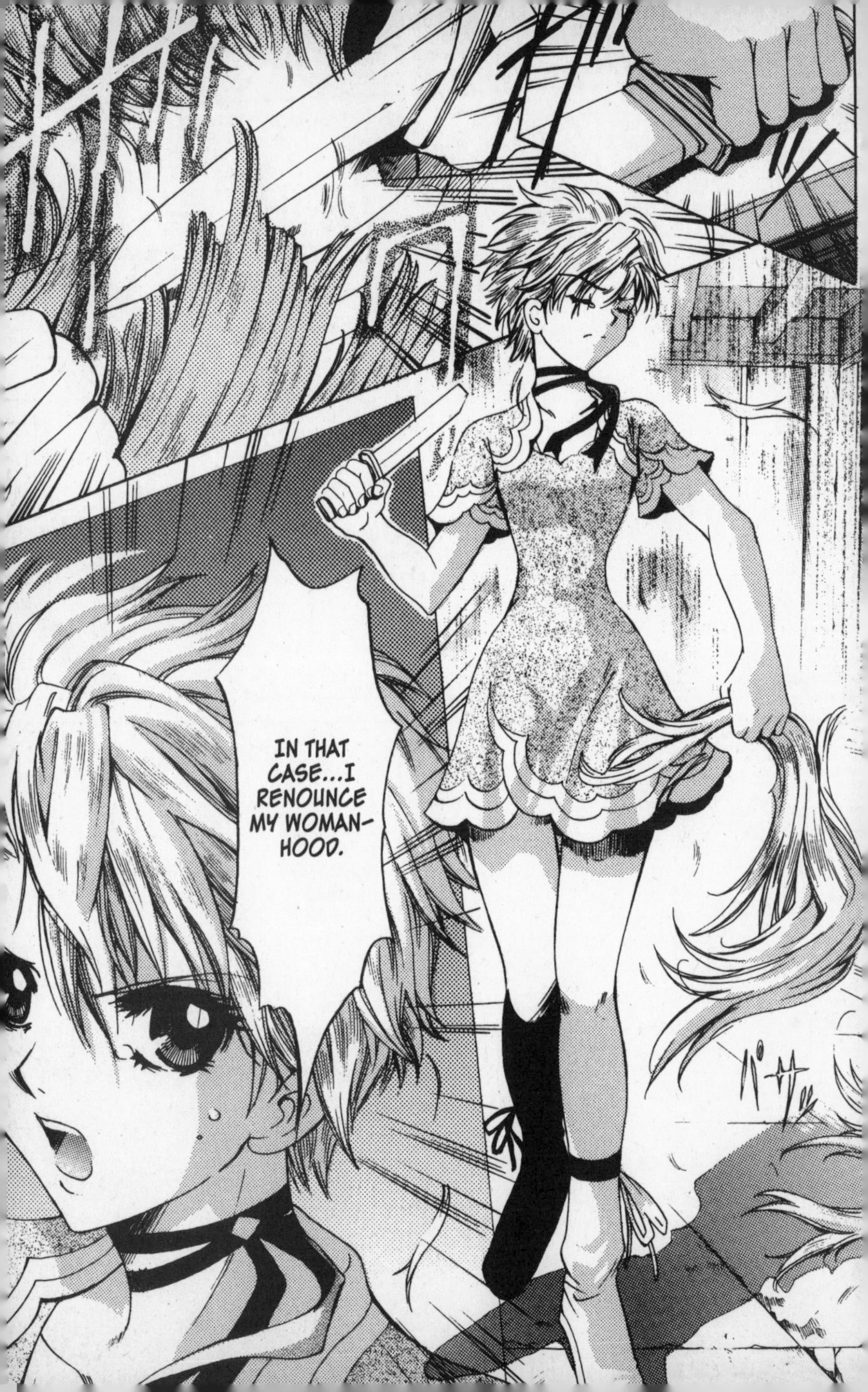
IN THAT CASE...I RENOUNCE MY WOMAN-HOOD.

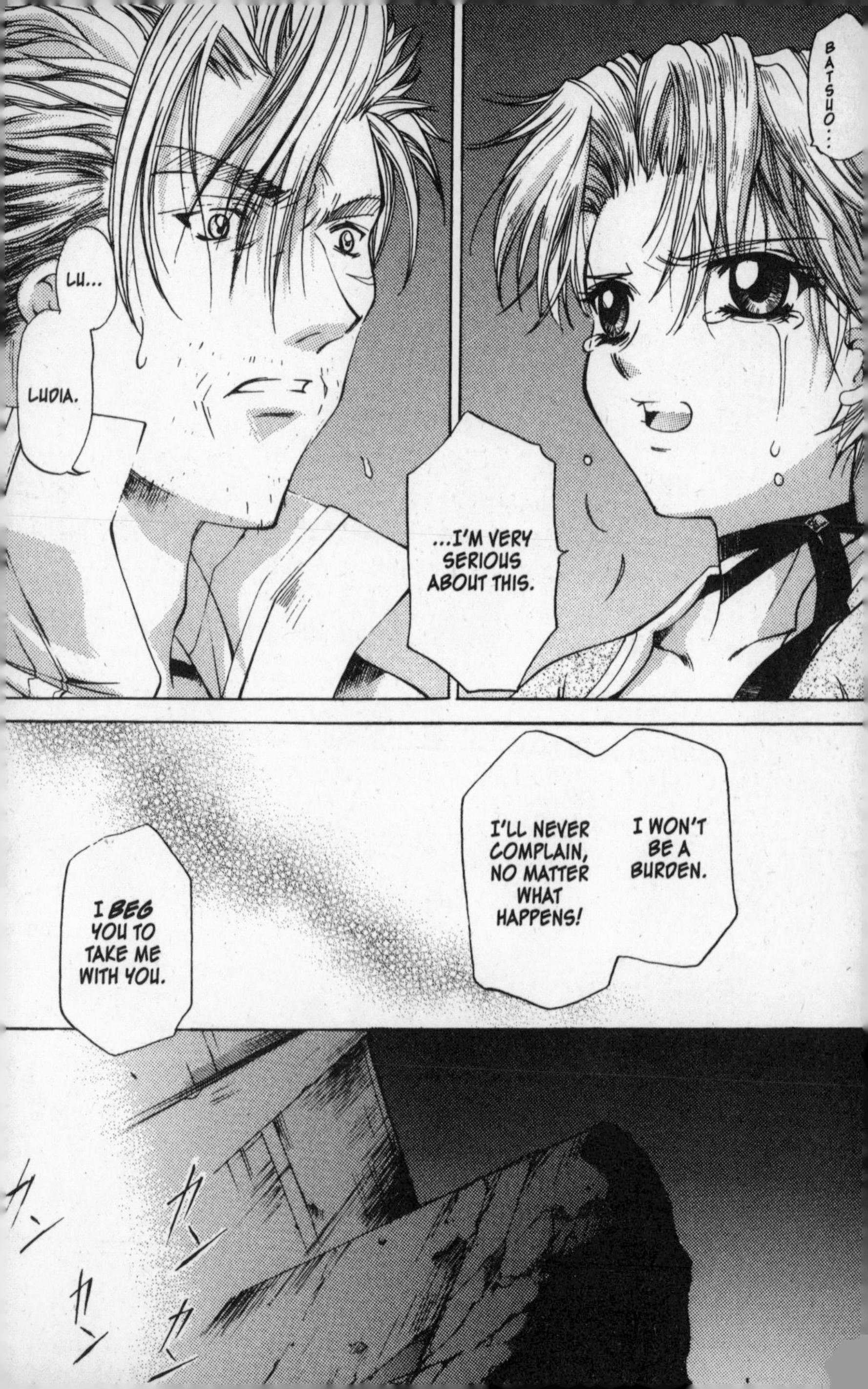
BATSUO...
...I'M VERY SERIOUS ABOUT THIS.
LU...
LUDIA.
I WON'T BE A BURDEN.
I'LL NEVER COMPLAIN, NO MATTER WHAT HAPPENS!
I BEG YOU TO TAKE ME WITH YOU.
カン
カン
カン

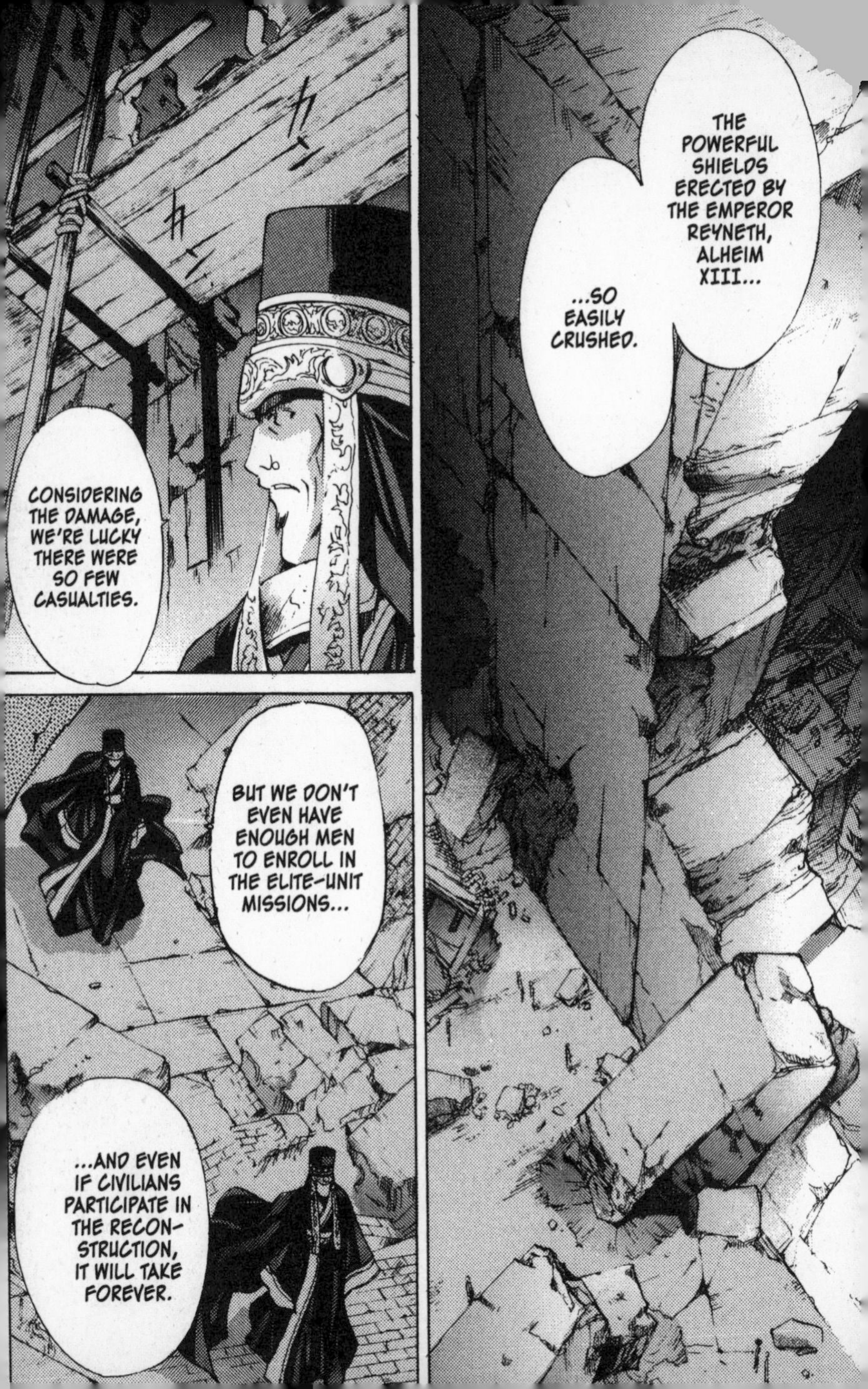
THE POWERFUL SHIELDS ERECTED BY THE EMPEROR REYNETH, ALHEIM XIII...
...SO EASILY CRUSHED.
CONSIDERING THE DAMAGE, WE'RE LUCKY THERE WERE SO FEW CASUALTIES.
BUT WE DON'T EVEN HAVE ENOUGH MEN TO ENROLL IN THE ELITE-UNIT MISSIONS...
...AND EVEN IF CIVILIANS PARTICIPATE IN THE RECON-STRUCTION, IT WILL TAKE FOREVER.

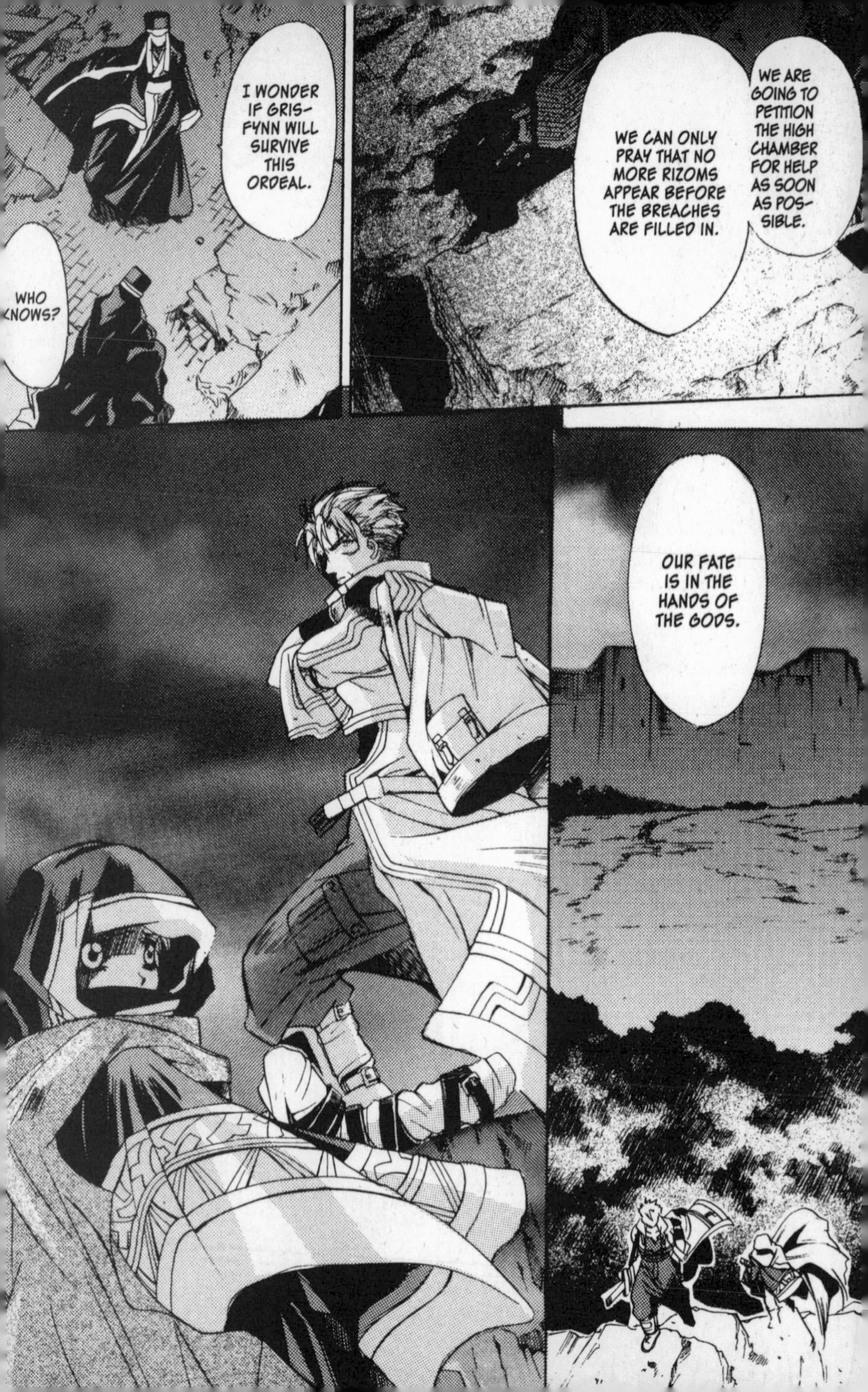
WE ARE GOING TO PETITION THE HIGH CHAMBER FOR HELP AS SOON AS POS-SIBLE.
WE CAN ONLY PRAY THAT NO MORE RIZOMS APPEAR BEFORE THE BREACHES ARE FILLED IN.
I WONDER IF GRIS-FYNN WILL SURVIVE THIS ORDEAL.
WHO KNOWS?
OUR FATE IS IN THE HANDS OF THE GODS.

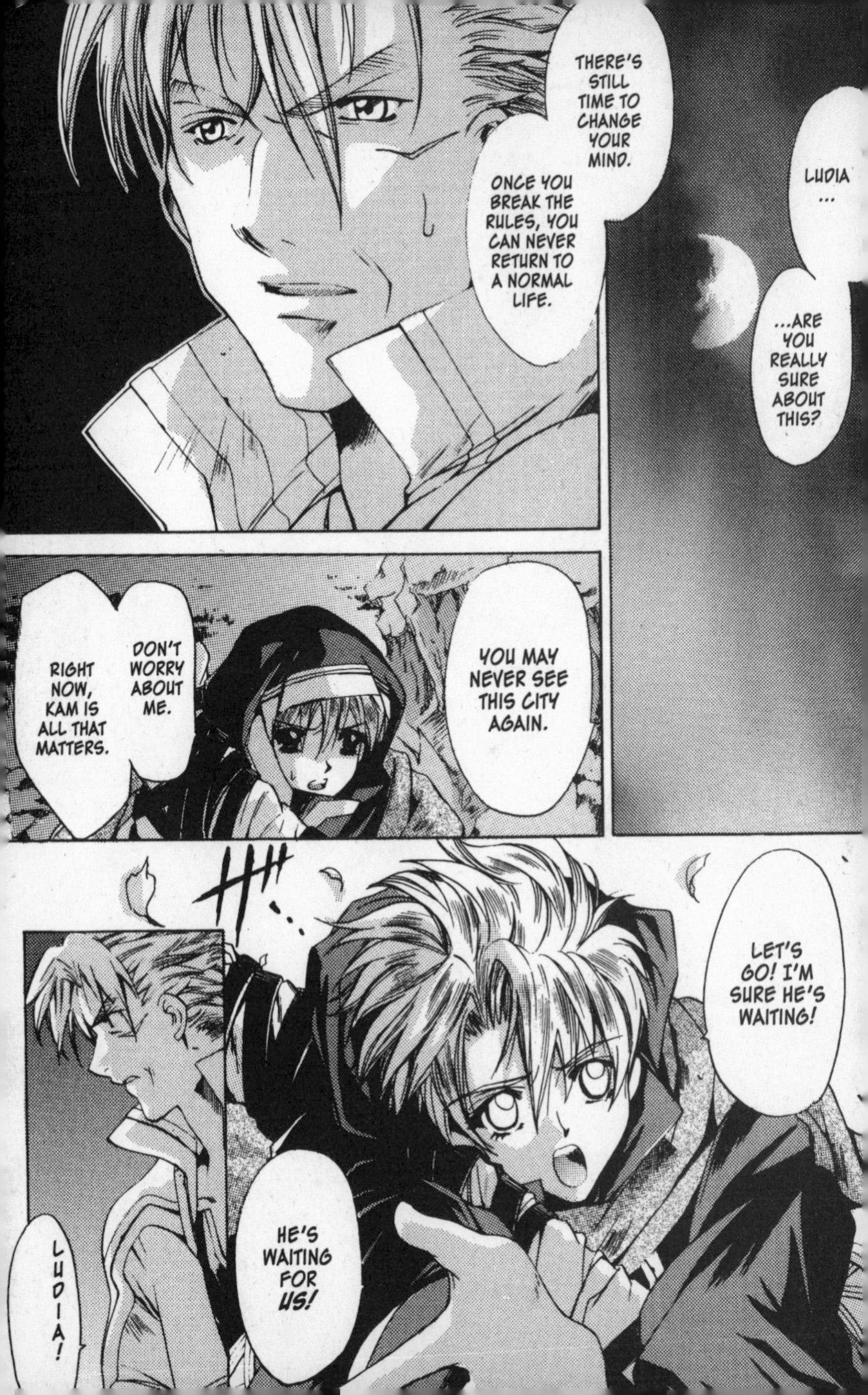
LUDIA ...
...ARE YOU REALLY SURE ABOUT THIS?
THERE'S STILL TIME TO CHANGE YOUR MIND.
ONCE YOU BREAK THE RULES, YOU CAN NEVER RETURN TO A NORMAL LIFE.
YOU MAY NEVER SEE THIS CITY AGAIN.
DON'T WORRY ABOUT ME.
RIGHT NOW, KAM IS ALL THAT MATTERS.
LET'S GO! I'M SURE HE'S WAITING!
HE'S WAITING FOR US!
LUDIA!

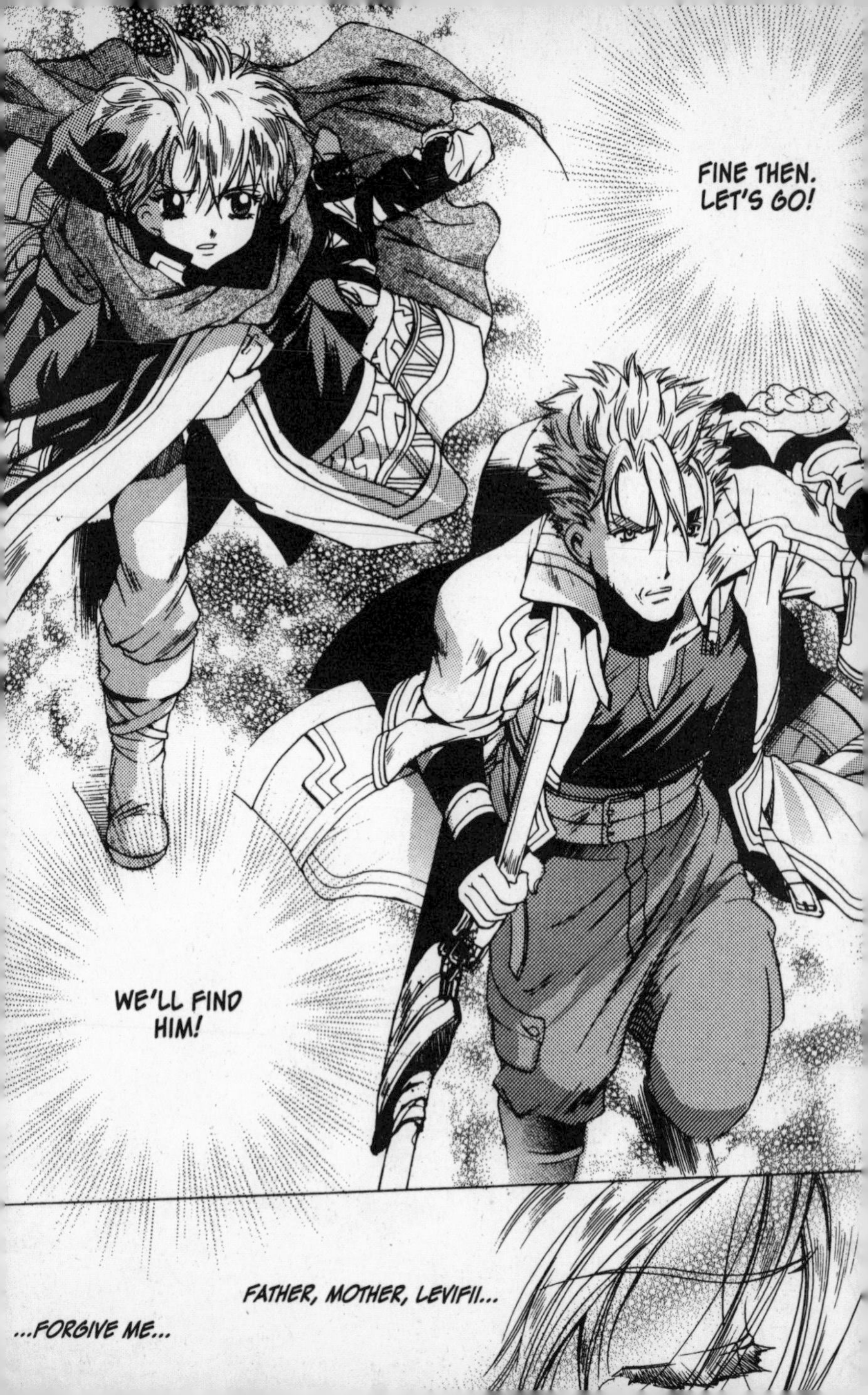
FINE THEN. LET'S GO!
WE'LL FIND HIM!
FATHER, MOTHER, LEVIFII...
...FORGIVE ME...

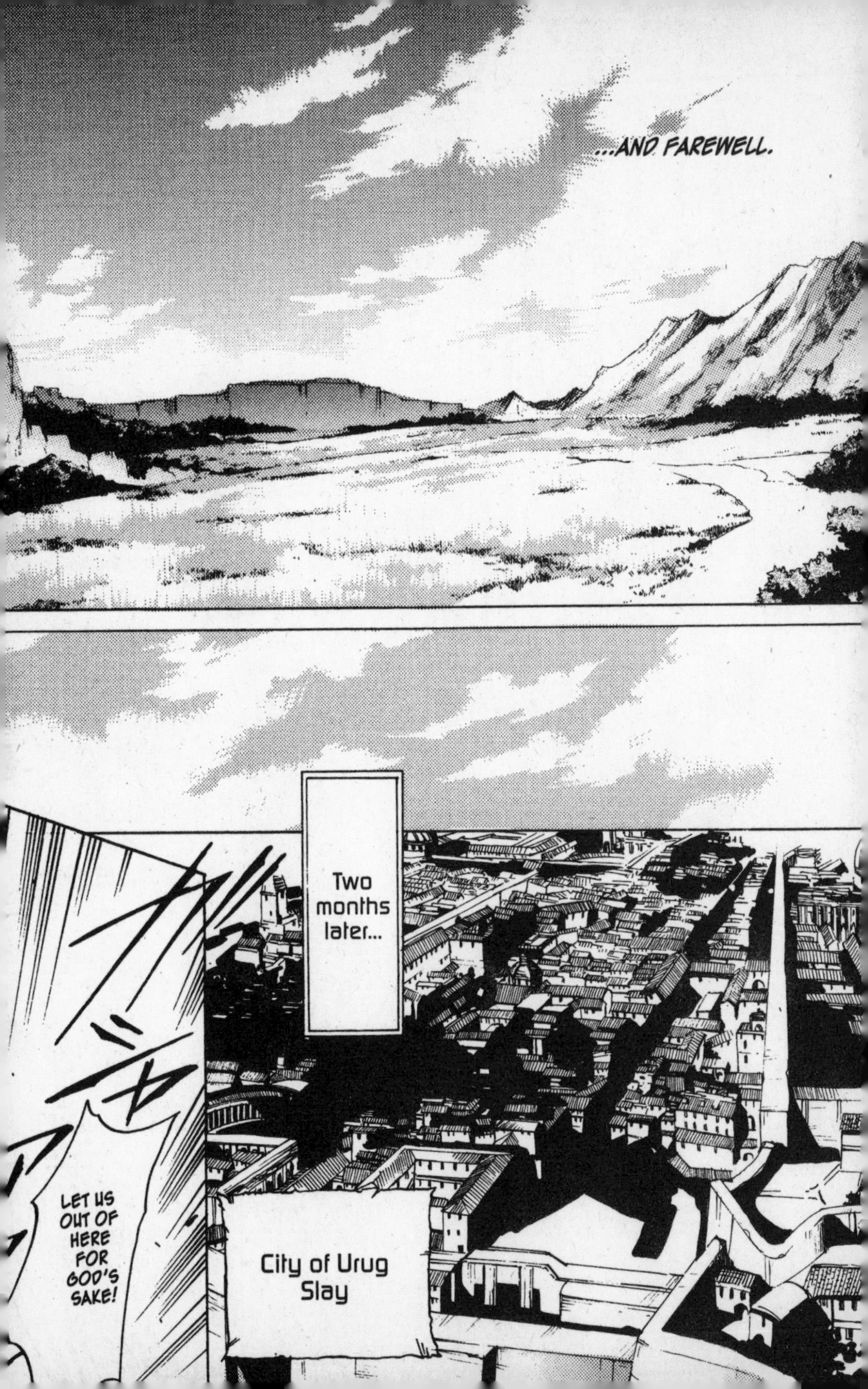
...AND FAREWELL.
Two months later...
City of Urug Slay
LET US OUT OF HERE FOR GOD'S SAKE!

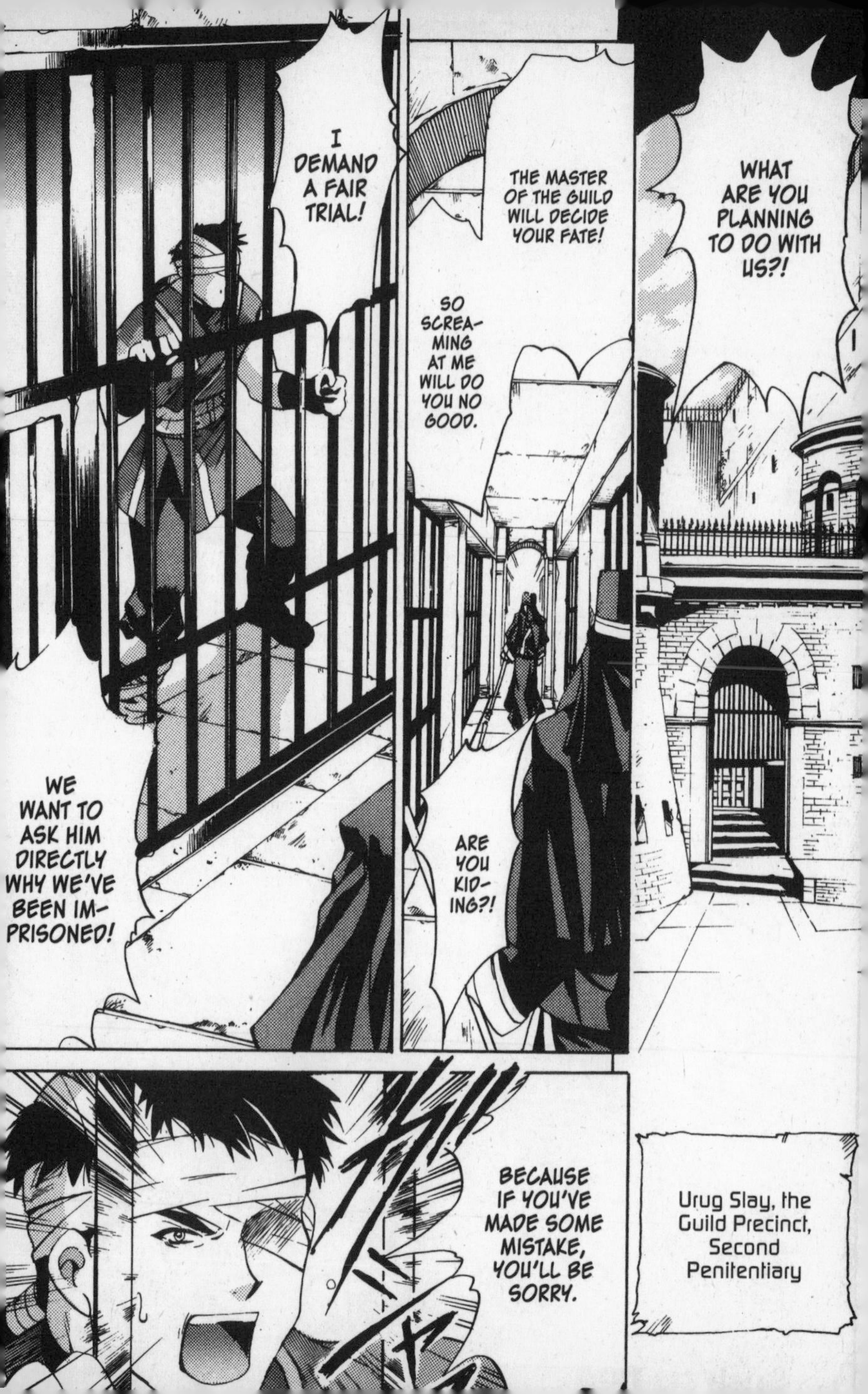
WHAT ARE YOU PLANNING TO DO WITH US?!
THE MASTER OF THE GUILD WILL DECIDE YOUR FATE!
SO SCREAMING AT ME WILL DO YOU NO GOOD.
ARE YOU KIDDING?!
I DEMAND A FAIR TRIAL!
WE WANT TO ASK HIM DIRECTLY WHY WE'VE BEEN IMPRISONED!
Urug Slay, the Guild Precinct, Second Penitentiary
BECAUSE IF YOU'VE MADE SOME MISTAKE, YOU'LL BE SORRY.

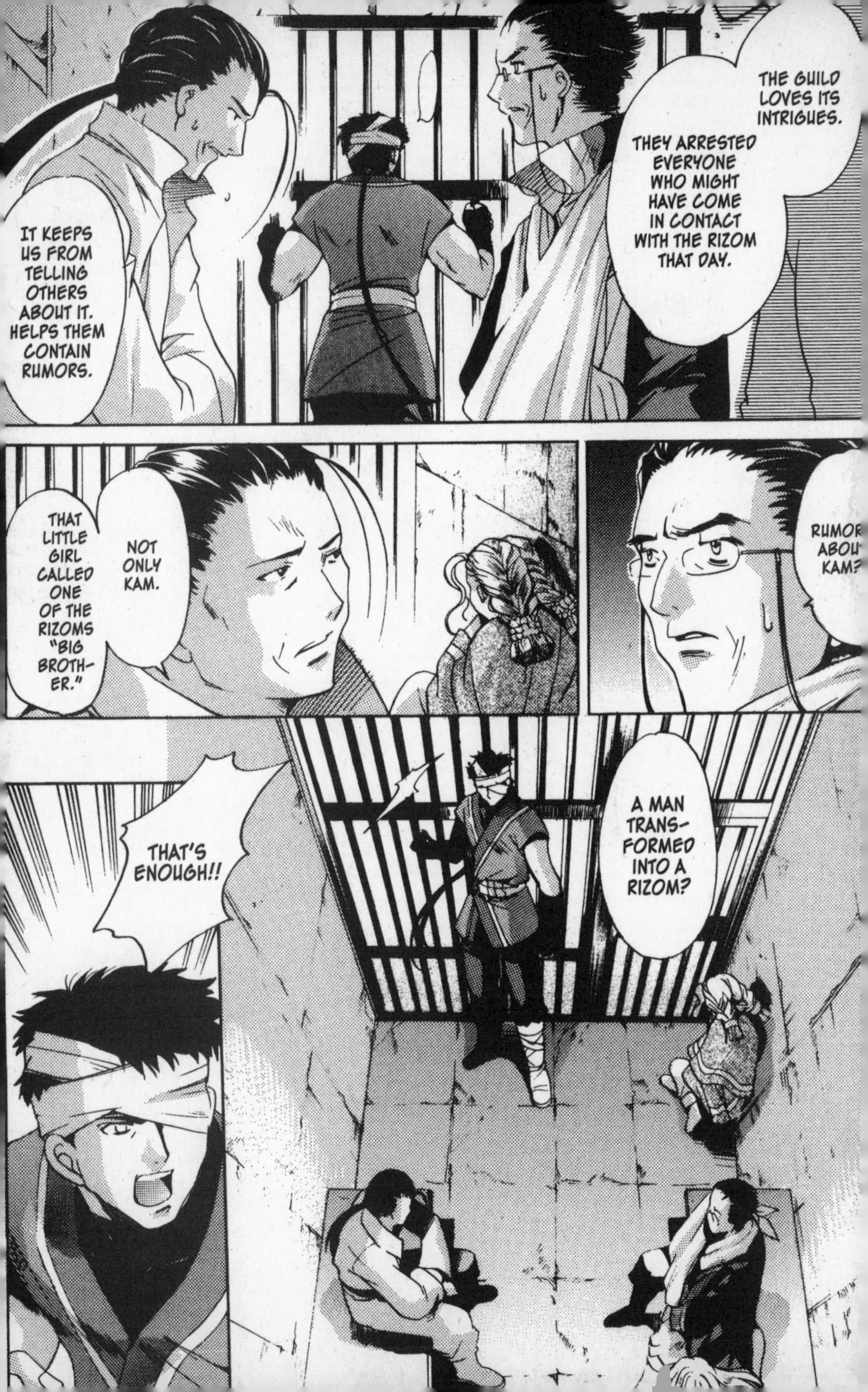
THE GUILD LOVES ITS INTRIGUES.
THEY ARRESTED EVERYONE WHO MIGHT HAVE COME IN CONTACT WITH THE RIZOM THAT DAY.
IT KEEPS US FROM TELLING OTHERS ABOUT IT. HELPS THEM CONTAIN RUMORS.
RUMOR ABOU KAM?
NOT ONLY KAM.
THAT LITTLE GIRL CALLED ONE OF THE RIZOMS "BIG BROTHER."
A MAN TRANSFORMED INTO A RIZOM?
THAT'S ENOUGH!!

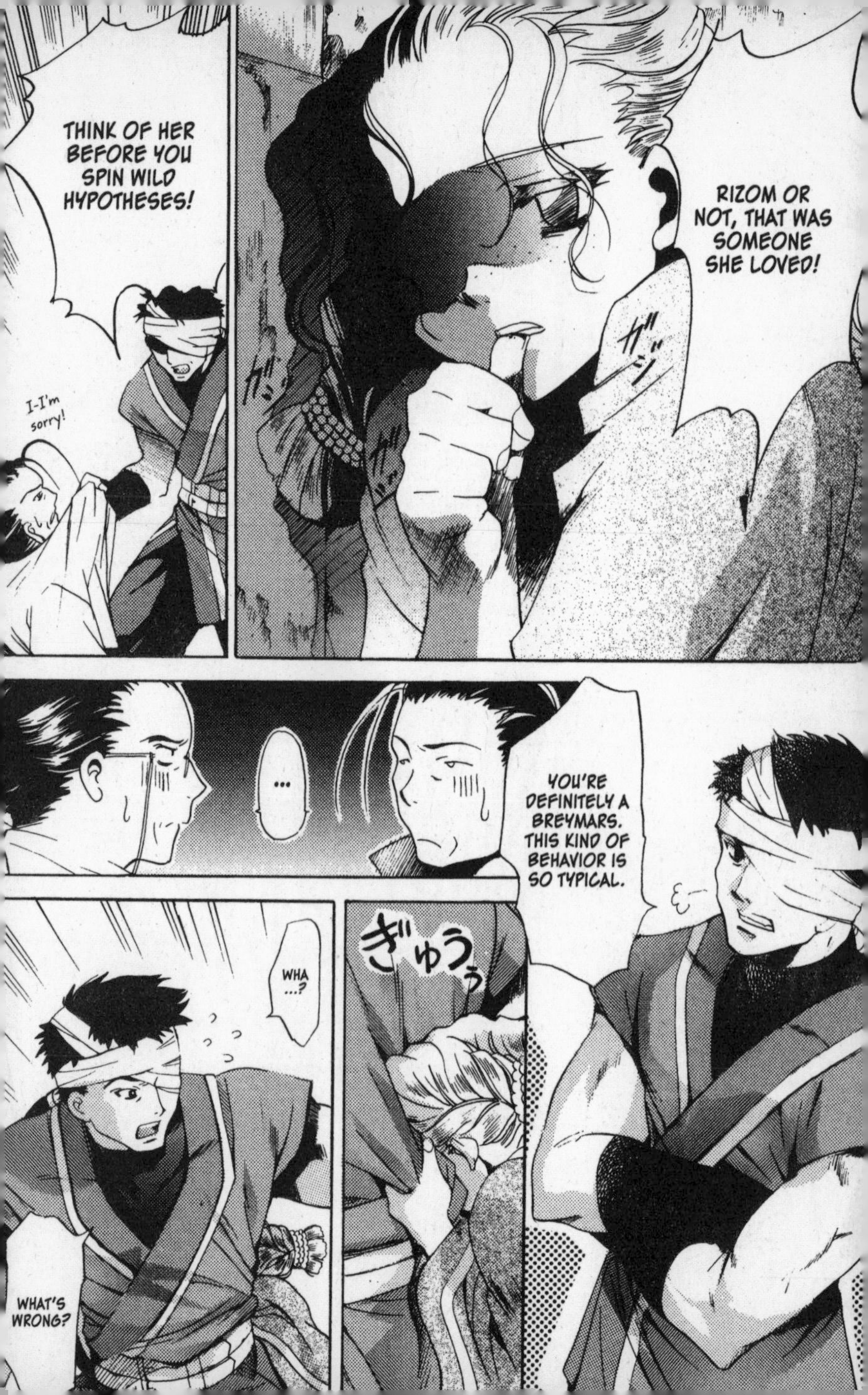
RIZOM OR NOT, THAT WAS SOMEONE SHE LOVED!
THINK OF HER BEFORE YOU SPIN WILD HYPOTHESES!
I-I'm sorry!
YOU'RE DEFINITELY A BREYMARS. THIS KIND OF BEHAVIOR IS SO TYPICAL.
...
ぎゅうぅ
WHA ...?
WHAT'S WRONG?

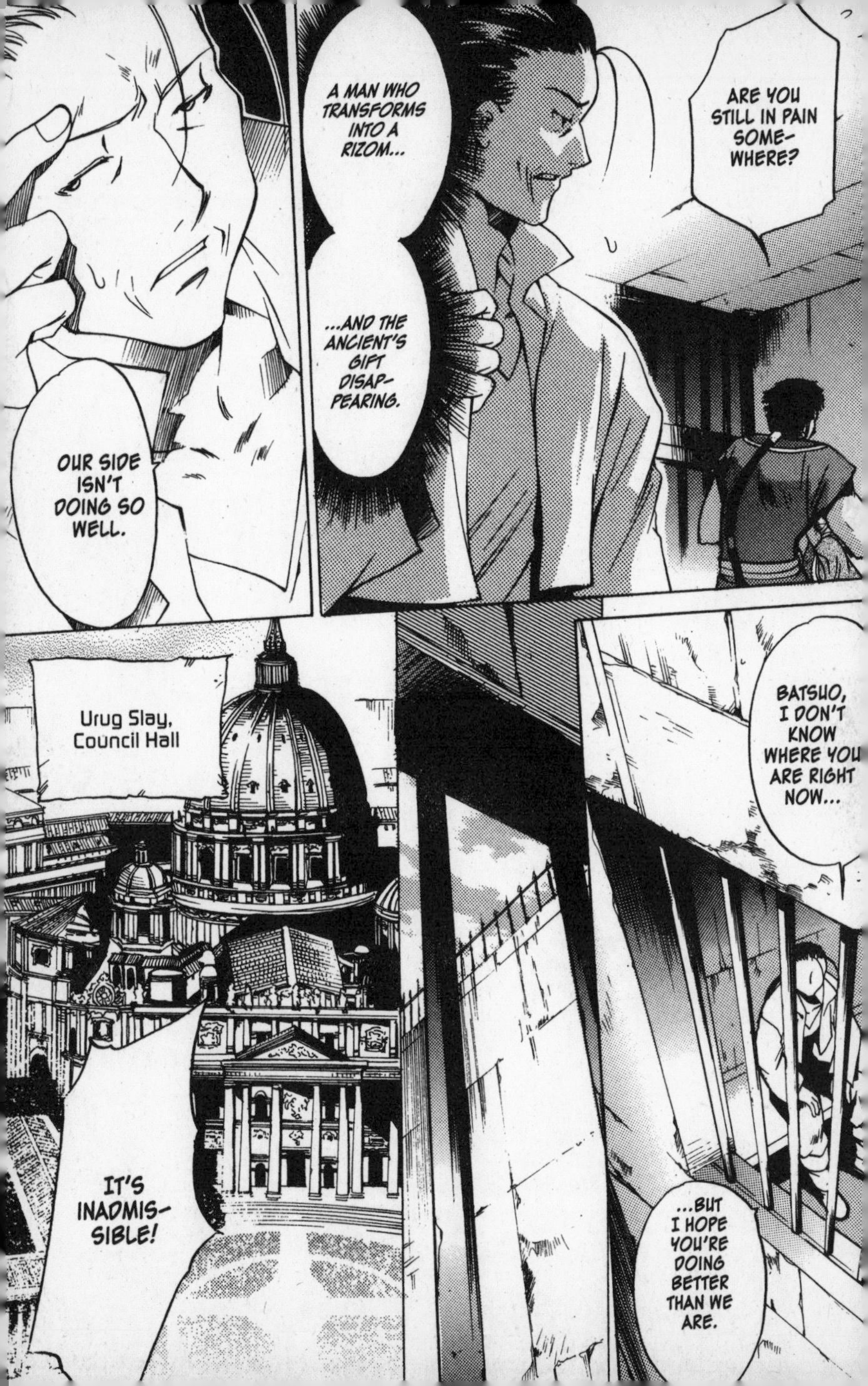
ARE YOU STILL IN PAIN SOME-WHERE?
A MAN WHO TRANSFORMS INTO A RIZOM...
...AND THE ANCIENT'S GIFT DISAP-PEARING.
OUR SIDE ISN'T DOING SO WELL.
BATSUO, I DON'T KNOW WHERE YOU ARE RIGHT NOW...
...BUT I HOPE YOU'RE DOING BETTER THAN WE ARE.
Urug Slay, Council Hall
IT'S INADMIS-SIBLE!

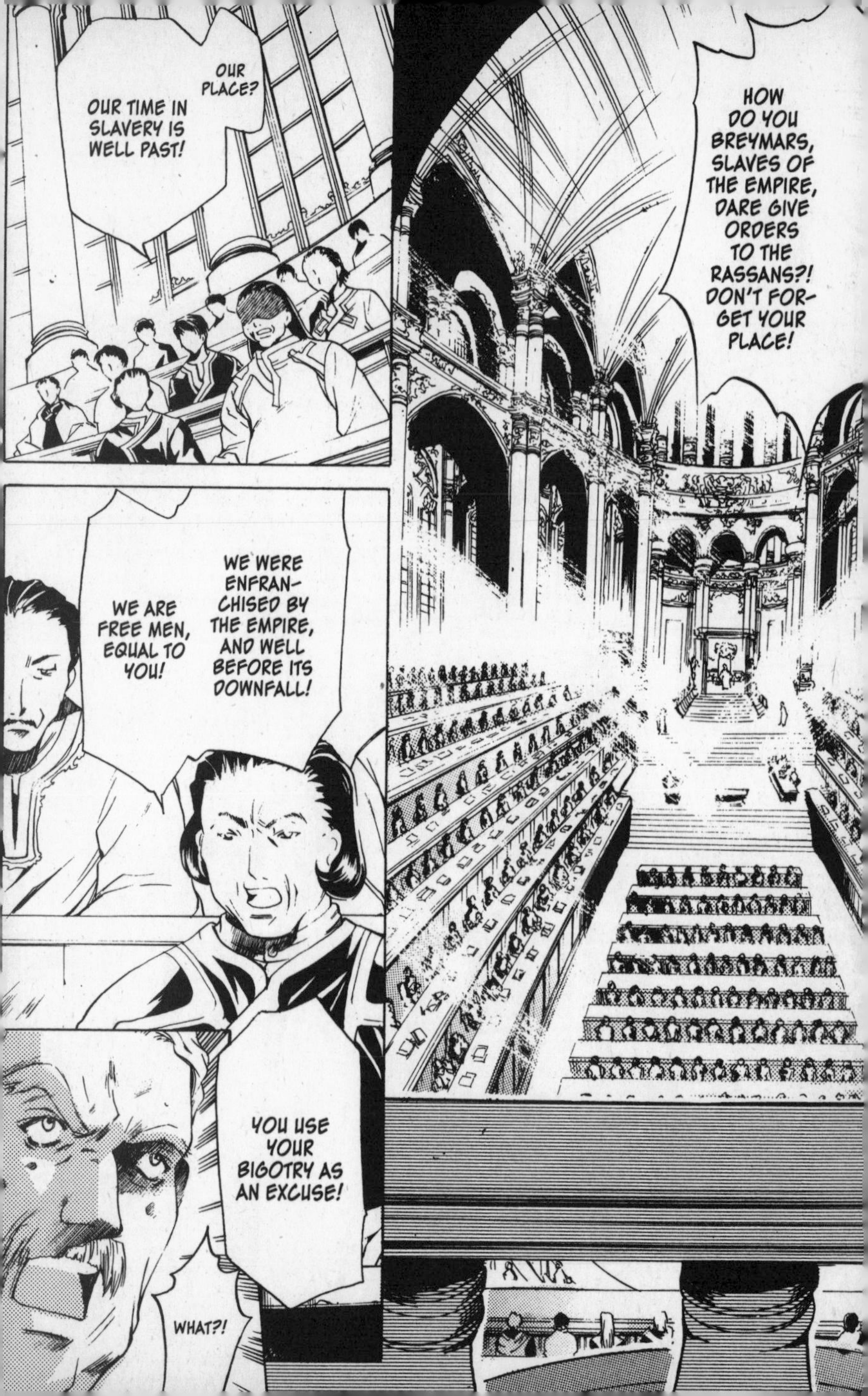
HOW DO YOU BREYMARS, SLAVES OF THE EMPIRE, DARE GIVE ORDERS TO THE RASSANS?! DON'T FOR-GET YOUR PLACE!
OUR PLACE?
OUR TIME IN SLAVERY IS WELL PAST!
WE WERE ENFRAN-CHISED BY THE EMPIRE, AND WELL BEFORE ITS DOWNFALL!
WE ARE FREE MEN, EQUAL TO YOU!
YOU USE YOUR BIGOTRY AS AN EXCUSE!
WHAT?!

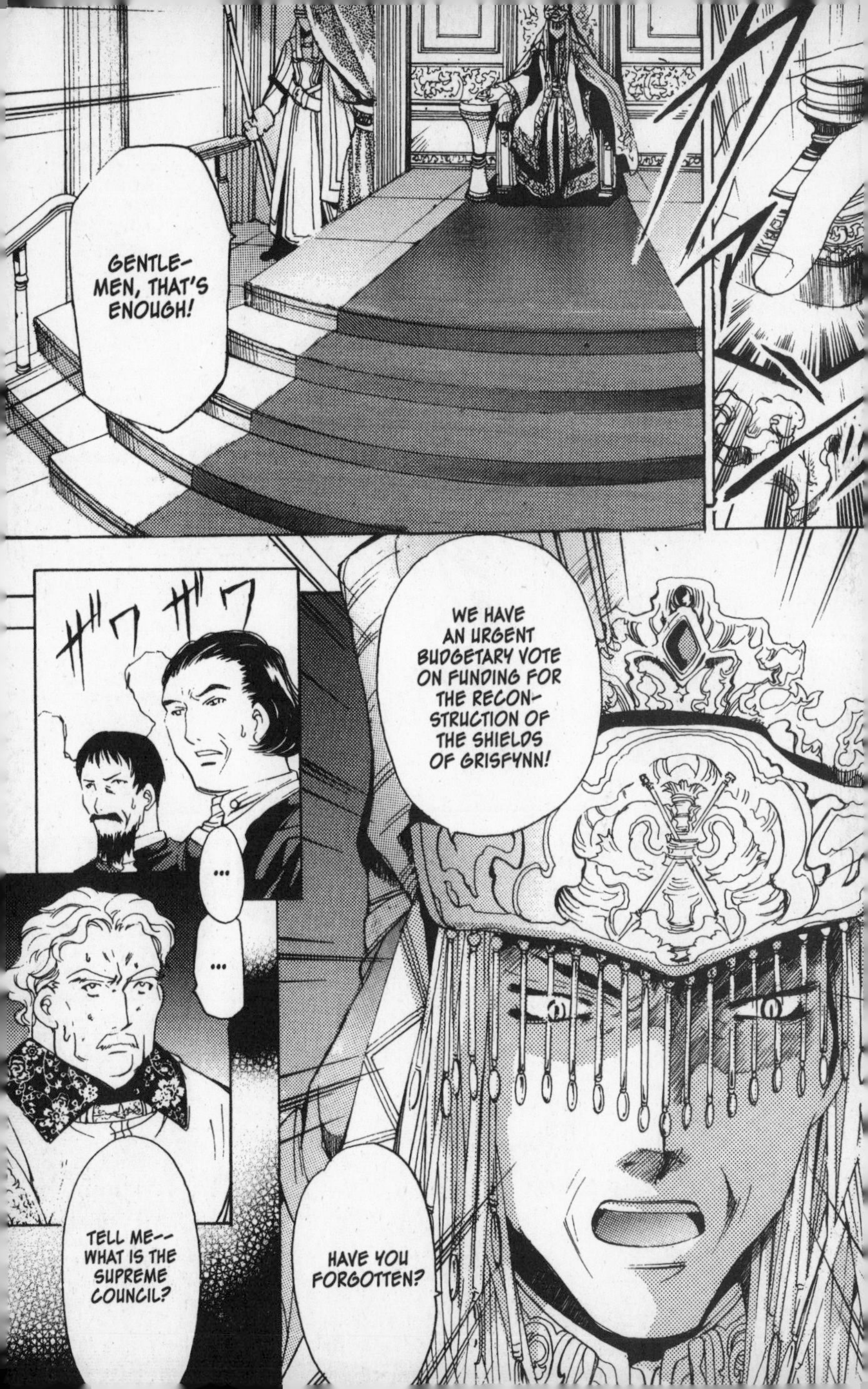
GENTLE-MEN, THAT'S ENOUGH!
WE HAVE AN URGENT BUDGETARY VOTE ON FUNDING FOR THE RECON-STRUCTION OF THE SHIELDS OF GRISFYNN!
ザワ ザワ
...
...
TELL ME-- WHAT IS THE SUPREME COUNCIL?
HAVE YOU FORGOTTEN?

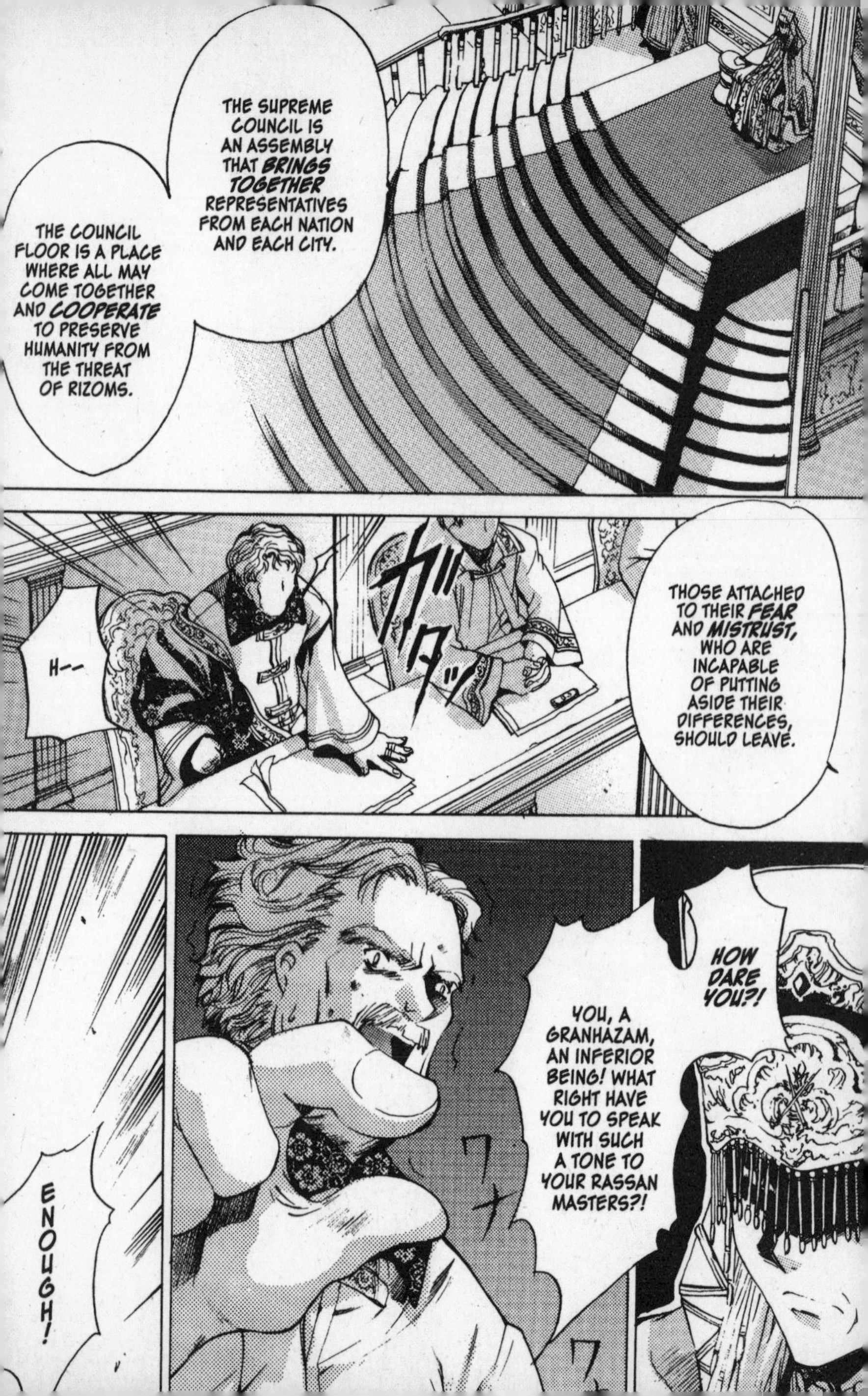
THE SUPREME COUNCIL IS AN ASSEMBLY THAT *BRINGS TOGETHER* REPRESENTATIVES FROM EACH NATION AND EACH CITY.
THE COUNCIL FLOOR IS A PLACE WHERE ALL MAY COME TOGETHER AND *COOPERATE* TO PRESERVE HUMANITY FROM THE THREAT OF RIZOMS.
THOSE ATTACHED TO THEIR *FEAR* AND *MISTRUST,* WHO ARE INCAPABLE OF PUTTING ASIDE THEIR DIFFERENCES, SHOULD LEAVE.
ガタッ
H--
HOW DARE YOU?!
YOU, A GRANHAZAM, AN INFERIOR BEING! WHAT RIGHT HAVE YOU TO SPEAK WITH SUCH A TONE TO YOUR RASSAN MASTERS?!
ENOUGH!

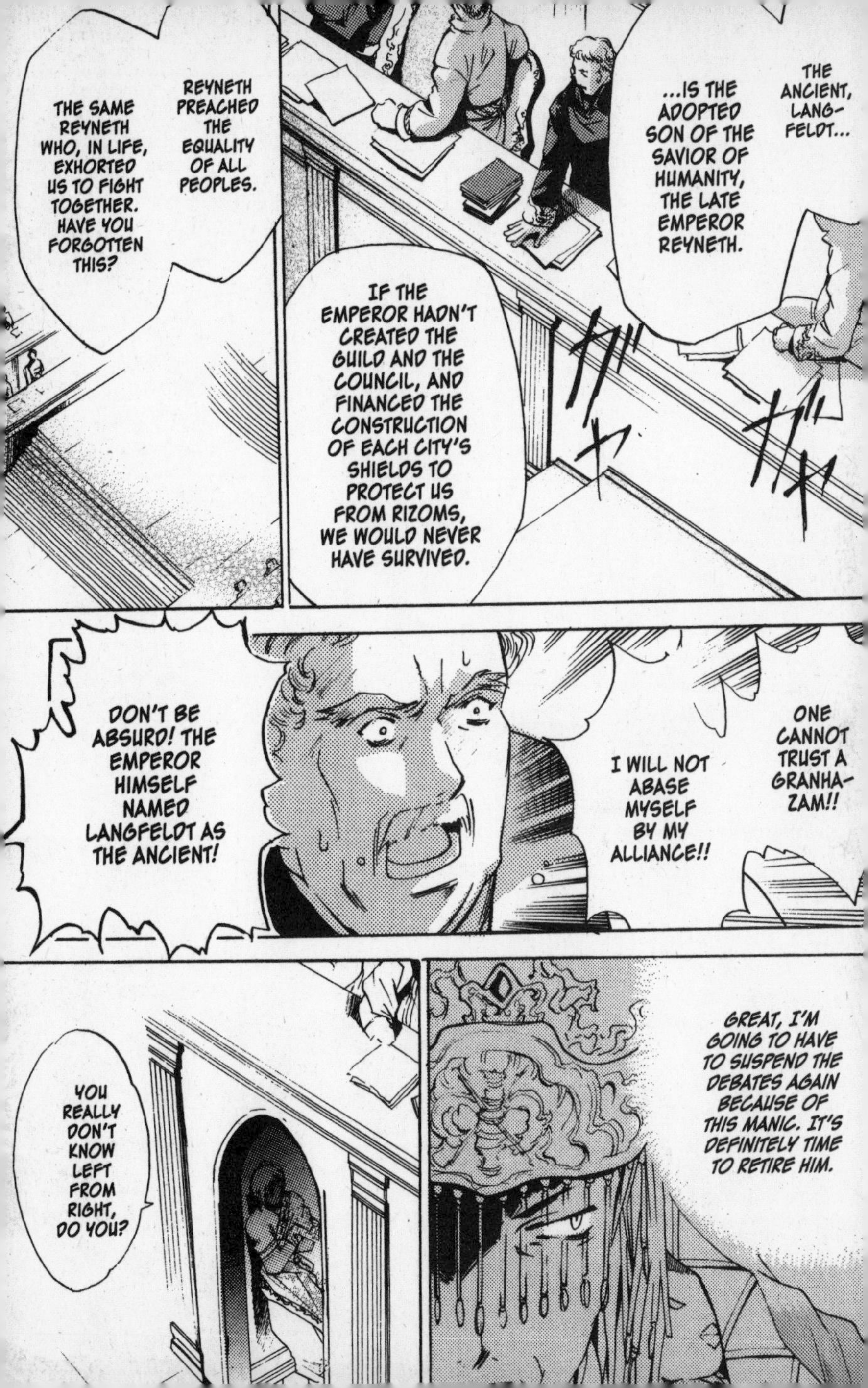
THE ANCIENT, LANGFELDT...
...IS THE ADOPTED SON OF THE SAVIOR OF HUMANITY, THE LATE EMPEROR REYNETH.
IF THE EMPEROR HADN'T CREATED THE GUILD AND THE COUNCIL, AND FINANCED THE CONSTRUCTION OF EACH CITY'S SHIELDS TO PROTECT US FROM RIZOMS, WE WOULD NEVER HAVE SURVIVED.
REYNETH PREACHED THE EQUALITY OF ALL PEOPLES.
THE SAME REYNETH WHO, IN LIFE, EXHORTED US TO FIGHT TOGETHER. HAVE YOU FORGOTTEN THIS?
ONE CANNOT TRUST A GRANHAZAM!!
I WILL NOT ABASE MYSELF BY MY ALLIANCE!!
DON'T BE ABSURD! THE EMPEROR HIMSELF NAMED LANGFELDT AS THE ANCIENT!
GREAT, I'M GOING TO HAVE TO SUSPEND THE DEBATES AGAIN BECAUSE OF THIS MANIC. IT'S DEFINITELY TIME TO RETIRE HIM.
YOU REALLY DON'T KNOW LEFT FROM RIGHT, DO YOU?

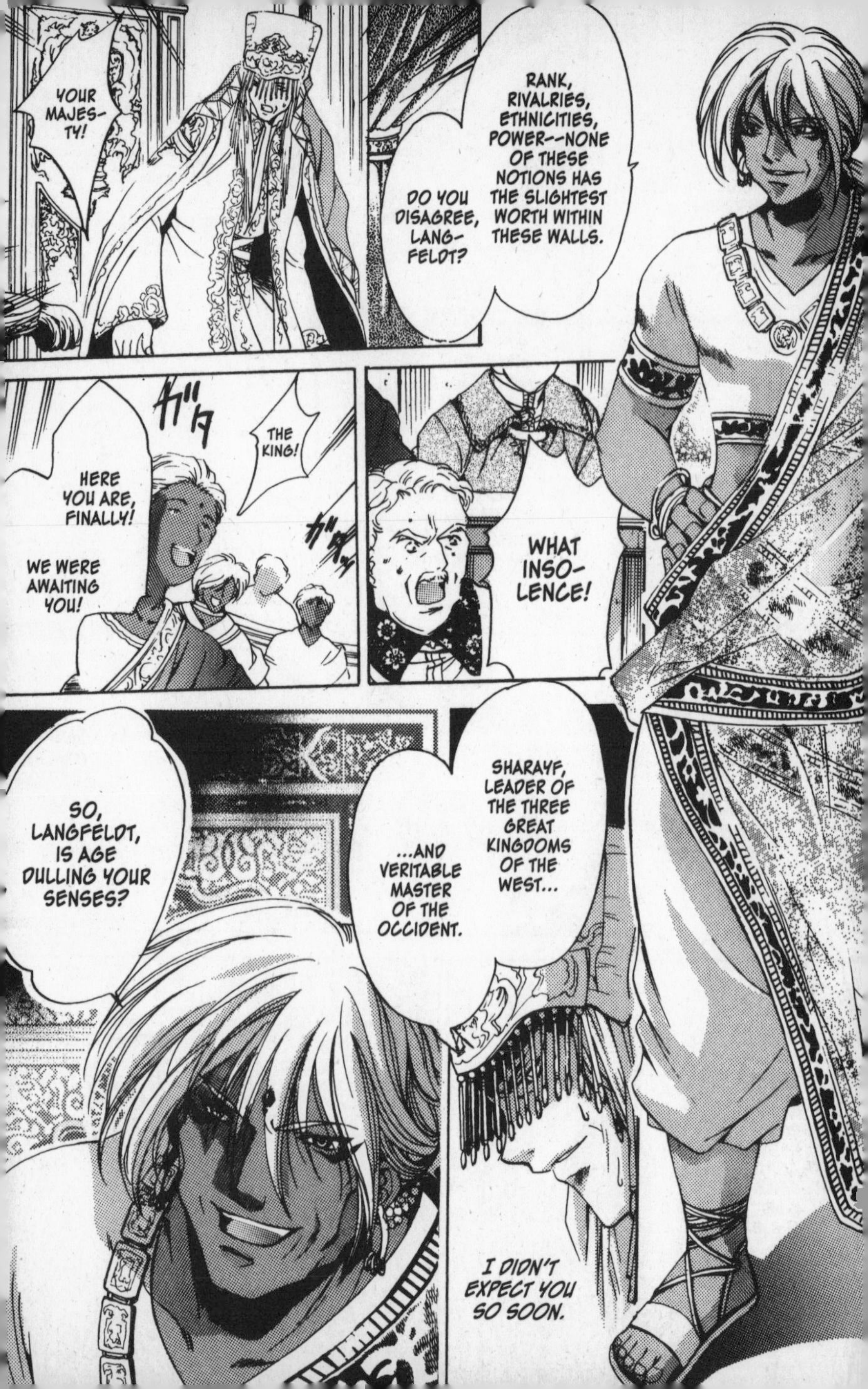
RANK, RIVALRIES, ETHNICITIES, POWER--NONE OF THESE NOTIONS HAS THE SLIGHTEST WORTH WITHIN THESE WALLS.
DO YOU DISAGREE, LANGFELDT?
YOUR MAJESTY!
WHAT INSOLENCE!
THE KING!
HERE YOU ARE, FINALLY!
WE WERE AWAITING YOU!
SHARAYF, LEADER OF THE THREE GREAT KINGDOMS OF THE WEST...
...AND VERITABLE MASTER OF THE OCCIDENT.
I DIDN'T EXPECT YOU SO SOON.
SO, LANGFELDT, IS AGE DULLING YOUR SENSES?

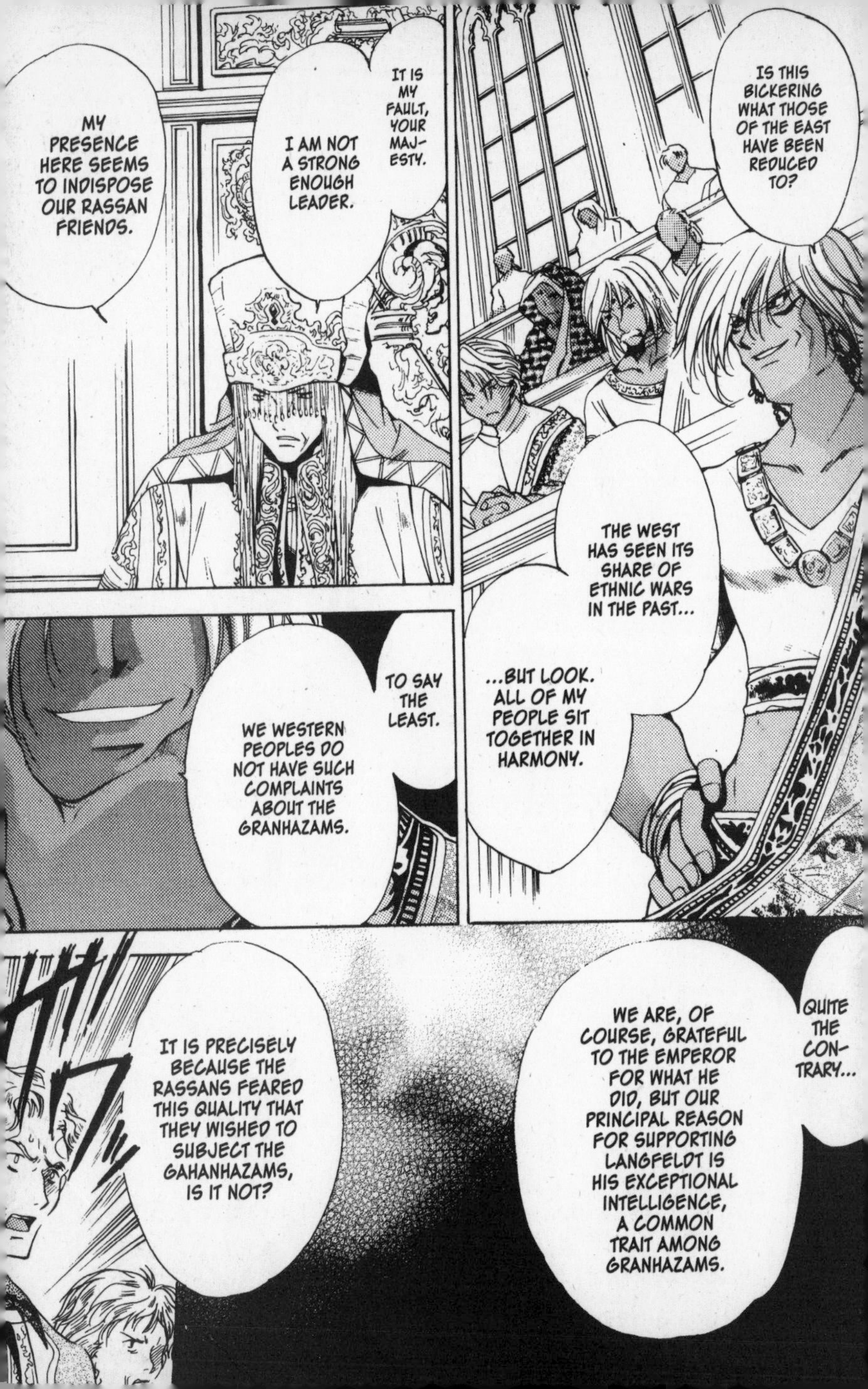
IS THIS BICKERING WHAT THOSE OF THE EAST HAVE BEEN REDUCED TO?
THE WEST HAS SEEN ITS SHARE OF ETHNIC WARS IN THE PAST...
...BUT LOOK. ALL OF MY PEOPLE SIT TOGETHER IN HARMONY.
IT IS MY FAULT, YOUR MAJESTY.
I AM NOT A STRONG ENOUGH LEADER.
MY PRESENCE HERE SEEMS TO INDISPOSE OUR RASSAN FRIENDS.
TO SAY THE LEAST.
WE WESTERN PEOPLES DO NOT HAVE SUCH COMPLAINTS ABOUT THE GRANHAZAMS.
QUITE THE CON-TRARY...
WE ARE, OF COURSE, GRATEFUL TO THE EMPEROR FOR WHAT HE DID, BUT OUR PRINCIPAL REASON FOR SUPPORTING LANGFELDT IS HIS EXCEPTIONAL INTELLIGENCE, A COMMON TRAIT AMONG GRANHAZAMS.
IT IS PRECISELY BECAUSE THE RASSANS FEARED THIS QUALITY THAT THEY WISHED TO SUBJECT THE GAHANHAZAMS, IS IT NOT?

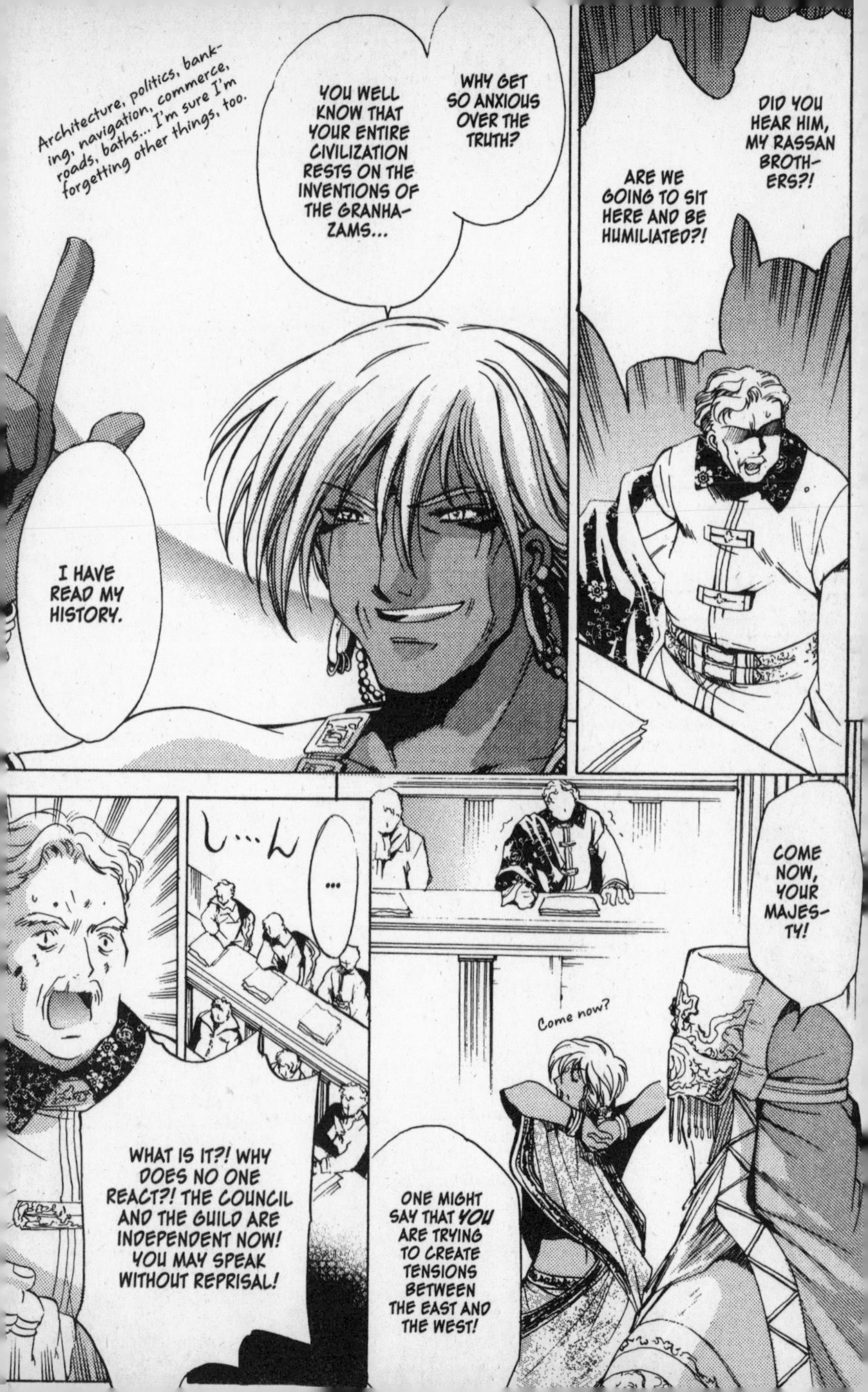
DID YOU HEAR HIM, MY RASSAN BROTHERS?!
ARE WE GOING TO SIT HERE AND BE HUMILIATED?!
WHY GET SO ANXIOUS OVER THE TRUTH?
YOU WELL KNOW THAT YOUR ENTIRE CIVILIZATION RESTS ON THE INVENTIONS OF THE GRANHA-ZAMS...
Architecture, politics, banking, navigation, commerce, roads, baths... I'm sure I'm forgetting other things, too.
I HAVE READ MY HISTORY.
COME NOW, YOUR MAJESTY!
Come now?
ONE MIGHT SAY THAT *YOU* ARE TRYING TO CREATE TENSIONS BETWEEN THE EAST AND THE WEST!
し…ん
...
WHAT IS IT?! WHY DOES NO ONE REACT?! THE COUNCIL AND THE GUILD ARE INDEPENDENT NOW! YOU MAY SPEAK WITHOUT REPRISAL!

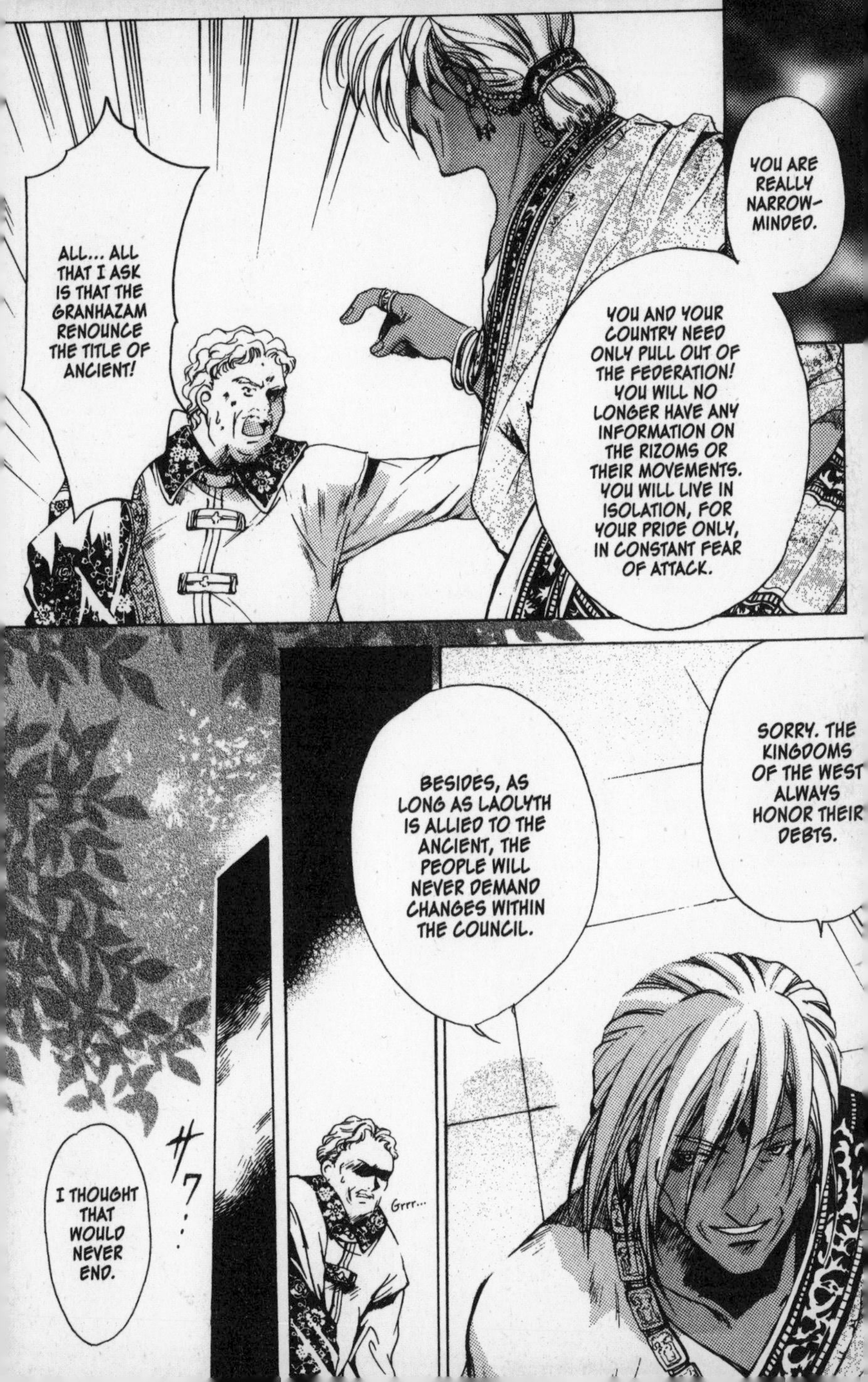

YOU ARE REALLY NARROW-MINDED.
ALL... ALL THAT I ASK IS THAT THE GRANHAZAM RENOUNCE THE TITLE OF ANCIENT!
YOU AND YOUR COUNTRY NEED ONLY PULL OUT OF THE FEDERATION! YOU WILL NO LONGER HAVE ANY INFORMATION ON THE RIZOMS OR THEIR MOVEMENTS. YOU WILL LIVE IN ISOLATION, FOR YOUR PRIDE ONLY, IN CONSTANT FEAR OF ATTACK.
SORRY. THE KINGDOMS OF THE WEST ALWAYS HONOR THEIR DEBTS.
BESIDES, AS LONG AS LAOLYTH IS ALLIED TO THE ANCIENT, THE PEOPLE WILL NEVER DEMAND CHANGES WITHIN THE COUNCIL.
Grrr...
I THOUGHT THAT WOULD NEVER END.

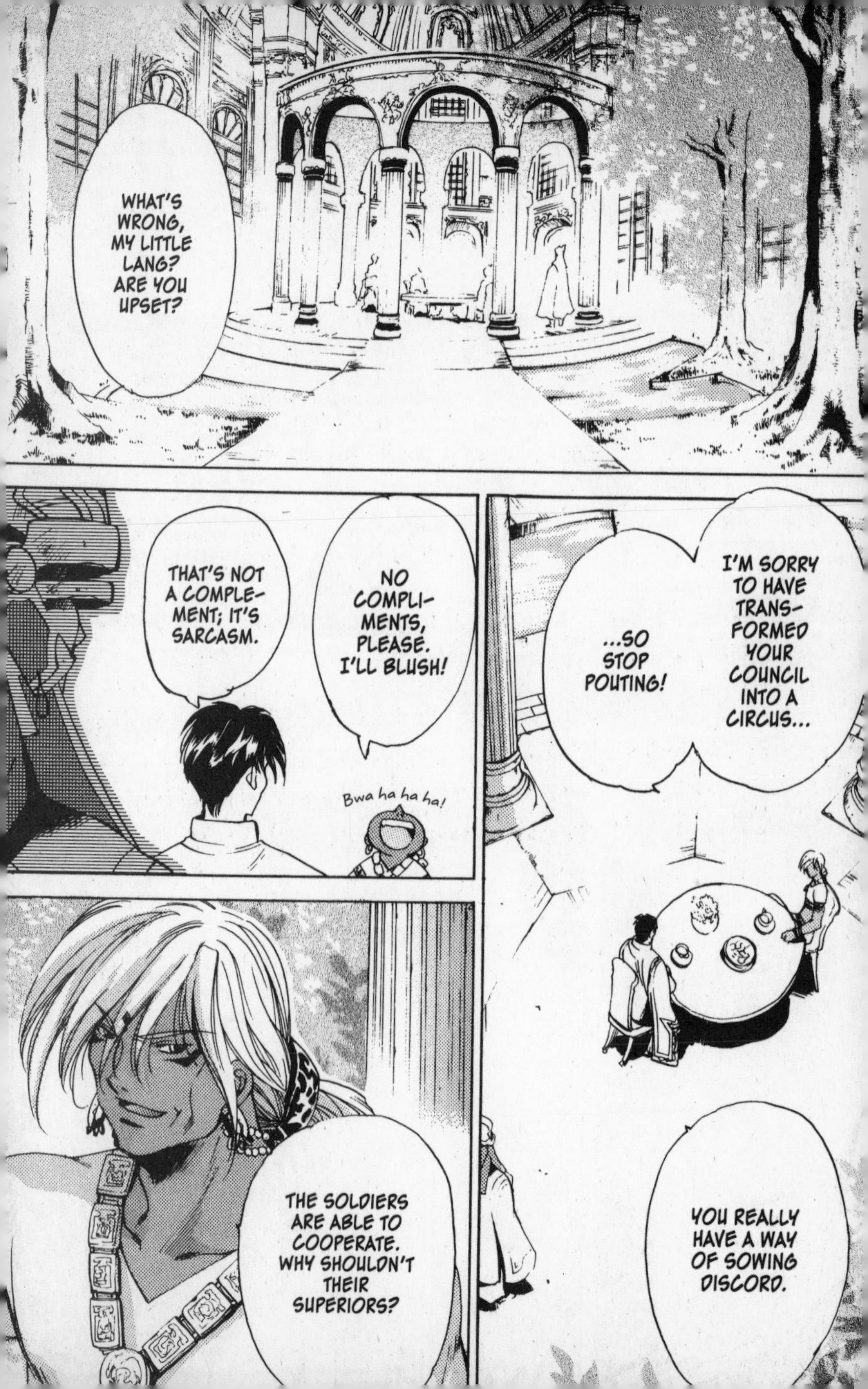
WHAT'S WRONG, MY LITTLE LANG? ARE YOU UPSET?
I'M SORRY TO HAVE TRANS-FORMED YOUR COUNCIL INTO A CIRCUS...
...SO STOP POUTING!
YOU REALLY HAVE A WAY OF SOWING DISCORD.
NO COMPLI-MENTS, PLEASE. I'LL BLUSH!
THAT'S NOT A COMPLE-MENT; IT'S SARCASM.
Bwa ha ha ha!
THE SOLDIERS ARE ABLE TO COOPERATE. WHY SHOULDN'T THEIR SUPERIORS?

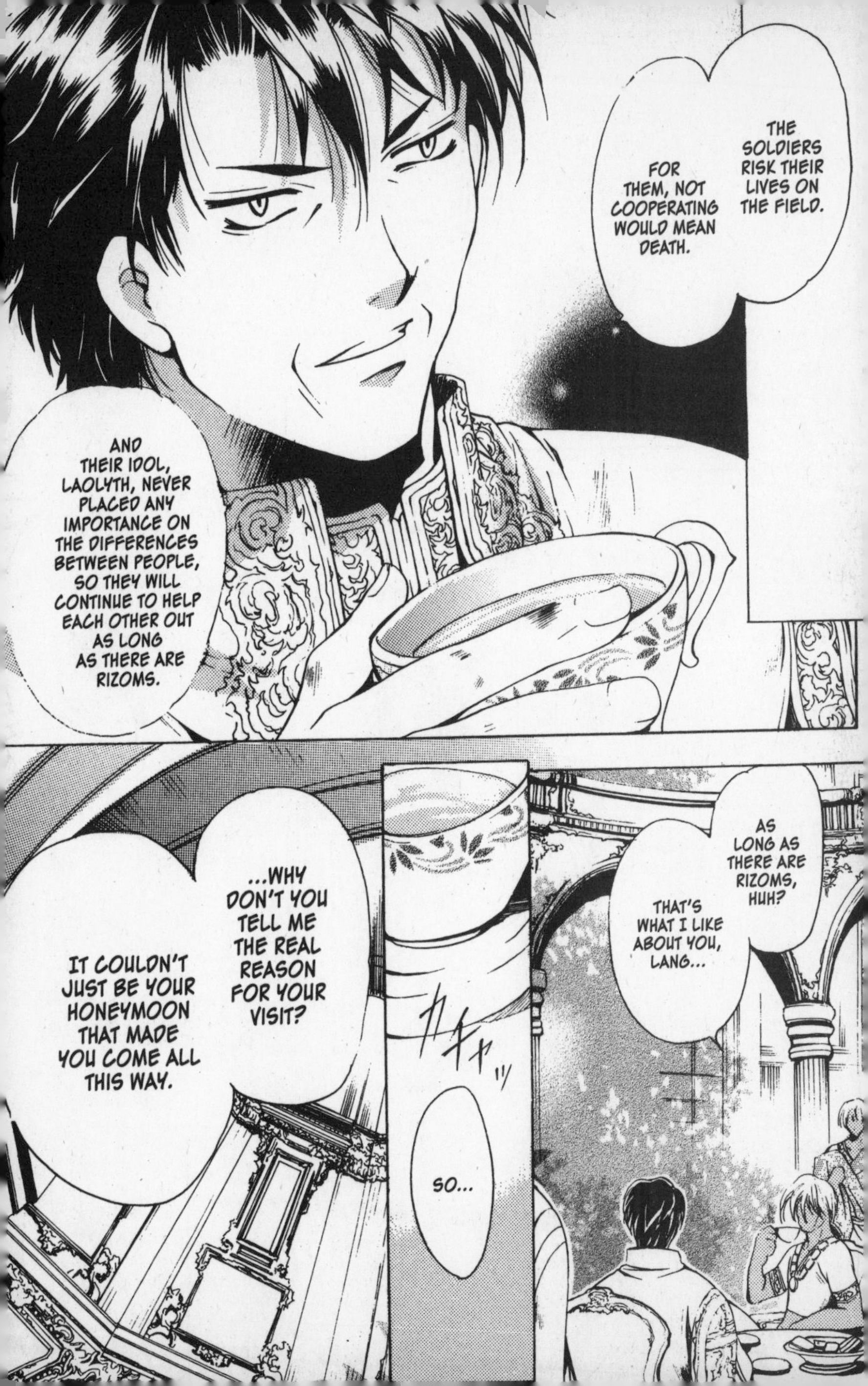
THE SOLDIERS RISK THEIR LIVES ON THE FIELD.
FOR THEM, NOT COOPERATING WOULD MEAN DEATH.
AND THEIR IDOL, LAOLYTH, NEVER PLACED ANY IMPORTANCE ON THE DIFFERENCES BETWEEN PEOPLE, SO THEY WILL CONTINUE TO HELP EACH OTHER OUT AS LONG AS THERE ARE RIZOMS.
AS LONG AS THERE ARE RIZOMS, HUH?
THAT'S WHAT I LIKE ABOUT YOU, LANG...
カチャッ
SO...
...WHY DON'T YOU TELL ME THE REAL REASON FOR YOUR VISIT?
IT COULDN'T JUST BE YOUR HONEYMOON THAT MADE YOU COME ALL THIS WAY.

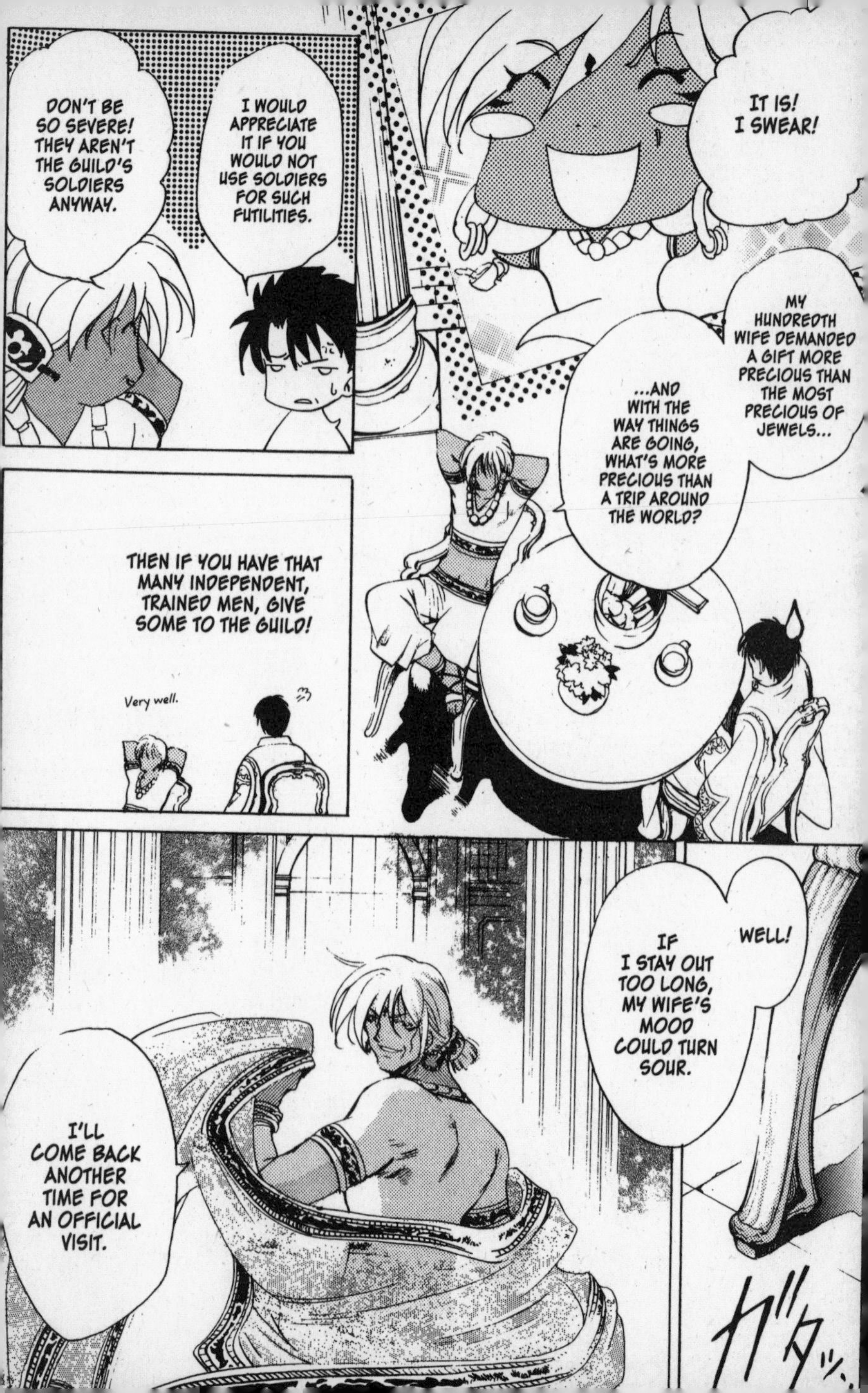
IT IS! I SWEAR!
MY HUNDREDTH WIFE DEMANDED A GIFT MORE PRECIOUS THAN THE MOST PRECIOUS OF JEWELS...
...AND WITH THE WAY THINGS ARE GOING, WHAT'S MORE PRECIOUS THAN A TRIP AROUND THE WORLD?
I WOULD APPRECIATE IT IF YOU WOULD NOT USE SOLDIERS FOR SUCH FUTILITIES.
DON'T BE SO SEVERE! THEY AREN'T THE GUILD'S SOLDIERS ANYWAY.
THEN IF YOU HAVE THAT MANY INDEPENDENT, TRAINED MEN, GIVE SOME TO THE GUILD!
Very well.
ガタッ
WELL!
IF I STAY OUT TOO LONG, MY WIFE'S MOOD COULD TURN SOUR.
I'LL COME BACK ANOTHER TIME FOR AN OFFICIAL VISIT.

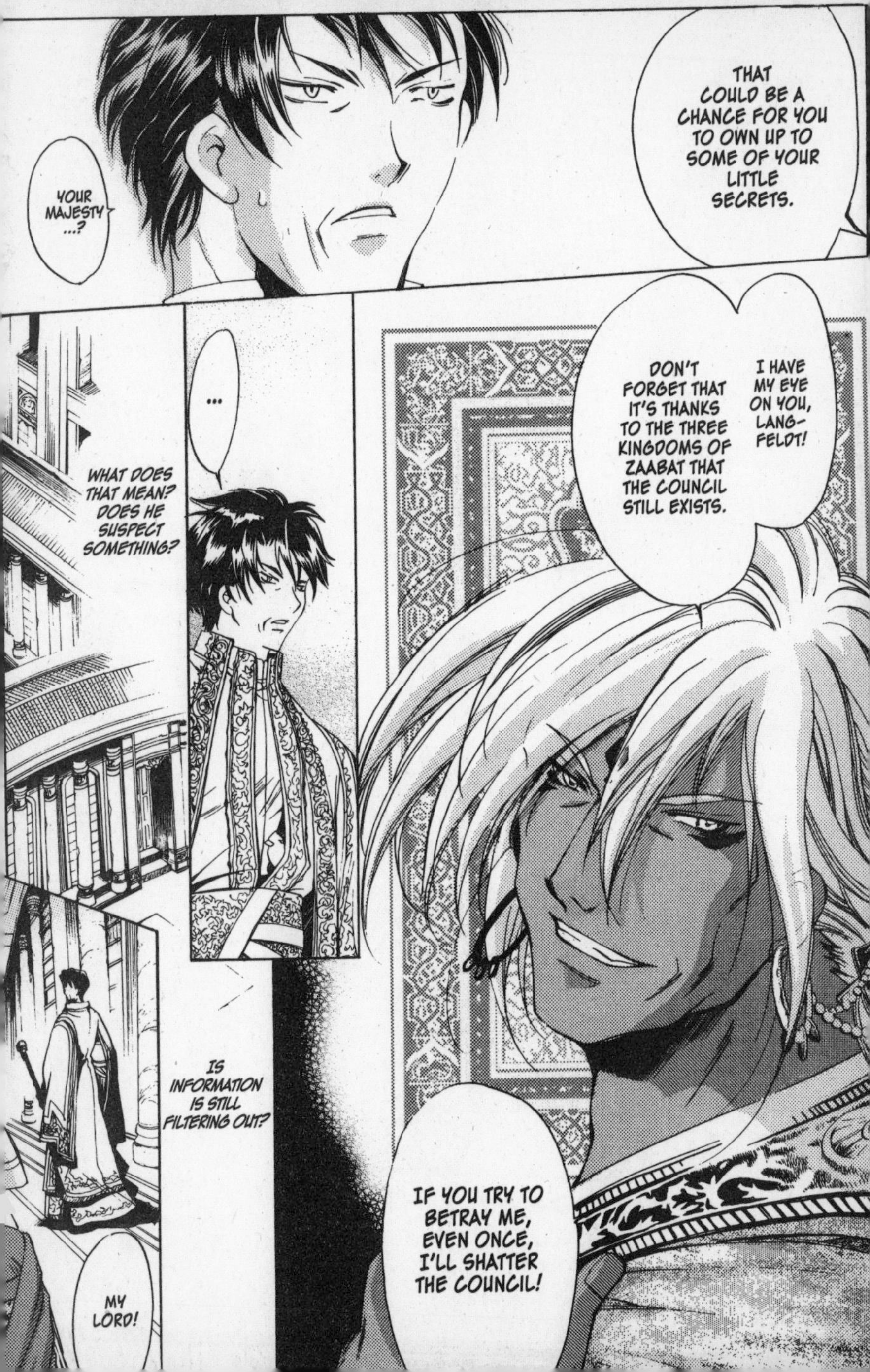
THAT COULD BE A CHANCE FOR YOU TO OWN UP TO SOME OF YOUR LITTLE SECRETS.
YOUR MAJESTY ...?
I HAVE MY EYE ON YOU, LANG-FELDT!
DON'T FORGET THAT IT'S THANKS TO THE THREE KINGDOMS OF ZAABAT THAT THE COUNCIL STILL EXISTS.
IF YOU TRY TO BETRAY ME, EVEN ONCE, I'LL SHATTER THE COUNCIL!
...
WHAT DOES THAT MEAN? DOES HE SUSPECT SOMETHING?
IS INFORMATION IS STILL FILTERING OUT?
MY LORD!

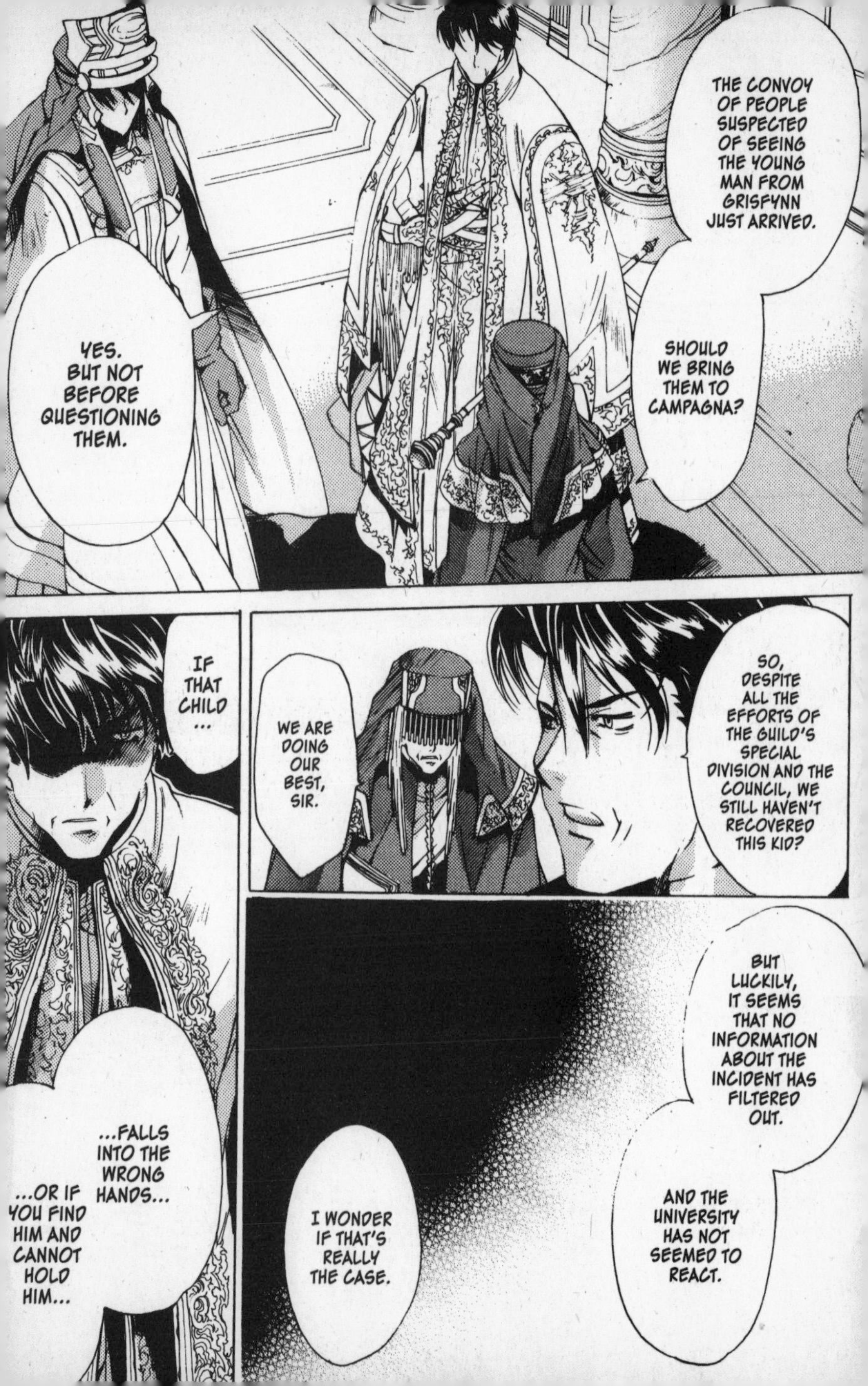
THE CONVOY OF PEOPLE SUSPECTED OF SEEING THE YOUNG MAN FROM GRISFYNN JUST ARRIVED.
SHOULD WE BRING THEM TO CAMPAGNA?
YES. BUT NOT BEFORE QUESTIONING THEM.
SO, DESPITE ALL THE EFFORTS OF THE GUILD'S SPECIAL DIVISION AND THE COUNCIL, WE STILL HAVEN'T RECOVERED THIS KID?
WE ARE DOING OUR BEST, SIR.
BUT LUCKILY, IT SEEMS THAT NO INFORMATION ABOUT THE INCIDENT HAS FILTERED OUT.
AND THE UNIVERSITY HAS NOT SEEMED TO REACT.
I WONDER IF THAT'S REALLY THE CASE.
IF THAT CHILD ...
...FALLS INTO THE WRONG HANDS...
...OR IF YOU FIND HIM AND CANNOT HOLD HIM...

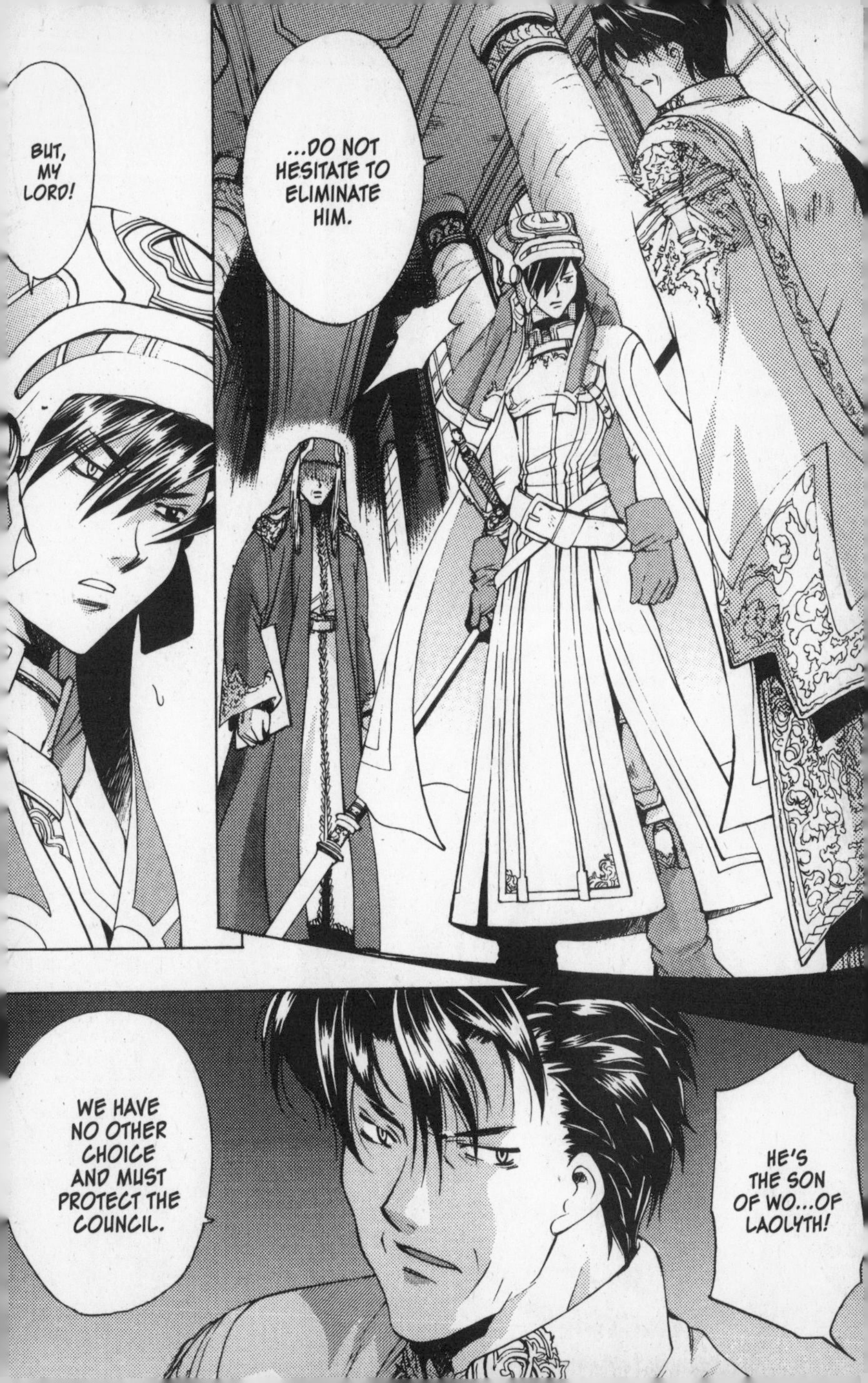
...DO NOT HESITATE TO ELIMINATE HIM.
BUT, MY LORD!
HE'S THE SON OF WO...OF LAOLYTH!
WE HAVE NO OTHER CHOICE AND MUST PROTECT THE COUNCIL.

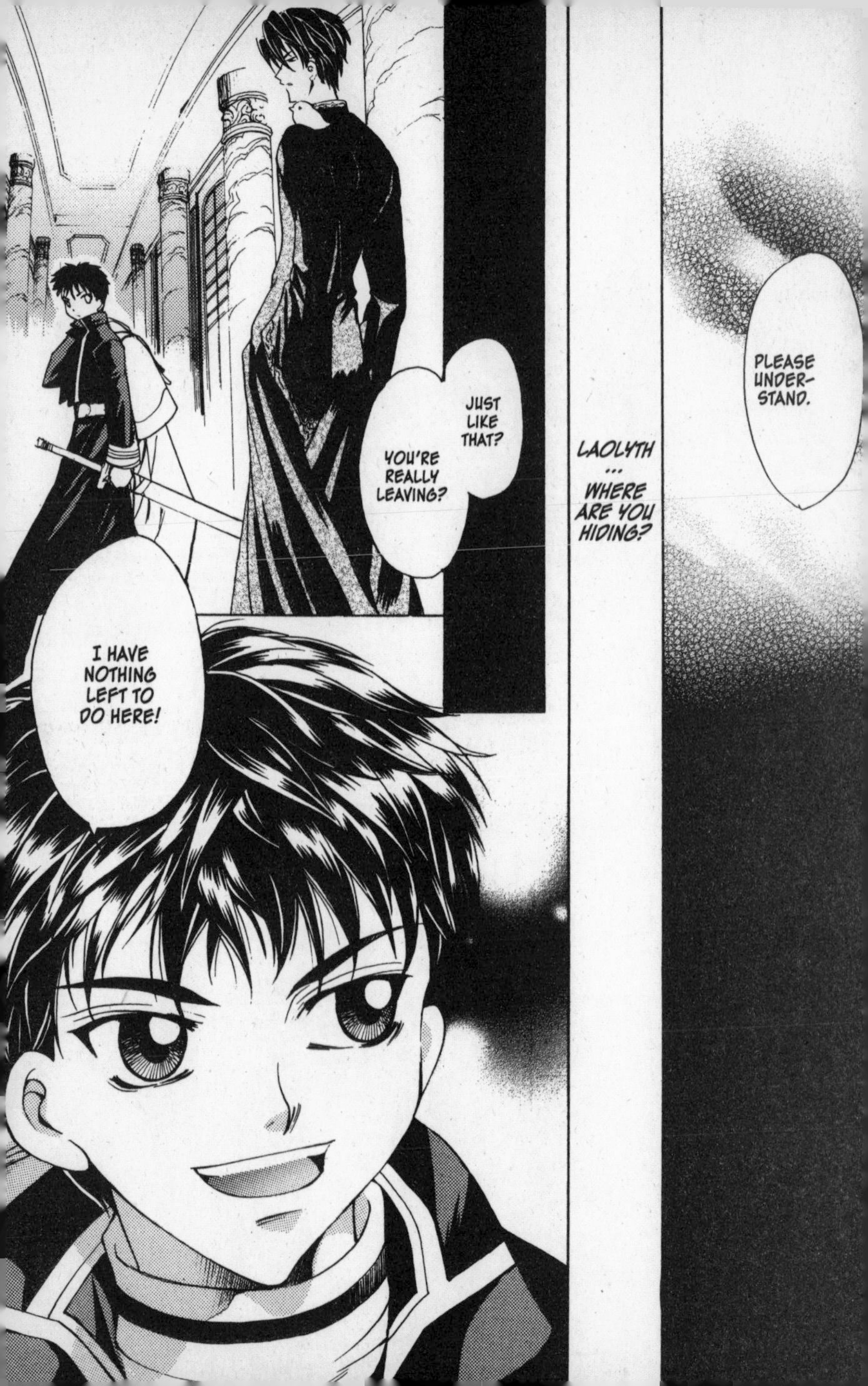
PLEASE UNDER-STAND.
LAOLYTH ... WHERE ARE YOU HIDING?
JUST LIKE THAT?
YOU'RE REALLY LEAVING?
I HAVE NOTHING LEFT TO DO HERE!

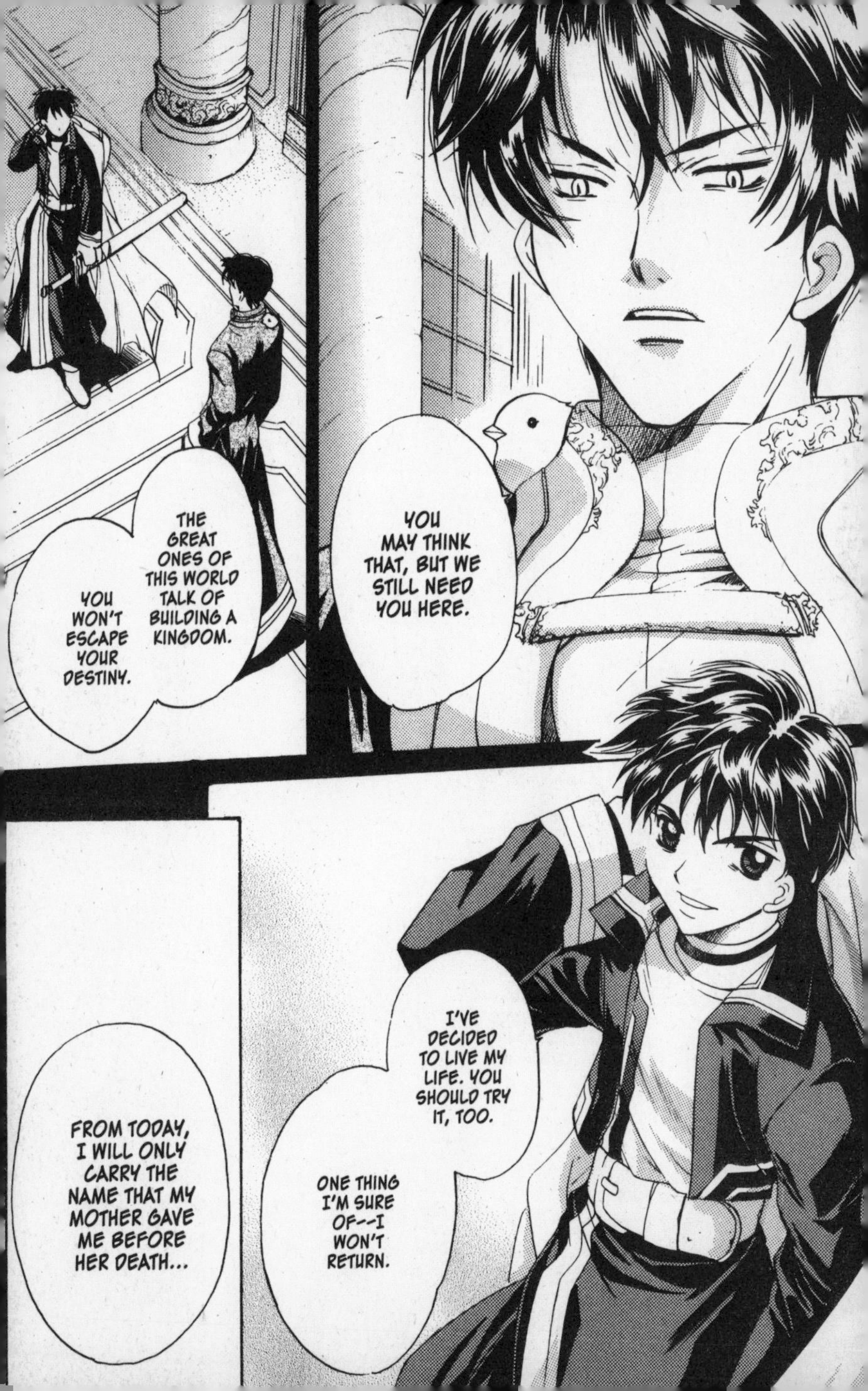
YOU MAY THINK THAT, BUT WE STILL NEED YOU HERE.
THE GREAT ONES OF THIS WORLD TALK OF BUILDING A KINGDOM.
YOU WON'T ESCAPE YOUR DESTINY.
I'VE DECIDED TO LIVE MY LIFE. YOU SHOULD TRY IT, TOO.
ONE THING I'M SURE OF--I WON'T RETURN.
FROM TODAY, I WILL ONLY CARRY THE NAME THAT MY MOTHER GAVE ME BEFORE HER DEATH...

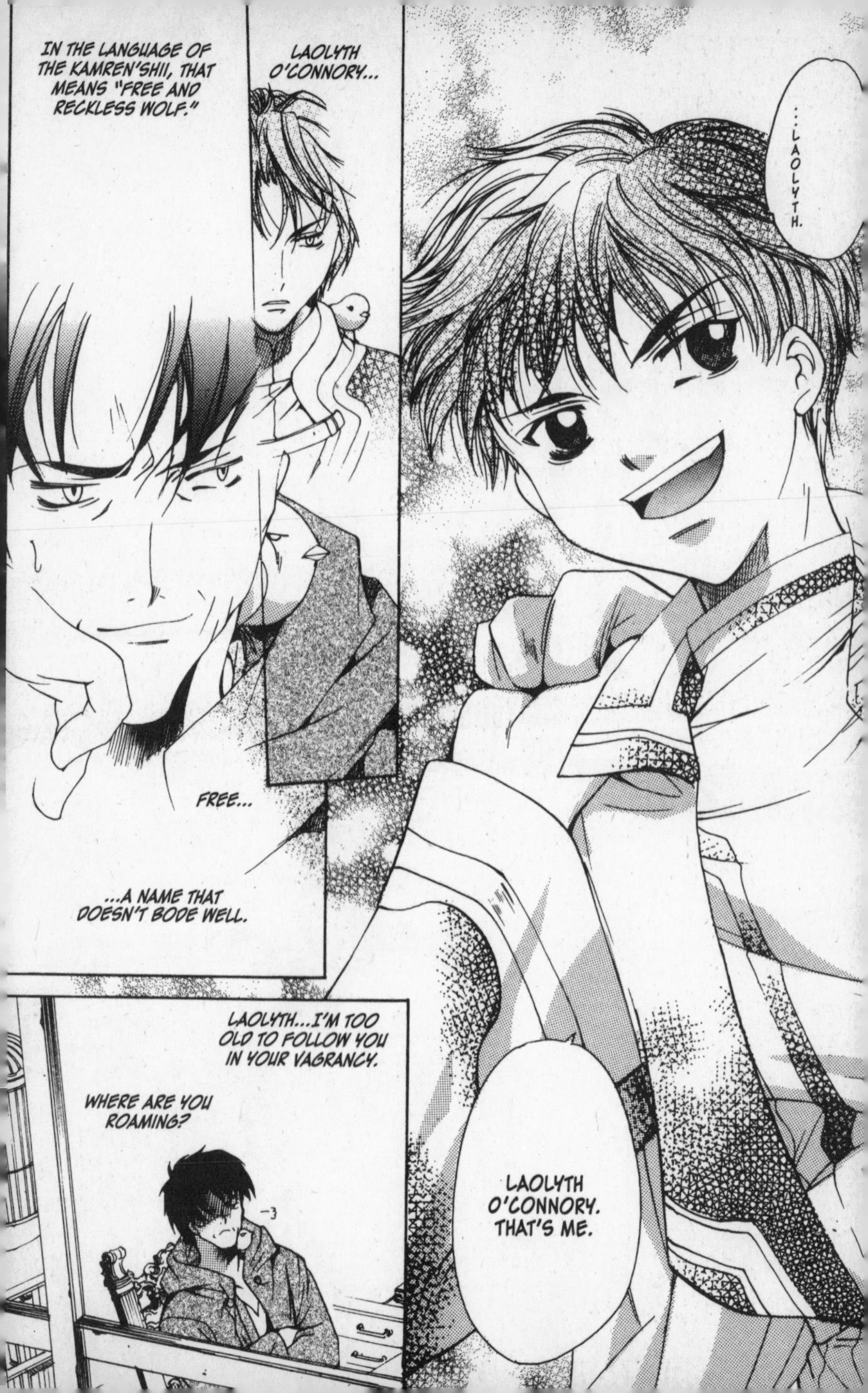
...LAOLYTH.
LAOLYTH O'CONNORY. THAT'S ME.
LAOLYTH O'CONNORY...
IN THE LANGUAGE OF THE KAMREN'SHII, THAT MEANS "FREE AND RECKLESS WOLF."
FREE...
...A NAME THAT DOESN'T BODE WELL.
LAOLYTH...I'M TOO OLD TO FOLLOW YOU IN YOUR VAGRANCY.
WHERE ARE YOU ROAMING?

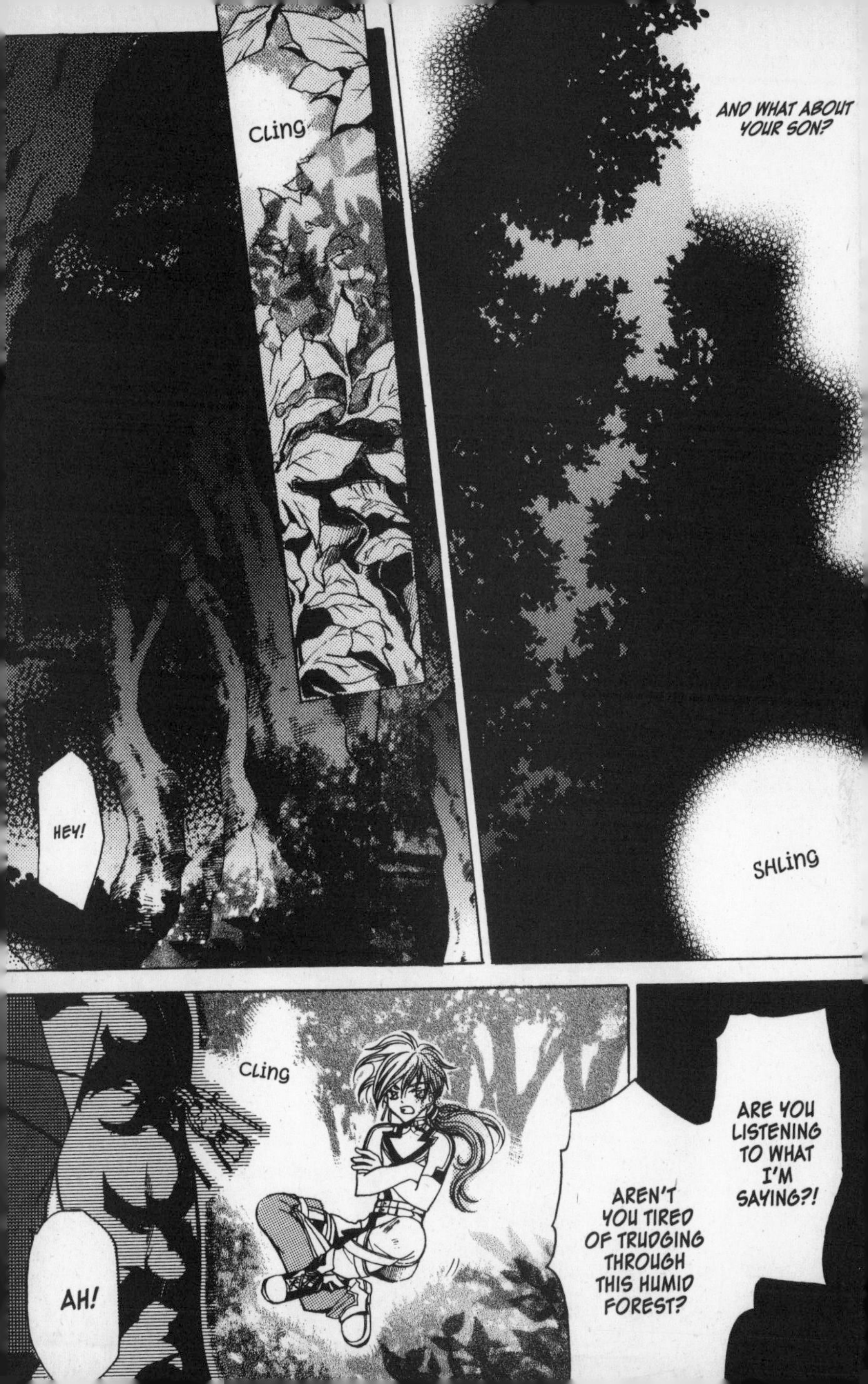
AND WHAT ABOUT YOUR SON?
SHLING
CLING
HEY!
ARE YOU LISTENING TO WHAT I'M SAYING?!
AREN'T YOU TIRED OF TRUDGING THROUGH THIS HUMID FOREST?
CLING
AH!

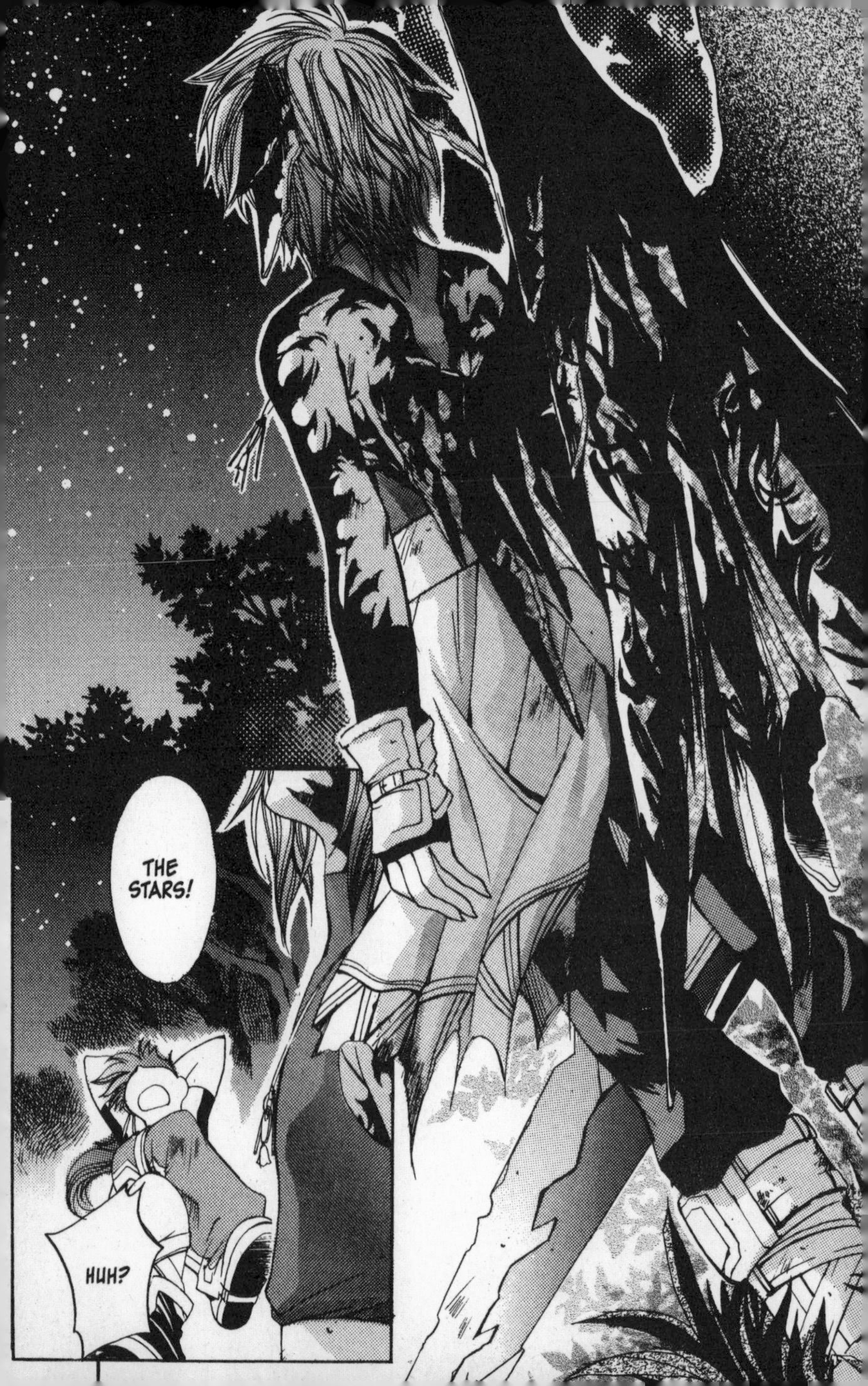
THE STARS!
HUH?

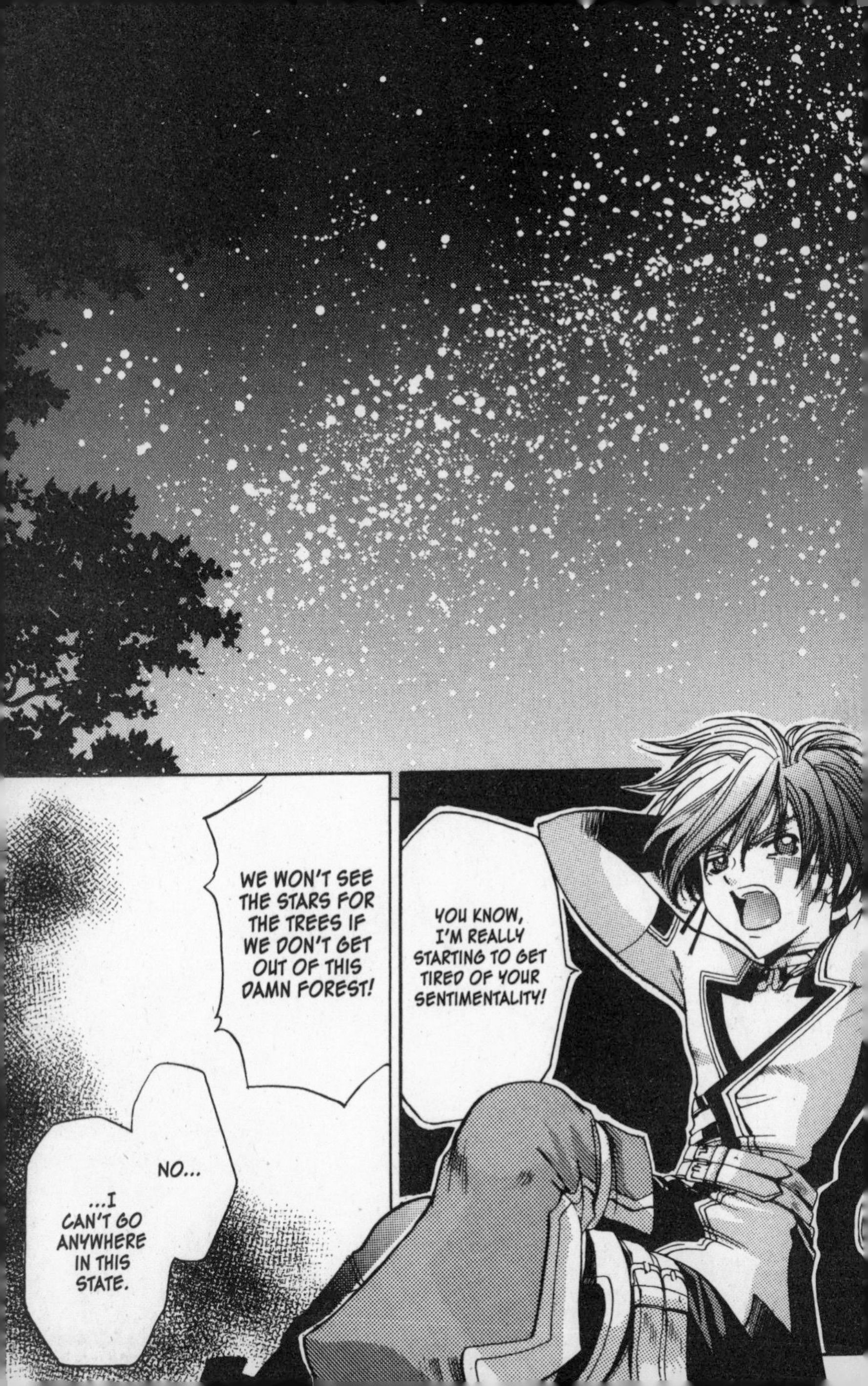
YOU KNOW, I'M REALLY STARTING TO GET TIRED OF YOUR SENTIMENTALITY!
WE WON'T SEE THE STARS FOR THE TREES IF WE DON'T GET OUT OF THIS DAMN FOREST!
NO...
...I CAN'T GO ANYWHERE IN THIS STATE.

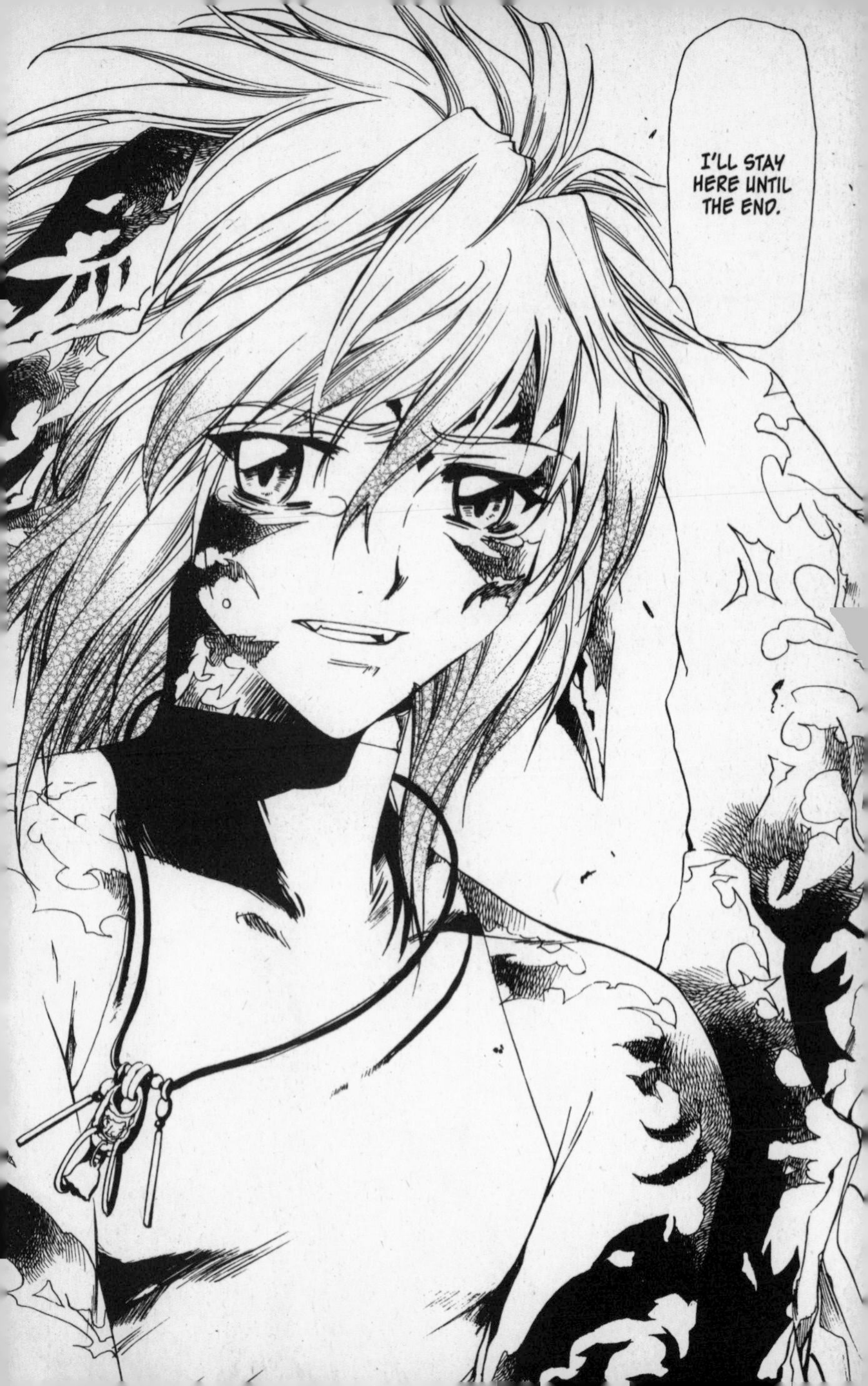
I'LL STAY HERE UNTIL THE END.

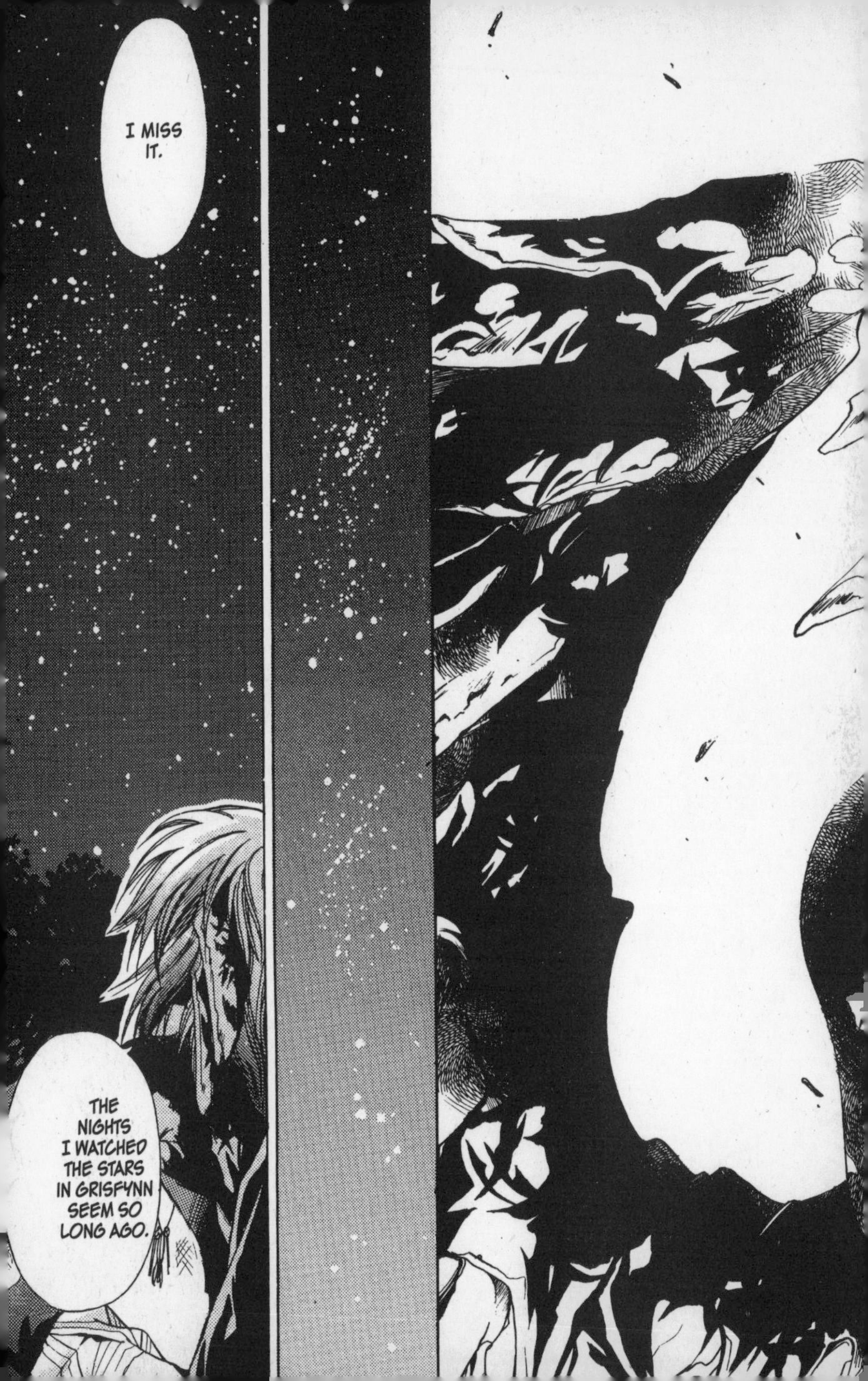
I MISS IT.
THE NIGHTS I WATCHED THE STARS IN GRISFYNN SEEM SO LONG AGO.

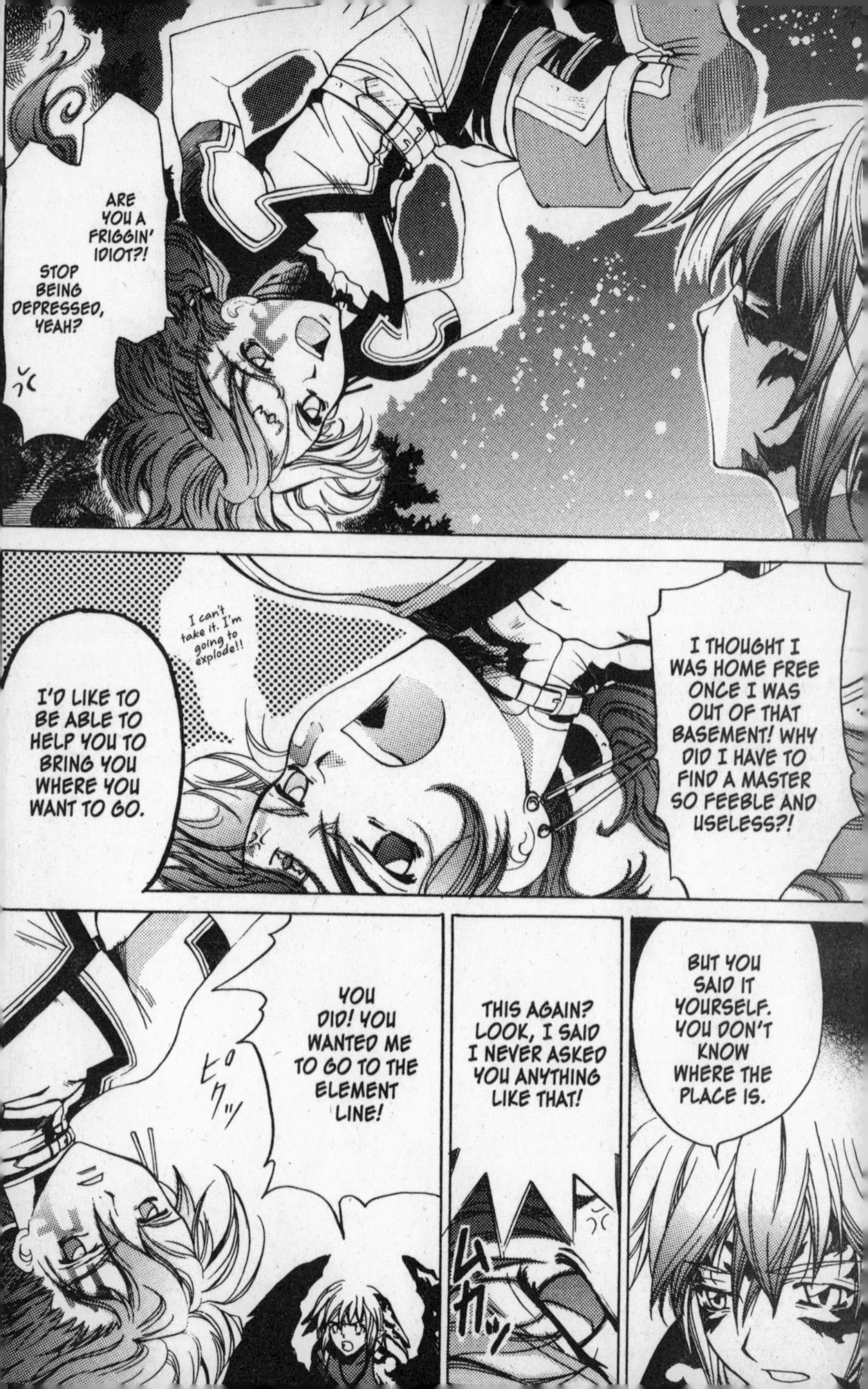
ARE YOU A FRIGGIN' IDIOT?!
STOP BEING DEPRESSED, YEAH?
I THOUGHT I WAS HOME FREE ONCE I WAS OUT OF THAT BASEMENT! WHY DID I HAVE TO FIND A MASTER SO FEEBLE AND USELESS?!
I can't take it. I'm going to explode!!
I'D LIKE TO BE ABLE TO HELP YOU TO BRING YOU WHERE YOU WANT TO GO.
BUT YOU SAID IT YOURSELF. YOU DON'T KNOW WHERE THE PLACE IS.
THIS AGAIN? LOOK, I SAID I NEVER ASKED YOU ANYTHING LIKE THAT!
YOU DID! YOU WANTED ME TO GO TO THE ELEMENT LINE!

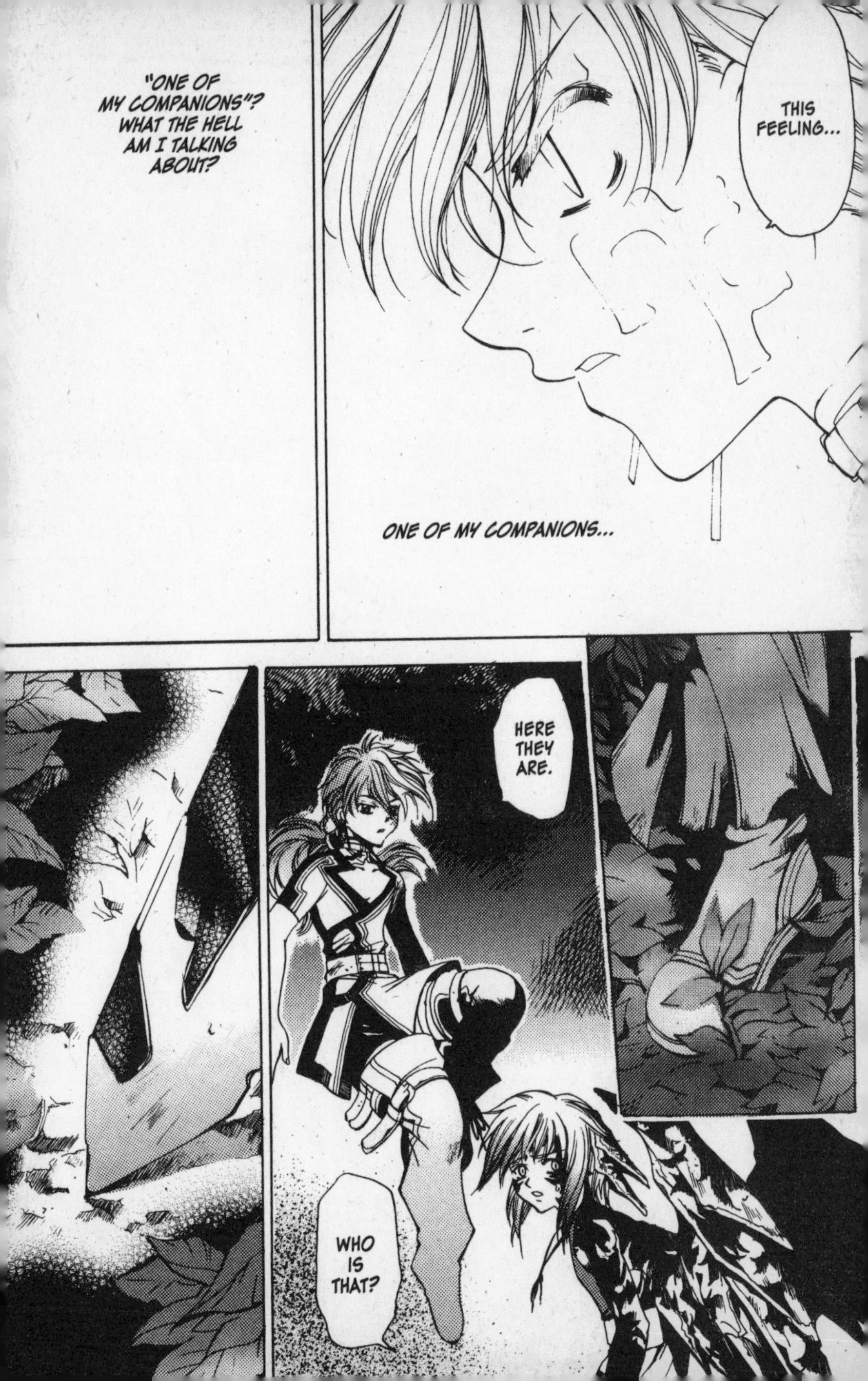
THIS FEELING...
ONE OF MY COMPANIONS...
"ONE OF MY COMPANIONS"? WHAT THE HELL AM I TALKING ABOUT?
HERE THEY ARE.
WHO IS THAT?

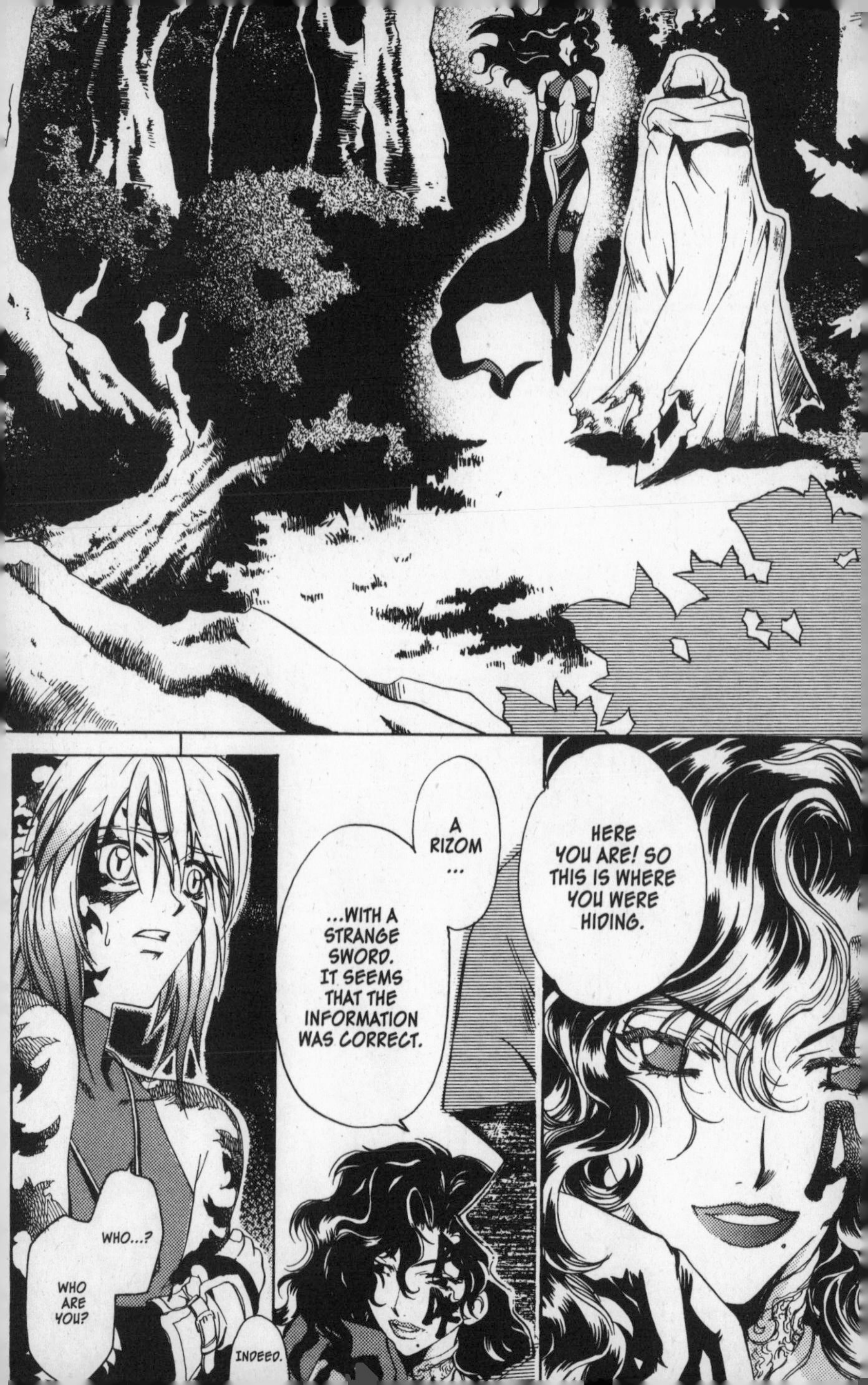
HERE YOU ARE! SO THIS IS WHERE YOU WERE HIDING.
A RIZOM ...
...WITH A STRANGE SWORD. IT SEEMS THAT THE INFORMATION WAS CORRECT.
INDEED.
WHO...?
WHO ARE YOU?

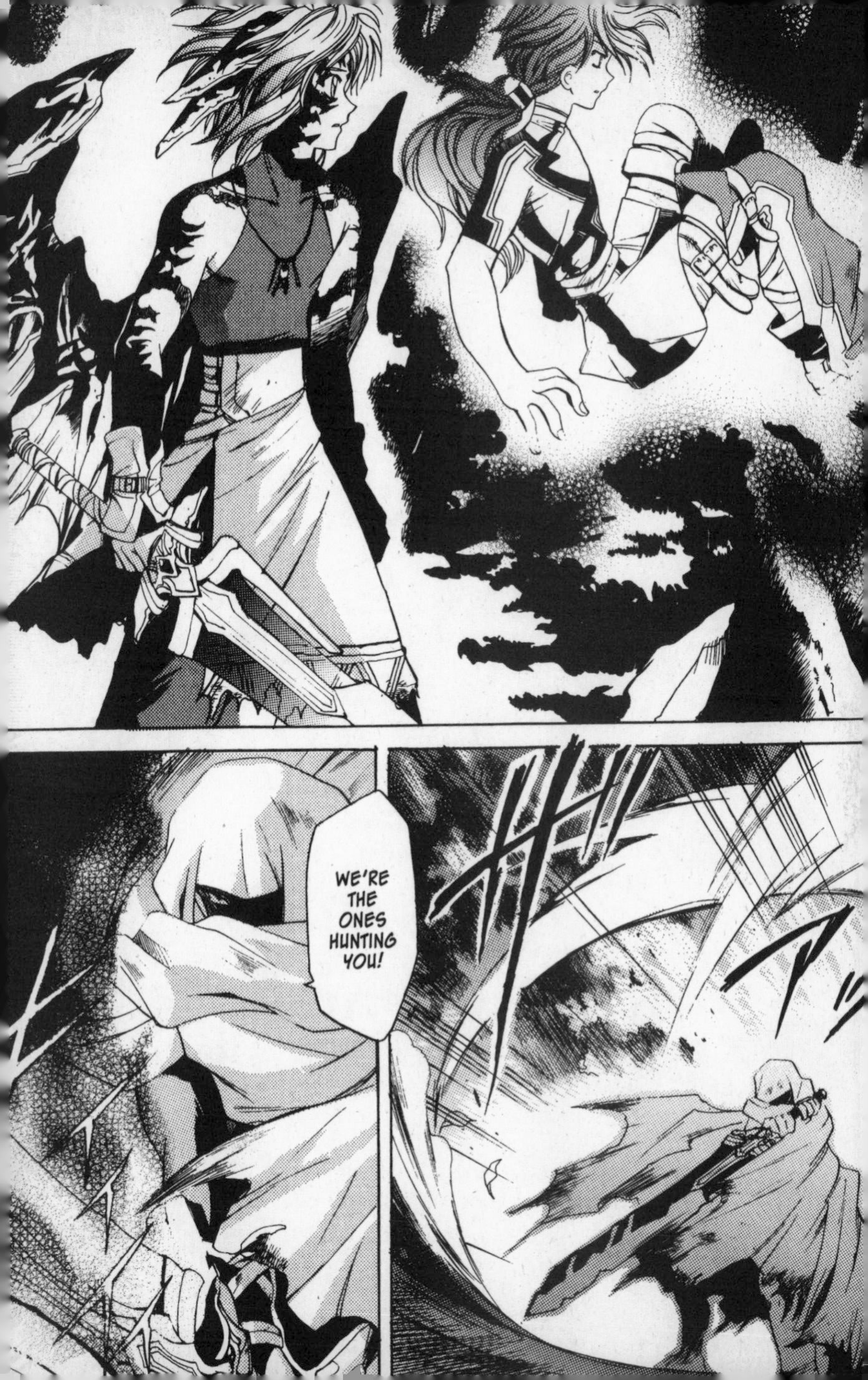
WE'RE THE ONES HUNTING YOU!

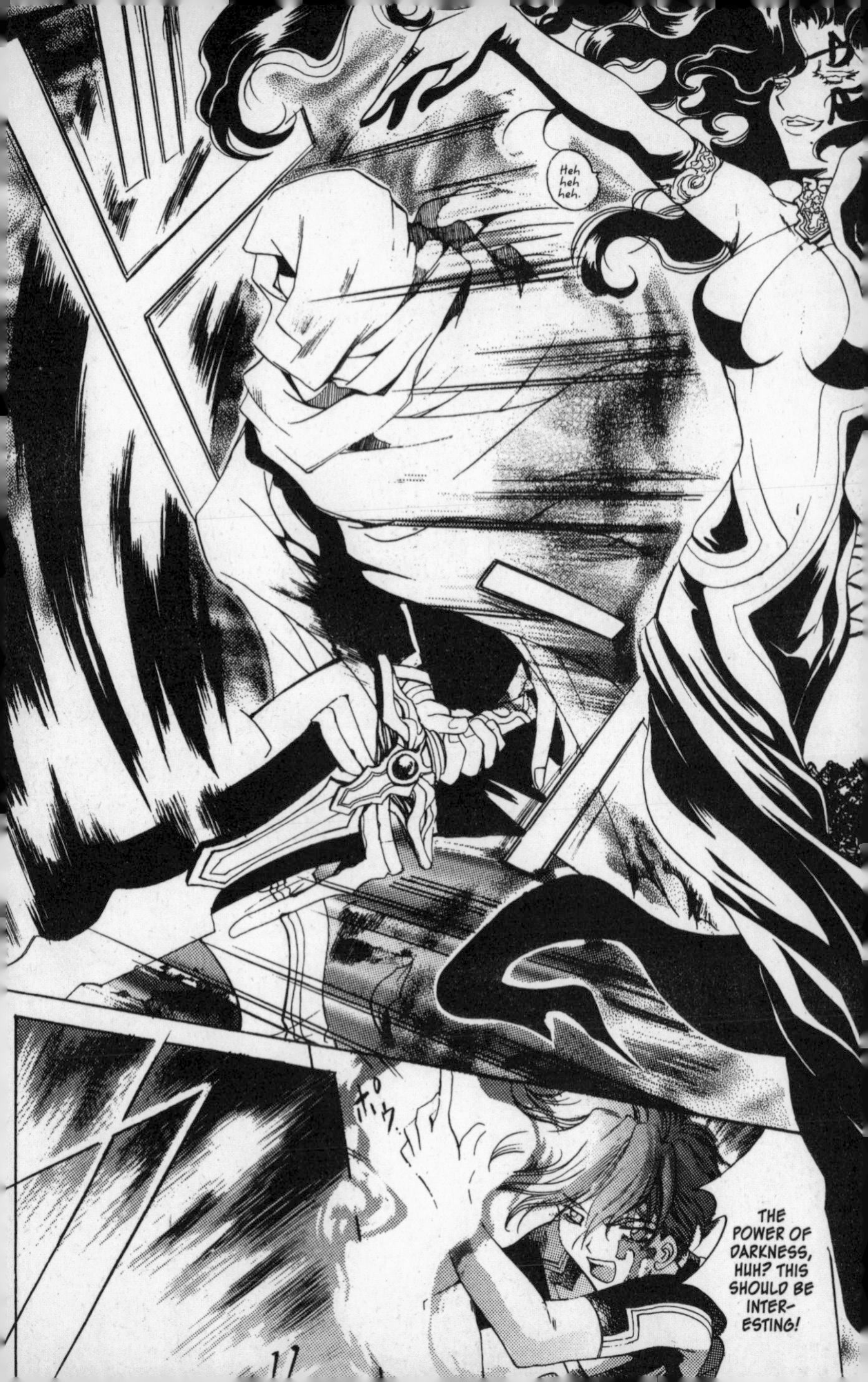
Heh heh heh.
THE POWER OF DARKNESS, HUH? THIS SHOULD BE INTER-ESTING!

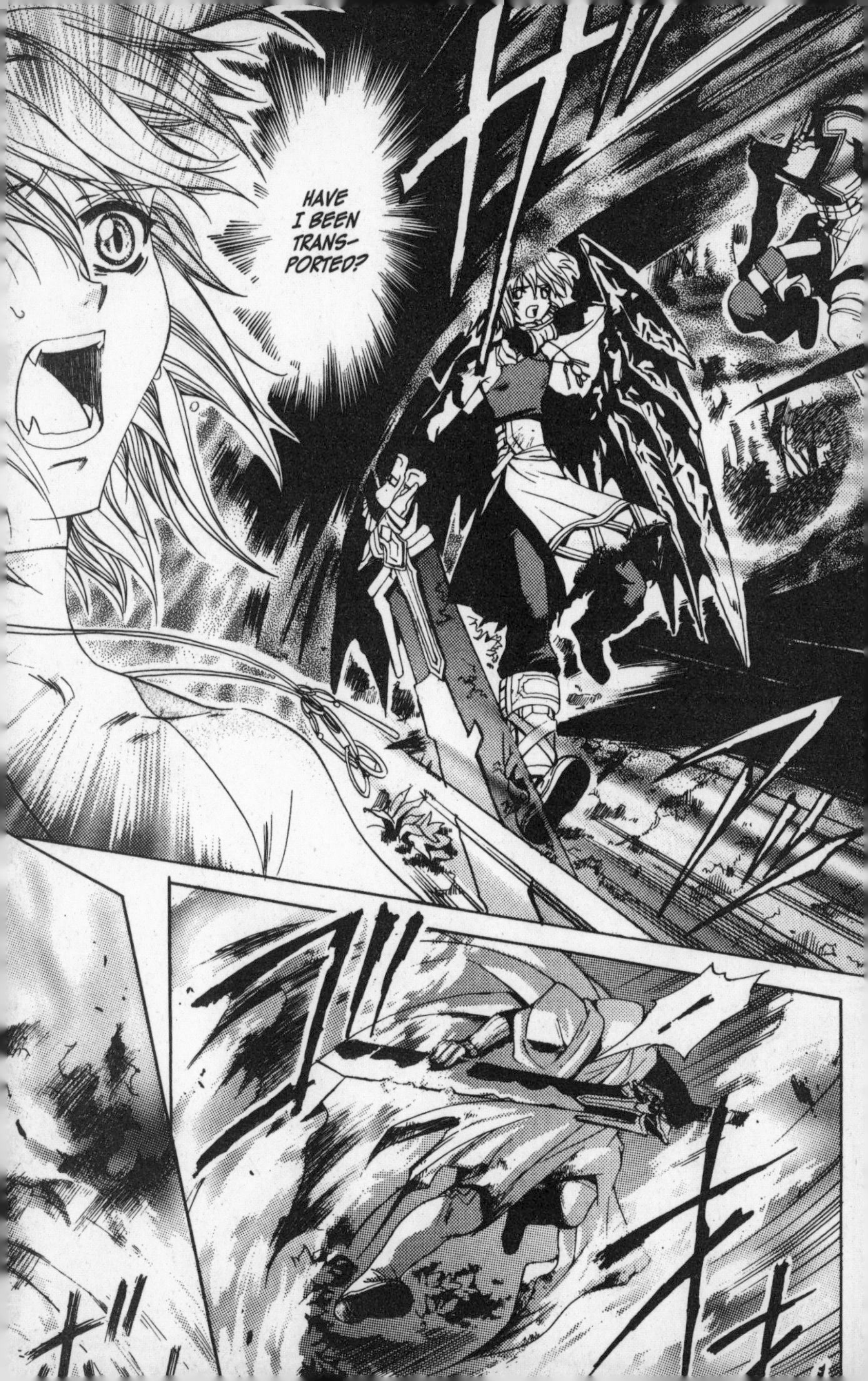
HAVE I BEEN TRANS-PORTED?

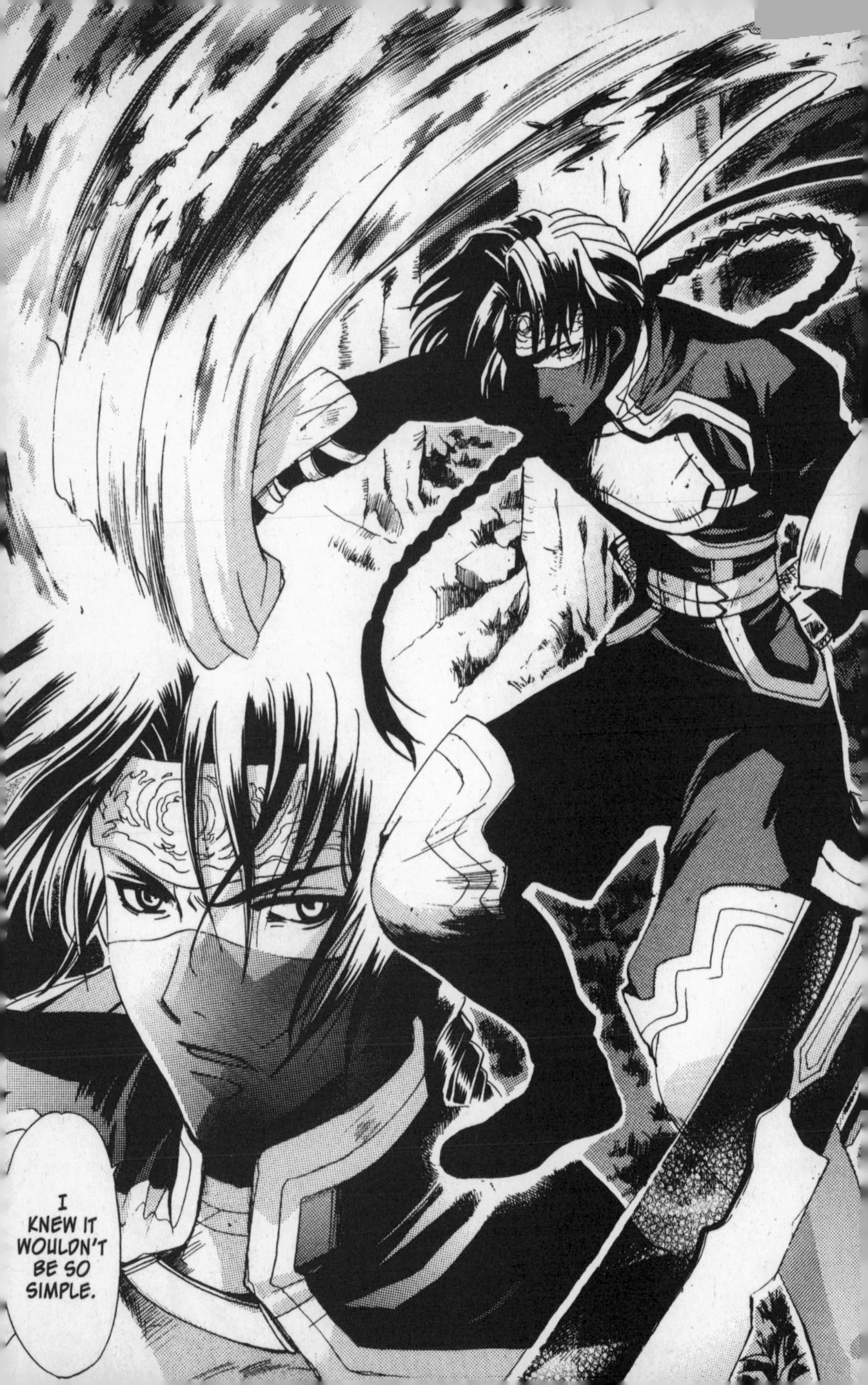
I KNEW IT WOULDN'T BE SO SIMPLE.

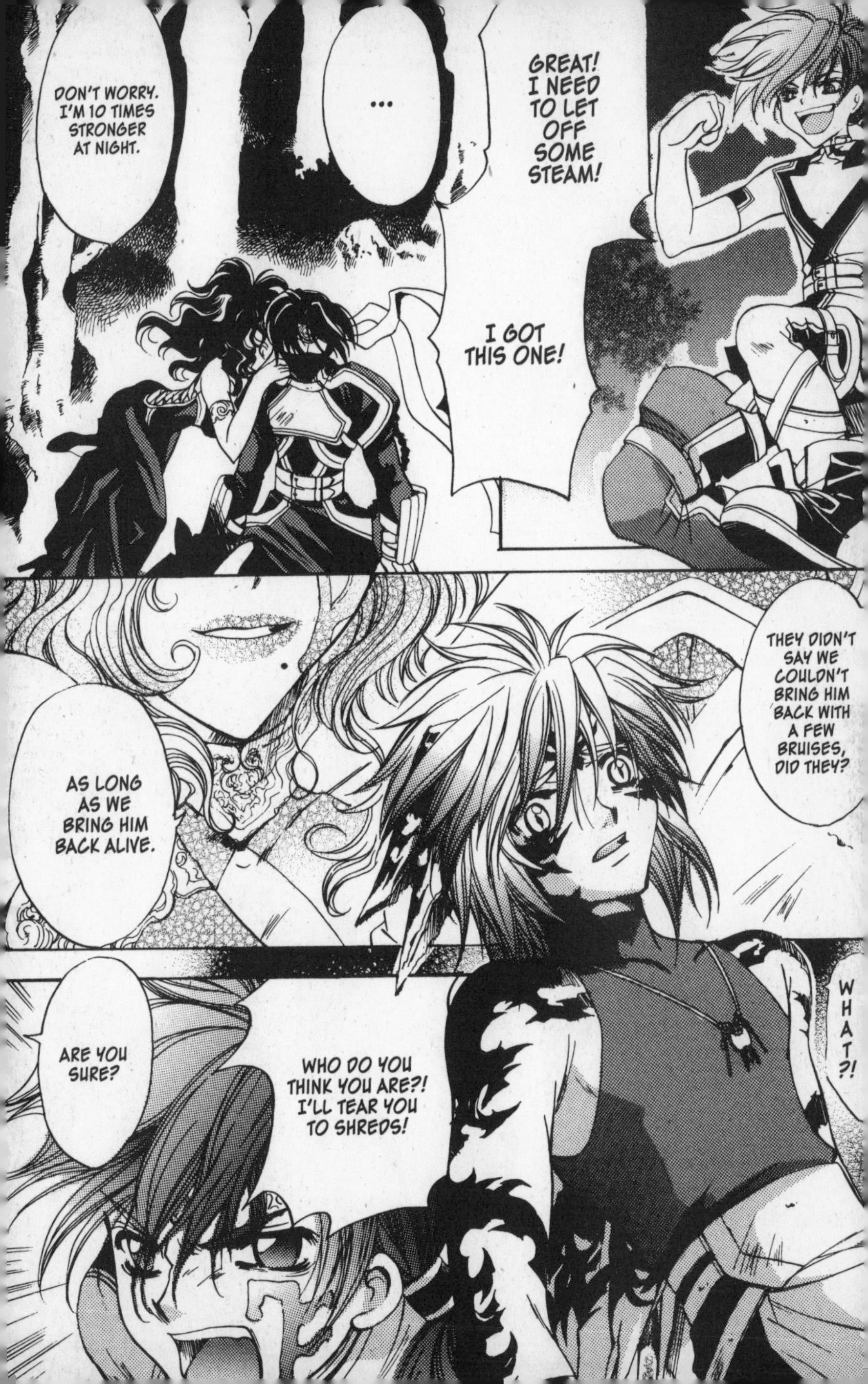
GREAT! I NEED TO LET OFF SOME STEAM!
I GOT THIS ONE!
...
DON'T WORRY. I'M 10 TIMES STRONGER AT NIGHT.
THEY DIDN'T SAY WE COULDN'T BRING HIM BACK WITH A FEW BRUISES, DID THEY?
AS LONG AS WE BRING HIM BACK ALIVE.
WHAT?!
WHO DO YOU THINK YOU ARE?! I'LL TEAR YOU TO SHREDS!
ARE YOU SURE?

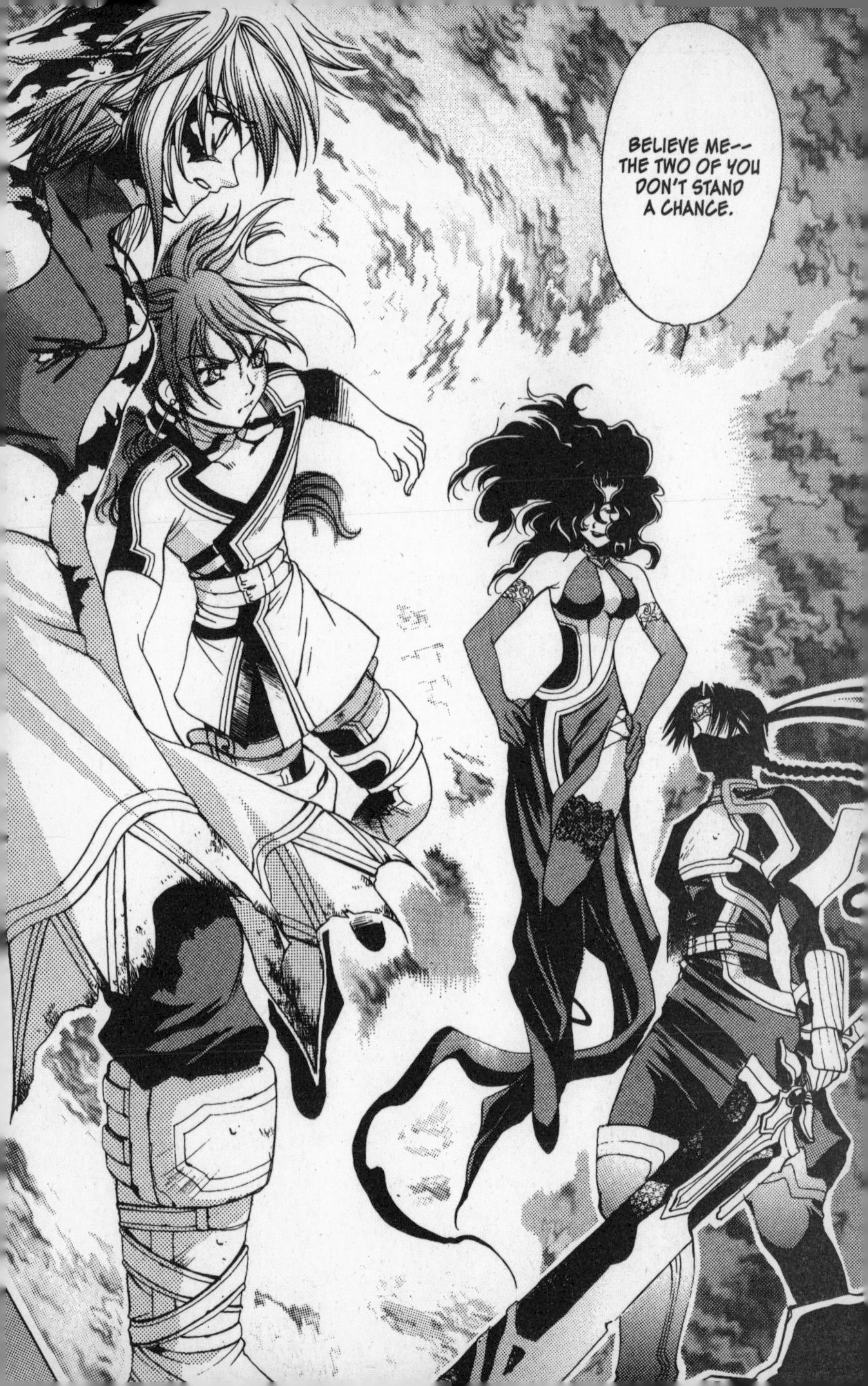
BELIEVE ME-- THE TWO OF YOU DON'T STAND A CHANCE.

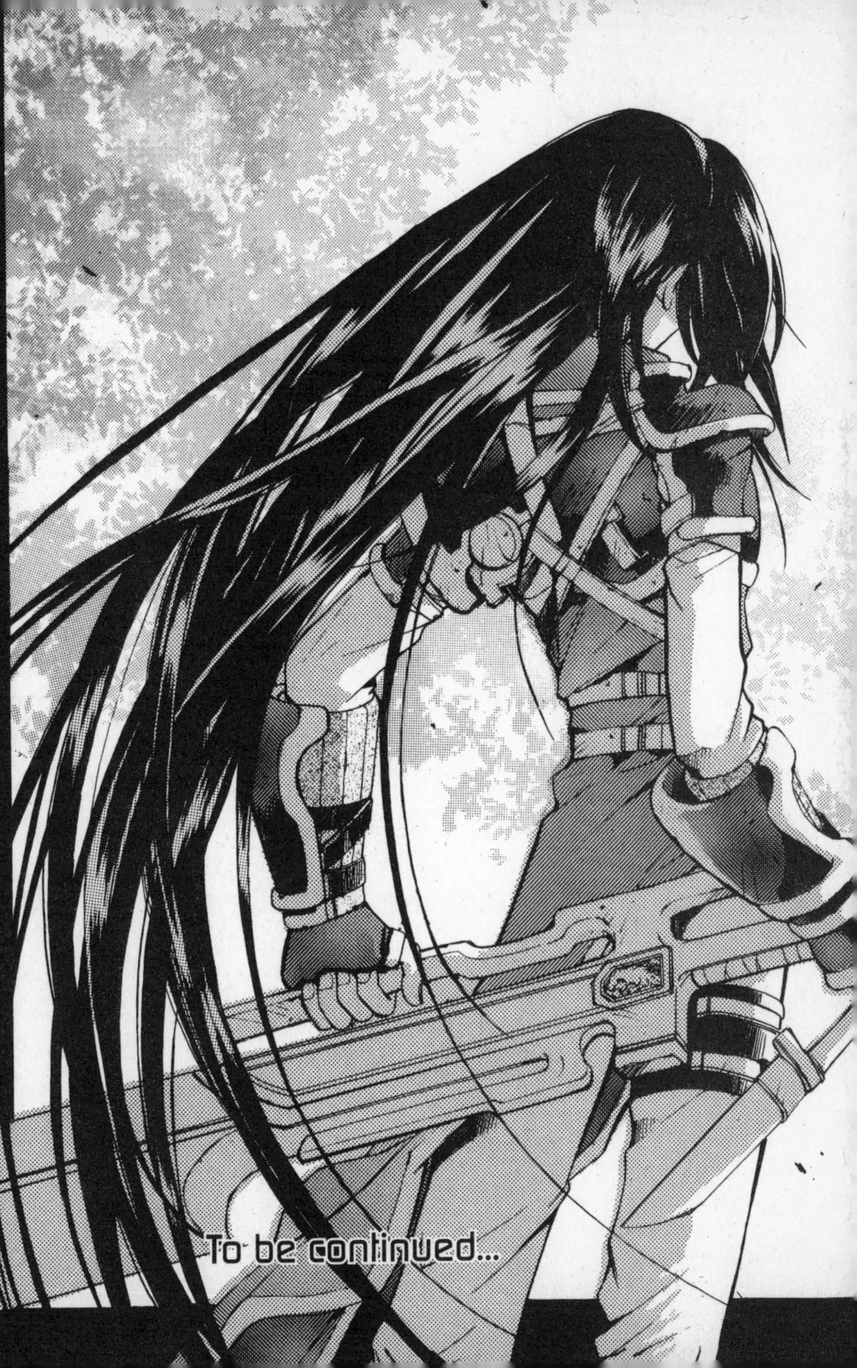
To be continued...

In the next volume of:

After searching for two months, Batsuo and Ludia are still not able to locate Kam, and Winslaks has not been able to break through his sword's seal to materialize long enough to help them. Meanwhile, Langfeldt and his people are also in search of Kam, believing he is the key to solidifying the Ancient's powers. However, soon enough, familiar and unexpected faces begin to appear. How will the people react with the discovery of none other than Laolyth?